Sustainable Cities

Regional Policy and Development Series

Series Editor: Ron Martin, Department of Geography, University of Cambridge

Throughout the industrialised world, widespread economic restructuring, rapid technological change, the reconfiguration of State intervention, and increasing globalisation are giving greater prominence to the nature and performance of individual regional and local economies within nations. The old patterns and processes of regional development that characterised the post-war period are being fundamentally redrawn, creating new problems of uneven development and new theoretical and policy challenges. Whatever interpretation of this contemporary transformation is adopted, regions and localities are back on the academic and political agenda. *Regional Policy and Development* is an international series which aims to provide authoritative analyses of this new regional political economy. It seeks to combine fresh theoretical insights with detailed empirical enquiry and constructive policy debate to produce a comprehensive set of conceptual, practical and topical studies in this field. The series is not intended as a collection of synthetic reviews, but rather as original contributions to understanding the processes, problems and policies of regional and local economic development in today's changing world.

Sustainable Cities

Graham Haughton and Colin Hunter

Regional Policy and Development Series 7

Jessica Kingsley Publishers
London and Bristol, Pennsylvania

Regional Studies Association
London

The right of Graham Haughton and Colin Hunter to be identified as authors of this work has been asserted by them in accordance with the Copyright, Designs and Patents Act 1988.

First published in the United Kingdom in 1994 by
Jessica Kingsley Publishers Ltd
116 Pentonville Road
London N1 9JB, England
and
1900 Frost Road, Suite 101
Bristol, PA 19007, U S A

with the Regional Studies Association
Registered Charity 252269

Second impression 1996

Copyright © 1994 Graham Haughton and Colin Hunter

Library of Congress Cataloging in Publication Data
A CIP catalogue record for this book is available from the Library of Congress

British Library Cataloguing in Publication Data
Haughton, Graham
Sustainable Cities. – (Regional Policy &
Development Series; Vol.7)
I. Title II. Hunter, Colin, III. Series
307.76

ISBN 1-85302-234-9

Printed and Bound in Great Britain by
Athenaeum Press, Gateshead, Tyne and Wear

Contents

Part B: Introduction to Pollution 125

The Nature of Pollution 126

Part C: From Principles to Policies: Addressing Urban Environmental Problems 199

Acknowledgements

The idea of writing this book came to us over four years ago, in a Paris bar after a long session with the Urban Affairs Group of the OECD, helping them to produce the book *Environmental Policies for Cities in the 1990s*. We are particularly grateful therefore to Ariel Alexandre and Siegfried Brenke, who indirectly provided the stimulation for this book, and also helped improve our understanding of the urban environment.

In the prolonged gestation period of this book, a considerable number of people have introduced new material to us, for which we are particularly grateful. Most importantly, a number of people read and commented on one or more draft chapters for us: Peter Roberts, Kevin Thomas, Lindsay Smales, Dave Gibbs, Graham May and David Whitney. We are extremely grateful to all of them for their advice: however we accept full responsibility for the text ourselves.

Alexandra Press for the diagram taken from *Built Environment 4*, 2, 101–110 by N. Lee and C. Wood (1978) on p.258

Ashgate Publishing for the diagram by P. Newman and J. Kenworthy taken from *Cities and Automobile Dependence* on p.86

Pergamon Press for the diagram taken from *Progress in Planning 32*, 3, by K.J. Button and D.W. Pearce (1989) on p.237

PART A

SUSTAINABILITY AND URBAN DEVELOPMENT

Interest in the urban challenges raised by the growing debates on sustainable development and global environmental change has increased very rapidly in recent years. This book builds on this growing interest in the role of cities in the sustainable development process, examining both specific problems of urban environmental degradation and the contribution cities can make to broader goals of attaining global sustainability (Box A.1).

Box A.1 Some Changing Urban Environmental Challenges

- The increased capacity of the human race to provoke adverse environmental change on a truly global scale – something to which urban populations make a major contribution.
- The increased size of cities, in terms of both their population and their land consumption, which has intensified adverse environmental impacts, particularly on a regional scale.
- The accumulation of different historical additions to the built environment and social and economic life has given cities an ever more clearly defined, and often more fragile, environment of their own.
- The rise of the automobile has added to environmental decay in most cities, many of which face difficulties in physically absorbing the demands placed on them.

Cities have long experienced environmental problems, not least in respect of overcrowding; air, water and noise pollution; poor sanitation; and poor housing. Such long-recognised problems persist in virtually all cities, but they are also being added to, as it becomes apparent that urban problems are intimately tied up with the concerns of global environmental sustainability.

Box A.2 Phases of Human–Ecosystem Relationships

Phase One: Primeval phase

By far the longest phase, in which human populations differed little from other omnivorous mammals in their interactions with the other components of the ecosystems of which they were part (the main exceptions being the use of fire and use of simple tools). Daily energy consumption per capita: 2000 kcals.

Phase Two: Early farming phase

Beginning around 12,000 years ago in some regions. Spreading domestication and advancing farming techniques led to humankind beginning to change the face of the Earth, altering the environment on a large scale, with deforestation, erosion, changes in dominant vegetation, a shift towards monoculture and selective breeding of plants and animals. The shift away from nomadism to permanent shelter in most societies brought some benefits, but was also associated with deteriorating relations between human populations and microbial, protozoal and metazoal parasites and pathogens. Environmental impacts were mainly local and short-term, involving vegetation destruction and animal slaughter. Daily energy consumption per capita: 4–12,000 kcals.

Phase Three: Early urban phase

Initiated five thousand years ago in Mesopotamia, and not long afterwards in China and India. Increased density and crowding of urban living came to be associated with 'stressed' human populations, whilst pestilence became a distinguishing trait. Occupational specialisation gathered pace, creating more rigid, more extreme and more permanent divides in society, which also found a spatial manifestation in divided cities. More productive rural agriculture led to surpluses which could support growing cities, with immediate rural hinterlands of greatest importance in feeding the cities. Diets often came to rely on single staples (e.g. rice, wheat, maize, potatoes), with this narrowing of diets contributing to certain diseases and also to vulnerability to famine. Daily energy consumption per capita: 26,000 kcals.

Phase Four: The urban industrial phase

Began with the industrial revolution in Europe and North America around 200 years ago. This phase is associated with a major mechanisation of production and massive increases in energy consumption, both overall and in per capita terms. Cities grew rapidly in size and in terms of their share of total population. Increased energy usage has involved fossil fuels in particular, with daily energy consumption at 50,000 kcals per capita. Major impacts also on biogeochemical cycles, for instance nitrogenous human wastes which formerly would have been recycled being lost, largely to the rivers and oceans. Many environmental impacts at local and regional scales, notably urban pollution.

Phase Five: The global interdependence phase

The global economy has been transformed in recent years, becoming economically and environmentally more interconnected. Cities act as the nodal points of unprecedented flows of resources, wastes, traded products and services, finance capital and labour. Environmental problems are local, regional and global in scale increasingly involving major damage to the global ecosystem, whilst using resources at unprecedented, unreplenishable rates. Daily energy usage per capita averaging 300,000 kcals. Particularly important has been the growth of transfrontier environmental problems, such as acid rain and global warming.

(Adapted in part from Boyden *et al.* 1981, pp.9–18; Boyden 1984, p.9; and Kemp 1990,p.3)

Environmental concerns appear to have entered a new era in terms of the scope and scale of problems associated with human activity. With urban residents likely to account for 50% of the world's population by the year 2000, the changing role and functions of cities are necessarily central concerns for policy makers.

The enormous diversity of urban development histories, and contemporary forms of urban development, make any attempt at categorisation of urban ecosystem development a difficult task. Drawing in particular on the work of Boyden *et al.* (1981), but also that of Kemp

(1990), it is possible to construct a five-phase model of human ecological existence (Box A.2). According to Boyden (1984) the fourth phase, that of modern industrialisation (termed the 'urban industrial' phase in Box A.2), is one which could not last indefinitely, given its growing use of extrasomatic energy and non-renewable resources, and the growing amounts of gaseous and chemical wastes. Moreover, this phase has been deemed non-sustainable in large part because of the inefficient, highly resource-hungry nature of cities, so that entering into a new, more ecologically sustainable form of world development would require future cities to be fundamentally different from those of the present. It is now possible to identify a fifth stage in human–ecosystem relationships, where the impacts of human activities can, for the first time, create serious dislocation to the balance of the global environment, as witnessed by the discovery of holes in the ozone layer and the emergence of the enhanced 'greenhouse' effect.

As the Earth enters this fifth phase, humanity faces a new series of environmental challenges, created largely by its own activities. Both the scale and scope of environmental degradation present fundamental challenges to the stability of the global environment, possibly posing a threat to the very survival of the human species. Some of these threats have been apparent for many years, with a particularly notable staging point in terms of an international approach being the United Nations Conference on the Human Environment in Stockholm, held in 1972. At this stage the developed nations wanted to meet to discuss international pollution, whilst developing countries wanted a forum for the articulation of their own more immediate concern with the 'pollution of poverty', not just the 'effluence of affluence'. In the period since then concern over the environment has grown, with some fluctuations, eventually emerging as a global political priority in the late 1980s in response to increased information and understanding of the impacts of human activities on the environment, especially a growing awareness of new forms and intensities of pollution, from radiation pollution, to acid rain, ozone layer depletion, and global warming (Box A.3).

Political leaders reacted initially on an issue-by-issue basis, if at all, notably with the Vienna (1985) and Montreal (1987) meetings on reducing the emissions of ozone layer-depleting substances. In 1987 the World Commission on Environment and Development (WCED), produced *Our Common Future*, also known as the Brundtland Report, after Gro Harlem Brundtland who chaired the Commission. This report popularised the concept of sustainable development and set the tone for much of the ensuing debate, particularly concerning the need to bring about forms of economic growth which are compatible with a maintained – or improved – environmental quality for present and future generations, whilst also emphasising the role of social inequalities and poverty in bringing about unsustainable behaviour. This report included a chapter on the particular problems facing cities, which stressed the complementary nature of urban and regional strategies and the importance of developing secondary urban centres as a means of controlling the growth of very large cities, seen as particularly problematic.

Box A.3 Contemporary Global Environmental Concerns

Biodiversity. The rapid rate of species and habitat loss threaten to reduce nature's store of hidden resources. This is illustrated by the rise in commercial use of rainforest plants in medical treatments, although source countries, often developing nations, argue that the more developed countries exploit these resources, with few benefits for source countries.

Hazardous substances. The movement and storage of toxic and radio-active substances, especially waste products, has become an increasingly important issue as more and more substances are found to be hazardous to human health and the environment.

Climate. Of particular concern is the *greenhouse effect*, with the warming of the Earth's climate predicted to involve sea level rises, melting of the polar ice caps, changes in regional climate patterns and greater weather instability.

Oceans. The world's oceans are important not simply because of the anticipated rises in sea levels resulting from global warming, but also because they play an important role in regulating the world's climate and in neutralising some of mankind's polluting activities.

Pollution. This has many forms: air, water, land and noise pollution. Particularly important is the recognition of some of the potentially dangerous interactions between different contaminants and the cumulative effects of these. Also important is the rise in transfrontier pollution, most notably acid rain.

Desertification. This is a rapidly growing problem in Africa in particular, driven by unsustainable agricultural practices in the face of growing population and resultant food demands.

Deforestation. This has risen to prominence because of the rapid rate at which it occurs, undermining tropical rainforest resources in particular, and also possibly affecting the global climate, since forests may play an important role in converting carbon dioxide into oxygen.

Indigenous peoples. The pressure on resources which is contributing to deforestation is also leading to indigenous peoples being deprived of their homes and means of living.

Resource-base depletion. This refers especially to the depletion of non-renewable resources, such as fossil fuels, but also to the deterioration of renewable resources, such as soils and forests.

Overpopulation. The anticipated doubling of the world's population in the next 50 years and the pressures to improve standards of living could create huge pressures on the environment if we were to remain reliant on existing technologies, consumption habits and known resource stocks.

Consumption. Resource-base depletion is not simply a matter of the pressures of rising numbers of people, but also of continually rising standards of living, resource-use profligacy, and non-sustainable consumption habits.

Technology. Some new technologies have brought major changes in the environment, from the spread of cars to the creation of new toxic chemicals. There is a continuing debate about the relative merits of high technology as opposed to intermediate technology.

Biotechnology. The rise of new scientific techniques, such as genetic engineering, may bring some important benefits to mankind; unless properly controlled and monitored, they may also unleash some social and environmental problems.

Inappropriate development. This is a particularly important issue in areas such as aid for developing countries, which in many instances has been environmentally insensitive, for instance, building large dams which necessitate the removal of whole villages and which may obliterate scarce fertile agricultural land.

Military. Two elements concern commentators: the devastation which accompanies war, and the distortion of the market created by government support for the military. Many people argue that finances for military research and weaponry would be better spent on initiatives to tackle environmental and social problems.

Trade. Uneven terms of trade are for some commentators central to the underdevelopment of developing countries, a condition which in turn undermines attempts to improve the environment.

(Sources include: Allaby 1989; MacNeill, Winsemius and Yakushiji 1991; Vidal and Chatterjee 1992)

It took the Earth Summit held in Rio de Janeiro in 1992 to bring global leaders together to confront the wider range of environmental challenges. This meeting has been criticised by some for failing to come up with policies of a sufficiently radical nature to tackle effectively the problems confronting the world. Nonetheless, the Rio Summit did result in a wide-ranging programme to tackle these global problems, with Agenda 21 providing the centrepiece for international cooperation and coordination (Quarrie 1992). This international programme is to be accompanied by national and local responses, with local authorities being asked to enter into a dialogue with their citizens, local organisations and businesses aiming to adopt a local Agenda 21. Within Agenda 21 some important urban and regional concerns are highlighted (see Chapter Eight). Governments are advised to delegate decision-making to the lowest level of public authority consistent with effective action and a local approach. Community participation in environmental programmes at all stages is stressed, as is the development of 'sustainable city networks' to encourage international information-sharing on initiatives. Comprehensive approaches to urban planning are advocated which recognise the individual needs of cities and are based on ecologically sound urban design practices. In the Rio conference follow-up meetings held in Manchester in 1993 and 1994, sustainable cities were the central concern.

The problems facing cities have changed considerably over time. Hough (1990), for instance, argues that since the nineteenth century the evolution of cities has seen improved human health and deteriorating environmental conditions. Certainly in prosperous cities, problems related to the condition of the basic infrastructure and prevalence of disease among the human population have diminished. It is rarely the case, however, that there has been a simple improvement in urban environmental conditions: as industrial sulphurous smogs have become less common in deindustrialising prosperous cities, photochemical smogs (see Chapter Four) have often become more common. In a similar vein, it is possible to see that the dominant causes of urban environmental problems vary around the world. In prosperous – or, more popularly, developed – countries, problems relating to production, housing and basic infrastructure (water, electricity) have tended to diminish, whilst consumption problems (e.g. high waste flows) and traffic problems have increased. In the former communist countries of central and eastern Europe many production-related problems persist in industrial cities. Alternatively, in some of the state capitals there are now fewer production-related problems, but traffic-related problems are growing. In the remaining communist countries, problems are more difficult to classify: in China production-related problems remain intense in some heavily polluted cities, whilst in Cuba financial problems are impeding the provision of adequate housing and other basic infrastructure. It is in the cities of the developing – or Third World – countries, however, that problems are most acute, with cross-cutting problems related to production, (under-) consumption, underprovision and poor maintenance of the basic infrastructure and, increasingly, traffic problems.

In addition to these broadly constituted differences, it needs to be remembered that every city will have its own unique set of circumstances, from economic well-being to local topographic conditions which affect its environment. The perspective of this book is international, within the limits of unevenly available information about the different regions of the world and their cities. We seek to examine a wide range of causes and impacts related to urban environmental problems. Inevitably, at times this involves some oversimplifications, not least because academic understanding of urban environmental issues across the world is still underdeveloped.

The three chapters in Part A examine the changing nature of cities in the context of the emerging sustainable development debate. Chapter One introduces some of the main challenges for urban development raised by contemporary concern over global environmental change, and, in particular, the sustainable development debate; Chapter Two concentrates on urban growth and economic restructuring; and Chapter Three looks at the changing internal form and function of cities, discussing the implications of these changes for encouraging more sustainable forms of urban development. Part B contains two chapters which examine aspects of the urban natural environment, concentrating on urban air and water pollution. The three chapters in Part C examine principles and policies for promoting sustainable urban development, concluding with a review of the political and management challenges for moving from principles to policies.

CHAPTER ONE

Urban Development
and the Environment

The future will be predominantly urban, and the most immediate environmental concerns of most people will be urban ones.

World Commission on Environment and Development (1987, p.255)

1.1 CITIES AND THE ENVIRONMENT: PROBLEMS AND POTENTIAL

For most of us, cities are incredibly phantasmagorical. The same city at different times we can know and not know, love and hate, revere and revile, yearn to leave and ache to return to. It is not only in this subjective sense that the city continually changes. In an objective sense too the same city can rapidly transform itself, not least physically: morning smog followed by clear evening skies, parched land turning to mud slurries. In economic and social terms too, cities are continually in flux, one day with a dominant polluting employer, the next with five thousand more redundant workers. Nothing about the city is static: everything about the city is continually in change. Barbara Ward (1975, p.39) went further than this, declaring that 'the very word "settlement" is in some measure a contradiction. In many ways modern man is living with "unsettlement"'. Our places of work, recreation and residence all differ and change over time, so that in our assorted roles as residents, commuters, producers, consumers, migrants, leisure-seekers and tourists, we are always on the move within and between our cities, whilst the cities themselves continually change and develop in both form and function.

Yet from this richness of urban diversity and dynamism it is possible to construct an understanding of what it is that drives cities. Moreover, there are a number of issues unique to cities which need to be addressed by city analysts and city dwellers, issues which are not entirely separate from non-urban settlements and economies, but which are none the less distinctively urban. Perhaps foremost amongst these is the issue of the

quality of the urban environment. The great variety of urban environmental issues is important to note here, since the problems associated
with low-density sprawl are very different from those of high-density
cities, and the issues facing smaller cities may be very different from
those facing a large city.

The reasons for adopting an urban focus on environmental problems
and potentials are compelling. It is at the urban level that many environmental problems are sourced and where many environmental problems
are experienced at their most intense (OECD 1990). Indeed, Breheny
(1990, p. 9.4) finds it surprising that the debate on planning cities for
sustainability is so underdeveloped, given that they 'are obviously both
great consumers and degraders of the natural environment'. This lack
of debate may in part reflect the disdain with which cities have long been
regarded, with commentators from the nineteenth century to the present
day challenging the very basic premises of urban living, demanding a
more rural lifestyle, a return to nature. From this perspective, cities are
almost inherently undesirable in environmental terms, not just because
they are polluted, degraded places in which to live, but because they are
held to distort rural economies and foster lifestyles which are energy-intensive and remote from contact with nature.

As cities continue to grow in size and in their share of the growing
global population and economic wealth, their environmental impacts
will of necessity continue to be a central theme in the move towards
global sustainability (Box 1.1). As Chapters Four and Five demonstrate,
cities can also have major environmental impacts at both local and global
scales. Cities can act as early-warning indicators of more deep-seated,
broader-reaching environmental crises too, since problems often emerge
there more quickly, more intensely and more acutely than elsewhere
(Commission of the European Communities 1990). Urban populations
are also major energy users, especially in low-density sprawling cities,
making them major contributors to global warming (see Chapters Three
and Four).

Another justification for an urban scale of analysis, however, is that
cities are in themselves a unique form of natural, built and cultural
environment. As a natural environment, cities have their own distinctive
properties, such as the urban heat island, wind tunnels created by large
buildings, and air-inversion effects, which can intensify environmental
problems (see Chapter Four). In contemporary Rome for instance, long
blocks of high rise flats have been built on the edge of the city, in part
preventing the sea wind from bringing cooling breezes (the *venticello
stuzzicarello*) into the city. Added to the effects of high rise buildings in
the city centre itself and the exhaust fumes of 100,000 cars in the narrow

streets of the centre, a new urban microclimate has emerged in which the city is reputedly turning into a furnace (Endean 1993).

Box 1.1 Cities and Wider Environmental Issues

- 42.6% of the world's population was urban in 1990: 72.6% in developed countries, 33.6% in developing countries.
- 60% of the world's gross national product is produced in cities.
- 65% of cities with over 2.5 million people are coastal, several already at or below sea level.
- On average, each city of one million people daily consumes 625,000 tonnes of water, 2000 tonnes of food and 9500 tonnes of fuel, and generates 500,000 tonnes of waste water, 2000 tonnes of waste solids and 950 tonnes of air pollutants.
- Urban populations in different countries vary hugely in their environmental demands. Urban residents in developed country cities generate on average 0.7–1.8 kg of domestic waste daily, compared with 0.4–0.9 kg daily in developing countries.
- In the USA, almost a third of urban land is now devoted to the needs of the car.
- Idling car engines in traffic jams in the USA in 1984 alone accounted for 4% of petrol consumption.
- Land loss has become a pressing problem: in Egypt, for example, more than 10% of the most productive farmland has been lost to urban encroachment over the past three decades. In many Western European countries it is estimated that 2% of agricultural land is being lost to cities each decade.

(Hardoy, Mitlin and Satterthwaite 1992, Quarrie 1992, Girardet 1992, Tolba and El-Kholy 1992)

Urbanisation brings with it many transformations of nature, including pollution, site transformations, such as river channel diversion, and changes to the functioning of local ecosystems, altering natural flows of energy, water, food and materials (Douglas 1989b). High-density urban living in particular fundamentally alters the ecology of an area, not least in terms of human health, often leading to more 'crowd infections' and physical injuries, from industry and transport (McMichael 1993). Urban sprawl can pose a particular problem by eating into valuable natural habitats, whilst cities also pass on some of their impacts, making intensive demands on the environmental resources of their hinterland areas, such as quarries for building materials. Some forms of pollution are, in fact, distinctively urban in source, impact, or both. On a related matter, it is important to recognise that the interaction of polluting elements often intensifies problems: it is within cities, the source of so many contaminants, that the scope for such combinations is greatest (OECD 1990). Added to this is that the very concentration of polluting activities in cities increases the chances of breaching local environmental tolerance limits.

Cities also constitute an important cultural environment, not least the accumulation of different human-made artifacts in the built environment, from grand Renaissance cathedrals and neo-Gothic town halls to terraces of solid Victorian artisanal dwellings. There is a real tension here with aspects of the natural environment, well illustrated by the recent decision of the Indian authorities to close down polluting industries close to the Taj Mahal to prevent further deterioration of this international treasure. A city's individual sense of place is heavily influenced by the way in which the inheritances of the built environment are used in contemporary social and economic practices. In fact, it is possible to go so far as to see much of the physical fabric of cities as a non-renewable environmental resource in itself, meriting some degree of environmental protection (OECD 1990). The city needs to be seen as an asset in the widest sense: not just its individual parts, but the urban whole (Solesbury 1990). Socially and economically, cities can be regarded as important resources which provide a productive base for economic growth and improving living standards, although it could be argued that many of these urban advances are at the expense of rural areas. Breheny (1990, p. 9.7) draws a link between natural environmental resources and a city's economic and social resources, arguing that 'the natural world supports the city, but the city's man-made resources, in turn give the city its distinctive, dynamic character'.

It is not only the nature of the problems which give rise to the need for an urban focus to environmental issues. Cities are also potentially more environmentally friendly than many realise (Box 1.2). As Elkin, McLaren and Hillman (1991, p.45) point out, 'Cities have great capacity to be more resourceful ... Urban design integrated with nature can both save resources and allow city dwellers to enjoy a more natural environment'. Banister (1992), for instance, finds that travel in cities is less energy-consuming than in small towns and rural areas, in large part because journey lengths are shorter, so people can walk and cycle more, whilst in large cities public transport is commonly better developed and more widely used. Well-designed and well-managed cities can reduce travel distances and therefore energy usage, be culturally and environmentally stimulating (many of our greatest buildings and parks are urban), reduce some of the pressures on rural land which contribute to overintensive farming, whilst in many societies the large concentrations of population can create a huge popular voice against immediate environmental degradation.

Box 1.2 The Urban Environment and Potential for Improvement

- Changing the shape, size, residential density, layout, and location of activities in cities can bring energy-demand variations of up to 150%.
- Studies have shown that low-density cities use twice as much energy as high-density cities, taking account of climate and income variations.
- On average, each resident in most low-density Canadian cities emits around 20 tonnes of CO_2 a year; in higher-density Amsterdam the equivalent figure is 10 tonnes.
- Increasing the percentage of people travelling by public transport is generally easier in higher-density, compact cities. Increased use of public transport can bring about major energy savings, reducing the emissions of pollutants. In Tokyo, 15% of commuters drive to work, compared to 90% in Los Angeles.
- Some cities have retained a strong urban agriculture sector and are virtually self-sufficient in food, including 14 of China's largest 15 cities.

(Alcamo and Lubkert 1990, Rees and Roseland 1991, Girardet 1992, Owens 1992)

Improving the global environment requires that cities make a major contribution, a contribution that will require not just a pro rata, per capita change in habits, but a more fundamental look at the ways in which cities work and the ways in which they might be structured in the future, in order to enhance the capacity of their businesses and populations and to contribute more fully to the global sustainability drive. The environmental problems of cities do not simply relate to the numbers of people living there, nor to the problems of overcrowding. Instead, the design of the city can be the central issue in shaping the way in which environmental resources are used. Changing the size, shape, population densities and internal ordering of cities can all lead to reductions in energy use in particular. It is not cities as such which are necessarily bad, then, but the ways in which they are built and used – most notably how buildings, railways, highways and open spaces are designed, laid out and located (see Chapter Three). The Sears Tower in Chicago brings home the potential impact of urban activities on the global environment, since 'this ugly monster uses more energy in 24 hours than an average American city of 150,000, or an Indian city of more than one million inhabitants' (Hahn and Simonis 1991, p.12).

1.2 CITIES AND SUSTAINABLE DEVELOPMENT

1.2.1 Cities

The term 'cities' is an elastic concept. There is no absolute definition which is satisfactory in all circumstances. What constitutes a city may well vary between nation-states, with smaller thresholds in countries with smaller population size. It can also vary according to the settlement context of an area, since in many cases, a small town in or close to a large conurbation will effectively and functionally be part of the city, whereas a similar-size town in a largely rural area may well be a small market town. Robertson (1989, p.17), makes a similar point in highlighting that what people regard as their own locality can differ according to local circumstances, from vast spaces in remote rural areas to small city neighbourhoods. Also, as the Commission of the European Communities (1990) point out in a useful review of many of the definitional problems involved, cities and their hinterlands are increasingly indistinct from each other, linked by better communications and increasingly exposed to similar cultural influences.

Because of the many ambiguities surrounding what constitutes a city, this book tends to refer loosely to all urban areas as cities, be they small towns, conurbations or megalopolises. Following the definition of Cappon (1990, p.9), a city is regarded as 'a more or less regular and recognisable agglomeration of buildings and thoroughfares, where people live and work', and also engage in many of their social and cultural activities, usually requiring at least 10,000 residents. The physical distinctiveness and the proximity of people, work and services is still a defining urban characteristic, despite the various passing infatuations with the liberating effects of improved communications technologies.

There is still no real sign that Melvin Webber's 'non place urban realm' is about to emerge, where high mobility will lead to the dissolution of localised senses of community, and their replacement with more functional communities (Webber 1964, Self 1982). What is perhaps most important to bear in mind is the sheer variety of cities, in terms not only of their internal form, functions and driving dynamism, but also in terms of their regional and national contexts.

1.2.2 Urban environment

The *urban environment* is complexly structured and richly textured in its interweaving of a mixture of natural, built-form, economic, social and cultural dimensions. For the sake of convenience, the overall urban environment can be said to consist of natural, built and social components. The natural environment includes air, water, land, climate, flora and fauna, whilst the built environment encompasses the fabric of buildings, infrastructure and urban open spaces. The social component embraces less tangible aspects of urban areas, including aesthetic and amenity quality, architectural styles, heritage, and the values, behaviour, laws and traditions of the resident community (OECD 1990).

It is possible to see the urban environment as either a distortion of natural ecosystems, or as an ecosystem in its own right, characterised by high artificial flows of energy, as a result of the heavy reliance of most cities on imported fossil fuels. Newcombe (1984) describes the ecosystems of most developing country cities as 'immature', following from Odum's (1969) definition. They

> ...grow rapidly, use the available energy resources inefficiently, have negligible re-use of vital materials such as nutrients and water, and are subsequently more highly dependent on, and vulnerable to, changes within their hinterland (or forage areas). Their infrastructure development is low, with relatively simple structures of short half-life, and with high gross productivity. (pp. 91–2)

In a similar vein Odum (1989, p. 17) claims that 'the city is a parasite on the natural and domesticated environments, since it makes no food, cleans no air, and cleans very little water to a point where it could be reused'. Other doom-laden views of the city abound: for Friedman (1984, pp.48–49) the city is a cancer, 'an overgrown organ which takes all the food, so much food it can no longer perform its proper function: and cancer is a lethal illness'. According to Mayur, (1990, pp. 37–38) cities are 'overgrown monstrosities with gluttonous appetites for material goods and fast declining carrying capacities... Only catastrophe awaits such a system of disharmony'.

As has already been emphasised, the urban environment is an open, dependent system, which necessarily interacts with the environments and economies of the city's hinterland, a hinterland which has become increasingly global rather than regional. More self-reliant cities are sometimes said to be more akin to a natural ecosystem (Friedman 1984). Generally speaking, larger cities are more open, and also tend to involve greater resource consumption per capita (Douglas 1989a). The important point is that the openness and the environmental impacts of city ecosystems can and do vary markedly over time and between places. Whether there is such a thing as a separate urban ecosystem is still open to debate, since the city is quintessentially part of the global ecosystem, possibly also overlaying a number of regional ecosystems.

1.2.3 Sustainable development

Sustainable development is a phrase which quickly entered into the common vocabulary with the heightened environmental awareness of the late 1980s. There is no commonly accepted single definition of sustainable development; indeed, Pearce, Markandya and Barbier (1989) in an appendix to their book *Blueprint for a Green Economy* quote twenty-four separate definitions. The most widely cited definition is that of the World Commission on Environment and Development (WCED 1987), also known as the Brundtland Commission:

> Sustainable development is development which meets the needs of the present without compromising the ability of future generations to meet their own needs. (p.43)

The growing numbers of people and their changing technologies have rapidly increased the capacity of the human race to make fundamental changes to the present and future state of the global environment. This critically alters the parameters of the environmental debate, as the increased scale and scope of environmental problems is recognised.

We would argue that there are three major principles which must underpin the process of sustainable development: inter-generational equity, intra-generational equity and transfrontier responsibility (Box 1.3). All three elements need to be considered in any discussion of sustainable development. The sustainable development debate implies tremendous political challenges, not least since the very configuration of political systems at global and local scales has previously allowed – indeed possibly encouraged – undesirable environmental impacts. Particularly important has been the uncompensated displacement across political boundaries of the costs of environmental exploitation associated with economic development. In effect, sustainable development says that the true costs of environmental exploitation are not being recognised because they are being shared inequitably socially and geographically, in terms of both present and future generations.

Box 1.3 Three Basic Principles for Sustainable Development

Principle of inter-generational equity. In considering any human activity, the effects on the ability of future generations to meet their needs and aspirations must be considered. This is sometimes also referred to as the *principle of futurity*.

Principle of social justice. This is concerned with current generations, where poverty is seen as a prime cause of degradation. Sustainability requires that control over distribution of resources be more evenly exercised, taking account of basic needs and common aspirations. Wider participation in environmental strategies and policies is an integral element of achieving this aim, sometimes also known as *intra-generational equity*.

Principle of transfrontier responsibility. At the broad level, stewardship of the global environment is required. More specifically, transfrontier pollution needs to recognised and controlled. Where feasible, the impacts of human activity should not involve an uncompensated geographical displacement of environmental problems. Rich nations should not overexploit the resources of other areas, distorting regional economies and ecosystems. Similarly, the environmental costs of urban activities should not be displaced across metropolitan boundaries, in effect subsidising urban growth.

The essential, defining characteristic of sustainable development is its emphasis on *futurity* or *inter-generational equity* in terms of access to beneficial aspects of the environment. Such inter-generational equity requires that natural capital assets of at least equal value to those of the present are passed on to future generations (we return to the 'constant natural assets' rule below). This is a more difficult concept than it at first seems, since society still has an imperfect knowledge of the value of the natural environment, ranging from still undiscovered or little-understood rainforest plant and animal life to broader issues, such as the role of the atmospheric ozone layer and the oceans in mediating global climatic patterns. Because of this, it is difficult to value the environmental stock of the present and indeed to know exactly what it is we are passing on to future generations. This also involves an intersection with concerns over environmental values in a broader sense: do we use financial values, moral and ethical values, quality of life considerations, or other ways of assessing value? Inevitably, we must use all these categories of value, but at the present we lack the basic tools to measure – let alone integrate – the different facets of environmental value. Furthermore, since some of these values are necessarily qualitative, whose values do we accept as dominant?

Some headway into resolving some of these dilemmas can be made by looking at our current understanding of the benefits of natural environmental resources. These can be categorised into three key areas (Jacobs 1989). Firstly, there are natural resources for production and consumption, principally raw materials and energy. Secondly, as the natural environment operates as a sink for society's waste products, the sustainability requirement is not to overload the Earth's natural capacity to absorb and (preferably) recycle waste streams, whether air and water pollution or landfill sites for domestic and industrial waste. Thirdly, the environment provides a series of 'free services' which must not be impaired; an example is the role of the ozone layer (see Chapter Four). Integral to such considerations is the notion of the Earth's carrying capacity for particular human activities insofar as they have an impact on the environment. Although much attention is rightly paid to global impacts, local environmental tolerances are also important. For instance, the capacity of rivers to absorb pollutants is finite, and when overloaded can lead to a greatly reduced range of aquatic life. Cities, as the major sources of pollutants within small areas, frequently breach local environmental limits in respect of one or more polluting agents.

These, then, give an indication of some of the underlying ecological requirements of sustainable development, considerations which operate at all scales from local to global. It is fundamental to sustainability, however, to look beyond these (in some senses) rather narrow parameters to consider the economic, social and political circumstances which have led the world to its current condition. Particularly important is the need to understand the significance of the drive to economic growth and the combination of historic and contemporary social and economic inequalities which have patterned economic growth.

Economic growth was a central concern of the Brundtland Commission and has also emerged as a central concern in the new awareness and practice of environmentalism (e.g. Jacobs 1989, 1991; Singh 1989). For some 'deep green' or 'deep ecology' writers, there is a total incompatibility between continued high levels of economic growth and sustainable development, as the one systematically undermines the other

(Seabrook 1990). This is not dissimilar to the views espoused in *The Limits to Growth* by the 'Club of Rome' (Meadows *et al.* 1972), a seminal document which declared that the growth of the world's population could not be sustained by the world's stock of resources, therefore a global crisis was imminent; this probably constituted the most stern rebuke to unlimited population growth since Malthus. This model is not without its critics, who point to the unrealistic assumptions which underpin it of continuing exponential population growth and a finite resource stock (see Owens and Owens 1991). Similar views on the unsustainability of current economic growth patterns can be found in the *Ecologist*'s (1972) much-quoted 'Blueprint for Survival' and in the work of Mishan (1967), who provided one of the earliest denunciations of a naïve faith in the redemptive power of science to solve existing and future environmental problems.

At their most extreme, 'ecocentric' views have been characterised as eco-fascism (Pepper 1984), in which ecological imperatives wholly overshadow prevailing political imperatives, encompassing a need to halt or even reverse both population growth and economic growth. A related uncharitable view in the 1970s was that these 'trendy' ecocentric views had a class bias, and that those involved would simply climb up on to their wealthy pedestals and kick the ladder down behind them (see Owens and Owens 1991). This fear was to re-emerge twenty years later, with similar accusations of 'eco-imperialism' by developing-country governments over attempts to achieve global protocols on pollution (Buttel, Hawkins and Power 1990).

At the other extreme are those who believe that the combination of the abundance of nature and the ingenuity of the human race will always find new solutions to newly emerging problems, with the best way forward being continued economic growth and investment in techno-logical capacity to cope with any problems which this growth creates (Simon 1981, Simon and Kahn 1984). Economic growth then becomes necessary to sustainability, as it alone can provide the necessary financial resources and technological capacity required to deal with environ-mental problems. As Redclift (1987) has pointed out, there are, however, severe limits to our reliance on these anticipated 'technical fixes'. For instance, the development of nuclear energy may reduce the pollution of carbon-based fuels in conventional power stations, but brings with it a range of problems such as coping with radiation leaks both during and after its use in generating electricity. In consequence, such technical solutions as may emerge through scientific investigation should always be regarded as complementary to sound conservation policies, not as replacing them. More than this, society needs to reorganise its activities in ways which prioritise preventing environmental problems arising, not simply responding to each new crisis as it emerges.

In between these two extremes of environmentalism are a whole range of views, most of which involve a sustained critique of the failings of conventional economics, of the capitalist mode of production and of the former centrally planned economies of Eastern Europe and the Soviet Union (Johnston 1989, Singh 1989). One way through this maze of arguments is to interpret sustainable development as not so much the 'limits of growth', more the 'growth of limits' (MacNeill, Winsemius and Yakushiji 1991). Certainly, experience tells us that technological advances will bring some solutions to environmental problems: the trick seems to be avoiding some of the problems which technology also tends to bring with it, as in the case of cars, chlorofluorocarbons (CFCs) and nuclear energy. These concerns are at the centre of the formulation of the 'precautionary principle' in sustainable development that is, if in doubt about an activity's likely environmental consequences, do not take it further (see Chapter Six).

As the sustainability debate has developed, it has become possible to distinguish between weak and strong notions of sustainability, which in some senses reflect longer-standing differences between 'deep green ecology' and 'light green' environmentalists. The 'weak sustainability' position regards natural environmental capital as potentially replaceable with human-made capital stock. In this view, new technological products can in some cases replace natural environmental goods, so that the overall level of capital in the system is retained at a constant or growing level. More controversially, we could have more roads and less environment, or vice versa, under this rule (Turner, Pearce and Bateman 1994). There are many complications here, including whether capital stock should be measured using physical units, economic value or price (Pearce 1992). Using the weak sustainability definition, achieving economic development compatible with environmental protection is fairly easy. Sustainable development from this perspective may simply just become a new set of words to justify maintaining current patterns and processes of economic growth (Rees and Roseland 1991).

The 'strong sustainability' position, alternatively, holds that human-made capital stocks and natural environment capital stocks are not always interchangeable. One of the rationales for supporting this position is that human-made capital can readily fluctuate up or down, whilst if natural capital assets are depleted beyond certain levels, the effect is irreversible, possibly involving extinction. A form of sustainability which sees a growth in natural capital stock may also increase the resilience of the environment and indeed the economy (Pearce 1992). Finally, since the poor are generally more reliant on natural capital assets, any risks and uncertainties in replacing these are borne disproportionately by this group (Pearce, Markandya and Barbier 1989).

Sustainable development, then, is a term which is far from value-free. Instead the term raises an enormous number of contentious issues, so that its use as political mantra quickly emerges as unsatisfactory and deceptive. For O'Riorden (1989, p.93), 'Sustainability is becoming accepted as the mediating term which bridges the gap between developers and environmentalists. Its beguiling simplicity and apparently self-evident meaning have obscured its inherent ambiguity'. The reasons why global change arguments have been accepted so rapidly, whilst the *Limits to Growth* arguments of the 'Club of Rome' in 1972 were so hotly disputed, tells us something of the interpretations being placed on sustainability by some politicians and businesses. Where *Limits to Growth* called for a steady state economy with a halt to unbridled growth, global change may bring new business opportunities in environmental technology, such as CFC replacements. The contrasts are particularly apparent for carbon-based energy sources: where *Limits to Growth* emphasised the depletion of fossil-fuel stocks, 'global change' arguments tackle their abundance and overuse (Buttel, Hawkins and Power 1990).

The nature of the argument has shifted in some respects, then, but the fundamental challenge to economic growth and social justice issues remains central to both approaches: sustainable development and 'limits to growth'. The capture of the sustainability agenda by the liberal establishment, however, may prove to be yet another instance of what Susan George (1984, p. 55) so memorably termed 'appropriate terminology', an echo of the appropriate technology debate (see Chapter Two). Harvey (1993) also warns of the capture and appropriation of the 'green' or 'environmental' agenda by those who have other underlying objectives.

Strong notions of sustainable development represent a profound challenge to the existing status quo, requiring a break in the 'growth mentality' of most existing institutions of economic investment and resource allocation (O'Riorden 1989, 1990; Blowers 1993). Singh (1989, p. 224) goes further and proclaims sustainability as a revolutionary goal, which will require a thorough-going societal transformation to 'install justice, equity, peace and eco-protection as absolute values'. More than this, sustainability is said to require a new political economy, one which will involve fundamental changes in international development, changes which prioritise the needs of the world's poor and which challenge the right to polarised standards of living which favour rich nations as well as rich individuals (Redclift 1987, Johnston 1989). This line of thought is one which can readily be traced back to similar arguments used in both *The Limits to Growth* (Meadows *et al.* 1972) and

'Blueprint for Survival' (*Ecologist* 1972). This emphasis on people is important, since virtually all commentators prioritise the need to engage people in the decision-making and implementation processes of sustainable development, both through non-governmental organisations and directly in their own communities. This principle of participation is also a notable theme in Agenda 21, issued after the Earth Summit at Rio in 1992, with particular attention paid to the role of indigenous peoples and women.

There remains, nonetheless, a continuing tension in the environmental debate, between rich and poor countries. Whereas the richer countries can frame their concerns over maintaining the value of the environment in the long term, and over the value of a good environment for businesses and high quality of life for consumers, in the poorer countries the destruction of the environment creates much needed short-term economic growth (Redclift 1992). Here the tension between meeting basic survival needs and improving lifestyles is keen, and it is for this reason that social justice – or intra-generational equity – considerations are always at the forefront in the sustainability debate. Thus, where stabilisation of, for instance, CO_2 emissions may be politically difficult in countries such as the USA, in poorer countries with much lower energy consumption per capita and rapidly increasing populations, it is near impossible (Rees 1991).

This concern with social justice issues in turn relates to a broader perception – shared to varying degrees by the Brundtland Commission, O'Riorden, Singh and others – that a narrow concern with the environment alone is an impediment to solving the environmental problems of the world, since so many of these problems are rooted in social malaise and inadequately functioning economic systems. In the (rather emotive) words of Commoner (1973):

> When any environmental issue is pursued to its origins, it reveals an inescapable truth – that the root cause of the crisis is not to be found in how men interact with nature, but in how they interact with each other – that to solve the environmental crisis we must solve the problems of poverty, racial injustice and war; that the debt to nature which is the measure of the environmental crisis cannot be paid, person by person, in recycled bottles or ecologically sound habits, but in the ancient coin of social justice; that, in sum, a peace among men must precede the peace with nature. (p.23 cited in Singh 1989, p. 155)

In this view, the problems of the environment must be traced to dominant modes of production, consumption and reproduction (Johnston 1989, Robertson 1989, Singh 1989). Whether capitalist or centrally planned 'communism', the outcomes have been remarkably similar, an *undervaluation of environmental resources* which has encouraged overexploitation of natural resources by the human race (Pearce, Markandya and Barbier 1989), and also exploitation of individuals by each other (Singh 1989).

The obstacles to sustainable development from this perspective revolve around institutional blockages created and maintained – sometimes unwittingly – by the major international power players, the rich nations and their support institutions. In addition, the adoption of 'weak sustainability' positions by most rich countries has led to the so-called consensus in international policy being labelled a sham, where prosperous countries continue with 'business as usual', hoping for technical solutions to problems, whilst the poorer countries can see little advantage for themselves in pollution controls (Rees 1991). In this context, O'Riorden (1990) argues that the new environmental imperatives of impending global disaster require the rise of a new breed of politician, the global politician who prioritises global survival over the narrower short-term interests of national and local economic growth.

The combination of the undervaluation of environmental resources, and the existence of global political and economic systems which have in considerable part relied upon uneven development, has meant that regional economic growth has frequently been achieved by the passing-on of the burden of environmental costs across political borders. In a similar vein, underdeveloped political systems for fostering stewardship for the global environment, have for many years allowed transfrontier pollution to go unchecked. The fragmentation of political responsibilities and economic systems was central to a growth machine which disregarded all but the most immediately apparent, that is locally apparent, environmental costs of human behaviour. Now that the capacity of the human race to alter the global environment is better understood, the principle of transfrontier responsibility, or global stewardship, can be seen as an integral dimension of sustainable development. Policies for sustainable development require a perspective which transcends national boundaries, and at the local level, policies for sustainable urban development must transcend metropolitan borders.

1.2.4 Sustainable urban development

The final challenge in this section is to set out the concept of sustainable urban development. It is helpful to begin by briefly reviewing how others have set out agendas and objectives for improving the urban environment.

As we have already seen, many commentators see cities as parasitic on their hinterlands, and therefore unsustainable. Peter Berg (1990c), for instance, argues that

> Cities aren't sustainable because they have become dependent on distant, rapidly shrinking sources for the basic essentials for food, water, energy and materials. At the same time they have severely damaged the health of local systems upon which any sensible notion of sustainability must depend ... In addition, the social systems that make cities liveable, such as a sense of community and wide civic participation, are more typically eroded rather than strengthened. (p.104)

The natural region (or bioregion) of a city is seen as a particularly important focus for change: it is usually defined as following natural environment boundaries, such as a watershed. Focusing on such natural regions is thought to help ensure that urban residents are not divorced from nature, both as a resource provider and as a source of personal well-being. To become 'green', Berg argues that cities should not just clean themselves up, they need to become life-enhancing and regenerative, 'securing reciprocity between the urban way of life and the natural web that surrounds it' (1990a, p.141). The key ingredients in creating a green city are seen to be the need to look at the city in its bioregional context, and to bring about fundamental changes in the ways in which people treat nature, and treat each other. A fairly typical strand of 'deep green' city thinking is that urban residents need to engage in more cooperative forms of activity, frequently involving setting up a viable internal economic and social structure, usually on a small scale (Mollison 1990). The deep green city is generally small, cooperative and moving towards total economic and environmental self-reliance.

Whilst most radical green city commentators have seen the advantage of starting from scratch on a new site, others apply some of the same philosophy to changing existing cities. Mayur (1990) believes that:

> A green city is a living city by definition. It is an existing city, where the full potentials of all the intricately interconnected forces of nature are realised. In a sense, a green city is complete in its survival capacity. (p.38)

The multi-sectoral approach to creating a greener city is common to virtually all work on sustainable urban development, with increasing reference being made to the role of cities within broader environmental systems. Using the insights of work in Latin America, Leff (1990) argues:

Greening the city in the context of the urban explosion of Third World cities implies a reconstruction process that goes beyond anti-pollution measures, conservation of green areas, and reforestation of the surrounding environment of the city. As well, it goes way beyond better transportation systems, public services, and waste recycling technologies to rationalise the use of resources and energy with the urban ecosystem. (p.55)

In fact, it is necessary to look beyond the urban ecosystem to broader ecosystems. Leff goes on to argue and develop exactly this point:

Greening the city implies the articulation of urban functions in an overall sustainable development process. It implies new functions for the city and its reintegration into the overall productive process through a more balanced spatial distribution of agri-ecological, industrial, and urban activities. (p.56)

Others have emphasised the potential for changing the internal economic, social and spatial organisation of the city. This level of approach is particularly important in transforming existing large cities, which have evolved physical characteristics which run counter to the imperatives of sustainable development. For Elkin, McLaren and Hillman (1991), for instance:

sustainable urban development must aim to produce a city that is 'user-friendly' and resourceful, in terms not only of its form and energy efficiency, but also its function, as a place for living. (p.12)

It has also become increasingly common to link urban environmental policies to social and economic development policies. Achieving economic growth is a particularly important theme in the cities of poorer countries. The World Health Organisation (1992), for instance, says that

'sustainable urban development' should have as its goal that cities (or urban systems) continue to support more productive, stable and innovative economies, yet do so with much lower levels of resource use. (p.102)

Making some important additional links with the current sustainable development debates Breheny (1990) has suggested that urban sustainability involves:

the achievement of urban development aspirations, subject to the condition that the natural and man-made stock of resources are not so depleted that the long-term future is jeopardised. (p.9.7)

Breheny in this way attempts to bring into the equation inter-generational equity considerations, whilst recognising that in the city the loss and replacement of some human-made capital stock, such as buildings, is both inevitable and indeed desirable.

Intra-generational equity is also an important component in bringing about sustainable urban development. Policies are needed which link the urban environment, urban poverty and urban economic development, since all three are implicated in urban deterioration. Promoting sustainable development at the local level requires not only improvements to the physical environment, but also sustainable local economies and communities. This integration of concerns manifests itself in a number of ways:

- It is politically difficult to prioritise global environmental problems in the face of local unemployment, poverty and poor housing.
- Urban systems and markets tend to draw together poor people and poor environments.
- Poverty creates its own externalities, including deterioration of the built environment.
- Poor-quality urban centres promote a flight to the suburbs and a downward spiral of decline in the centre.
- Improving depressed neighbourhoods can and should have wider positive environmental impacts, for instance with housing insulation, traffic calming and local recycling initiatives.
- The mixture of land uses and functions at the local level can affect the demand for energy and transport.
- Green spaces can improve neighbourhood quality aesthetically, through noise reduction, and bring beneficial localised climate modification.
- High-quality environments are increasingly necessary to attract jobs in the shape of mobile firms.

(Maclennan and Mega 1992, pp. 6–7)

Enhancing urban economic and environmental self-reliance is a valuable and necessary policy direction for sustainable urban development, but total urban self-reliance may be neither a realistic nor a desirable goal (see Chapter Two). Taking this further, so well-connected are rural and urban areas that it can be reasonably argued that policies in pursuit of sustainable urban development always need to be framed together with policies for sustainable rural development (World Health Organisation 1992).

In practice, the objective of moving towards becoming a more sustainable city needs to be set in the context of a broader sustainable society, and related to its contribution to global sustainable development

(Leff 1990, OECD 1990). As an essentially human-made artifact, however, the sustainable city needs to aim towards more than just ecological balance at all these geographical scales, it also needs to sustain its own unique contribution to the environment, in terms of its built form in particular. A city which allows its handsome cathedrals and city halls to be taken down and replaced with aesthetically unpleasing buildings or uses, damages its own environment in much the same way as one which surrenders itself to the private motor car. A sustainable city is not so much an entity, an end point, as a process of contributing to global sustainable development. It implies a state of dynamic equilibrium within the global environment, not simply a state of local equilibrium. As a working definition for the purposes of this book:

> *a sustainable city is one in which its people and businesses continuously endeavour to improve their natural, built and cultural environments at neighbourhood and regional levels, whilst working in ways which always support the goal of global sustainable development.*

1.3 SUMMARY: URBAN SUSTAINABILITY AND GLOBAL INTERDEPENDENCIES

As economies and environmental problems have become increasingly international in scope, it has become ever more difficult to view cities meaningfully in isolation from each other or their less urbanised hinterlands. This is far from a new insight: the characterisation of cities as open systems, integrated into broader systems of environment and economy has long been accepted by geographers and others (Perloff 1969). Most importantly, it is important to recognise the ways in which economic development and environmental change are connected, on urban and global scales. Cities are connected to each other – and to resource areas in particular – by an increasingly complex web of links, in production systems, in finance, in resource usage and in the environmental problems which they both create and face.

In terms of the root causes of many of the problems which cities face, it is important to understand the economic and social relationships on local and global scales which have caused them to become 'unsustainable'. This leads to an important question: since many of the problems of cities are related to the broader social and economic relations within which they must operate, to what extent can we look to cities to provide their own solutions to the problems they face?

There are no easy answers; dismissive pessimism is as unproductive as irresponsible anticipation of the redemptive powers of local action and future technological solutions. Global interdependencies require policy action at various geographical levels, from the local and the urban through to the regional and global. They also require a cross-sector policy approach, implying a more sophisticated understanding of the relations between environment, economy and society, not least in their urban manifestations. Urban residents, businesses and politicians can play an important role in shaping their economies, societies and environments, but they cannot do this in isolation of their role in the global economy.

This introductory chapter has highlighted some of the main environmental and urban development issues which currently preoccupy many policy-makers. What becomes clear is that notions of sustainable development and sustainable urban development are highly contestable. What is not contestable is that urban environmental problems are enormous across the world, but that they vary hugely in cause, scope, scale and intensity between cities. Chapters Two and Three examine the ways in which different cities have developed in recent years, economically, physically and socially, and link these variations to differences in environmental problems.

FURTHER READING

A good introduction to most aspects of the sustainability debate is provided by Turner, Pearce and Bateman (1994) in *Environmental Economics: An Elementary Introduction*. Adopting a more specifically urban focus, and also a more polemical approach, is Girardet's (1992) *Cities: New Directions for Sustainable Urban Living*. At a more advanced level is the Town and Country Planning Association's report (Blowers 1993) *Planning for a Sustainable Environment*. Perhaps most importantly of all, it is still valuable to read the book which brought the sustainability debate to the political fore: *Our Common Future* (World Commission on Environment and Development 1987).

KEY THEMES

- Sustainable development
- Inter-generational equity, social justice and transfrontier responsibility (global stewardship).
- Human-made and natural capital assets
- Global environmental and economic interdependencies
- The city as a non-renewable resource
- Sustainable urban development

DISCUSSION POINTS

- Expand on the reasons why so many commentators place poverty at the centre of their analysis of sustainable development. Draw out some of the implications of this approach in terms of urban poverty issues.
- Is economic growth necessarily inimical to environmental development? Consider both rich and poor countries in your analysis.
- What do you consider to be the main 'limits to growth' for cities?

CHAPTER TWO

Urban Growth and the Urban Environment

2.1 URBAN CHANGE AND URBANISATION IN SUSTAINABLE DEVELOPMENT

2.1.1 Introduction

This chapter examines the local, regional and global interdependencies involved in urban growth, economic development and environmental change. The growth of urban population can be measured both as the percentage increase in numbers living in cities, and as urbanisation, i.e. the growing proportion of a national or regional population that is urbanised (Oberai 1993). Both dimensions are widely thought to be important in terms of environmental change and development. Rapidly growing, very large cities are held by some commentators to be almost inherently environmentally unsustainable, although in truth it is the incapacity of fast-growing cities to meet even the basic infrastructure needs of their residents which is the main problem, not growth *per se*. In a similar vein, there is a long-standing concern that an increase in urbanisation causes the countryside to lose its distinctive characteristics; this leads to an alienation of urban people from nature, which in turn lends itself to the adoption of environmentally unsustainable habits (McMichael 1993). The present chapter focuses on the nature of urban environmental change from a predominantly economic point of view, encompassing the attempts of policy makers to influence urban development. In the next chapter attention is turned to the internal economic and social workings of the city.

Historically, the process of urbanisation depended in considerable part on the efficiency of agriculture – mostly rural – in providing food for city dwellers, and on the administrative capacity of a particular society to stimulate the production, storage, and distribution of food. The connection between individual cities and their immediate rural hinterlands has gradually weakened as transport and communications systems have improved, so that by the twentieth century, global food and energy trade patterns meant that most large cities came to rely increasingly heavily on global trading systems (MacNeill, Winsemius and Yakushiji 1991, Girardet 1992). In the process, cities have become able to support ever larger populations, in part, however, by relying on their global hinterlands, sometimes divorcing producers, consumers and policy makers from the immediate impacts of their behaviour in terms of sustainable development.

One result of the de-coupling of the close interdependency of cities from their immediate agricultural hinterlands, plus the growth of global production systems (section 2.4 see p.53) has been the growth in the twentieth century of what are variously termed giant cities, global cities, world cities, mega-cities, or megalopolises. These very large cities have often been seen as an unstable form of development and less desirable than smaller cities, bringing with them both an intensification of existing urban problems and new problems (Gottman and Harper 1967, Richardson 1993).

It is a central part of the present analysis that the environmental costs associated with urban development have been inequitably spread, both socially and geographically, and that this has had a more profound impact in underwriting, or subsidising, the processes of urban growth and wealth generation than is usually recognised. Socially, the problems of urban environmental despoliation usually have most impact upon those already marginalised in society, for instance those who can only afford to rent or buy houses next to dirty, noisy main roads. There are strong geographical themes which crosscut the uneven social spread of both adverse and beneficial environmental impacts of urban development, both within the city and in terms of interactions with a city's regional hinterland. Generally speaking, the urban poor are concentrated in areas with a run-down built environment, often experiencing pollution from neighbouring industries or nearby major roads. Those with greater wealth usually use the relative freedom this affords to buy houses in areas with better environmental conditions (Friedmann 1989). Moreover, urban resource demands and waste products can create major disruption or pollution in hinterland areas, with only 15–20% of urban-sourced nitrous oxide pollution, for instance, falling inside the city (Alcamo and Lubkert 1990). In consequence, the present analysis has at its heart an examination of global economic and environmental interdependencies, processes which also need to be seen as closely interconnected to those national political and economic structures which allow cities to absorb and distribute the environmental costs of their activities inequitably.

2.1.2 Population growth

In the year 1800 just 5% of the world's population was urban; by 1900 the proportion had risen to around 15%; by the year 2000 the proportion will have increased to around 50% (McMichael 1993). In the first 50 years of this century the average global population growth rate was 0.8%, rising to 1.9% per annum between 1950 and 1985 (World Commission on Environment and Development 1987). Although the growth rate is expected to subside from this high level, none the less population growth will continue to make increasing demands on scarce resources for the foreseeable future. As 90% of the anticipated growth will occur in developing countries, and as these countries seek to improve the standards of living of their populations, it may well be these which will place greatest additional demands on global resources, especially agricultural resources. The current low living standards of developing countries – as well as limited internal capacity to support growing populations – may lead them to reject calls on them by international bodies to reduce their resource usage on environmental grounds. The poorer countries would inevitably see such strategies as the rich climbing on to their prosperous plateau and 'pulling up the ladder behind them'. It is for such reasons that so many environmental commentators place analysis of developing countries at the heart of their discussions, together with a more general treatment of anti-poverty strategies (World Commission on Environment and Development 1987, Singh 1989).

Very high rates of global population increase, continuing rises in standards of living and the heavy reliance within existing consumption patterns on non-renewable resources have combined to place enormous stress on world resources. Rising standards of living are important, not simply in the sense that rising per capita consumption has increased overall resource consumption, but also in that the unevenness of this rising consumption means that the vast majority of the world's population still has considerable ground to make up before it can attain the standards enjoyed by the wealthier nations. Even the adoption of a no-growth policy by the richer nations becomes untenable under these circumstances. People in developing countries expect their standards of living to increase over time, as do those poorer sections of the community in wealthy nations. A no-growth policy without some form of redistribution of wealth at various scales would be politically unviable.

The world's population is not only growing rapidly overall, it is also quickly becoming more urbanised (Table 2.1). An estimated 80% of world population increase between 1990 and 2000 will be in urban areas. Urban change and urbanisation are both generally highest in countries with high population growth rates (Tolba and El-Kholy 1992). In the 70 years to 1990, the urban population of developing countries increased more than tenfold, so that by 1990 some 37% of people lived in cities. Urbanisation is anticipated to continue to be more prominent in developing countries than elsewhere, fuelled primarily by high in-migration, but also by high rates of natural population increase (World Commission on Environment and Development 1987). Current global urban hierarchies could quickly change in appearance as a result of the differential rates of urban growth across the world (Table 2.2). Tokyo will probably lose its current position as the world's largest city by the year 2000, overtaken by developing-country cities such as Mexico City and Bangkok (Milne 1988). Despite the spectacular population increases in a few very large cities, the bulk of the urban population in developing countries continues to be in smaller cities with a population of less than one million (Hardoy, Mitlin and Satterthwaite 1992).

Table 2.1 Trends and projections in urban population, by region, 1950–2000

Region	1950	1990	2000
Urban population (millions of inhabitants)			
Africa	32.2	217.4	352.4
Latin America & Caribbean	68.8	320.5	411.3
Asia (not incl Japan)	184.4	975.3	1485.7
Other	0.2	1.4	2.1
Third World total	285.6	1514.7	2251.4
Rest of the world	448.2	875.5	946.2
Percentage of population living in urban centres			
Africa	14.5	33.9	40.7
Latin America & Caribbean	41.5	71.5	76.4
Asia (not incl Japan)	14.2	32.6	41.5
Other	7.5	23.1	27.3
Third World total	17.0	37.1	45.1
Rest of the world	53.8	72.6	74.9

Source: United Nations Environment Programme (1991)

The total urban population in developing countries is already larger than the total population of Europe, North America and Japan combined (Hardoy and Satterthwaite 1991). The World Commission for Environment and Development (1987) put the problem for cities in developing countries very starkly, anticipating that within 15 years the developing countries will have to increase their ability to provide urban infrastructure, services and shelter by 65%. The sheer magnitude of this problem looks even more insurmountable in the context of rising external debts, limited financial resources, alternative priorities in countries with high poverty levels, continuing rural pressures and the existing backlog of unsatisfactory urban conditions currently requiring urgent remedy. In many cities in developing countries there is an inadequate housing stock, resulting in a mix of shanty town growth and pavement dwellers, a high incidence of disease, poor sanitation, inadequate and unreliable supplies of clean water, poor infrastructure – from sewerage to roads – as well as air, noise and water pollution (see Chapter Five). High-density living dominates, whilst open space is scarce. There is a danger of oversimplification in the kind of generalisations used here, given the enormous variability in the form and rate of urbanisation between different countries, and in the environmental problems which they face (Leff 1990). What can not be denied, however, is the scale and intensity of the problem which urbanisation is already posing for many developing countries.

Whilst many writers have tended to fix on the urban problems of anticipated growth for very large cities such as Bangkok and Shanghai, based on official projections, Hardoy and Satterthwaite (1990) exercise a degree of scepticism. They have pointed to the very tentative nature of estimates for forty or more years hence, with the official caveats attached to the initial projections of bodies such as the United Nations often ignored by subsequent writers. Instead, Hardoy and Satterthwaite point to the need to understand the social and economic factors which contribute to the demographic changes of individual cities, with a view to avoiding the emergence of narrow assumptions of extrapolated exponential expansion, rather than some form of deconcentrated urban growth, as in some Western countries. This is to an extent already apparent in India, where the annual growth of Calcutta and Bombay is high at 4%, but is less than that of medium-sized towns such as Bangalore with 7% annual growth (Correa 1989, see also Hardoy and Satterthwaite 1990, pp. 88–9). They conclude that the issue of how fast a city is growing is secondary to increases in economic growth and standards of living, since the main problems of most Third World cities relate to poverty, which size may exacerbate but not necessarily create.

Table 2.2 Examples of rapid population growth in Third World cities (in millions)

City	1950	Most recent figure	UN projection for 2000
Mexico City	3.05	16.0 (1982)	26.3
Sao Paulo	2.7	12.6 (1980)	24.0
Bombay	3.0 (1951)	8.2 (1981)	16.0
Jakarta	1.45	6.2 (1977)	12.8
Cairo	2.5	8.5 (1979)	13.2
Delhi	1.4 (1951)	5.8 (1981)	13.3
Manila	1.78	5.5 (1980)	11.1
Lagos	0.27 (1952)	4.0 (1980)	8.3
Bogota	0.61	3.9 (1985)	9.6
Nairobi	0.14	0.83 (1979)	5.3
Dar-es-Salaam	0.15 (1960)	0.9 (1981)	4.6
Greater Khartoum	0.18	1.05 (1978)	4.1
Amman	0.03	0.78 (1978)	1.5
Nouakchott	0.0058	0.25 (1982)	1.1
Manaus	0.11	0.51 (1980)	1.1
Santa Cruz	0.059	0.26 (1976)	1.0

Source: WCED 1987, p.237

2.1.3 The changing function of the city in the global economy and global ecology

A central feature of urban dynamism is the changing economic roles of cities. At one level this can be seen in the light of broad functional shifts, for instance shifts through such stages as market town, industrial city and service centre to international trading centre. It is also possible to examine the changing roles of cities in terms of the evolving capitalist mode of production. Harvey (1989a, p. 53), for instance, sees different roles for the city over time in terms of 'the mobilization of surpluses in the mercantile city, the production of surpluses in the industrial city, and the absorption of surpluses in the Keynesian city', that is, the economic surpluses in the form of profits intended for capital accumulation. It is not possible or desirable to derive from this a model for the general evolution of city functions which each city must go through (see below on the dangers of 'developmentalism'). It is possible, however, to draw some distinctively environmental themes from this type of analysis. For instance, in the mercantile city many of the environmental costs of urbanisation were borne outside the city, in the agricultural hinterlands in particular, which generated the economic surpluses that were transferred into the cities; in the industrial city the environmental costs associated with production were much more clearly felt within the city itself, particularly in the form of air pollution; in the contemporary Western post-industrial city, many of the environmental costs associated with industrial production are gradually being displaced directly from the largest cities as they deindustrialise, only to be replaced by the environmental costs of high consumption, such as the problem of waste disposal.

Useful though these insights are in respect of Western urbanisation, they lose some of their power when applied to cities elsewhere. In particular, the contemporary Third World city offers a very different perspective, since in many cities a greater proportion of the environmental costs of development are to be found in the home and in the workplace, in part owing to different attitudes and priorities in the regulation of urban growth and of the labour market. In the past thirty years most of the largest cities in developing countries have suffered cumulative environmental problems, most notably industrial pollution and road traffic-related pollution and congestion. It is important here to note that whereas in the West urbanisation was largely led by industrialisation, in developing countries urban expansion has tended to precede industrialisation, and indeed industrialisation has often been seen as the means of coping with high urban population growth, through modernisation and job creation (Gilbert and Gugler 1992).

Urbanisation linked to industrialisation was, for much of the latter half of the twentieth century, seen as an integral and necessary part of the modernisation of national economies in developing countries, bringing them closer to the idealised standard of the Western industrial nation. This perspective is now widely rejected as a facet of misconceived developmentalism (see Taylor 1989). Instead of projecting historical development paths on to less-developed countries and their cities (see for instance the 'development stages' models of Rostow 1960, and Taafe, Morrill and Gould 1963), whereby they would need only aspire to the Western development path and their problems would be solved, commentators have increasingly emphasised the centrality of the notion of interdependencies between nations' and cities' economies at a global level (Wallerstein 1979, see also Brookfield 1975).

The various development stages models also tended to see urban systems as the key to modernising 'backward' regions, with beneficial modernising effects expected to gradually spill over from large cities to smaller cities and rural areas (see Gilbert and Gugler 1992 for a review). The more prevelant form of analysis in recent years has been to examine urban development, not in terms of the position of particular cities within their national urban hierarchies, but as part of a global process. Radical development critiques argue that each nation and city cannot aim along the same preordained development trajectory, since the possibilities for progress are constrained by limited global resources and the existing success within global capitalism of particular regions (Gore 1984, King 1990a, 1990b; Knox and Agnew 1989). Capitalist development in this system *requires* polarisation between rich and poor regions, rather than providing the motor for poor countries to become richer. Some formulations of this approach may have overreacted to previous work which ignored interdependency, arguing that the capitalist system necessarily denies modernisation and development to regions on its periphery (see Corbridge 1986), which, as the recent rapid growth of economies such as those of Taiwan and Malaysia illustrates, is not necessarily the case. Most commentators, however, argue that it is the overall differentials which are increasing at the global scale.

An increasingly important theme in development debates has been an examination the role of a system of world cities, metropolitan core areas which are seen as providing the critical nodes in the articulation of production, services and cultural transactions on a global scale (Sassen-Koob 1984). That is, the emergence of a global trading place is articulated primarily through the control functions of a few very large world cities, providing specialised services, high-level management and command functions, both political and economic (King 1990b). From this perspective 'the metropolis is indisputably a global settlement, an international phenomenon, a nodal point in the international division of labour. It serves multiple social, economic and cultural functions across national and international borders' (Angotti 1993, p.3). The growth of very large cities is regarded as integrally related to the growing internationalisation of capital in the post-war years, involving the emergence of growing global trade in production and services, articulated around a continually changing global division of labour, the search for new markets and the continuing concentration and centralisation of capital (King 1990b). We have here an interesting and closely interconnected parallel to arguments that the growth of large cities was fuelled initially by rising rural agricultural productivity and later by the emergence of global agricultural hinterlands. The growth of very large cities may well be a matter of national concern, in terms of internal urban hierarchies, but the economic forces fuelling this growth are largely global, making local attempts to curb large city growth all the more difficult to address in policy terms.

Contemporary metropolitan cores such as New York, Los Angeles, Frankfurt, Tokyo and London were not always in this dominant position, nor can they be expected always to remain as 'world cities'. Economically successful world cities have been a central feature of many of the newly emerging growth nations in the global economy, with the success of the city-state nations of Hong Kong and Singapore pointing to something of the central role of cities with strong internal political and economic structures in achieving rapid economic transformation. As small island states they also demonstrate the importance of global hinterlands in fuelling metropolitan growth. Alternatively, one reason for the fall of some former dominant cores – for instance early Rome – may have been their unsustainable environmental exploitation of their hinterlands (Girardet 1990). With the emergence of global hinterlands for very large cities, such immediate connections between metropolitan growth and decline, and environmental deterioration are becoming less relevant. Large cities are at the centre of very complex global economic and environmental interdependencies and can quickly shift the foci of their exploitation from one set of countries to another.

As we have already intimated, these insights from the political economy of urbanisation are important in achieving an understanding of the environmental concerns of cities. The intermeshing of the world's economy and the Earth's environment has emerged as a central theme in the sustainability debate, in particular the emergence of what have been termed the shadow ecologies of Western nations (MacNeill, Winsemius and Yakushiji 1991).

> Economic activity today is concentrated in the world's urban/industrial regions. Few, if any, of these regions are ecologically self-contained ... the major urban industrial centers of the world are locked into complex international networks for trade in goods and services of all kinds, including primary and processed energy, food, materials and other resources. The major cities of the economically powerful Western nations constitute the nodes of these networks, enabling these nations to draw upon the ecological capital of all other nations to provide food for their economies, and even land, air, and water to assimilate their waste by-products. This ecological capital, which may be found thousands of miles from the regions in which it is used, forms the 'shadow ecology' of an economy. The oceans, the atmosphere (climate), and other 'commons' also form part of this shadow ecology. (p. 58)

These shadow ecologies, or 'ecological footprints' (Hardoy, Mitlin and Satterthwaite 1992) of cities, leave their imprint across the world, not just in immediate hinterland areas. World trading means that individual cities (and nations) can become less dependent on specific hinterlands as trade is switched between areas, becoming less vulnerable in the short term to loss of supplies. However, the ability to sidestep the problems which urban demands create may have contributed enormously to global environmental deterioration and vulnerability.

2.2 WHY CITIES GROW

2.2.1 The contemporary forces of urban growth and urbanisation

Many reasons have been put forward for why human settlements exist, ranging from their role as administrative centres for territorial control and the defensive role of walled cities, to human social needs, including the role of close contact in cultural, artistic and scientific development, all of which may help foster urban and indeed national economic growth (Richardson 1978). In addition, cities, by virtue of their population size and relative wealth, can support various levels of functional specialisation, not least in terms of social and cultural facilities, health care, education and retailing. Cities can also provide a well-spring of innovation, resulting from the richness of social interaction, which in turn results from the very fact that so many people live and work in such close proximity (Jacobs 1984, Bairoch 1988). It has even been argued that 'without cities there could have been no real civilisation' (Bairoch 1988, p.1). Cities can also be symbolic of a nation's values and its achievements, albeit often those of a limited political and economic elite (HABITAT 1987). The Commission of the European Communities' (1990) *Green Paper on the Urban Environment* claims that it is a combination of economic, social, cultural and political dynamics which stimulate urban growth (Box 2.1).

Cities attract people and businesses to them for many reasons, but perhaps foremost amongst these dynamic impulses is the search for jobs and wealth-creation opportunities. It is important therefore to understand the main economic rationales of cities, and also to see how they interconnect with other growth impulses. Also important to bear in mind are the historical private and public urban infrastructure costs tied up in the built environment of large cities, which can both facilitate and impede contemporary forces of urban change.

Cities can decline, but they generally do so relatively slowly, and in recent centuries very few have disappeared altogether, except perhaps some on the resource frontier, one-industry towns dependent on the extraction of a finite resource, often in hostile environments. Lewis Mumford (1961) in *The City in History* and Colin Ward in *Welcome Thinner City* (1989) have both observed that every city tends to have its one 'golden era', but for many decline quickly ensues. Part of the fascination of twentieth-century urban change has been the attempts of some older cities to 'reinvent' themselves after initially being written off following rapid deindustrialisation. Active restructuring policies have been pursued in many older cities seeking to achieve a second golden era, sometimes drawing on the legacy of the built environment inherited from the first golden era. Notable examples include Baltimore in the USA, Lille in France, Halifax in England, and Glasgow in Scotland. Cities, then, are not simply subject to the whims of changing external economic pressures: urban governments, communities and business leaders can seek to reposition themselves within the global economy in an attempt to revive their prosperity.

Box 2.1 The Dynamics of Urban Growth

The Economic Dynamic. The city is synonymous with proximity, providing the multiple contacts and activities which make it a hub of information and a creative centre. It is this ability to assemble the economic factors involved in all stages of production, research and consumption that draws firms to the urban centres.

The Social Dynamic. The city brings together a wide variety of social facilities (nurseries, hospitals, social service agencies, etc.) whose role is becoming increasingly important as populations are marginalised by underemployment, unemployment and poverty. Indeed, the concentration of social problems makes it possible to define and pursue specific rather than general remedial policies. The city also concentrates employment opportunities: this represents one of its great attractions. More generally, the city represents choice: of social relations, of education, of services and of work.

The Cultural Dynamic. As in the social sphere of which it is a part, the city's cultural role depends on density, proximity and choice. These factors facilitate the 'production' of culture as much as its 'consumption'. In addition, the historic heritage of the city allows unique economic activities linked to culture, including tourism.

The Political Dynamic. More than any other place, the city must respond directly to the demands by its citizens for 'good government'. It is a place where direct participation is possible and increasingly practised, and where the individual can develop most freely a sense of personal and civic value. It is no accident that 'citizen', 'citoyen', 'cittadino' or 'Bürger' denote the political sovereign in our languages.

(Adapted from Commission of the European Communities (1990) *Green Paper on the Urban Environment*, pp. 20–21)

In terms of the present-day dynamics of urban development, Harvey (1989a) has sought to examine how cities have evolved new strategies and new roles to bring about renewed economic growth. This analysis is based around the notion of cities transforming themselves from being centres of production to centres of consumption, and also centres of information processing. In adapting to new conditions Harvey sees four different competitive elements for cities attempting to restructure themselves:

1. **Competition within the spatial division of labour.** The combination of improved transport and communications systems, enlarged scales of production, where fragmentation of the production process is possible, and more rapid technological turnover with shorter investment cycles has fuelled a rapid and increasingly dynamic globalisation of production systems (Dicken 1992). In consequence, production processes can be located on a global scale to exploit the localised availability of cheap resources, cheap labour and lax environmental standards. The tendency under the post-war international division of labour has frequently been to locate routinised aspects of mass production, which require only low skilled labour, in cheap labour locations. Although this summary is a tremendous simplification of what are in reality a complex series of often contradictory social, political and economic pressures, it is possible to see that cities increasingly have to compete with each other on a global scale in order to attract multinational investment and to deter indigenous employers from moving to other locations. The old assumption that once a manufacturer has made an investment in a locality, the plant is there for ever, no longer holds. Cities must compete to minimise their financial and legislative demands on employers, in order to create local conditions conducive to investment, from low pay or highly-skilled labour pools to attractive environments for executive living.

2. **Competition within the spatial division of consumption.** The emerging importance of spatial divisions of consumption, in terms of consumption behaviour (such as leisure, vacations, entertainment), is little remarked upon, yet it has now become an important critical dimension of economic activity. Increasingly, consumption can be seen to separate itself from the normal routines of work and household living, with new forms and styles of consumption. This in turn requires new spaces for consumption and a further fragmentation within and between cities. In this context, cities are now having to compete for a role as consumption centres, as witnessed by the rising investment in leisure com-

plexes, in re-enforcing positive cultural heritages, in new retail complexes and in providing waterfront amenity areas, for instance.

3. **Competition for command functions.** Cities also compete with each other for the often highly-centralised high order functions of high-finance and government, plus attendant support industries. An example is the competition between European cities in the early 1990s to host the ten new European Union insitutions. In recent years, the key to success in this sphere has been to improve centrality and efficiency as a global information-gathering centre by building on existing reputations and facilities, not least to provide effective transport and communications infrastructures. It is in this context, rather than that of comprehensive inner-city renewal, that schemes such as London Docklands need to be seen.

4. **Competition for redistribution.** Finally, cities compete for redistribution of economic power and financial resources, both through government policies – not least urban and regional assistance – and through other channels, such as religious and voluntary organisations, trade unions and so on.

If we accept that these factors will be the main driving forces for urban development in the next few decades, what then are the environmental issues which arise from this analysis? Perhaps the most important is that the notion of a post-industrial city hides some interesting tensions. Most urban leaders will still want to compete for mobile industrial investment, including those whose cities are also seeking to improve their position in terms of command functions. There is a tension here, in that in order to improve their position in terms of the spatial division of consumption, these same cities will not tolerate environmentally despoiling industry to the extent they did in the past. Alternatively some cities, seeking to improve their position through increased industrial investment, will find that competition in the spatial division of labour forces them to offer ever less stringent environmental controls on consumption of resources, pollution and landscape degradation. For other cities, attempts to improve their position in terms of global and national redistribution mechanisms may, if successful, allow a buffer against lowering environmental standards and a means to improve environmental conditions. Experience suggests that both national and international aid programmes come with strings attached, many of which have directly or indirectly contributed to environmental degradation (Conroy and Litvinoff 1988, Hardoy, Mitlin and Satterthwaite 1992). This said, agencies such as the World Bank have become more sensitive to criticisms of adverse environmental impacts associated with projects which they fund. Also, as Turner (1991) points out, adjustment policies funded by global institutions do not necessarily degrade the environment: much depends on the form of policy adopted and the sectors of the economy affected.

The attempts of urban civic leaders to mould the growth of their cities has led to some important distortions in investment priorities for large cities. For instance, in Istanbul during the early 1980s the election of a new entrepreneurial mayor led to the city investing in high-profile, symbolic infrastructural projects for eight years, aiming to project an image of the city as being of world city status. One notable example was the decision to raze some thirty thousand commercial and residential buildings along the shores of the Golden Horn, including some of architectural and cultural signficance, replacing them with formal gardens and a large autoroute (Keyder and Oncu 1993). In this process of generating showpiece investments, not only were the infrastructural needs of existing rundown neighbourhoods neglected, but the very success of the strategy in linking Turkey to the global economy was instrumental in increasing migration to Istanbul, in turn creating additional housing pressures and a growing marginalised pool of workers seeking jobs.

There are some important issues here. The process of urbanisation is not a'natural' one, subject to a set of abstract economic or other laws. Rather it is very much guided by the political structures and priorities involved, and by existing social and economic conditions. According to some commentators, metropolitan development in developing countries has been fuelled by a political and economic system which displays persistent *urban bias*. Tanzania's Julius Nyerere (1968), for instance, argued that the repayment of overseas loans used to fund urban development is ultimately made by the rural population, through the sale of peasant produce. In effect, the urban population achieves the benefits of investment in roads, hospitals, electricity and water supply, not the rural people whose endeavours earn the foreign capital used to pay off the loans.

The consumption demands and the political power of urban areas can distort resource and investment allocations in favour of urban priorities and against the needs of the rural poor (Lipton 1977, Keyfitz 1991). The range of distorting mechanisms is extremely diverse, with interrelated industrial policies providing further indirect forms of urban subsidy (Lipton 1977, Gugler 1988, Oberai 1993, Richardson 1993). Examples include: the allocation of government spending to prestige urban investments; direct subsidies of urban food, infrastructure provision, health and education; measures raising the price of industrial goods relative to farm prices, in the process diverting rural, urban and overseas capital to the more profitable opportunities afforded by urban industry;

the provision of urban educational facilities which attract the more able members of the rural population. It has also been argued that civil servants in capital cities tend to allocate resources to where they can most obviously see the impacts – in their own city – and where they can help assuage some of the immediate political pressures of the urban classes.

One policy implication of accepting the urban bias thesis is the need to moderate the exploitative implications of urban expansion by shifting the emphasis in government policy towards rural development and even to curb the growth of cities, in particular by seeking ways to limit rural–urban migration. The urban bias case, however, remains contentious, with some analysts pointing instead to a bias against the urban poor, which has fuelled uneven metropolitan growth in part at their expense, and the nature of bias within the rural sector, which has favoured privileged groups such as rich agriculturalists (see Gilbert and Gugler 1992).

2.2.2 Migration and cities

Migration can play a central role in the urbanisation process, although its contribution to urban growth varies considerably between different cities and different nations. International migration is linked to environmental degradation in several ways, as both outcome and cause. Land degradation and water shortages may be contributing to a growing class of environmental refugees, flowing across national borders, into both refugee camps and already crowded cities (MacNeill, Winsemius and Yakushiji 1991, Tickell 1991). In Australia there is a major on-going policy debate over the role of high immigrant flows on the urban environment, since the majority of immigrants are destined for cities. The concerns here are many (see Fincher 1991), including the belief of some that Australia has already reached its optimum 'carrying capacity' and that adding further population adds to pressure to maintain agriculture in marginal lands, sustained only by government subsidy and chemical inputs. It is also argued that since Australians generally have a higher consumption of resources per capita than the countries from which immigrants come, the net effect is to increase global resource consumption. This form of disingenuous analysis masks the remnants of a nationalist way of thinking which previously found its expression in the 'white Australia' immigration policy. Fincher concludes her review of the issues involved in the case of Australia by pointing to the multi-faceted, multi-causal nature of environmental degradation, which makes it unhelpful to isolate just one factor, such as immigration. Immigrants are not necessarily more profligate in their resource consumption than any other sections of the community. Indeed, the impacts of immigration on Australian cities have to be seen in the context of various forms of out-migration from cities, and the positive social and economic impacts of the activities of immigrants.

Internal, domestic rural–urban migration is usually a major element of the demographic change of those cities which are still growing rapidly. In the older industrial nations net rural–urban migration has generally ceased, sometimes to be replaced by a drift out from the cities. Historically, the drive towards urbanisation was largely economic, with people attracted by the prospect of higher wages and undeterred by the very real environmental problems of cities. Bairoch (1989) summarises these tensions for Western European cities (Table 2.3), concluding that whilst urban–rural wage differentials increased through the nineteenth century, health differentials declined.

Table 2.3 Urban–rural differences in wages and infant mortality in Western Europe

	Differences in wages in favour of the city	*Differences in infant mortality in favour of the countryside*
c.1815–40	15–20%	50–70%
c.1900–14	25–30%	10–20%

Today, rural–urban migration is most strongly associated with cities in developing countries, although with major variations between nations. In general, about a third of the urban population increase in Africa and Asia comes from migration or reclassification of urban areas, as opposed to 58% in Latin America (Tolba and El-Kholy 1992), with the remaining growth largely due to internal urban population increases.

There are many types of rural–urban migration (from seasonal to permanent), which change over time and vary between cities and nations, whilst an extremely wide range of economic, social and even environmental push-and-pull factors are involved in stimulating these widely varying migration patterns (see Gunn 1978, Jones 1990, Gilbert and Gugler 1992, Goldstein 1993). Economic factors are usually said to dominate in the migration decision, as individuals seek to improve their income levels and to gain access to the wider range of jobs, occupations and investment opportunities which can be found in cities relative to rural areas (Gugler 1988). Paralleling these economic factors, is the lure of the relatively sophisticated social and cultural facilities found in the cities. In cities, the health care infrastructure is usually better, children are more likely to get better schooling, bus and train networks allow access to a wide range of services from retailing to theatres in different parts of the city, houses are often better built and more likely to be connected to electricity and to mains water and sewage outlets. Urbanisation is generally more costly in this respect for a nation than rural development, in part because of the need to provide such basic infrastructure for the inhabitants (Lewis 1978), and in part because of the higher costs of building it (Richardson 1993).

A further problem associated with high in-migration for a rapidly expanding city is that not all migrants get jobs immediately in the formal sector of the economy, and remain largely outside the domain of the tax system. As with other marginalised people in the city, the problem is largely one of poverty rather than immigration *per se*. However, migrants do place additional demands on the urban infrastructure without necessarily making a significant contribution to the costs of providing and maintaining it, either in that they are not fully employed in the formal sector and paying taxes, or those who are may simply be displacing people with jobs, involving no net gain in tax revenue. Unsurprisingly, city governments have frequently been unable to provide basic infrastructure sufficiently quickly to meet rapidly rising demand.

This is not purely an issue for cities in developing countries, but their problems have tended to be of a much higher magnitude than elsewhere, especially in the form of homelessness and widespread shanty town growth. There are now a billion people living in shanty towns around the world, including half the populations of Calcutta, Lusaka and Colombo and over two-thirds in Mexico City and Lima (Tolba and El-Kholy 1992). These settlements are usually only illegally connected to water and electricity supplies and often not at all to piped sewerage outlets. This has made a major contribution to continuing poor environmental health conditions, which have in turn contributed to the spread of infectious diseases (see Chapter Five). Rapid rates of urban growth, without parallel improvements to basic urban infrastructure, can be a major contributor to environmental degradation, and insofar as high in-migration can be one factor in high population growth it is a cause of concern to many policy-makers.

Wilbur Zelinsky's (1971) Mobility Transition model provides an interesting attempt to relate patterns of rural and urban migration to stages of a nation's development. In this model, rural–urban migration is seen as an important element early in a country's modernisation progress, later becoming superseded by migration between cities, and counterurbanisation, where some people move out from the cities to rural areas. Taylor (1989) dismisses the Mobility Transition model as the pinnacle of geographers' misplaced developmentalism (see section 2.1.3 p.35). It is not necessarily the case then that developing countries and their cities will or should follow this trajectory: the implication that rural–urban migration patterns and related environmental pressures will decline as modernisation advances needs to be treated cautiously.

Falling foul of some of the same criticisms is the urban life cycle model, which draws largely on the European experience (see Hall and Hay 1980, Fielding and Halford 1990, Hay 1990). This model argues that is possible to identify a cyclical pattern of urbanisation, suburban-isation, counterurbanisation and reurbanisation. Suburbanisation arises as the central city loses its attraction to businesses and residents, with the outward movement of both facilitated by improved public and private transport. Counterurbanisation then follows, as employers and workers react to the disagglomeration economies of large cities, such as congestion, high land prices and social, economic and environmental decay. Reurbanisation may then follow, as the dilapidated inner urban areas previously deserted by outward migrants are recolonised and revitalised, most notably through housing gentrification. Whilst this cyclical model has been seen as a basis for policy prescription, its value is undermined by its reductive nature, which emphasises pattern over process, that is: it tells us how things have changed in some contexts but very little about why. It is difficult to accept this as a general model of urban change.

It is possible to begin to understand some of these same trends in a very different way when the analysis takes as its starting point the need to understand underlying processes of change, rather than simply iden-tifying patterns of change. Walker's (1981) analysis for instance points to the development of suburbanisation as a means of transforming a flagging capitalist economy. Suburbanisation from this perspective in-volved a radical restructuring of space, which turned the consumption of cars, petrol, tyres – and even larger houses – from luxuries into necessities, invariably with the connivance of the state. American capi-talism from the 1920s in this analysis actually required the investment opportunities created by urban expansion, in part as it fled the con-straints of the inner cities with their more organised and more costly labour forces. From hidden government subsidy of road building pro-grammes to private-sector manipulation of markets, suburbanisation was not a simple 'natural' law of urbanisation in motion, but a shift fuelled by the search for commercial gain, from property developers, road builders, oil companies and automobile manufacturers. Perhaps most disturbing is the case of the General Motors subsidiary, National City Lines, which during the 1930s and 1940s bought and then closed down the networks of electric street cars and trolley buses in 45 cities

in 16 states (Stretton 1978, Adams and Brock 1986). According to
Bradford Snell in 1974 (cited in Adams and Brock 1986), in evidence
to the Senate Subcommittee on Antitrust and Monopoly:

> Thirty-five years ago Los Angeles was a beautiful city of lush palm
> trees, fragrant orange groves and ocean-clean air. It was served then
> by the world's largest electric railway network. In the late 1930s
> General Motors and allied highway interests acquired the local
> transit companies, scrapped their pollution-free electric trains, tore
> down their power transmission lines, ripped our their tracks and
> placed GM buses on already congested city streets. The noisy
> foul-smelling buses turned earlier patrons of the high-speed rail
> system away from public transit and, in effect, sold millions of
> private automobiles. Largely as a result, this city is today an
> ecological wasteland: the palm trees are dying of petrochemical
> smog; the orange groves have been paved over by 300 miles of
> freeways; the air is a septic tank into which 4 million cars, half of
> them built by General Motors, pump 13,000 tons of pollutants
> daily. (p.6)

According to Walker's analysis then, a particular form of urban growth,
low-density suburbanisation, was preferred not for its efficiency, but for
its profitability, and powerful forces ensured that very little got in the
way of the quest for profit. This is a simple caricature of a much richer
analysis of suburbanisation processes (see also Berry 1984), which also
focuses on the role of residential class segregation in cities as a means
to creating localised capacities for the extraction of high rents for the
owners of land and property. Thus, for instance, working class people
get 'trapped' in certain districts, which then allows landlords to charge
extraordinary rents, thereby increasing their profits. Migration to and
within cities emerges from this analysis as a fundamental aspect of the
capital restructuring of an economy, not simply a necessary concomitant
of modernisation. It is not sufficient to look at past patterns of migration
urban development, and extrapolate from them: rather, we need to
understand the underlying causes of change relevant to each area and
to different historical periods.

2.2.3 Agglomeration economies and diseconomies

For the conventional economist, the economic rationale of cities lies
principally in the efficiencies which can result from agglomeration
economies, with economies of proximity and scale especially important.
Economies of proximity refer to the fact that it is cheaper to exchange
goods and services between nearby suppliers. There are also major
savings for producers located close to their raw materials where the

production process involves considerable weight loss. Economies of scale can occur where marginal unit costs are reduced with increased production or services levels. This can benefit larger cities: for instance, relatively it may be cheaper to run a bus service of fifty vehicles than of one, as the owner can jointly advertise all services, buy discounted buses in bulk, and so on. Beneficial agglomeration economies can also occur through economies of density and scope (Button and Pearce 1989), such as the advantages of access to a greater range of financial services and transport support infrastructure, and the shared costs of common facilities, such as access to tool makers in a jewellery quarter or cold stores in a fishing port, and access to a particular labour pool, be it skilled or cheap unskilled labour that is required.

It is important to recognise here that the economic advantages of urban agglomeration can also imply environmental efficiency. For instance, proximity can cut down on the environmental costs of transport, both through reduced travel distances between producers, and the potential to reduce commuting distances. The tendency towards larger-scale production can potentially produce energy savings too, though again this is not always the case. For example, in the case of energy generation, neighbourhood combined heat and power (CHP) provision is often both economically and environmentally more efficient and less costly than relying on the large electricity generating plants which currently dominate production in the Western nations (OECD 1990, Hutchinson 1992).

Positive agglomeration economies such as these are important elements in improving the productivity of urban businesses generally. What they do not do is provide a linear path, where the larger the city, the greater its productivity, efficiency or desirability as a centre for production or service industries, or for habitation. This in part relates to the agglomeration diseconomies associated with very large cities, e.g. higher land costs, higher labour costs (more evident in affluent cities than in developing-country cities), congestion, stress, noise, air pollution and so on.

In any city there will always be a mixture of agglomeration economies and diseconomies. In general, agglomeration diseconomies begin to dominate in larger cities, as the benefits of agglomeration begin to diminish and even disappear, and as the disadvantages become more prominent in both absolute and net terms (Richardson 1978). To use a simple example, as cities grow in size, traffic congestion often increases, journey times increase, motor vehicle fuel efficiency diminishes, noise levels rise and air pollution becomes more concentrated, counteracting some of the advantages of close proximity. The effects of agglomeration economies and diseconomies, however, are frequently too complex to reduce to simple directionalities. For instance, the disagglomeration effect of high land prices may well force industry out from the city centre, but this can also be seen as advantageous. Indeed in some areas, where high land prices bring about higher residential densities, this may have a positive impact in terms of supporting local services, including public transport (see Chapter Three).

The search to identify environmental and economic efficiencies associated with urban agglomerations tells us only so much about the forces which power urban growth. As the previous sections have highlighted, the ways in which cities begin to restructure economically, socially and demographically are incredibly complex, responding to a wide range of global and local structures and dynamics. Large cities may well become in some ways more economically and environmentally inefficient as they grow in size, but for a variety of reasons, including the continuing value of investments in different aspects of the built environment, they rarely collapse. The search for urban agglomeration efficiencies, then, is only a very partial explanation for urban growth and decline, and provides little justification for limiting the size of very large cities.

2.3 EXTERNALITIES AND THE URBAN ENVIRONMENT

It is important to examine in some detail the ways in which economic systems draw upon environmental resources and capacities, not least since the failure of these systems to account fully for environmental costs of economic growth is widely held to be the root cause of many contemporary urban – and indeed global – environmental problems. In economists' terms, some costs lie outside the market pricing mechanism and are not therefore distributed by the market in a 'rational' manner. These hidden costs are generally referred to as *environmental externalities*. They include those environmental burdens created by producers, consumers and others, which are not taken into account in pricing mechanisms, in effect passing the burden on to others.

A prime example of environmental externalities is the suburban resident who drives into work daily in the centre of the city, in the process polluting the inner urban atmosphere, contributing among other things to ill-health, low house values close to major roads and building decay. Those who create environmental damage do not necessarily suffer from this themselves, but others do, and in this process very strong social and geographical inequalities are created. (Chapter Seven provides a more detailed examination of this issue.)

Changing the pricing structure of goods to incorporate external costs can help change producer and consumer behaviour, for example introducing pricing differentials between leaded and unleaded petrol through the tax system in the UK, has encouraged a rapid spread in the availability of unleaded petrol and encouraged consumers to switch to lead-free fuels where possible. There are, however, important ethical questions involved in raising prices through externality pricing in isolation from redistributive policies, since higher prices may in effect simply allow the rich to buy the right to pollute others. Similarly, increasing fuel prices is an excellent way of attempting to curb urban car use, but it can penalise people who live in rural areas, remote from shops and other services and with poor public transport provision. Taken to their extreme, market solutions which individualise the problems work against collective solutions. For instance, the market solution to global warming for the individual might be to invest in air-conditioning; for dirty water problems the answer would be to buy bottled water or invest in filters; to avoid smog either be in a car yourself, wear a gas mask or escape to furthest suburbia.

This is related in part to what has been termed the 'tragedy of the commons' (Hardin 1969, see also Johnston 1989), where the individual acts outside the broader sense of societal well-being. According to this view, it is inherent within the nature of individuals operating outside of a collectivist agreement that they will each seek to use 'common' natural resources without a long-term regard for sustainable yield. For instance, twenty farmers may graze twenty sheep for years on a piece of common land within the land's carrying capacity, but one other person adds just one more sheep to this grazing and all the common land quickly becomes degraded and fails to self-replenish. The costs are not borne solely by the farmer who adds the one sheep, but instead are shared equally by all twenty-one farmers. The tragedy is that in the short term the one additional farmer gains equal benefits to the others, and so continues in a habit which will ultimately cause the demise of the livelihoods of all the farmers.

In this way, the free market becomes conducive to the short-term interests of continuing to overexploit the land for the benefit of the individual, whilst the broader, long-term communal interest is undermined. Persuasive though the tragedy of the commons argument is, it must be remembered that in virtually every society there exists a framework of formal and informal societal regulatory controls which seek to prevent such antisocial behaviour, protecting the common good through collective social responsibility and sanctions. It is only when such systems are broken down that the 'tragedy of the commons' becomes relevant at the local level. Indeed, rather than advocating a market based solution, it may well be the increasing 'commodification of nature', where everything has its price, that is undermining communal stewardship and replacing it with the vagaries of private property ownership.

There is a parallel argument (Owen 1969) concerning the growth of cities, where

> growth by accretion has occurred because of individual decisions to take advantage of the urban infrastructure, its markets and of the external economies available in a settled community. But these decisions are made without appropriate actions to compensate for the resulting social costs. For instance, a new plant coming to New York benefits from existing markets and infrastructure, and from the great variety of service industries already there to meet its requirements and reduce its risks. The fact that this newly arrived enterprise may increase the congestion and costs of urban living for everyone does not influence the location decision. The city continues to grow because newcomers can still benefit, even if their arrival is detrimental to those already there. (p. 208)

Many urban analysts have noted that historically urban development has been fuelled in part by the exploitation of labour and nature, but also through the efficiency of the built environment as an arena for capital accumulation and centralisation (Harvey 1989a). Remarkably little, however, has been made of the ways in which cities distribute environmental costs unevenly both within the city and externally, a process which has been of central importance in reducing urban costs and fuelling further growth. This is not to say that the role of nature has not played a central part in some explanations of uneven regional and urban development: it has (Smith 1990); or that uneven access to environmental goods has not been widely remarked upon: it has (Harvey 1973, Dicken and Lloyd 1981). Harvey (1973, pp.69–70), for instance, uses the case of urban open space to demonstrate his thesis that accessibility or proximity to certain resources affects the 'real' income of individuals.

The argument stated here, however, is more fundamental than this. Cities are the centres for the creation and redistribution of major environmental externalities. These are then passed on unevenly, both within the city and outside, with crosscutting uneven social redistributive effects. To caricature this rather crudely: city factories may obtain their coal from surrounding pit villages, which bear the costs of environmental pollution associated with coal extraction, whilst the miners bear the costs of poor health related to their occupation; the factories then pollute the air around them and most affect those living close by, those who cannot afford to move to cleaner suburbs; the factory owners do not pay for the costs imposed on others, only for internal production costs. One policy objective might therefore be to cost these environmental impacts and make the factory bear them as part of its production costs. The counter-argument for some economists is that we need to examine the substitution costs of alternative social arrangements in an attempt to maximise society's total production output. In this argument, rather than limit production or compensate the polluted living next to a factory, it might be cheaper to move the people away (Coase 1960), a solution which might suit economists' abstract models but which holds little sway with those who feel ties to a particular community. Nonetheless, Coase's argument does illustrate that it is important to be aware that the benefits of reducing pollution impacts in one place might also have some counterbalancing detrimental impacts, such as job losses in the local community. Pricing all externalities into the market is a necessary policy direction, but it raises major challenges in terms of addressing social and geographical inequalities in adverse environmental impacts. Chapter Seven returns to this theme with a look at economic tools for improving the urban environment.

2.4 URBAN ECONOMIC RESTRUCTURING

2.4.1 *Big is beautiful?*

Just as very large cities have established global hinterlands in environmental terms, so they have become enmeshed in complex global trading networks, whilst smaller cities have also become increasingly linked into this global metropolitan core, directly and indirectly. The globalisation of production and services has involved a major restructuring of most urban economies over the post-war period, the results of which have been significant in altering the size, functions and physical form of cities.

In some countries, there has been a major redistribution of industry in the present century, away from the old industrial cities and towns of the industrial revolution, involving in particular a major deindustrialisation of the metropolitan cores. The old links between urbanisation and industrialisation, and the resultant environmental degradation, have been broken. Alternatively, for cities in developing countries, as we have already seen, for a variety of reasons industry has continued to be attracted to the large cities, which in consequence provide major concentrations of both production and trade. Increasingly, however, both domestic and overseas investment appears to be turning to the smaller, secondary cities of developing countries, such as Chiang Mai in Thailand, bringing industrial pollution problems to these areas too.

For some commentators, in many of the older industrial countries there has been a functional reversion of cities to their pre-industrial past, where commerce, administration and cultural activities again dominate (Cheshire 1988). The outcomes of this transformation have been far from uniform, so that it is far from a simple path to the revitalisation of all cities (Begg and Moore 1990). To understand why this is, we need to take a closer look at the processes of urban deindustrialisation and economic transformation, bearing in mind always that economic, social and environmental transformations tend to be processes which interact with one another.

The main features of urban deindustrialisation are fairly widely agreed upon and include: decline in manufacturing output; high levels of unemployment and underemployment; a loss in unskilled manual work in particular; reduced private-sector training; rising crime levels and other indicators of social stress; out-migration of skilled labour; low average income levels; a reduction in the local tax base; an increasing demand on welfare services such as health and social security benefits; and a serious deterioration in the local physical environment, in particular derelict land and buildings (Button and Pearce 1989). In some cities there has been a sufficient rise in service-sector employment to balance industrial job losses, but even here these new opportunities have rarely been suitable for those losing their jobs, and have frequently been low paid, temporary or part time, and in sales, clerical and personal service occupations. Generally speaking urban deindustrialisation has entailed massive transition costs, mainly borne by the individual and the household unit.

There are two main schools of thought on the causes of urban deindustrialisation, one which centres its analysis on urban land markets, the other on urban, and indeed international, labour markets. The two are not quite polar extremes, since the main protagonists of each option appear to concede a degree of relevance to the analysis of the opposing viewpoint (Massey and Meegan 1985). The urban land market analysis, most convincingly pursued by Fothergill and Gudgin (1982), starts from an analysis of the differing patterns of industrial change between large cities, smaller cities, industrial towns and rural towns. The evidence for Britain in the 1960s and 1970s suggests that deindustrialisation has been most acutely felt in the larger industrial towns and cities, whilst the smaller country towns, especially those in rural areas have shown either less decline or some degree of growth in industrial employment. Fothergill and Gudgin conclude from their analysis that the problem of deindustrialisation in large cities stems primarily from their land problem, most notably the lack of large plots of land suited to the needs of large-scale manufacturers, who tend to prefer extensive single-storey buildings to multi-storey premises on smaller sites. Related considerations include high land costs, inner-area congestion, archaic road systems with narrow, restrictive roads, the high cost of reclaiming much urban ex-industrial land, and the difficulty of land assembly because of the historical legacy of small, fragmented land holdings. Other commentators have also pointed to the high urban land and property taxes imposed by some local authorities, though there is no evidence to suggest a direct correlation between these taxes and the rate of deindustrialisation. This analysis has some important elements of explanation within it, but is at best only partial.

The alternative perspective is to look at the competitive nature of firms themselves, particularly in terms of their changing position within, and their use of, the international division of labour. The emphasis here is very much on the attempts of large employers to reduce their costs, both directly by keeping their own wages costs to a minimum, and indirectly through subcontracting work to smaller companies, who in turn reduce their costs through lower labour costs. According to this analysis, many employers leave high labour cost urban locations in favour of low labour cost suburbs, small towns or even overseas.

Central to this process was the rise of mass production and a finer detailed division of labour, associated with the potential for a greater fragmentation and compartmentalisation of the production process into individual component stages. With the parallel rise in cheaper mass transportation and better telecommunications, as well as improvements in process technology, it became increasingly possible to separate different parts of the production process, and to locate these on a global basis, close to cheap raw materials, cheap labour or lax environmental regulation, as appropriate to each stage, in an attempt to reduce production costs. Multi-plant, multinational companies began to create global production systems in response to these enabling factors, the drive to lower costs and the possibilities of creating global markets. Thus the Ford motor company, which in large part introduced the concept of mass production lines to the world in the 1920s (hence the term Fordism as a popular, if misleading, shorthand for mass production), moved on in the 1960s to produce the 'world car' concept. In this system components for a car could be sourced from around the world, and then assembled at a few strategic sites, close to the major markets.

Where in the past world trade was dominated by global movements of raw materials and finished goods, from the 1950s a so-called New International Division of Labour emerged, involving a search by globally mobile investors for cheap labour locations in which to place the most routinised, often deskilled, segments of a production cycle. It is important not to overplay the role of labour, since one of the main reasons for internationalisation was the search to open up new markets, markets required to make large-scale production systems cost-effective (Dicken

1992). As a result of these tendencies, international trade began to grow rapidly, and has come to involve growing flows of semi-completed products. Most importantly, the very mobility of capital meant that multinational companies were able to stimulate competition between nations and cities to create the conditions which would attract companies to locate there, including government subsidies, low taxation, controls on trade union activities, lax health and environmental regulation standards and guarantees of political stability.

The resulting shifts of capital have been complex, and there is not the space here to deal in detail with the many dimensions of these changes (see instead authors such as Henderson and Castells 1987, and Dicken 1992). In summary, global investment trends since the 1950s have involved some shift from Western nations towards cheaper producers in developing countries, almost invariably involving the larger cities because of their better accessibility. In recent years, there has been some reversal of this pattern, with investment moving back to Western nations, in part as these have deregulated their labour markets. Also, throughout this period, there have continued to be other major flows of investment, most notably between richer countries, as multinationals have sought to gain entry into protected regional and national markets (e.g. Japanese motor company investments in the UK, motivated in part by the need to improve access to the European market). In addition, there have been increasing overseas investment flows from the growing number of developing-country multinationals.

Most importantly of all perhaps, these shifts in mobile capital have been highly selective, involving only certain elements of the production cycle, in particular routinised mass production. Alternatively, those parts of the production cycle involving recent innovations and higher capital investment have more usually been located in the home country of each multinational, along with research and development facilities and much of the management hierarchy.

Although the academic literature has concentrated largely on the role of labour in these changing global investment patterns, it has become increasingly clear that the movements of some forms of production have been motivated by environmental considerations. Talking about health hazards resulting from certain manufacturing operations, in June 1978 US Congressman David Obey noted that

> there is apparently a growing trend towards moving such manufacturing to countries where knowledge of the health hazards is limited or where concern about worker and public health is secondary to economic development goals. The result is that citizens of foreign countries sacrifice their health, U.S. workers lose their jobs, and ethical businessmen [*sic*] who go to the expense of implementing

needed safeguards are undercut by those who knowingly poison foreign workers and their communities in order to gain competitive advantage. (Cited in Hasson 1985, p.7)

On the Mexico–USA border, American companies have rushed to invest in Mexican factories, gaining access to cheap labour (around 60 pence an hour), but also causing massive migration to the border towns, with not all migrants getting jobs. Over 2000 manufacturing plants have been set up since 1969 under the *maquiladora* system of encouraging firms to relocate by removing import and export duties on components and finished products for the US market (Reid 1993). In the case of Nuevo Laredo (Freedland 1993):

> The result is dozens of Third World shanty towns attached like growths to the city: shacks of cardboard, plywood and tarpaulin, housing whole families in single rooms. There is no sewerage, no running water, no electricity. Tuberculosis and typhoid are rife... The population explosion has caused a human and environmental disaster in Nuevo Laredo and in places like it all along the Mexican border... Foreign firms have set up maquiladores not just because labour is cheap, but because Mexico's environmental and safety rules are looser and rarely enforced. (p.40)

Although *maquiladores* are legally required to take hazardous solid waste back to the United States, according to Reid (1993) illegal dumping is still rife. In the 1990s the rapid growth of industrial production in southern China's Special Economic Zones began to present similar problems. Attracted by cheap labour and land, and by lax environmental and health and safety regulations, foreign investors have set up operations in the Guangdong province north of Hong Kong. In Shenzen Special Economic Zone a series of blasts in a chemical factory killed between 15 and 70 people and injured 200 in August 1993, and in November 1993, 81 workers making dolls for export were killed in a factory fire, where windows and doors had been locked to prevent thefts. In a similar incident, 188 Thai workers were burned to death in a locked toy factory outside Bangkok in May 1993.

The release of lethal gas (methyl isocynate) at Bhopal in southern India from the Union Carbide plant in 1984 officially was responsible for 2988 deaths, with an additional 100,000 injured and 200,000 people evacuated (United Nations Environment Programme 1991). According to Dinham (1985), other Union Carbide plants in the US and France were equipped with considerably more sophisticated plant-wide emergency safety systems, which could have provided a quicker warning and possibly a quick remedy to the problem. Such accusations are part of a long history of exporting environmental risks and hazards, with certain

US insurance companies recognising the problems of asbestos as early as 1918, causing some producers to move away to circumvent regulatory control and high insurance rates (Hasson 1985). The international division of labour has a close partner in the international division of industrial and environmental health hazards. In addition, there are important links to the creation of new international markets for goods regarded as hazardous in some way in Western nations, and therefore to varying degrees regulated, from cigarettes to baby milk and certain pesticides.

The selective nature of these global investment shifts has in some part contributed to the deindustrialisation of large Western cities and to the growing importance of their role as service centres, linked into global production and producer services trading networks. On the one hand there has been a decentralisation of some industrial processes away from the large Western cities, frequently accompanied in the metropolitan core areas by a centralisation and concentration of service-sector activities, plus certain high value-added products such as computers. Higher-order services have been attracted to the metropolitan cores by the highly skilled workforces and the conducive environments offered in terms of the rich textures of access to other business decision-makers, finance sources, political networks and educational services, which are important in information-processing, decision-making, coordinating and marketing (Knox and Agnew 1989). This very much links into Harvey's (1989a) analysis of the repositioning of cities within changing spatial divisions of labour and consumption, and competition in respect of command functions and redistribution mechanisms. The result is that there is considerable variance in the experience of deindustrialisation in Western cities: not all cities have lost industrial employment to the same extent, and probably none have stopped searching to increase industrial jobs within their boundaries.

Indeed, the reductive nature of global competition for scarce investment has led to deteriorating conditions in some countries, including the USA. Frequently this has seen the emergence of a growing number of sweatshops operating outside the formal regulatory system, and the introduction of enterprise zones, which have included proposals to remove or lower property taxes, reduce environmental and health and safety at work regulations, and further weaken trade union rights (Smith 1987). As such, cities such as Los Angeles and New York have continued to polarise, with central areas host to the large office buildings of multinational companies, whilst adjacent Latino neighbourhoods play host to small sweatshops producing goods often under subcontract to these same multinationals, and almost invariably with underpaid migrant labour working in poor – indeed illegal – conditions. Similarly, piecework homeworking in industries such as clothing carries the pattern of exploitation into the home. This process of 'bringing the Third World home' provides one of the least savoury aspects of the emergence of globally mobile capital and the intense competition between localities for the few jobs which it can bring with it (Sassen-Koob 1984), involving relaxed labour market, health and safety at work and environmental regulatory standards, and limited policing of those laws which remain.

Whilst both the land- and property-led and the labour-led approaches to urban deindustrialisation acknowledge some degree of parallel deterioration within the urban environment, neither, rightly, prioritises this as a *cause* of decline. That said, there is evidence that environmental degradation may be a key contributory element in instigating and maintaining a spiral of urban decline, influencing the investment intentions of industrialists. Furthermore, the legacy of environmental external costs such as contaminated land and derelict buildings imposes further costs on those attempting to break out of the downward spiral of urban change, whether through reindustrialisation or residential, leisure or commercial usage.

To regard environmental degradation simply as a *consequence* of urban economic restructuring is not helpful, then, not least since there is much evidence to suggest that the state of the local environment is an important contributory factor when industrialists are seeking new locations, particularly so in the case of high technology industries. Indeed, it is quite possible to see that although deindustrialisation may make cities less attractive in some regards in the short term, with abandoned buildings and contaminated land, in other respects it may contribute to environmental enhancement, depending on what eventually replaces the industrial usage.

2.4.2 Flexibility is beautiful?

The role of the environment in newly emergent forms of urban economic restructuring also requires consideration, from the possibilities for decentralising some service sector tasks to the home, through the spread of telecommuting, to the shift from large-scale mass production systems towards more fragmented production networks. Telecommuting may encourage certain types of work to be undertaken at home, reducing the need to commute physically between home and work. A study in Los Angeles found that new telecommuters did change their habits significantly, making fewer and shorter car journeys, travelling only one-fifth of their previous distances (Kitamura 1991). Likewise, 'teleshopping' and home deliveries may result in journey reductions (Ekins, Hillman and Hutchinson 1992). The savings in terms of energy consumption, demands for roads, urban congestion and time available for leisure are potentially quite large from such advances. The relevant technologies remain embryonic and unevenly spread, particularly in rural areas. Gillespie (1992), however, warns that the impacts of telecommunications technologies are likely to be complex, resulting in fewer but longer journeys, with the new links often supplementing rather than replacing face-to-face contact. Moreover there are considerable grounds for concern about the marginalising effects and psychological impacts which home-based working may entail for workers, leading in some cases to loneliness, family tension, illness and poor work organisation and discipline (Forester 1992, Clark, Burral and Roberts 1993).

This said, in the case of Britain it has been estimated that telecommuting would decrease national energy consumption by 0.06% for every 1% of the workforce who telecommute, an implied maximum saving on the national energy bill of 6% if every single worker took up telecommuting (British Telecom study, cited by Gibbs 1993). An earlier study in the US following the 1973 oil crisis estimated that for every 1% of the population who transferred from car commuting to telecommuting oil consumption would be reduced by 5.4m barrels a year (Nilles, Carlson, Gray and Hannemann 1986). The potential for reducing commuting journeys appears to be significant in some sectors of the economy, and whilst the traditional workplace office is unlikely to disappear in the foreseeable future, the number of journeys required by workers may well diminish.

The era of mass production emerged as the dominant form of production from the 1950s, bringing economies of scale to large-scale producers of relatively uniform products. For many commentators the hegemony of this form of production in capitalist economies came under threat from the 1970s onwards, and is now being challenged by alternative forms of production system. Of these, flexible accumulation is seen by many as the most likely successor to Fordism. In summary, mass production is seen to have become too rigid to satisfy the demands created by rapidly changing consumer tastes and the increasing desire for non-standard products. Fordism has also been implicated in the neglect of the environmental impacts of production (Lipietz 1992). Moreover, the social organisation of large-scale plants with their detailed division of labour involved in deskilled routine production tasks came to be regarded as less productive, requiring a shift towards more flexible, more rewarding work tasks for a core of skilled workers. Alternatively, non-core workers still involved in routine production tasks find themselves more likely to be subject to unfavourable work conditions, with growing use of short-term contracts. It is also increasingly common for work to be subcontracted to smaller firms, many of which exercise tighter work discipline and offer lower pay.

In addition, there has been a shift towards shorter production runs of more customised, higher value-added products. This trend has been assisted by improved telecommunications for linking consumers, retailers, wholesalers, market researchers, designers and producers, plus more flexible production technologies. In consequence of these labour process and product market changes, the vertical and horizontal integration of the previous production regime is becoming more fragmented. The work of single large-scale factories is increasingly being spread among different firms in different, often smaller plants, involving a rather different division of labour.

It is possible see some potentially environmentally and socially benign effects in the flexible accumulation model. In one variant of this theme, flexible specialisation, successful localised clusters of similar producers are said to be emerging, sometimes referred to as 'new industrial districts'. Firms operating in these local clusters are seen to benefit from mutual subcontracting work, by sharing the burden of some overheads, such as training and marketing, whilst also helping spread technologies either purposefully to ensure quality along the production supply chain, or simply as an accident of intense local competition encouraging product improvement (Piore and Sabel 1984, Porter 1990). Whilst this may mean that communities will emerge where it will be difficult to tell where society ends and economy starts, and where workers are valued as a key resource, not a commodity to be exploited (Ekins, Hillman and Hutchinson 1992), it is unlikely to work out in quite this way.

Instead, the emergence of a divide between core and periphery workers may simply involve some workers becoming more secure whilst others become further marginalised. The notion of 'new industrial districts' emerging out of virtuous economic and social forces which draw firms together to provide a model for economic transformation may be similarly ill-conceived, for whilst such tendencies may be discernible in some sectors in some areas, more generally it can be seen that close proximity of firms across fragmented production chains is not a prerequisite for success. Some firms will continue to fragment their production on a national and international basis in search of specialist services, cheap labour and raw material inputs. Moreover, the spread of work to smaller subcontractors is not in itself a necessarily benign process, and indeed small producers are frequently associated with poor observation of health and safety regulation and labour laws (Rainnie 1989).

One area where the processes of flexible accumulation may prove in some part beneficial is in the further fragmentation of the production process, which may see a shift away from large-scale mass production sites in favour of small factories and offices. This in turn may lead to new possibilities for integrating some factories back into the urban fabric, meeting the calls of some commentators to move away from the exclusionary planning zoning practices which arose with mass production (Commission of the European Communities 1990). These zoning practices are said to have encouraged large-scale industries to locate either on the edges of the city or in other areas, in both cases increasing commuting and freight traffic distances, whilst also fuelling the shift towards road transport. This argument is something of an oversimplification, since as we have already noted much of the movement out of central areas predated widespread zoning policies, and was also stimulated by the search for larger sites.

A reversion to more mixed-use zones, involving the location of some smaller scale production units closer to where people live, may help reduce some journeys and add to the variety and diversity of neighbourhood life. However, this is only likely to affect a relatively small number of businesses, with the old demands for separation of housing and industry likely to remain powerful forces, especially where hazardous products and processes are involved. Indeed, encouraging more mixed industrial and residential land use may not in itself prove to be wholly benign in net environmental terms, as it would require more trips by lorries into the middle of these mixed residential areas. Similarly, where the further fragmentation of production processes does not lead to specialised industrial clusters, it implies considerably more journeys being undertaken within any production process. The resulting environmentally negative effects will be exacerbated where just-in-time procedures place great emphasis on regular batches of component parts, requiring more journeys, many by road (Gibbs 1993). Fragmenting and localising aspects of global production systems does not, then, appear likely to be the key to restructuring industrial systems towards a more environmentally sustainable mode of operation.

2.4.3 Small is beautiful

The most widely advocated proposals for restructuring local economies towards greater environmental awareness are those predicated on the twin concepts that 'small is beautiful' and that local self-reliance needs to be increased. The small-is-beautiful school has its roots in the hugely influential work of E.F. Schumacher (1974) in particular. Drawing on

Gandhi's saying, that the poor of the world cannot be helped by mass production, only by production by the masses, Schumacher argued that

> The technology of *mass production* is inherently violent, ecologically damaging, self-defeating in terms of non-renewable resources, and stultifying for the human person. The technology of *production by the masses*, making use of the best of modern knowledge and experience, is conducive to decentralisation, compatible with the laws of ecology, gentle in its use of scarce resources, and designed to serve the human person instead of making him [*sic*] the servant of machines. I have named it *intermediate technology* to signify that it is vastly superior to the primitive technology of bygone ages but at the same time much simpler, cheaper, and freer than the super-technology of the rich. (1974, p.28)

From this perspective, work should be satisfying in its own right, designed to make it rewarding to each individual, not to maximise profits in a spiral of uncontrolled production and consumption increases, fed not by meeting basic human needs and desires, but by the imperatives of capitalist growth. The notion of socially useful work has also taken on a particular poignancy as workers have sought to identify alternatives to job losses generally, but particularly in declining military industries (Collective Design/Projects 1985). A common theme in the socially useful production debate has been the desire to create local jobs to meet local needs, creating good quality jobs in socially and environmentally ethical businesses.

Schumacher also argued for a reversion to small communities, smaller producers and smaller governments. Cities are regarded as alienating women and men from nature, and there should instead be a return to the land, an anti-urban sentiment which as we have seen in Chapter One has a considerable pedigree. The disdain for large central governments is also a strong theme in town planning history, with Peter Kropotkin in 1920 for instance arguing that the twelfth century saw a rapid spread of urban fraternities and guilds within the major towns, which acted in effect as free states, providing a series of liberties which in turn provided the basis for enormous intellectual ferment and economic growth, and later became suppressed by the rise of centralised states in the sixteenth century (see Hall 1988, for a fuller discussion). What is interesting in the case of Schumacher is that his anti-urbanism is tied in with a distrust of large-scale organisations generally, as these are held to lead almost invariably to ecological devastation:

> Although even small communities are sometimes guilty of causing serious erosion, generally as a result of ignorance, this is trifling in comparison with the devastations caused by gigantic groups moti-

vated by greed, envy, and the lust for power. It is moreover obvious that men [*sic*] organised in small units will take better care of *their* bit of land or other natural resources than anonymous companies or megalomaniac governments which pretend to themselves that the whole universe is their legitimate quarry (1974, p. 29).

There is an element of patriarchal thinking in some of Schumacher's search for apparent simplicity, in particular when he tells us that women do not need work outside the home, and that large-scale employment of women should be seen as a sign of serious economic failure, especially where it leads to children running wild! (p. 47) Men alone appear to be nature-designed to work, and women alone to have responsibility for children. Despite such occasional grating sentiments, the overall thrust of Schumacher's work has met with widespread popular acceptance, although very little of substance in terms of government policy. His critique of the brutalism of Fordist mass production systems remains as compelling and convincing today as it was in 1974, indeed even more so as these systems appear to be waning, in considerable part because of the problems which Schumacher diagnosed. But in his search for telling portraits of villains and victims Schumacher did occasionally overstate his case, and it remains to be proven that small is always necessarily better than large, as Al Rainnie (1989) quite forcibly argues in the case of small firms.

Schumacher also promoted greater local self-reliance since 'production from local resources for local needs is the most rational way of economic life, while dependence on imports from afar and the consequent need to produce for export to unknown and distant people is highly uneconomic and justifiable only in exceptional cases and on a small scale' (p. 49). This is a theme which has proven attractive to many subsequent environmental commentators, again sometimes mixed in with a call for a reversion to smaller communities as the basic unit of society, sometimes in the form of a shift away from cities, sometimes as enhancing the role of neighbourhoods within cities in shaping their own economic and social destinies (Robertson 1978, Brown 1981, Elkin, McLaren and Hillman 1991). The value of this approach is its stress on increasing the use of local resources and opportunities in order to satisfy primarily local needs (Ekins, Hillman and Hutchinson 1992). Again, this approach has a considerable pedigree outside the current environmental debate, with early landmarks including Robert Owen's unsuccessful attempt to create a self-supporting community in 1825 when he bought the village of New Harmony in Indiana, USA. Apparently 'the idealism and limited material capacity for self-sufficiency did not take long to fail' (Collective Design/Projects 1985, p.11), but along with his earlier New Lanark experiment in Scotland, New Harmony did provide a model which others subsequently sought to emulate. Kropotkin, too, gained a popular audience for his views on the need to establish dispersed communities, which would act as the centres of networks of small-scale producers in industrial villages who would engage in production for local needs.

The drive to increase economic self-containment in one form or another is one which many cities are already attempting to foster, in particular aiming at import substitution. Policies range from relatively conventional attempts to increase the numbers of locally-owned small businesses, whether operated as private businesses, cooperatives or community businesses, to moulding enterprise structures and dynamics towards meeting local social and economic needs, and to attempts to break away from the mainstream economy with community-based exchange initiatives. The advantages of creating small businesses include greater awareness of local needs and resources and less vulnerability to branch plant closures following decisions taken by corporate head offices in another continent to pull out of an area (Dauncey 1986). Policies to encourage businesses to change their behaviour range from diversification strategies in favour of socially useful products, as already noted, to tying public assistance for companies to social and environmental issues, such as equal opportunities, industrial democracy and wage levels, as happened with the former Greater London Council. Local authority support for locally-based, environmentally friendly firms through purchasing policies and in the investment of pension funds has also been advocated (Dauncey 1986, Gibbs 1991). On a more esoteric level, at the moment there are initiatives such as Local Exchange Trading Systems (LETS), which according to their proponents provide 'a remarkable tool for strengthening local communities' (Linton and Greco 1990, p. 155). The aim of LETS is to break away from the cash-based exchange system to create a new local currency system based on the imputed value of services which are exchanged between members. For example, a plumber may fix a tap for a member of a LETS, the value of which may at some stage later be offset when another member of the system provides a service for the plumber. In this system cash does not change hands, and the exchange of services and goods need not be directly reciprocal between two people, using a centrally maintained 'accounts' system. The advantages of such systems include their contribution to building community spirit, reducing leakage of spending from an area, and increasing the ability of members without a formal cash income to enter into local goods and services exchanges. These exchange systems are not necessarily a form of black economy, and indeed US and UK tax offices do consider these barter arrangements potentially taxable. They have an interesting parallel in self-build housing initiatives, where people with different skills come together to build their own houses drawing on the collective skills of the group, rather than each individual seeking to become an expert joiner, bricklayer, plasterer, electrician, plumber and so on.

This shift away from a cash-based urban economy is one which finds many proponents, and certainly has much to recommend itself as an antidote to the over-commodification of many social and environmental goods, services and relationships, from childcare, to cleaning up a street or small patches of over-grown, abandoned land. It is one element among the widespread calls for measures for economic growth other than Gross National Product (GNP), where progress is measured only in monetary flow terms and excludes community and other self-help schemes, and issues of standard of living or environmental capital. Hiring a baby sitter may add to GNP: using a family member will not; similarly a short-term spurt of growth based on a non-renewable resource can appear as growth, when in truth in many respects it represents a decline in ecological wealth (see Chapters Six and Seven). Cities are at the exchange core of their societies, where for a variety of reasons, more goods, services and relationships become formalised and commodified, providing them with a spurious measure of well-being compared to rural areas where less formal arrangements exist. High living standards in cities and rapid rates of urban economic growth may be something of a chimera, if what we are really trying to gauge is quality of life using inappropriate measures.

Moving towards what James Robertson (1978, p.80) calls a sane, humane, ecological future, is said to require as an integral element a shift away from the institutional economy based on money and jobs towards the gift-and-barter economy of households and local communities. In this process, local cooperatives and community enterprises will provide a key element in creating local products and services geared to the needs of local people, thereby creating local jobs and training (Ross 1986). So far, the alternative economy of small cooperatives and businesses responsive to the moral imperatives of ecological production remains small and largely confined to metropolitan areas. In the case of the former West Germany, this 'alternative economy' accounted for an estimated 25,000 fully-employed people in the late 1980s, whilst other environmental industries employed between 400,000 and 500,000 people (Ossenbrugge 1988).

There are some important tensions between such local self-containment policies and the global nature of the capitalist economic system, in particular the search for innovation, which is worldwide. An area which successfully isolated itself in a self-contained local economic system would after a time find itself denying residents the opportunity to buy the new products and cheaper mature products which rapidly-spreading innovation elsewhere has brought about. A successful self-contained economy of the 1950s might begin to rue this 40 years later if residents were still stuck with high-cost, heavy fuel-consuming cars and washing machines, black and white televisions and so on. Shell UK in its evidence to the House of Lords Select Committee on the European Communities (1993) argued that economic development is a motor for environmental improvement, citing the declining intensity of energy use in the UK since 1950 as an example of greater efficiency in resource use. Most proponents of local self-reliance are alert to these contradictions, with Galtung (1986), for instance, advocating a nesting of self-reliance at local, regional and national levels, where each level seeks to improve self-reliance at that level and in the case of local areas 'trading with suitable communities defined by [their] vicinity and/or affinity' (p. 104). In this view the self-reliant local community should seek to find traders in the same country, and if trading internationally should do so with those with a shared regional identity, except in the case of rich nations where recognition of power inequalities may lead to a diversion of trade to those areas which need it most.

Jane Jacobs (1984) provides an alternative view of the value of increasing self-reliance in *Cities and the Wealth of Nations*. In this intriguing and challenging book she argues that cities are the driving economic force of the world economy, and that trading between cities underpins successful urban economies. As part of their continuous process of economic renewal, cities need to innovate internally, in part responding to external competitive pressures. This competition promotes vigorous product substitution, as businesses seek to improve on imported goods and services in both quality and price. According to Jacobs, cities which fail to respond in this way and which orientate themselves to either export-only, or domestic-only markets, tend to decline, whilst the import-substituting metropolis continues to expand. This analysis points to the tremendous tension involved in balancing how cities link into the global economic system. Too much self-reliance and too little self-containment can be equally damaging to urban economic development. Increasing local economic self-reliance is a legitimate objective for sustainable urban development, but it does need to be treated creatively as a *direction* of change, rather than having an objective of total self-containment. Most importantly, such a shift should involve a shift towards greater urban ecological self-containment (see Girardet 1990), where the emphasis is on reduced demand (through efficiency gains or consumption changes), re-use, repair, reconditioning and recycling.

Whilst the alternative economics movement has captured the moral high ground in this debate, with its emphasis on community-based industries which aim to meet local needs with local resources, with minimum waste and maximum re-use of materials, there is also an important role to be played by conventional businesses in greening both the global and local economies. Increasingly in the past ten years businesses have begun to respond to environmental concerns, from making their existing processes more environmentally benign, to seeking to create and satisfy new markets for environmentally friendly products and services (Elkington and Burke 1987, Hutchinson 1992, Roberts 1992). In addition, insurance companies have increasingly adopted environmental screening of firms (Roberts 1992). The rationales for such changes in behaviour are diverse, from simple moral duty, to increasing government environmental regulation, the threat of expensive litigation for environmental damage, and the growing consumer pressures for products which are more environment-friendly. In response, some companies have been active in moving towards lean production and cleaner production, in creating new 'environmentally friendly' products and processes, in devising corporate environmental policy statements, in providing publicly available environmental audits of their work processes, in eco-labelling, and in adopting a supply-chain perspective to their production processes, ensuring that subcontractors maintain high levels of environmental awareness (Clement 1991, Confederation of British Industry 1991, House of Lords Select Committee on the European Communities 1993).

There have been widespread fears that the shift towards more rigorous environmental standards will lead to job losses; however, the experience of the former West Germany has been that jobs in the new environmental industries have outnumbered those lost (Ossenbrugge 1988, 1991). In Sweden the introduction of rigorous environmental legislation in 1969, requiring all new plant investments to curb pollution whilst subsidising anti-pollution measures in existing plants for five years, resulted in the creation of 4600 person-years of jobs (OECD 1977).

Encouraging though trends in corporate environmental responsibility are, the shift towards greater environmental consciousness and greater acceptance of the need for fundamental changes to environmentally damaging products and processes is extremely patchy, and indeed there have been undoubted 'bandwagon' jumpers, who claim to be environmentally friendly in one aspect of their product (e.g. reduced packaging for washing powders), whilst neglecting other damaging aspects of their product (e.g. high phosphate content in washing powder). The evidence of green consumerism leading to some important product and process innovations is strong, but to make any major impact this nascent trend will need to be backed up by internationally imposed standards of consumer information so that decision-making is not distorted, whilst legal minimum standards need to be applied with rigour (see Chapter Six). Economic restructuring forces within the market system can move towards greater environmental awareness, but without some form of global standard-setting and regulatory controls, this is likely to continue to be an uneven process across companies and areas.

Some important themes emerge from this analysis. Firstly, it highlights the difficulty of simply attempting to 'buck' the dominant global capitalist system, which has its parallel in the difficulties of redirecting this system to achieving a more environmentally sustainable form. Secondly, in attempting to reform and gain some control over economic restructuring forces, viable, rigorously maintained regulatory systems are required to establish and police agreed minimum standards of environmental behaviour, for both producers and consumers. Thirdly, these regulatory systems need to be operationalised at a variety of levels, from global protocols to systems which can set local standards and controls. Fourthly, successful environmental restructuring requires that individuals and communities become more active in bringing about economic restructuring in their local economies. Finally, empowering local communities will entail changing attitudes towards local governance, where greater powers and resources are devolved to local communities. For urban areas, as elsewhere, there is a continuous need to 'think globally, act locally', to encourage the broader planetary stewardship for which we are all responsible.

2.5 CITY SIZE AND SETTLEMENT PLANNING

2.5.1 For and against very large cities

Rapid urbanisation is frequently seen as potentially undermining the overall efficiency of a country, because it supposedly creates an unbalanced settlement pattern, especially in the case of urban primacy, where cities are exceptionally dominant in relation to the rest of the country, such as Mexico City and Mexico. Regarding the growth of very large cities, there is particular concern about whether they are economically efficient in their own right and about whether they effectively drain their hinterland areas of natural, financial and human resources, weakening these economies in the process.

It is not just economic arguments which have led to unsympathetic views of the desirability of very large cities, since environmental degradation is commonly held to increase with city size. One of the most important environmental dimensions of urban growth is that for many resources consumption per capita increases with city size. For instance, water usage per capita tends to increase in this way, as more water is used in parks, gardens, street cleaning, fire fighting, and so on (Douglas 1989a), although it is difficult to disentangle the size effects from issues of wealth and development density, which are also important elements in increasing water demand.

In general terms it is also true that the larger the city, the more dependent the city becomes on external ecosystems, not only because consumption rises, but also because the internal capacity for food and energy production is reduced. This reduction occurs in part as the intensity of land use increases, itself a function of the rising land values throughout the city which accompany urban growth. The evidence on pollution levels increasing with city size is equivocal, appearing to be weak for air pollution but rather stronger for water pollution (Orishimo 1982).

Loss of agricultural lands at the expanding periphery of large cities and the reduction in urban agriculture in large cities provide further elements of negative environmental change. Although the loss of urban food production capacity is typical of cities in general, in many cities in developing countries, urban agriculture remains an important ingredient in the local economy, albeit appearing to diminish with increasing city size. Indeed in some smaller African cities the production of urban food is the main occupation of many (Lado 1990).

The emergence of the metropolitan area in the twentieth century represents a qualitatively new form of human settlement (Mumford 1961, Angotti 1993). It is larger, more complex and plays a more commanding economic, political and cultural role than the industrial city which preceded it. It is possible to see this as either a progressive or regressive trend. Certainly, most very large cities appear to have a considerable range of both economic and environmental problems associated with them. Alternatively, Angotti (1993) argues that historically, large cities have been a largely progressive force, bringing new opportunities, new ideas and new wealth to increasing numbers of cities. Following from this, he argues that the problem is not so much with size as the internal organization of cities, in particular low-density sprawl cities. From either perspective, the question remains: if large cities have the potential to be so bad, why do we continue to allow them to expand? The answer is probaby because we have never developed tools sufficiently powerful to contain the growth of dynamic large cities, and in part because there remain considerable doubts about the desirability of attempting to control urban expansion.

There are some important issues here, as it does appear that technological innovation rates are positively correlated with increasing city size, and that technological diffusion occurs more rapidly in larger cities, although the distinctive urban contribution to innovations has tended to decrease over time (Bairoch 1988). According to Bairoch, there are five main reasons for the positive association of urban size with innovation rates. Firstly, high population density facilitates human contact and accelerates flows of information. Secondly, the diversity of the urban economy is conducive to technological advances achieved in one sector being applied in others. Thirdly, cities have concentrations of educational and research facilities which encourage original thinking and systematic reflection. Fourthly, cities tend to attract the more creative people from their hinterlands because of their greater economic and social opportunities. Finally, echoing Jacobs (1984), cities serve as the main gateways for links to other cities, with their concentrations of innovative ideas, links made through trading and migration.

In economic development terms the large city has many advantages: a wide range of producer services, a large skills pool and lower communication costs (Brotchie 1992). High rates of economic development frequently continue to be positively related to city size (Bairoch 1988). If productivity can be measured by income per capita (a rather contentious proposition), large cities are more productive than smaller ones, though in Australian cities the differential between large and small cities fell by 50% between the 1970s and 1980s, possibly reflecting improvements in communications technologies (Brotchie 1992).

According to this perspective, it is not size *per se* which is the problem of large cities, rather it is the internal form of the city and poor management of the urban city region (see Chapters Three and Eight). Nonetheless, considerable prejudice continues against allowing the continued expansion of very large cities, most notably arguments that the distinction between rural and urban areas is diminishing, so large cities should be contained in order to help the distinctiveness of rural areas to survive. In the West, much of this distinctiveness has long been on the wane, fuelled by the growing integration of rural production systems within the metropolitan-led capitalist system. In developing countries rural distinctiveness remains in the sense of highly unequal divisions, in terms of wealth, wages and access to services such as hospitals. This continues to provide an important rationale for national settlement planning and rural development programmes to spread the benefits associated with very large cities to other areas of the country. Alternatively, concern has rapidly grown since the 1960s over the internal metropolitan divisions in wealth, opportunity and environmental quality, in part following racial tensions in cities in the USA and the UK, but also following work on the relationships between urban form, access and mechanisms of income redistribution in cities. The economic, social and environmental sustainability of cities requires looking both outward and inward in managing the processes of change.

2.5.2 Very large cities: optimum size and regional planning

The debate over the desirability of allowing very large cities to expand unimpeded, accompanied by academic discussion of themes such as the rank size rule and central place hierachies, led to urban and regional policy regimes designed to avoid over-large, over-dominant cities, in favour of 'more balanced' settlement patterns (see Lloyd and Dicken 1977, for a review of these models). The evidence linking urban size and settlement hierarchies to economic growth, economic efficiency or pollution is equivocal (Findlay 1993, Richardson 1993). None the less, this mode of thinking still permeates planning and development practice, with both World Commission on Environment and Development (1987) and the Rio Earth Summit for instance advocating the promotion of intermediate urban centres as counterpoles to large cities (see Chapter Eight).

Following from the various critiques of the problems of large cities, there has also been considerable debate over the notion of ideal or optimum city size, attempting to establish at what stage size became problematic, so that policies could be instigated to restrain further growth. For Ebenezer Howard (1898), the founder of the Garden City movement – perhaps the single most influential figure in town planning history – the ideal population size for his new Garden Cities was to be 32,000, on a site of 1000 acres, surrounded by another 5000 acres of green-belt farm land. This limit must be seen as related to the infrastructure and technologies available at the time. Interestingly, however, Howard spoke of the emergence of the Social City, where as the new town reached its maximum capacity, an additional, linked town would be set up nearby. In this way, a series of connected towns would build up, in effect a sort of multi-centred metropolis but interwoven with considerable amounts of green belt. In a diagram in the first edition of Howard's book (not subsequently reprinted) a central town of 58,000 is shown surrounded by six 'garden cities' around its circumference, each with 32,000, providing a city of 250,000 people. This is not all that dissimilar to the colonial systems of the ancient Greeks, who used to start up a new city when a certain size was reached, largely because of the need for reliable water supplies.

Jean Gottman (1967) points out in a review of ideal city size proposals, that the suggested optimum size among European planners has tended to gradually increase over time. Certainly, the early British New Towns tended to take 30,000 as an ideal size, but this was increased in subsequent rounds to 100,000 and ultimately 250,000 (e.g. Milton Keynes), as planners began to realise the importance of minimum-size thresholds in enabling cities to achieve economic takeoff, and in particular in supporting key service functions.

The British Garden City and New Town experiments were a hugely influential policy-expression of concern over the problems of large cities, in this case over the fears of congestion in London. New Towns and Growth Pole policies have since been widely adopted as a tool of urban planning in France, Australia, China, Russia and in some developing countries, with planners attempting to rewrite national settlement geographies by purposefully creating new settlements. Growth Pole theory has been particularly influential, postulating that it should be possible to set up new centres around particular propulsive economic sectors (e.g. petrochemicals complexes, steel production, and related suppliers and manufacturers further along the production chain), which would provide sufficient internal economic coherence to enable these centres to take off economically in their own right. These growth centres could be located in 'backward areas' as an instrument of regional policy because, over time, it was envisaged that there would be positive spill-over effects to surrounding areas, as demand for agricultural products rose and as producers moved out from the core area. In the event, the experience of the new growth centres has been equivocal: there have been some successes, but not to the extent envisaged, with beneficial linkages into surrounding areas only materialising on a relatively small scale. Interestingly, the current plans to create an Earth Centre in the former coal mining area of the Dearne Valley near Rotherham, UK, seek to provide a local growth pole, centred around a museum for sustainability and attracting new environmental industries.

Experience shows that attempting to rewrite settlement geographies in order to syphon off the growth of large capital cities is fraught with difficulties. At worst, these policies have merely created new urban problems in new locations whilst undermining the economic viability of the older, large cities. It is perhaps too easy to be harsh in judgement of the new towns, some of which have matured well, creating pleasant living and working environments, particularly relative to some of the central city slums, from which many of the original residents moved out (Stretton 1978). Most of the difficulties of the new towns relate less to their design and environmental impacts, and more to underestimations of the minimum city size required to achieve successful economic takeoff, and also to changing economic circumstances. The final waves of British new towns coincided with massive deindustrialisation on a national level, destroying the base of mobile capital which held the key to the jobs that the new towns needed to attract.

The parallel arguments for urban containment policies are well articulated in the literature, and indeed have for much of the twentieth century provided a key rationale for land use planning, in the West involving green belt and urban consolidation policies in particular (Hall *et al.* 1973, Hall 1982). Green belts around the edges of cities have sought to limit their outward spread for a variety of reasons, not least to prevent cities and rural areas losing their distinct characters, an argument perhaps more relevant to densely populated countries, such as the UK, than less densely populated countries such as Australia. Green belts have had some limited beneficial impacts in urban containment, but criticism of this policy has been gaining momentum as it becomes apparent that there is some element of boundary-jumping, simply creating new commuter towns on the far side of the green belt, whilst also preserving the privileges of a good residential environment close to the countryside mainly for those already financially well-off. Similarly, curbing personal mobility in the form of laws to prevent rural–urban migration, as has happened in China, is widely seen as curbing basic personal freedoms, and even where it has been enacted it has failed to work.

Other policies which aimed to deflect urban economic growth to peripheral regions have also been experimented with, most notably with the limits on industrial and office development used in Britain in the 1960s to encourage manufacturers to leave London, in particular, in favour of peripheral regions. These restrictions on expansion in the capital city were accompanied by grants to assist the transfer of operations to the distant areas. This policy fell into disuse during the 1970s as national industrial expansion turned into rapid deindustrialisation, limiting the amount of mobile investment available; this was accompanied by a growing concern over the declining employment opportunities in the inner-city areas of London, and evidence emerged that many new plants which had been forced to move out to distant regions appeared to be closing prematurely.

In many developing countries, settlement policy has been heavily influenced by the urban bias debate already alluded to. Urban primacy is generally more marked in these countries than elsewhere, fuelling concerns that the settlement pattern should be altered, with a combination of policies to promote second- and third-tier cities and to engage in strong rural development policies, aiming at stemming the flow of rural migrants. Arguments that the capital costs of developing smaller cities are lower, in part because of cheaper land and labour, are similarly found to be less important than expected, with Richardson (1993) estimating the resulting savings at only around 4–7% of total urban capital costs. Policies to favour small- and intermediate-size urban settlements have met with uneven success, in part because the ways in which they are meant to achieve the elusive notion of balance are ill-understood, whilst policies have tended to be inadequately attuned to the unique circumstances of each secondary city and city region (Hardoy and Satterthwaite 1986, Gilbert and Gugler 1992). Nor are environmental conditions of smaller cities necessarily better than those in large cities: because local authorities in small cities tend to lack the financial resources and legislative powers of larger cities, many basic facilities are underprovided, and land-use and pollution-control powers are often less effective. In most developing countries for instance, smaller cities tend to have lower proportions of their population serviced by piped water systems and sewerage connections (Hardoy, Mitlin and Satterthwaite 1992).

As the urban capital costs associated with population absorption in megacities are four to six times higher than those for rural absorption, the case for promoting rural development is clearly a strong one (Richardson 1993). Policies aimed at improving rural infrastructure (e.g. roads from farm to market, land irrigation) have had some notable successes; however, generally speaking, such policies have not met with a great deal of success in stemming rural–urban migration in most developing countries. Indeed Richardson also notes that any gains in lower capital costs may be offset by losses to GNP. This point leads neatly to the arguments of Jane Jacobs (1984), who argues that so central are the world's large cities to the economic vitality of the global economy and individual national economies, that permanent transfer payments to develop 'backward' areas are entirely undesirable:

> ...feeding as voraciously upon city earnings as they do, they reduce intercity trade in favour of trade between cities and inert economies; divert earned city imports to economies that cannot replace imports; and reduce cities' abilities to serve as good customers for one another's innovations. Subsidies milked from cities are for these reasons profoundly antidevelopment transactions. (p. 193)

There is no easy conclusion to these debates about the very validity of regional planning as a mechanism for containing large city expansion and redistributing economic wealth. But it is interesting to reflect on the extent to which the debate has come to be framed largely in economic and social terms, since historically there has also been a strong environmental dimension to regional policy. In particular, the Regional Planning Association of America, which was formed in 1923 and included Lewis Mumford amongst its founders, was influential during the 1920s and 1930s in setting the regional policy agenda. Friedmann and Weaver (1979) summarise that:

...the RPAA's goal was ecological reconstruction of the physical environment to promote high cultural development and a biotechnical economy. Their planning strategies were based on decentralization and resource conservation through technological improvements: highway construction, rural electrification and new towns. (p.34)

At the heart of this philosophy was Benton MacKaye's (1928) assertion that:

Cultural man [*sic*] needs land and developed natural resources as the tangible source of bodily existence; he needs the flow of commodities to make that source effective; but first of all he needs a harmonious and related environment as the source of his true living.

These three needs of cultured man make three corresponding problems:

(a) The conservation of natural resources.

(b) The control of commodity-flow.

(c) The development of environment. (pp.29–30)

Environmental considerations lay at the core of regional planning, then, in its formative years, along with a belief in the need to diffuse the metropolis, using the possibilities of technological advances, such as electricity generation, to fuel the decentralisation of industry and population. By the 1960s and 1970s regional policy had sufficiently lost sight of its origins in some countries to allow regional grants to subsidise the creation of ecologically-damaging industrial clusters in peripheral regions, such as the petrochemical complex on Teesside in northern England. However, in the 1990s, regional planning is once again beginning to look to environmental considerations as a fundamental part of its own rationale, and therefore of its everyday practice. Regional planning can be redefined to place at its heart the need to support businesses to make a positive contribution to improved sustainability, including policies to reduce pollution and excessive resource demands, and policies to reduce transport needs for raw materials, goods and services. Here it is not so much the size and location of settlements that take centre place, but the relationships between individual activities, and the implications of this for energy and transport demand. Chapter Three returns to this theme, examining the internal form of cities and city regions.

One of the problems with attempting to limit large city expansion is confusion over what a city is, where it starts and where it ends, and how its size, land area, economic wealth, population, or possibly even environmental disturbance should be measured. Following from this point, one option might be to frame policies not in terms of the usual absolutes of physical spread or resident population, but instead in terms of urban environmental impact. For instance, it might be desirable to say that a city with average annual pollution levels above certain standards should be refused permission to add new net houses or industries. A similar approach operates already in the USA, where new industrial polluters are discouraged from setting up in areas with high pollution, unless the new pollution is 'offset' against reduced pollution from existing sources in the area (see Chapter Seven). This policy direction could be framed to take account not only of urban ambient pollution levels, but also the 'export' of pollution to neighbouring areas. The incentive would then be provided for urban government and businesses to work together to improve the environment of their city. Although technically it is difficult, if not impossible, to do this with complete accuracy, it may be helpful to move in this direction. Certainly there needs to be a shift away from some current government systems, which encourage further urban expansion as a means of widening the city's tax base without considera- tion of the environmental impacts of further growth.

Creatively used regional planning can be an important element in redistributing the concentration of wealth and opportunities within a nation. However, if poorly applied it can undermine the success of growth cities, and instead simply create new declining peripheral settle- ments. Regional policy at its most effective seeks to balance these tensions and provides a cross-sectoral approach to policy coordination, in particular seeking to prevent market and political distortions which favour cities over peripheral areas. Particularly important are policies to ensure that those living and working in cities are aware of the environ- mental impacts of their activities outside the urban area. This requires political and economic systems capable of identifying and remedying the uneven spread of deleterious impacts of urban activities. This is one reason for empowering a regional tier of governance, backed by a national government willing to develop powers and resources for envi- ronmental management to the regional and local levels. The alternative is to see a continued balkanisation of urban and regional space, as happens in parts of the United States, as local communities in privileged areas seek to set up their own local government, reaping the advantages of low taxes resulting from their privileged position, but avoiding meet- ing the full costs of their residents' activities within the broader social city region (Fox 1985, Issel 1985).

2.6 CONCLUSIONS FOR SUSTAINABLE URBAN DEVELOPMENT

When looking at the processes of urban change in a world of complex global interdependencies, it is essential to examine external dynamics and structures of change. Indeed it is most certainly true that it is pointless to plan for the sustainable city without planning for sustainable rural areas at the same time. Adapting cities to the imperatives of sustainable development requires more than just limiting urban growth because it is assumed to be environmentally damaging. Similarly, aiming to internalise a city's environmental impacts, in the sense of seeking to become almost wholly self-contained, makes little sense given the complex global forces shaping economic and social change. Cities are fundamentally about the exchange of materials, products, services, people and ideas. The need is not to negate this function but to adapt it creatively.

Although very large cities do indeed have global economic and environmental hinterlands, they also are still usually heavily reliant on their more immediate bioregional hinterlands, whilst smaller cities will often be even more integrated within an interdependent regional environmental, economic and social complex (Andruss et al. 1990). It may therefore be preferable to return to and to adapt either bioregional boundaries, or to revert to Ebenezer Howard's concept of the social city region, a notion which has recently attracted the support of the Town and Country Planning Association (Breheney and Rookwood 1993).

Regional settlement planning may have had its problems but that is not a reason for rejecting it; rather it is a reason for learning from past experience in different nations, and seeking to improve upon the past, most importantly by working creatively with those responsible for other policy regimes who are seeking to effect similar changes. Regional planning needs its visionaries, creating new town ideas, but it is likely that new towns will only ever have a marginal role in the move towards a greater urban contribution to global sustainability. It is policies to re-fashion existing cities, not simply by limiting size, but by more fundamental alterations to the internal structure and dynamics of cities, which will contribute most to global sustainability. It is these issues of the internal workings of the city which form the focus of the next chapter.

FURTHER READING

Bairoch (1988), in *Cities and Economic Development*, has produced a wide-ranging historical and contemporary overview of the growth of cities and their contribution to economic growth. In addition, Lewis

Mumford's (1961) *The City in History* is still a splendidly idiosyncratic, well-informed and highly enjoyable read. Reinterpreting history from an environmental perspective, Ponting (1991), too, provides an excellent read, albeit not placing the development of cities at centre stage. Also taking a more global view, MacNeill *et al.* in *Interdependent Development* give a lucid account of the contemporary links between global economic and environmental development. Hardoy *et al.* (1992) provide a valuable summary of the urban experience in developing countries.

KEY THEMES

- Environmental externalities
- Global commons
- Optimum city size
- Social city region

DISCUSSION POINTS

- Provide a checklist of the likely advantages and drawbacks of a sustainable development policy which seeks to limit settlements to a maximum size of 15,000 people.
- Outline and evaluate the arguments for and against regarding cities as environmental free-loaders (cf the global commons debate).

CHAPTER THREE

Inside the Social City Region

In many countries the use of urban space has altered dramatically over the twentieth century. In some cities the space demands of the motor car now account for almost a third of urban land, rising to two-thirds in inner Los Angeles (Girardet 1992, McMichael 1993). None the less, in European cities, often considered as densely populated, over half the urban area is open space in some manifestation (Girardet 1992).

Unfortunately, much of the change in the ways in which we use urban space has been to the detriment of the natural, cultural and social environments. Historic buildings have been torn down unnecessarily, open spaces have been built over, whilst homes, shops and offices have tended to be located further and further apart from each other, increasing the amount of energy and time used in travelling from one place to another.

Policies to change the internal structure and functioning of the city are central, therefore, to improving the urban environment, and have the potential to bring about major reductions in urban energy demands. They can also be important in increasing economic efficiency, improving the social fabric of the city and adding to the city's aesthetic appeal. In addition, as Chapter One emphasised, the existing built environment of the city can also constitute a valuable aesthetic and cultural resource, so that in altering the city from within, it is always important to seek to enhance existing positive design features, including historic buildings and precincts, open spaces and other assets. This chapter examines some of the most important aspects of the changing internal form and functioning of the city over the past hundred years, starting with urban density issues, followed by sections on urban form, urban design and the social and economic disadvantage associated with the nature of the built environment.

3.1 URBAN DENSITY AND URBAN SPRAWL

During the twentieth century cities have extended outwards, upwards and even downwards in ways never before envisaged. The internal structure of activities within the city has also changed markedly over time, across a range of dimensions, a trend which is especially evident in the low-density sprawling metropolitan regions. These areas have been radically altered by a combination of the decentralisation of population and businesses, large scale exclusionary land-use zoning within the city, and the increasing amounts of space given over to the demands of the motor car. Amidst all these changes, the population densities of cities have also changed, most notably in North America and Australia, where low-density suburban sprawl has become almost a defining feature of their twentieth century development.

Urban population density is a rather vexed issue which has long confounded the attempts of city planners to use their understanding of it as a means of improving the urban environment. In broad terms, urban population density is perceived as both an urban planning and an environmental issue because of the costs of urban infrastructure provision, which vary with density of development, and the perceived over-crowding of some cities, which is said to be correlated with increasing social stresses in particular. Arguing in favour of high density living, many contributors and policy makers within the sustainable urban development debate claim that the compact-city solution helps reduce the tendencies to peripheral urban sprawl and also stimulates urban dynamism and vibrancy (Commission of the European Communities 1990, Elkin, McLaren and Hillman 1991, Unwin and Searle 1991).

According to Angotti (1993, p.152), historically the range of urban densities has not increased dramatically: in pre-industrial cities, densities ranged from 200 to 5000 people per square kilometre, the same range as can be found in US cities today. Other examples which Angotti cites include the ancient city of Ur at around 6300 people per square kilometre, the same as contemporary Brussels, whilst Bogota in Colombia had a density of around 2300 people per square kilometre in 1670, the same as contemporary Cologne. Contemporary residential densities per square kilometre vary widely, with 14,600 in Beijing, 13,000 in central Tokyo and Osaka, to 9000 in New York City and 4000 in Los Angeles, and 210 in the Dallas metropolitan area (Smil 1984; Angotti 1993, pp. 13–14).

Generally speaking, urban densities peak in the inner residential areas and decline towards the outer suburbs (see Richardson 1978). Over time the density gradient usually falls, as a certain drift from the centre occurs. However, in recent years, a re-centralisation of urban population has emerged in many European, North American and Australian cities, as residential preferences have changed. The return to inner suburbs of the wealthier classes has been facilitated by a number of trends, notably: as industry has left the city and the aesthetic appeal of many older houses and mixed use neighbourhoods has been rediscovered; as household structures have changed in favour of dual income units, smaller families and later child-rearing; and as overburdened transport infrastructures have increased the difficulty of long-distance commuting. In developing-country cities, density gradients tend to be steeper, especially where poor transport links reduce the attractiveness of the outer areas, a factor which also contributes to the continuing preference of higher income groups for central living.

3.1.1 Against high-density living

High population density has been long derided as it is widely believed to be associated with antisocial behaviour, such as crime, delinquency, ill-health and so on (Michelson 1970). In the 1960s, considerable numbers of studies showed a link between overcrowding and antisocial behaviour among rats in experimental conditions, and sought to make tenuous links with human behaviour (Howard 1976), although now very few people would accept the validity of such links (Newman and Kenworthy 1989). Generally speaking, among humans the most important indicator that links overcrowding to human stress and psychosis is numbers of people per room, whilst numbers of household units per building or hectare are relatively unimportant (Howard 1976). None the less, post-war European housing policy was often based on these household-density measures. The coexistence of areas of high-density population with low levels of social disorder, for instance in parts of Hong Kong and Boston (USA), and of low-density areas with high levels of social disorder, such as some of Sydney's (Australia) western suburbs, seem to indicate that the real issues at stake are more likely to be a combination of social and economic factors, such as low income, poor education and social isolation (Alexander 1967, Newman and Kenworthy 1989). According to Alice Coleman (1985), reductions in density following residential redevelopment in North Peckham, London, resulted in soaring crime rates and very high rates of domestic arson. In many cities in developing countries, the main fears surrounding high-density living concern overcrowding and the rapid spread of disease. High density does not necessarily equate with overcrowding, there being a world of difference between high-density living in high-rise residential blocks with low numbers of people per room, and overcrowding in low-rise shanty town developments, with high numbers of people per room. We will return to some of these issues below.

One further possible complicating factor concerns cultural and national differences between people as a conditioning factor in their attitudes to proximity and crowding (Hall 1966, Howard 1976). Edward Hall (1966) argued that people from different cultures differed in their need for community involvement, with Puerto Ricans for instance having higher involvement than those of Germanic origin. Those cultures with higher involvement tend to prefer higher densities than others, possibly accompanied by greater screening from outsiders. There are so many complicating factors of social organisation, class and inurement to particular patterns of involvement, sometimes resulting from lack of opportunity to break out of these particular traditions, that it is important not to take such findings as universal truths, more as indications that community aspirations may indeed differ in respect of styles and density of urban residential living. Most importantly, the complicating factors surrounding urban density should make us wary of falling for the implicit environmental determinism which is sometimes found in arguments both for and against high-density living.

3.1.2 For high-density living

High urban population densities are still seen by many policy makers and urban development professionals as conducive to creativity: built-up central city areas are said to be vibrant, whilst suburbs are monotonous. The Commission of the European Communities (1990, p.19), for instance, talks of 'the failure of the periphery: the absence of public life, the paucity of culture, the visual monotony, the time wasted in commuting. By contrast, the city offers density and variety; the efficient, time- and energy-saving combination of social and economic functions; the chance to restore the rich architecture inherited from the past.' Even more dogmatically, the architect-ecologist-philosopher Paolo Soleri (1990) proclaims in the curious style of some urban 'visionaries' that

> The lesson is clear: life is where crowding is immense. Death comes when the system uncrowds... When the hyper-organism, the city, surrenders its makers and dwellers to the dimly alive pseudo-organism called suburbia, death is dancing... No 'eco-thinking' can ignore the miracle of crowding-living. To do so is to indulge in incoherent fantasizing. Worse, it is to betray Gaia, the opportunistic coherent game enacted by the proto-conscious realm. *The city, a mind product, is a crowding phenomenon. The city is a life maker.* (p.21)
> [italics original]

Soleri is currently building his model community, Arcosanti, in Phoenix, based on these and other elements of his theories. Elements of the reasoning sound alarmingly similar to Le Corbusier, usually credited with inspiring the development of mass-produced, high-rise housing (see below).

Environmental arguments in favour of high-density urban living frequently stress that this option is more efficient than low-density sprawl in terms of lower rates of domestic consumption of energy for heating, electricity and water, whilst scale economies can result in lower infrastructure costs, and critical mass thresholds are more likely to be reached to justify the provision of energy-efficient modes of public transport (underground metros, trams, etc.) (Angotti 1993). In addition, higher-density urban development is seen to economise on street lighting and to reduce transport needs, particularly where cities are so arranged that people can readily walk or cycle to work and to services, such as schools and shops. A further positive feature concerns the range of functions which well-designed neighbourhoods with high concentrations of population can support, in terms of health care, schools, shops and so on. As we have already seen, the opponents of high-density living might dispute most of these claims. Perhaps the most important arguments for high-density living, however, involve a strong reaction against the perceived problems of low-density living.

3.1.3 Against low-density living

The low-density suburban sprawl found in cities in the United States and Australia is frequently seen as the worst kind of urban structure (Angotti 1993). This form of suburbanisation is held by some to lead to atomised lifestyles which deny the emergence of a true sense of local community, and to encourage the 'cult of domesticity' (Walker 1981). Low-density suburbs of privately owned houses are seen as socially stultifying, where residents lead uniform, dull, conformist lives, in part because of the lack of social and economic diversity.

Within the sustainable urban development debate, those calling for higher-density residential development have been particularly concerned with the environmental implications of low-density urban sprawl which has characterised twentieth-century suburban expansion in some Western nations, most notably the USA and Australia (Box 3.1).

Whatever the balance of environmental advantages, one thing is certain, low-density sprawl has been facilitated by the rise of road transport, especially the private motor car. To varying degrees low-density suburban sprawl has also been subsidised by the state in some countries where associated infrastructure has been provided below cost, not least roads.

Box 3.1 Environmentally Undesirable Features of Low-Density Urban Development in Australia

- Consumption of large tracts of productive farmland for both housing and roads
- Increased area of paved and built-on surfaces, boosting urban run-off of rainwater and of petroleum and other deposits
- High storm water pollution relative to high-density areas
- Increased water consumption for garden use
- Increased energy usage and air pollution caused by decrease in viability of public transport, walking and cycling
- Increased energy consumption in single-storey, detached developments, because of poor thermal qualities relative to more compact housing forms
- High per capita petrol consumption and resultant polluting car emissions
- Poor recycling rates, due to relatively higher costs of collection

(Adapted from: Unwin and Searle 1991, p.2, and Newman and Mouritz 1991, pp. 13–14)

In their much-cited work on cities and automobile dependence, Newman and Kenworthy (1989) compare cities according to their petrol consumption and their urban density. A clear relationship emerges between low-density urban areas and high per capita petrol consumption (Figure 3.1). This leads the authors to conclude that high-density urban areas need to be encouraged, with policies to revitalise urban centres, to restrain car usage, and to provide better public transport. Although Gordon and Richardson (1990) argue strongly against the Newman and Kenworthy findings and policy conclusions on the grounds of failing to account for national lifestyle differences, the lack of emphasis on economic pricing policy tools and the claimed dubious viability of some public transport infrastructures, much of the validity of the original findings still holds (Breheny 1990). In a subsequent exercise (McGlynn, Newman and Kenworthy 1991), a range of cities from across the world is classified into five categories, from large-sprawling, US-style cities with high automobile dependence to more compact cities, with low automobile dependence. Here again a very strong correlation is found between what appear to be relatively environmentally benign traits in high-density cities, and the extreme profligacy in sprawling cities in terms of fuel consumption, space devoted to car parking and so on.

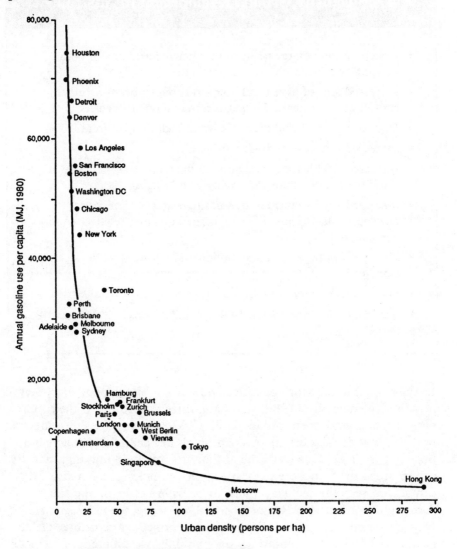

Source: Newman and Kenworthy 1989

Figure 3.1 Gasoline use per capita versus urban density (1980).

Such data provide ready ammunition for those arguing for urban consolidation policies that would bring more people and jobs closer to each other in higher-density, mixed-use inner areas. There is a need to exercise some caution here, however. It is not simply low residential density that is causing energy consumption profligacy, although it is certainly a major component. Also implicated are urban form and the separation of functional activities within very large cities which gives rise to the need for more and longer automobile journeys. This is something to which we turn in Section 3.2.

3.1.4 For low-density living

Those who argue against low-density suburbia commonly point to social stultification, environmental costs and high infrastructure costs. As Hugh Stretton (1989) points out, whilst the stereotype of slumbering suburbia may have some basis in fact in some areas, it is in truth a tremendous oversimplification, forgetting the organic growth within suburbs over time and the fact that some people lead very dull lives in the inner cities and in remote country towns. Indeed, some people are best able to express themselves creatively from a base in the privacy of their own suburban family house and garden. It is not the suburbs which are necessarily bad in themselves (Oliver, Davis and Bentley 1981).

Stretton also castigates those who make simple-minded accusations that suburbs are particularly bad for women, who may come to feel imprisoned in their suburban homes (see section 3.3). This sense of isolation is very similar to the more general 'transitional neurosis' or more popularly 'New Town blues' syndrome remarked upon in some post war British housing (Goodey 1974). Though some women may feel isolated in low-density suburbia, Stretton argues that large numbers of surveys show that most women prefer to live in a suburban house with garden than elsewhere (see also Cooper Marcus and Sarkissian 1986). Life in more densely populated inner-city areas may well be preferable for some people at some stages of their life cycles, and with the rise of numbers of single- and two-person household units this trend may well be increasing, but this does not make it necessarily the preferable option for all. Stretton also derides the notion that high-density urban life is preferable because it stimulates more casual relations with passing adult strangers, and that these are somehow more valuable and stimulating than the more routine family relationships, relationships at work, and those within a close (inner-area or suburban) community which domi-nate most lives. This slightly misses the point that, as Appleyard (1981) illustrates, well-designed residential neighbourhoods can be conducive to casual contact and, over time, lead to friendships growing.

Conceding that people may need the fun and vibrancy of city centres, Stretton argues that they don't need to live there, just close by. In Sweden, planners view access and proximity to the city centre as so important that they aim to ensure that there is a railway station within 900 metres of most housing, and that all residents should be no more than 30 minutes away from the city centre (Newman and Kenworthy 1989). More recently, the case for greater contact between people and access to urban facilities has become infused with an environmental tinge in Sweden, and policy makers have become increasingly concerned not to develop peripheral open space, preferring higher densities, either in existing centres, or in separate towns within commuting distance (Orrskog and Snickars 1992).

Most famously, Stretton (1989) praises low-density suburbs and the typical quarter acre-plot, which is the aspiration still of many Australians, because of its contribution to family life. The large suburban house and garden

> reconciles access to work and city with private, adaptable, self-expressive living space at home. Plenty of adults love that living space and subdivide it ingeniously. For children it really has no rivals. At home it can allow them space, freedom and community with their elders; they can still reach bush and beach in one direction and in the other schools to educate them and cities to sophisticate them. About half the lives of most of us are spent growing up then bringing others up. Suburbs are good places to do it, precisely because they let the generations coexist, with some continuing independence for each. These are the gains our transport costs buy for us. (pp. 21–22)

Here we have a well-developed counter-argument to Jane Jacobs' (1961) plea for fostering high-density urban neighbourhoods, supporting a fine-grained mélange of diverse services, jobs, and peoples. Interestingly, Stretton does not call for rigid planning zoning and separation of functions, and indeed suggests that his beloved suburbs might benefit from some loosening of planning controls. In presenting the case for suburbia, his intention appears to be to retain a heterogeneity of residential densities and living styles across each city, recognising that the preferences of people will differ, and indeed for any individual will change over the course of their lifetime. It is also worth noting that in environmental terms, too, low-density living can have its advantages (Box 3.2).

Box 3.2 Environmentally Desirable Features of Low-Density Urban Development.

- Large gardens may reduce summer temperatures: important in hot countries.
- There is greater potential for own food production, including reuse of domestic organic wastes as compost.
- There are greater opportunities to collect and use rainwater.
- It promotes affinity with nature.
- There is more space for solar energy panels.

(Beaumont and Keys 1982, Troy 1992)

3.1.5 Policies for raising urban population densities

Until recent years, in many countries the state was prepared to assume much of the financial burden of suburban infrastructure development, for instance: providing local sealed roads and sewage connections (Birrell 1991, Spiller 1993b). However, this situation has rapidly changed as governments have sought to reduce their spending and promote development within the city, and to reduce pressures for outward expansion. Whilst it is not desirable or feasible to introduce user charges on all elements of public infrastructure, it is certainly desirable to move in that direction in order to reduce the public subsidy to private sector-led low-density suburban expansion. (See Vittorio 1992 and Spiller 1993b, for an indication of the range of infrastructure involved and the current allocation of funding responsibilities in Australia.)

Urban consolidation policies have moved to the fore on the policy agenda and involve measures to promote more house building within existing city areas, usually medium-density housing. These policies have been seen as a means of making savings on infrastructure costs, reducing demand on edge-of-city land, reducing travel distances, and possibly helping promote increased use of public transport. Urban consolidation policies have typically included (Roseth 1991, Unwin and Searle 1991):

- infill on non-developed urban land
- residential plot subdivision in countries with a history of large residential plot sizes

- reducing minimum residential plot sizes in land use plans for residential developments
- allowing medium-density housing in areas previously designated for low-density housing in local plans
- a shift towards two- or three-storey housing.

Each approach has drawn some criticism. The opponents of using land currently designated as non-residential point to the loss of valuable open space, whilst higher population densities simultaneously increase the demand for public open space. Existing local residents also often see higher residential densities as detracting from the value of their own properties, although at least one study indicates that this is a false fear (Babbage 1993). Residential plot subdivision in Australia has allowed up to six household units to be built where previously one single-storey house stood in its quarter-acre plot of land.

It is generally held that both physical and social elements of urban infrastructure are cheaper to provide in high-density inner areas than low-density inner areas. For example, adding a new outer suburb would require considerable new road building and the laying of basic infrastructure for public services such as water pipes, whereas these facilities are largely already provided in inner areas, making attempts at regeneration and at increasing residential density potentially cheaper to provide for. In terms of social overhead costs, too, the state will be expected to provide new schools, police stations and so on in the new suburbs, whilst in the inner areas depopulation – caused in particular by a decline in the number of people per household unit – may be undermining the viability of schools, public transport systems and so on (Searle 1991). However, it is necessary to offset these savings with the need to construct higher buildings to achieve higher density, which frequently cost more to build and maintain than low-rise residential units (Hoch 1969, Stretton 1978, Elkin, McLaren and Hillman 1991). In a related vein, Stretton (1978) argues that suburban low-rise plumbing can make more use of gravity, whereas high-rise buildings will require greater use of pumps, and high-rise residential blocks will require electrically powered elevators. In addition, inner-area land is usually more expensive, and where it has been previously used rehabilitation costs in some cases can be very high, negating any savings in providing basic infrastructure.

Until recently, surprisingly little work had been undertaken to compare the infrastructure costs of urban consolidation and suburban development (Birrell 1991). However, a report for the New South Wales (Australia) state government apparently concluded that the costs of physical infrastructure development for each new dwelling in existing inner-urban residential areas were A$17–30,000 less than in the suburbs. Of these costs $8–14,000 constituted non-coverable public expenditure, whilst facilities such as main road provision, schools, hospitals and public transport services were not included (Roseth 1991). Troy (1992) disputes the estimate of cost savings of A$41,600 per dwelling unit quoted in a similar study undertaken by a consultancy firm for the City of Melbourne. He argues that many of the benefits are illusory: there is relatively little spare infrastructural capacity in the inner-city areas, and much of the existing infrastructure may well be approaching the end of its productive life span, most notably the water pipes, whilst the huge costs of retrofitting to upgrade drainage in existing built-up areas is, misleadingly, left out of calculations. In a similar vein, Troy argues that the notion that the inner-city resident is subsidising outer-city residents becomes more complex when the lower level of service accessibility and usage (especially public transport) in the outer city is taken into account, implying a reverse flow in subsidy in city regions with a unified government and tax system.

In some more densely populated city regions, land scarcity combined with attempts to remove high-density, low-rise housing slums in older cities, led to attempts to change urban density through building high-rise residential towers. In many cases these proved unsuccessful, using building materials and technologies of unproven capabilities, and in the case of public-sector housing, having been managed in such a way as to make them socially unworkable (Stretton 1978, Ravetz 1980, Coleman 1985, see also section 3.3 below). The development costs per household unit of these high-rise blocks and their land consumption were generally higher than for equivalent low-rise developments, with the difference in space accounted for by the provision of large tracts of poorly designed and poorly used open space around them (Stretton 1978, Ravetz 1980). The failure of some high-rise public-sector housing should not blind us to the possibilities of thinking of the three-dimensional city, however. After all, some high-rise private-sector residential housing is successful. It was not high-rise as such which was bad, but the 'hidden agenda' of cost-cutting and social engineering (see Hackney 1989).

In the three-dimensional city elevated roads are also generally poorly regarded because of their visual blight and their ability to divide neighbourhoods (Hoch 1969). Underground railways and road tunnels, alternatively, are seen as improving accessibility in city centres, reducing congestion and adding to property values. Similarly, underground car parks reduce surface space demand and the visual intrusion of the motor car. In countries such as Russia and Sweden, far-reaching experiments have placed other structures underground, including civil defence and military installations, convention centres and civic centres. A study comparing an underground and an overground plant in Sweden found the overground plant had greater absenteeism, whilst the underground plant had fewer accidents, but higher levels of headaches and psychosomatic problems (Hoch 1969).

The use of the emotive term 'town cramming', current in British planning circles, rather than 'urban consolidation' is an indication of the wariness with which some commentators understandably view the prospect of further attempts to increase urban densities, especially in older cities (Breheny 1992, Breheny and Rookwood 1993). The compact-city solution is not without its critics, some of whom prefer solutions chosen from a more varied selection (Breheny and Rookwood 1993), undoubtedly a sensible approach, given the problems associated with virtually every visionary or masterplan solution produced in the history of architecture and town planning. Having been easy game for the pseudo-philosophies supposedly underpinning earlier radical grand designs, contemporary planners have become more wary of single, grand-gesture approaches which sweep away all before them, all that went before and all the alternatives which might have been.

3.2 URBAN FORM AND FUNCTION

3.2.1 The case for a reversion to mixed land uses

Urban economic and social restructuring exert hugely varying impacts across cities and nations. In the developing countries the flight out of the city by the wealthy classes has been considerably less pronounced than in developed countries. In this section, however, the emphasis is very much on the Western experience. Where early cities were complex mixes, ranging across all social classes, the late nineteenth and much of the twentieth centuries saw the flight from the cities of increasing numbers of those who could afford to go, leaving behind a deteriorating housing stock, inhabited by the poor in environmentally degraded urban centres, where air pollution, noise, water contamination and insanitary housing conditions were all at their worst (Sherlock 1991). Though never as homogeneous in class and residential terms as the concentric zone theories proposed by the Chicago School, the many different areas within Western cities did none the less become less socially heterogeneous as part of this process.

According to Colin Ward (1989),

> The traditional city had a fine grain. Apart from its large public buildings it had developed as a series of small building sites... This fine-grained development, despite its complexity, was transparent to the user, by comparison with the sheer opacity of the modern

city... The functions and functioning of the city were apparent from its built form. (pp.22–23)

The 'fine-grained' city was quickly dispatched with the advent of the industrial revolution in the late eighteenth century. The building of seemingly ever larger factories required the rapid construction of large numbers of houses for the workers, a process which saw one of the first attempts at mass-produced, large-scale neighbourhood building. In Britain, the houses for the poorest workers were usually small and badly built; overcrowding was a major problem and became a significant cause of environmental health hazards (Burnett 1978).

Yet in these nineteenth-century neighbourhoods, the romanticised view is that cohesive communities quickly established themselves. To an extent they did, and undoubtedly the existence of local 'corner shops' and other service provisions helped this process. But a note of caution must be sounded at this point: communities here as elsewhere evolved gradually; they were not built overnight, nor were they achieved by purposeful urban design. Grinding poverty and reliance on a common employer were factors which encouraged community support systems, neither of which are usually desirable features in urban development.

In US cities, the development of 'large-grain functional differentiation' also started with the shift of production away from small-scale, home-based craft working towards large factories, separating production from consumption, workplace from home (Walker 1981, p.386). Even the rigid gridiron development pattern of cities in the USA was originally based upon small lots, whether for industry, commerce or housing (Ward 1989). Large-scale factories, became the norm in the twentieth century, often located away from the centre of the city, sometimes on the edge of town, changing dramatically the layout of the city and the flows of goods and workers across the urban space. Industrialisation linked with suburbanisation led to an increasing divide between work and home, between the public and private realm (Pratt 1989; see section 3.3 below). Physically, socially and economically, the city became more internally divided. More purely residential suburbs emerged, physically separated from increasingly distinctive industrial zones.

It is in the present century that the greatest changes in urban form have come about. Three main factors have facilitated an unparalleled physical expansion of large-grain cities. Firstly, the rise of motorised road transport liberated industry from the need to locate near its old break-of-bulk points, encouraging the shift of jobs towards the edge of the city. For the individual, too, the rise of the motor car has increased personal mobility, again fuelling the outward spread of suburban development and increasing journey-to-work distances. Secondly, the growth of large-scale businesses and governments was important in creating new large-scale factories and offices, attracting large flows of commuters and goods to them. As we noted in Chapter Two, industry and government also worked both separately and together to create the conditions necessary for the success of the shift towards car-based suburbia, such as removing public transport, building new roads and providing other forms of subsidised infrastructure. Thirdly, there was the emergence of functional zoning as a central tool in land use planning. Land use zoning became a popular tool in meeting the increasingly vocal call to separate industry from housing, in an attempt to improve the immediate environment of those faced with the prospect of living close to a large polluting factory. The first US zoning ordinance was enacted in New York in 1916, largely in response to the negative effects of skyscrapers, such as shadowing neighbouring buildings. Here we have the roots of exclusionary zoning. Although it has fallen into disrepute in some of its manifestations, at the time it represented a major achievement by separating residents from industrial pollution in particular. It would be unfair to say that large-scale zoning was forced on cities by planners alone: many businesses, land developers and residents vigorously campaigned for some form of exclusionary zoning.

In the vanguard of criticism of exclusionary zoning legislation as the basis for urban planning was Jane Jacobs (1961), who claimed that the very vitality of the city needed the ordered chaos which mixed neighbourhoods represented. Areas without a mixture of housing types, social groups, shops, workshops, offices and factories, became a form of potentially unsustainable social monoculture. The clamour for a return to the mixed uses of the fine-grained city has grown in recent years, largely because of its perceived potential to reduce car journeys within the city (Owens 1986, 1992; Ward 1989; Sherlock 1991; Breheny and Rookwood 1993).

Cities with dominant centres are increasingly seen as a central part of the problem of a deteriorating urban environment, creating a reliance on mass flows of people, materials energy and information, and causing a build-up of complex infrastructures veering towards overload and potential catastrophe. According to Stretton (1976, 289), 'no urban form is so vulnerable to shortages of energy, to "complexity breakdowns" or to aimless summer riots or deliberate sabotage'.

Alternatively, the concentration of traffic flows along radial routes has, in some cities, helped maintain the viability of the public transport infrastructure, reducing car journeys in the process. In this context the growth of out-of-town retail and employment centres and the associated decline in some city-centre locations may undermine the viability of some public transport systems. A further ingredient in the fragmentation of traffic flows within the city has been that many smaller, locally based shops and other public facilities such as hospitals, schools and libraries, have been closed, amalgamated or replaced by distant facilities. In these processes, those without access to private transport have been most disadvantaged, not least women who generally have more limited access to cars than men (Bowlby 1988). It is difficult to be sure of the impacts of the growth in dual-income households over the past thirty years. By and large, women have tended to work closer to home than males as they seek to accommodate work and family commitments within a limited time and financial budget (Pickup 1988). In this context, household location strategies within the city are increasingly being decided by accessibility not just to local facilities (shops, schools) and a single work place, but by more complex considerations concerning multiple jobs, access to more centralised retailing centres and public services, public transport access and car ownership.

One of the interesting features in the recent development of the sprawling cities of the USA and Australia has been the rise of strong suburban centres, which have themselves become the magnets for decentralising jobs. In a study of the 20 largest US cities, 46% of commuting trips involved shorter journeys across the outer suburbs in 1980, compared to 38% in 1970 (Gordon, Kumar and Richardson 1989a, 1989b). Taking such findings into consideration, Brotchie (1992) argues that in existing sprawling cities, commuting times are likely to increase with uniform density increases across the city and continued centralisation of jobs; however, journey times would be reduced where growth is focused on multiple suburban areas. Seeking to disperse activities relatively uniformly across the urban fabric would probably result in greater complexities of traffic and energy flows, undermine the viability of public transport and lead to a greater reliance on cars.

A more sophisticated approach than applying urban consolidation measures across every city area is evidently required. Increasing urban population densities without consideration of urban form makes little sense. It is now widely argued that within large cities it is appropriate to foster the development of a number of strong sub-centres within the city (Beaumont and Keys 1982, Brotchie 1992), concentrating traffic flows sufficiently to encourage public transport provision. A further advantage of centring development around strong sub-centres within the city is seen to be the support of local centres which can foster a rich mixture of activities, like a traditional city-centre area.

3.2.2 Energy, transport and urban form

The current built form of cities is, in many nations, an outcome of centuries of development and represents a major cultural and physical investment. Although Mumford (1961) says that, historically, cities have risen and declined both often and rapidly, the evidence of the last two centuries is that demise is increasingly rare: most of our existing large urban areas are here to stay (Owens 1992). As urban infrastructure is so expensive to provide it needs to be designed with the greatest prospect of being adaptable to changed future priorities and possibilities (Stretton 1976). In this respect, the two main likely future challenges of cities concern their high energy consumption and the heavy reliance of the petrol-powered motor vehicles. Linking urban form and energy use, Sue Owens (1986; 1992, p. 92) notes that

- interspersion of activities can change trip requirements, especially length bringing energy demand variations of up to 130%
- the shape of the urban area can lead to variations in energy demand of 20%
- density or clustering of trip destinations can bring about energy savings of 20%, mainly by facilitating public transport
- dense or mixed-use zones, facilitating combined heat and power systems, can increase the efficiency of primary energy use by 100%
- layout and orientation of buildings can lead to energy savings of 12% through passive solar gain
- siting, landscaping, layout and materials can produce energy savings of up to 5% through modifying microclimates.

As we have already argued, there is a strong relationship between land use patterns, overall transport demand and motor vehicle use. Motor vehicles continue to make increasing demands on urban space, create major pollution problems and major urban congestion problems (Box 3.3; Chapter Seven). Car travel has been increasing rapidly in recent years, mainly as a result of larger distances travelled per trip rather than more individual journeys (Gossop and Webb 1993), with longer journeys to work the most important element of this increase. This said, car journeys for social and entertainment reasons, and for shopping and personal business, are the main reasons for journeys, not travel to work or at work. Recreational travel also increased more rapidly than work-related travel between 1979 and 1986, as people gained more leisure time and greater access to cars (Banister 1992, Jones 1993).

Box 3.3 Car-Related Urban Problems

- In the UK, road transport accounts for 18% of all carbon dioxide emissions, 85% of carbon monoxide emissions, 30% of volatile organic compounds, and 45% of nitrous oxides, about 80% of which are released in urban areas.
- Only 15–20% of urban nitrous oxide emissions are deposited in the city, with the rest transported outside.
- In OECD countries, transport is responsible for 50% of atmospheric lead emissions, 80% of all benzene emissions, and about 50% of total hydrocarbons in urban areas.
- In the heavily polluted Athens basin and Mexico City motor vehicles account for 83% of air pollution.
- The manufacture of cars constitutes a major environmental impact in itself, in terms of materials and energy use.
- Air conditioning for cars accounts for 10% of global CFC-12 usage.
- Public transport is less land-intensive, with the passengers of two hundred filled cars able to occupy one tram car, on average.
- Roads demand more land in construction than rail, and cost up to eighty times as much to build.
- Material and energy use in road construction is high, as is disruption to nearby residents and ecosystems.
- In cities in the USA and Australia, road supply per capita tends to be three to four times as high as in European cities and seven to nine times higher than in Asian cities.
- Cities in the USA provide 80% more car parking spaces per 1000 workers than European cities, and six times more than in Asian cities.
- Road transport is associated with high accident and death tolls, and can deter cyclists and pedestrians.
- Congestion costs are high: in Athens city centre, road traffic moves at an average of just 7–8 km/hour, in Paris 18 km/hour and in London 20km/hour.
- The occupancy rate of cars is generally low: in Paris 1.25 passengers for every 4.5 seats

> - In OECD countries the social costs of road transport are estimated at 0.1% of GDP for noise, 0.4% for air pollution and 2.0–2.4% for accidents.
>
> (Thomson 1977; OECD 1988, 1990; Newman and Kenworthy 1989; Alcamo and Lubkert 1990; Hass-Klau 1990; Barton 1992; Gossop and Webb 1993; Tolba and El-Kholy 1992; Whitelegg 1993)

The increasing sprawl of the city and the functional separation of activities have added to the demand for motor cars and tended to reduce the viability of public transport in all but the largest and most densely populated towns and cities. The problems associated with high urban car usage have led to widespread calls, from the European Commission amongst others, to alter the balance of passenger movement away from private and towards public transport. Generally speaking, the most energy-efficient forms of travel are cycling, walking, buses, rail and then the car (Owens 1992, Banister 1992). Promoting public transport has implications for urban form, not just in the sense of creating stronger sub-centres within the city fabric, but also encouraging linear development of cities along public transport routes (Owens 1992). The relationships between urban density, journey lengths and choice of transport mode are complex, but it does appear that coordinated land use and transport planning is essential if car-dependence is to be reduced (Owens and Cope 1992, Jones 1993, Box 3.4).

In general, it appears that the greatest fuel energy savings are to be had from concentrating development in relatively remote smaller towns, or by changing the patterns of activities within the city, again sometimes concentrated at nodal points across the city (Owens 1991, Banister 1992, Rydin 1992b). The advantages of small settlement development include lower land costs and avoiding urban congestion, whilst among the disadvantages is loss of amenity in terms of access to a wide range of services and job opportunities. The advantages of changing towns and cities from within are primarily high energy saving and greater efficiency in the use of existing infrastructure (Banister 1992, Owens 1992).

Box 3.4 Rationales for Coordinating Land Use and Transport Planning

- Greater population densities tend to mean more services can be supported at neighbourhood level, encourage greater walking and cycling in preference to car usage and can increase the viability of public transport provision.
- Larger cities tend to be more self-contained in terms of jobs and services, which makes some journeys shorter, and are better able to support public transport.
- Journeys tend to increase in distance with urban size, negating some of the beneficial impacts.
- Centralisation of activities at selected points within the city region encourages the use of public transport.
- As public transport frequently offers the main viable alternative to the motor car, policies to reduce car dependence need to emphasise coordinated investment in public transport.

In summary, more than any other single development, the motor car has reshaped the twentieth-century city. On one level, this has been beneficial, allowing greater individual mobility for some, greater speed of movement of people and goods, and a growth outwards from the city. On another level, the costs have been enormous, in terms of pollution, space consumption, and the separation of urban functions.

3.2.3 Fostering diversity in urban form

In recent years there has been a rapid growth in the number of models of internal urban and regional form supposedly best suited to sustainable urban development (see also Chapter Eight). There are many who advocate denser living in an attempt to reduce travel times and distances, and to limit urban encroachment, with urban consolidation policies advocated by planners in Sweden, Australia and elsewhere. Others favour a shift towards decentralised concentration, developing smaller towns as overflow outlets outside the major cities. At the other end of the spectrum is a range of proposals for new ecological communities, based on notions such as permaculture; these aim towards greater self-reliance, moving back towards more rural-type settlements (Orrskog and Snickars 1992). Should our lifestyle become more urban, or more rural? The debate about the desirability and styles of urban living is as polarised now as it was in Europe and the USA in the nineteenth century. Breheny and Rookwood (1993) have argued that the shift towards the high-density, compact city would be premature and possibly undesirable as a policy for a whole urban area, not being sufficiently attuned to the different ways in which different parts of the city region are built and used, whilst the advantages remain unproven. Instead they propose an approach which identifies the different environmental problems associated with different parts of the social city region (centre, inner city, suburbs, rural areas) and propose different types of policies for each of them. This imaginative approach appears to provide a greater sensitivity to local differences and potentials, and to offer the greatest flexibility for individual choice about location and lifestyles within the city. The complex nature of the city and the people who live in it requires complex, multi-stranded and flexible strategies.

3.3 SOCIAL AND ECONOMIC DISADVANTAGE AND THE BUILT ENVIRONMENT

The changing form of the city and the very nature of the built environment have had dysfunctional and disempowering effects on some groups of people, from being denied access to a full range of services, to being obliged to live in some of the least environmentally attractive parts of the city. Alienation within the urban environment has become the lot of an increasing proportion of the urban population, disadvantaged not just in city centres but even in their own neighbourhoods.

Urban access issues are important for a wide range of social groups, according to sex, race, age, class, sexual preference, the homeless, the jobless and poorly paid, and many other social categories. For the physically disabled, poor urban design has frequently resulted in a worsening of accessibility, where even pedestrianisation schemes in city centres can quickly lead to further marginalisation of their position, unless special access and parking are provided. For some mentally ill people in Britain, the reality of the government's 'care in the community' policy has been the closing down of old mental health hospitals without adequate support being provided for those released. Instead, for many of the mentally ill, city centres have become magnets, particularly where personal poverty and homelessness have accompanied their condition. We know relatively little about the processes of homelessness more generally, including how it changes over time, how it varies between cities and the effects of the transient inner urban lifestyle for people in this condition, who are inevitably exposed to some of the worst which the urban environment can throw at them.

Acknowledging that urban access issues are multi-faceted, for the sake of convenience we shall use just one group of people to illustrate the nature of this debate: women. It is important to bear in mind here that disadvantage tends to be multi-layered, so that acute problems are particularly likely to be felt by those disadvantaged across more than one dimension, for instance black working-class women will usually face different kinds of disadvantage to white middle-class women, and in most cases experience a greater severity of disadvantage. Similarly, the nature of disadvantage may change over a person's lifetime, not only in response to external conditions, but also to alterations in an individual's family responsibilities (Mackenzie 1988).

After years of neglect on this issue, in recent years there has been considerable interest among many writers in how women have dispro-portionately borne many of the environmental and social costs of built urban environments, environments developed largely by and for men. According to England (1991),

> the location of residential areas, work-places, transportation net-works, and the overall layout of cities in general reflect a patriarchal capitalist society's expectations of what types of activities take place where, when, and by whom. (p.136)

Within this patriarchal, capitalist system, the role of women has been primarily as sources for the reproduction of labour power and cheap, often impermanent, labour. Women's work, both paid and unpaid, has been used throughout the capitalist mode of production to subsidise the pursuit of profit, both historically and in contemporary times. For instance, the much-vaunted rise of female participation rates in Europe, North America and Australia since the 1960s has been associated in considerable part with a rise in casualised, low paid, temporary labour. In recent years there has been a reworking of the old distinctions between the private and public realms, where following industrialisation and the separation of work (public) from home (private), women were frequently relegated to the 'invisible' activities of domestic life, i.e. of reproduction, and cities shaped to meet the demands of the public needs of men in the production sphere (Mackenzie 1989, Parham 1993). These distinc-tions have now been eroded to some extent, only to be replaced with new, more complex structures of disadvantage, not least of which is the continuation of land use zoning around old assumptions of a divide between the public and private, production and reproduction realms.

Specifically in terms of urban labour markets, many women have remained tied to working in close proximity to their place of residence, in particular because of continuing household responsibilities, such as childcare, and the lack of access to a car (Pickup 1988). The increasing costs and the declining efficiency and coverage of public transport in many cities disproportionately affects women, both in terms of access to paid work and their household responsibilities. These are of course interrelated, not least since extra time spent on domestic responsibilities and travel leaves less time for engaging in paid employment. The result is that many women operate in more geographically limited labour markets than men, reducing their range of opportunities and their bargaining stance within the labour market. Poor transport access is an integral element of the dimension of the disadvantage which some women experience within the city, echoing Alison Ravetz's (1980) comment that increasingly we can identify the emergence of two major new classes: the travel-rich and the travel-poor. Distant suburban locations, far from major sources of employment, can particularly disadvantage women for such reasons, not necessarily in every case (Stretton 1989), but certainly in some. And in recent years this problem has become more acute: as fewer women grow their own food, make clothes, repair goods and so on, so they have become more reliant on making trips out for these services. Those with restricted car access or who are served by poor public transport are consequently becoming more disadvantaged (Parham 1993).

It is possible to extend this argument and examine the ways in which urban planning practices in the twentieth century, with their rigid zoning of land uses, have codified and prioritised land use according to male values and male needs. So it is not simply that industry, office areas and residence are separately zoned, making it difficult for women in particular to combine their household responsibilities with work. On a simple level, the zoning of central business districts exclusively for office use and for up-market service facilities, such as photocopy bureaux, brasseries and winebars, and therefore not for daily shopping needs, symbolises starkly the dominance of male worker values. Artificially created work zones soothe the male corporate psyche as it briefly rests from the pursuit of business opportunities, whilst simultaneously alienating many women workers (see Huxley 1991). In a similar vein, Parham (1993) argues that the public–private realm dichotomy saw suburbs designed on assumptions of the female as passive and protected within the private sphere.

The subordinate role of women has become firmly enmeshed in the urban built environment: cities are not neutrally structured (England 1991). This can be seen in the position of women in urban labour markets, in the lack of emphasis on visibility and urban design to reduce the risk of physical attack for female pedestrians, and in the expectation

that women will absorb or take responsibility for many urban environmental externalities, such as the roar of daytime traffic past houses on
or near main roads, and the encroachment of private urban development
on open spaces.

The danger in such analysis is in underplaying the ability of women
to transform their own and their families' lives. As experience in many
Third World localities has shown it is often women who have taken
responsibility for transforming their local environments (Dankelman
and Davidson 1988). In a similar vein, imputing the desire for suburbanisation solely to men would be to miss the real point, which is that
both men and women can take the decision to live in suburban locations,
but that women bear the costs disproportionately and can become most
locked into an undesirable location, such as when their children leave
home.

3.4 DESIGN AND THE BUILT ENVIRONMENT

3.4.1 The rise and fall of large-scale, large-grained plans

The built environment of the city presents mixed challenges: reusing or
demolishing historic buildings, which are aesthetically pleasing but
seemingly functionally outdated; accommodating or removing ancient
patterns of narrow streets; encouraging daring new architectural designs, or insisting on reference to existing building styles. These and
many other challenges face those responsible for moulding the fabric of
the city, from private developers and land owners to local governments
and local communities. The public pronouncements of the Prince of
Wales have seen a rising popular interest in urban design issues in
Britain, and in particular have highlighted the problems of the modernist
project, raised questions over the value of pastiched vernacular architectural styles, and brought to the fore the need for greater community
involvement in the development process (Punter 1990). Concern over
the impact of urban design on women has also grown rapidly, as part of
a growing grassroots involvement in design, and has raised particular
issues of personal safety. In the USA popular critics such as Jane Jacobs
(1961) and Richard Sennett (1990) have similarly raised public awareness of the importance of urban design: both are critical of particular
aspects of urban planning, most notably zoning in the case of Jacobs, as
we have already seen, and gridiron street patterns in the case of Sennett.

The rigid gridiron layout of the city is far from unique to the USA,
but it is here that it is most common, and where it has been most
insensitively applied to the urban fabric. According to Sennett (1990),

The grid can be understood...as a weapon to be used against environmental character – beginning with the power of geography. In cities like Chicago the grids were laid over irregular terrain; the rectangular blocks obliterated the natural environment, spreading out relentlessly no matter that hills, rivers, or forest knolls stood in the way. The natural features that could be levelled or drained, were; the insurmountable obstacles that nature put against the grid, the irregular course of rivers or lakes, were ignored by these frontier city planners, as if what could not be harnessed to this mechanical, tyrannical geometry did not exist. (p.52)

For older cities, the tyranny was particularly acute, as grid planning for far-flung suburbs required the obliteration of existing hamlets and farmsteads. The new gridiron plans were 'spectacular in their inefficiency and waste', often failing to distinguish between main arteries and side streets, being built to the same width and with the same infrastructure (Mumford 1961, p.482). By failing to respect hill contours in cities such as San Francisco, people were forced to spend more energy in getting from place to place, later involving higher petrol consumption, whilst little or no attention was paid to natural factors such as prevailing winds, soil structure and the orientation of buildings to capture solar energy. In the case of New York too, the imposition of the grid in 1811 to 155th street, and in 1870 to the northern tip of the island, was pursued with little variation allowed, even where it would provide better use of a hill or suit the Manhattan water table (Sennett 1990). Nature, space and history were together awkwardly conquered by the rolling machine of grid development, a system of 'abstract units suitable for buying and selling, without respect for historic uses, for topographic conditions or for social needs' (Mumford 1961, pp. 480–81). This said, the gridiron frequently provided a convenient framework for public transport provision. For Sennett, the gridiron layout is instrumental in the creation of the 'compulsive neutralization' of the city, where the city is emptied of historical reference in order to facilitate its building and rebuilding.

'Make no little plans, for they have no power to stir men's minds' Daniel Burnham proclaimed in the earliest phase of modernist planning, towards the end of the nineteenth century (Harvey 1989b, p. 40; Mumford 1961, p. 459). Slum demolition, new council estates, major new roads, all would be coordinated by city planners, architects and transport engineers. In Chicago in 1909, in his most ambitious plan, Burnham set out to do for that city what Baron Haussmann had done for Paris in the previous century, attempting to restore a supposedly lost visual harmony and harmonious social order, overcoming the 'chaotic city', which he saw as brought about by over-rapid growth and an overly rich mixture of nationalities (Hall 1988). To rid the city of such chaos, he proposed new thoroughfares and the creation of new parks, combined with slum removal, and the elimination of industry and railroads along the waterfront, all with little or no attention to the neighbourhood as a place for living or to the need for family housing (Mumford 1961). The planned large-scale, monumental city was transferred from Europe to America; Europeans returned the compliment by studying the emerging American masterplanners, and soon the style was to be imitated around the world, albeit diluted by a swift reversion to the functionalist tool of zoning (Hall 1988). Just as much as gridiron development, modernist development required the virtual obliteration of history, a so-called 'creative destruction', in its quest to impose its own vision of rational planning, social order and economic efficiency (Harvey 1989b). This process was to be achieved by technocratic means: policies were devised and implemented by an elite corps of urban 'experts' with little reference to the communities whose lives were to be affected.

Designs and masterplans for the modernist city of the first seventy years of the twentieth century usually required starting afresh, building new cities stripped of the chaos of the nineteenth-century city and the dull provincialism associated with Ebenezer Howard's Garden City. The new cities were said to require the destruction of much of the old, and the construction of large-scale cities in conformity with visionary masterplans. Architects such as Le Corbusier sought to remove the evidence of the city as a gradual accretion of buildings and spaces, as an organically developing entity with historical reference points, a sense of narrative in the very accumulation of buildings and layouts evident at street and neighbourhood level.

Given their chequered history, most forms of urban monumentalism evoke very mixed responses in people. On the one hand, most people regard the monumentalism evident in the experiments with large-scale public flats as a failed exercise, where form triumphed over function. The symbols of the modernist city transferred to the residential sphere fundamentally challenged views of acceptable urban aesthetics, and failed to convince the majority of the public. Alternatively, President Mitterrand's celebration of Paris in the 1980s as a World City, with the building of twelve new Grand Projects, though disparaged as costly and vainglorious by some French people, is widely admired both internally and internationally as an expression of a particular confidence in urban living. It is not monumentalism as such which is of dubious value, then, rather the form it takes.

By the early 1970s large-scale masterplans for comprehensive urban development had began to lose their grip on the imaginations of people, politicians and eventually even planners, and the first of the demolitions of the modernist high rise residential blocks took place in 1972 in St

Louis, USA. Catching up rather belatedly, people like Douglas Lee (1973) provided detailed justifications for moving away from the large-scale models and masterplans still characteristic of urban planning, advocating a shift towards what were intended to be more locally sensitive forms of urban development. By then, however, some of the worst excesses of urban design ever seen had already been committed.

3.4.2 Bad buildings and designing against nature

In Europe and North America the public-sector tower block and the public-sector housing estate have come to be regarded as the antithesis of good design: sealed buildings in sealed areas, denied permeability in terms of both the natural environment and the social environment. We find echoes too of the over-zoning arguments of some critics. For Richard Sennett (1990),

> Faced with the fact of social hostility in the city, the planner's impulse in the real world is to seal off conflicting or dissonant sides, to build internal walls rather than permeable borders. Highways and automobile traffic, for instance, are used to subdivide different social territories in the city... Similarly, functional disaggregation has become a technique for sealing borders; the shopping mall that is far from tracts of housing, the school on its own 'campus', the factory hidden in an industrial parks. These techniques, which originated in the garden city planning movement to create a peaceful, orderly suburb, are now increasingly used in the city center to remove the threat of classes or races touching, to create a city of secure inner walls. (p.201)

It was not just that the buildings were poorly designed, but the spaces in which they were located were poorly designed, too. Cities not only became more divided, socially and economically, but neighbourhoods within them became monofunctional and monocultural, stripped of historical reference points and denied any possibility for a rich diversity of contemporary social reference points, as far as design alone can ever achieve this. This latter point is important, since people inevitably do adapt neighbourhoods, no matter what the original design intentions: they do not simply adapt themselves to the design of their living spaces.

At the level of the individual household, the grand strategies for urban redesign seem somehow remote and distant. But as the people who cleared out from inner-city slums to public-sector estates found, when the radical new architectural and planning theories were put into practice they had the power to devastate the lives of ordinary people. In particular, these policies came to be associated with the wholesale destruction of vibrant inner-city communities supporting a wide range of local services, replacing them with lower-density outer-urban estates or inner-city medium-rise developments (as in Hulme, Manchester, England) and tower blocks. Around the world, the attempts of transport engineers, public housing providers, architects and planners to alter the urban fabric from the 1950s through to the 1970s, to accommodate new motorways and comprehensive redevelopment, were largely disastrous. They failed both in the goal of creating a new social order with new urban monuments, and in the goal of providing better housing for citizens.

According to Hugh Stretton (1978) this was a period of divisive housing policy, where the desires of home buyers for low-density residential suburban development were accommodated, as part of the desire for lower population densities:

> But at the same time many of their public authorities were applying opposite principles to any housing they planned for poorer households. The public housing towers and wall-blocks, and the working class housing which government induced private investors to provide in France and West Germany, were not what most of their tenants wanted. They were often dearer to build and maintain than the types of housing the tenants would have preferred... Scarcely anywhere, ever, did their planners survey the housing preferences of the classes they were designed for. (pp.146–7)

Cheaply produced, usually public sector-owned, medium- and high-rise housing also alienated residents from contact with the natural elements, except the plagues of vermin and damp moulds which came to characterise this sort of accommodation. They were mass-produced to uniform design, and necessarily built on a large scale, so only large companies could undertake to construct them, too often attached to corrupt practices (Stretton 1978). Most developments were energy-inefficient, both in their construction and subsequently, proving difficult and expensive to heat.

Socially, too, the lack of 'defensible space' in and around public-sector medium- and high-rise residential developments, and indeed around certain types of low-rise housing developments, is deemed by some writers to have contributed to urban alienation, vandalism and crime (Coleman 1985). This issue is still controversial and fiercely debated: in particular, the assumption that urban form can create social ills and environmental degradation, independent of wider cultural, economic and social structures and dynamics seems misplaced (Holyoak 1993). A high-rise residential block in Hong Kong or a private high-rise harbour front residential block provide very different environments to most superficially similar British outer-city public-sector tower blocks, not least in terms of individuals' choice over where they live.

It is perhaps sufficient to leave this unfortunate period with Hugh Stretton's (1978, p.167) judgement on the British public housing experiments in high-rise during the 1960s: 'even now it is hard to grasp how pretentious and how bad that phase of planning was, in technical as well as in social ways'. In France, Italy, the USA, Australia and elsewhere the same judgement applies, yet well into the 1970s, and in some cases beyond, poorly designed high-rise housing blocks were still being built in many countries.

In offices, too, high-rise towers not only changed local microclimates in the city, but came to have their own internal microclimates of hot spots and cold spots, and with their closed ventilation and heating systems, and windows which could not be opened, they even developed their own diseases, such as legionnaire's disease or 'sick building' syndrome. These buildings were designed to keep nature out, replacing natural sunlight with artificial light, natural ventilation with artificial ventilation, raising energy requirements enormously (Dole 1989b, 1989c).

Designing against nature, and indeed against human nature, became the leitmotifs of this period, exacerbating tendencies evident since the industrial revolution. According to critics such as Lewis Mumford this approach was an inevitable concomitant of a particular doctrine which no longer saw the city as an organism, a nexus of civilisation and nature, with its own cultural and natural limits. Instead, a more mechanistic approach prevailed, which viewed not only the house but the whole city as a machine for living. In consequence, '[w]hen the city was viewed as a machine, people's function in the city changed from being a vital, indispensable link in the eco-system to being an anonymous and dispensable cog in the machine' (Engwicht 1992, p.24).

3.4.3 Building better, building greener

Environmental considerations in the sense of energy conservation have gradually begun to be taken more seriously in housing and office design in recent years. In the UK it is estimated that 50% of CO_2 emissions are from buildings, 60% of which is attributable to housing: there is reportedly scope for reducing these emissions by around 35% from better-built and better-designed buildings, and using more efficient household equipment (Rydin 1992a). In many modern offices, artificial lighting alone accounts for around 30% of energy consumption (Moran 1993), a dependence which better design to use natural sunlight can halve. Approaches to better building can include energy efficiency in equipping houses, such as wall and loft insulation, draughtproofing, and provision of solar panels for heating, choosing materials which are less energy-intensive to manufacture, and recycling of building materials (Dole 1989a, Rydin 1992b).

Also important are building design and layout considerations, such as designing houses to capture solar energy in winter months and to provide cool, shaded spaces in summer months (Correa 1989, Rydin 1992a). In local plans, people should gain priority in terms of solar heating gains, whilst warehouses, roads and car parks should be favoured less (Dole 1989a). Controlling wind speeds with wind breaks close to walls of buildings can be important in ensuring that solar gains are not dispersed in winter, whilst wind funnels should be avoided (Dole 1989c). Generally speaking, detached houses are more inefficient in their energy consumption than attached forms of dwellings, such as terraces and flats (Rydin 1992a). Courtyard designs can be used in cool climates to capture heat, and in warm climates to provide shade, reducing the need for air conditioning (Rydin 1989a, Correa 1989). Well-designed courtyards can also provide an attractive communal space, safe for children to play in and conducive for adults to meet in. Additionally, the internal design and equipping of housing can be made conducive to environmentally sensitive behaviour, such as providing space for bikes in garages, designing kitchens to facilitate recycling and composting, providing dual-flush toilet cisterns, using condensing boilers, and building ventilated larders to reduce the need for large refrigerators (Rydin 1992a).

In the office building sector too, energy considerations are beginning to make an impact upon design, in particular leading to a new generation of 'smart' buildings, smart not only in their accommodation of the trappings of advanced telecommunications and electronics systems, but also in their adaptation to the natural environment (Moran 1993). Rather than sealing buildings in order to control the internal environment, some new buildings are once again relying on opening windows and using natural air flows in the heating and cooling of offices, together with solar panels and heat exchangers.

3.4.4 Designing for or against the car

The growth of the car-centred city has attracted widespread concern in terms of more local-level impacts, leading for calls to revert to designing cities for people and social equity, moving away from recent policies which are seen to have favoured cars and economic efficiency. There remains a strong debate in the urban design movement about whether to design neighbourhoods for or against the car. At one end of the spectrum, there are policies to improve car circulation, and at the other, attempts to keep cars out of residential areas. Some of the earliest work aimed at improving car circulation can be traced to the Radburn neighbourhood units developed by Stein and Wright in the 1920s in the USA. Usually known as the Radburn style, roads were set out hierarchically, with distributor roads and cul-de-sacs. In Britain, most of the New Town experiments sought to develop these neighbour-unit ideas further in an attempt to foster 'neighbourliness', often with some success.

Following Alice Coleman's (1985) critique of public-sector housing, foreshadowed by Alison Ravetz's (1980) more wide-ranging treatment of post-war town planning, urban design during the 1980s in Britain in particular engaged in a reactionary method of designing suburbia in the inner cities (Holyoak 1993). Low-rise, medium-density housing became the preferred mode of development, private space preferred to public space, and cul-de-sacs preferred to connecting roads. More recently, cul-de-sacs appear to have begun to fall into disrepute, being blamed for social isolation and the absence of urban 'hustle and bustle': connecting roads are once more being advocated (Matthews 1993, Murrain 1993).

Outside the newly built residential areas, improved car access has generally resulted in poorer access for pedestrians (Ravetz 1980). The amount of space devoted to the car in terms of roads and car parking has grown throughout the twentieth century, albeit not commensurate with the increase in road traffic. Visual intrusion, increased noise levels and air pollution, as well as the greater risk of accidents, have undermined the creative use of urban space and in particular have made walking and cycling more difficult. This in turn has caused more people to resort to the car. At the neighbourhood level, streets are increasingly packed with parked cars and roads are made dangerous, especially for children at play.

These, though, are but the most tangible outward manifestations of a profound restructuring of urban space in many Western cities. As we have already noted, neighbourhood-level facilities have often been gradually reduced, with the loss of small shops and so on associated with the rise of large supermarkets, hospitals and leisure centres. This has meant that people have had to travel further afield to get to these services, leading to particular problems for people with limited access to cars, notably some women, the physically disabled, and the elderly. Those who cannot travel readily to these centralised facilities are more dependent on the lesser range and often higher prices of the reduced level of local facilities, or in the case of some services such as health and leisure, lower usage of public facilities. The car-based city has improved access to larger – and sometimes better – facilities for some, but reduced it for others. Engwicht (1992) estimates the size of this latter group at 40–60% of the urban population.

High road traffic levels can also have major impacts on the levels of social interaction and community cohesion at the neighbourhood level. Increased road traffic appears to be directly related to alienation. In a classic study of residential streets in San Francisco, similar except for levels of road traffic, Appleyard (1981) found many more instances of local acquaintances and friends in those streets with lighter traffic, where people had more chances of meeting, as people sat on the porch or gardened, and as children played on the street. In a similar vein, a large road through a neighbourhood can effectively cut it in two, limiting access to friends and services. For young children, too, the impacts of increasing numbers not being allowed to walk to school unattended, in large part prompted by fears of traffic accidents, are reducing the autonomy of children and imposing burdens on parents and minders (Whitelegg 1993). The loss of pedestrian activity on streets at night, as people resort more frequently to cars often entails areas changing or losing their identity, sometimes becoming more prone to crime, creating a self-reinforcing spiral of decline.

At the local level, many local authorities have attempted to redesign urban neighbourhoods in an attempt to minimise the intrusion of road traffic by prohibiting access to heavy goods vehicles, using traffic calming measures, providing cycle ways and bus lanes, constructing noise baffles, pedestrianising certain streets and declaring others play streets, providing parking permits for residents only, building safer pedestrian routes, and developing green links between pedestrian routes and public transport. Traffic calming in particular involves a major redesign of streets, narrowing entrances to roads, building chicanes, imposing lower speed limits, road humps, and introducing benches, trees and so on, to encourage greater pedestrian use. A study of controls in 65 residential zones showed that they led on average to traffic accidents falling by 9%, deaths by 11%, injuries by 10% and property damage by 5% (OECD 1990). Figures from German experiments show much higher gains, with major reductions in noise, and reductions in traffic injuries by 84% in Nippes and 74% in Agnesviertel (Whitelegg 1993).

Traffic calming measures are always best undertaken at the local level, requiring strong local government since they will frequently meet some objections. The objections are sometimes justifiable since some design measures are not without their problems. In the case of pedestrianisation, local businesses frequently object to the perceived threat of a loss of business from passing traffic, even though experience shows that turnover almost invariably increases with pedestrianisation (Roberts 1981). Much, however, depends on the type of pedestrian area being created: some new precincts were built which were relatively inconvenient, distant from bus stops and train stations, or only approachable through tunnels under major roads and therefore of limited access to the elderly and the infirm (Ravetz 1980). Alternatively, well-designed pedestrianisation of existing high streets has largely been successful, at its best associated with street music, street theatre, street traders and meeting places for shoppers, workers and those just passing through.

3.4.5 Currently favoured ingredients for good urban design

As we have already noted, a dominant theme in urban design and planning in Europe at present is a call for the return to fine-grained, mixed-use neighbourhoods. Some of the central ingredients of contemporary good design are now well established (Box 3.5), although all of them have their areas of ambiguity, and all are subject to capture, pastiche and abuse. Indeed, in a range of dubious attempts to promote community identity, whilst conveniently improving real estate and tourist destination marketability, some gentrifying inner-area neighbourhoods have had a local theme or design style created for them, usually based on some historical reference point. This is not so much an attempt to retain the urban narrative of different generations and functions of buildings as a commercial creation of pseudo reference points through selective drawing of indigenous styles and the global vernacular of the gentrified neighbourhood. The use of traditional materials has gained a resurgence in popularity, whilst pastiched vernacular architectural styles have found favour, as have 'old fashioned' street furniture styles.

For some commentators, the return to traditional values in housing styles and neighbourhood design has been a retreat into a non-existent, mythical past of societal well-being, representing a failure to meet contemporary and future challenges thrown up by the motor car in particular. Brian Goodey (1993, p. 56), for example, is concerned 'that the fundamental interplay of urban design factors – space and circulation use, facade design, landmark making, edge definition and furnishing – has failed to develop a new language in keeping with future rather than promoted traditional demands'. 'Back to the future' has become the prevailing theme of inner-urban contemporary urban design in many Western prosperous cities, where investors, urban decision-makers and even urban residents seem more comfortable with the past than either the present or the future. The sustainability debate, with its emphasis on the fine-grained city, and post-modernist architectural theory, have unwittingly combined to consolidate this rather unimaginative approach to contemporary urban design. Perhaps we should be grateful that some inner-urban neighbourhoods do not have the resources for this kind of

Box 3.5 Encouraging Diversity Through Good Urban Design

- **Variety.** Districts should be multi-functional; building styles should not be uniform, preferably with buildings of different ages and conditions.

- **Concentration.** There should be a sufficient density of people to maintain variety and activity, preferably including people who are resident; street blocks should be short, as this seems to encourage more diversity in the ways in which streets and buildings are used.

- **Democracy.** People should have a choice in where they conduct their activities, but not at the expense of the collective.

- **Permeability.** People should be connected, able to obtain easy access to each other and to general urban facilities, always with respect to the needs for privacy and security.

- **Security.** Open and connecting spaces should be designed to enhance personal safety for vulnerable groups, such as women, and to encourage safety for children at play.

- **Appropriate scale.** Developments should build on local context and reflect local conditions.

- **Organic design.** The design should be locally distinctive, building on local context, respecting historical narrative within the urban fabric.

- **Economy of means.** Design areas *with* nature, using the most environmentally efficient means of achieving an objective, including use of local materials as appropriate.

- **Creative relationships.** These should be promoted especially between buildings, routeways and open spaces.

- **Flexibility.** Buildings and spaces should be adaptable over time to meet emergent challenges.

- **Consultation.** Make sure that urban design meets local needs, respects local traditions, and taps local resources.

- **Participation.** Where appropriate, communities of need, interest, experience and geographical proximity should be involved in the design, maintenance and running of projects, whether housing or open space.

(Based in part on Jacobs 1961, Hough 1990, Punter 1990, Murrain 1993, Winifkoff 1993) commercial exploitation and remain unthemed, undertaking different routes to redefining their areas, such as the return to urban agriculture of some of the urban poor (Simmonds 1993).

3.4.6 'Organic' planning as fragmentation and privatisation

The abandonment of most of the trappings of the modernist project has left something of a vacuum in terms of overall urban development strategies, with the confidence and vision of many in the development professions wilting under the onslaught of popular and political criticism of some of the excesses of the 1960s in particular. In place of the single grand 'vision' there has been a growing emphasis on prestige, flagship, private sector-led developments, usually heavily underwritten by public subsidy. At the same time, much of the urban fabric has been left to deteriorate.

The celebration of the city witnessed in urban revitalisation strategies in America and Europe, cloaked in talk of celebrating separate and shared cultures, the designation of festival cities, and the creation of symbolic structures, is in many cases essentially an exclusionary rather than inclusionary economic development strategy, designed to protect the privileges of a few, in particular downtown land and property owners, anxious that their cities should not enter into a permanent downward spiral. Again, Lewis Mumford (1961, p. 507) is worth recalling in his lament for the loss of original urban functions, where 'the ultimate fate of the commercial city is to become a backdrop for advertising'. But far from signalling the end of the city as Mumford so gloomily prognosticated, the showpiece city with its new monuments to Mammon and to popular culture does indeed seem to be associated with the current phase of urban revival in many prosperous countries.

David Harvey (1989b, p. 42) refers to the emergent pluralistic urban development projects and strategies as creating a 'collage city'. In the collage city, pastiche vernacular styles are borrowed at random from centuries of architectural style to create a new style of post-modern architecture, rooted not in reforming ideas but a near dispensation with theory and responsibility. Particularly interesting is the use of space: where modernists used space as a subordinate element to be shaped towards social goals, the post-modernists saw space as more autonomous, related to aesthetic goals (Harvey 1989b, p. 66). Whatever the philosophical pretext, the design of urban space remains in many parts of many cities a simple exercise in investment return over a given period of time, where aesthetics matter largely as a means towards a higher or more secure return.

Social engineering through the manipulation of people within public and private space has been far from lost in the (possibly fleeting) passage of post-modernism, where privatisation of public space in support of the aesthetic element has become a central feature. In the development of large shopping centres, gentrified inner suburbs and festival harbour fronts, money is being invested in opening up access to the city to the privileged few, whilst denying it to those already marginalised, including the poor, the disabled, the elderly and teenagers: 'these were excluded from shopping malls through lack of car access, security, or spending power [and] are now being excluded from the tidy urban quarters for the same reasons' (Goodey 1993, p.55). So-called public spaces created in these developments, sometimes quite large in scale, are in truth carefully controlled environments. They are not the spaces associated with urban protest movements, purposefully designed in many cities in the nineteenth and twentieth centuries, nor do they approximate to Aristotle's view that an urban space of assembly should only be as large as necessary for a shouting voice to be heard. The new open spaces are not the democratic spaces of the popular urban voice.

Never was the urban environment more carefully controlled than when it was commodified, privatised, and sold as part of the spectacle of the revitalisation of city centres, harbour front developments, and the building of new sports stadia and conference centres. Simultaneously the post-modern city has commodified the history of places for elite consumption in preserved historical areas and museums, whilst architects have engaged in eclectic referencing not just of a place's history, but also of borrowed symbols of global culture (Harvey 1989b). During the bastardised revitalisation of urban centres in countries such as the USA and UK in the 1980s, a new 'hybrid city' was born, where publicly relevant buildings and open spaces were privatised and, in an attempt to ensure investment security, buildings and people became highly controlled, subject to camera surveillance and protection by private security armies (Butina Watson 1993). At its extreme, in some neighbourhoods in cities in the USA, private security firms are hired to keep out the so-called 'undesirables' (Davis 1990).

3.4.7 Shanty towns: the ultimate bottom-up approach?

Learning from these experiments, contemporary urban design has begun to pay more attention to what people say they want, rather than to what the grand theorists and remote central and local government officials say they should want. Residential development has self-consciously attempted to become more organic, building from an area's existing character, function and layout, making more use of traditional materials and design, and introducing change gradually rather than en masse. In the UK during the 1980s, community architecture became particularly important in the design of public-sector and housing-association dwellings, though less so in private sector building. Low- and medium-rise housing, provided with private gardens, has once more become the norm, together with public open spaces designed to facilitate greater use, improve neighbourhood security and allow the informal supervision of children. In developing countries, too, a new emphasis on low-rise housing may be emerging for a number of reasons: they are a means to achieving incremental change; they enhance local diversity; they display sensitivity to life styles; they are quicker and cheaper to build, and not reliant on relatively scarce, priority construction materials (Correa 1989).

Indigenous self-help strategies are nowhere more in evidence, however, than in the shanty towns, or illegal squatter settlements of cities in many developing countries. The shanty town is possibly the most distinctive feature of the built environment of some cities, accounting for over half the population in some. The self-built shanty houses present a mixed challenge. On the positive side, they are an expression of self-help, and can emerge as vibrant communities in their own right, with strong social organisational forms (Lemnitz 1988). Usually they are preferable to sleeping on the street, whilst their construction involves considerable reuse of materials. In the case of poor in-migrants, they may be all that can be afforded, marking a transitory stage towards better accommodation. Poorly serviced though they may be, a higher proportion of dwellings will be connected to electricity, for instance, than in some rural areas (Bairoch 1988). For these reasons, some governments have shifted away from policies of pulling down shanty towns, to helping residents improve their housing conditions and economic prospects, in particular by giving them legal rights to the land which they have illegally occupied and by providing access to basic services, since it is absence of these which has been a blight to so many of them (HABITAT 1987).

On the negative side, shanty town dwellings are usually cramped, sometimes flimsily constructed and often unserviced by basic facilities. Overcrowded shanty town houses often provide less than one square metre of space per person, increasing the risk of person-to-person disease transmission, notably tuberculosis, meningitis, measles, rubella and influenza (McMichael 1993). Related health risks include poor location, associated in particular with vulnerability to floods and landslides, lack of fire exits, and proximity to the air pollution of industry, airports and major roads. As many shanty towns are located on vulnerable flood plains and are also ill-drained, external pools and puddles can attract mosquitoes, which bring with them risk of malaria, dengue fever,

Japanese encephalitis and filariasis. Also implicated as health hazards are poorly maintained stairs, inadequate protection against the elements, from rain to cyclones, the use of unsafe materials such as asbestos and lead-based paints, poorly designed kitchens susceptible to fire, and inadequately ventilated living spaces, especially where these are used for homeworking (World Health Organization 1991). Poor building construction, mud floors, cracks in walls and poor maintenance can also provide the living space for infectious vectors such as rodents, fleas, bedbugs, ticks, flies and mosquitoes (World Health Organization 1991, McMichael 1993).

In terms of basic facilities, the lack of electricity forces use of internal open fires for heat and cooking, often without adequate ventilation, which brings both safety hazards and vulnerability to respiratory problems and certain diseases. Lack of cheap, safe water is associated with gastrointestinal diseases, typhoid, cholera, hepatitis, trachoma, skin infections and parasitic diseases (Chapter Five). Absence of sewerage connections increases exposure to diarrhoea, gastrointestinal infections, cholera and schistosomiasis, with inadequately disposed of excreta also attracting insect vectors (World Health Organization 1991). Poor waste disposal generally can also encourage breeding grounds for rodent and insect vectors for a range of diseases.

A reminder of the intensity and scale of these problems is perhaps a useful antidote to those who get worked up about the minutiae of urban design problems in the West, such as pastiched vernacular styles. Aesthetic appeal should always be an integral element of good urban development, not least as it helps bring economic prosperity, but in some cases of extreme poverty aesthetic considerations must necessarily be subordinate to the immediate demands of survival. Shanty town development, although laudable in some respects, is so closely associated with poor health that it necessarily points to the limits of self-help solutions to urban problems (see Chapter Eight). Of course self-help is not just about poor-quality housing construction, nor is it restricted to developing countries, being particularly important in some Western cities and in Eastern Europe during its communist period (Ward 1985). Most importantly, self help in housing brings a sense of ownership, encourages rehabilitation over technocratic clearance and mass-build projects, increases skills amongst those involved, is more sensitive to local conditions and reuses materials. Self-help is a necessary but not sufficient precondition of building sustainable cities: it needs to go hand in hand with adequate resourcing, training, minimum standards and planned provision of collective services, from schools to water pipes. Unfortunately, the attitude of most governments has been to deny access to these elements necessary to support self-help.

3.5 URBAN DESIGN AND THE NATURAL ENVIRONMENT

Whilst the theme of design for open spaces in housing areas has already been alluded to briefly, it is also important to consider the broader role of design and the natural environment. Chapters Four and Five examine the nature of the urban climate and urban hydrology in some detail: the concern here is largely with the flora and fauna of the city. Many writers argue that wildlife in cities is an essential adjunct to city living, providing a sensory stimulus for residents, and a connection with nature which makes them more environmentally sensitive in their behaviour (Hough 1984, 1990; Goode 1990). Moreover, the natural environment in cities can still play a major role in moderating the impacts of human activities, for example, the role of green plants in absorbing pollutants and releasing oxygen: a Douglas Fir is capable of removing 18kg of sulphur dioxide from the atmosphere a year without harm to itself, and roadside plants help to reduce carbon monoxide levels (Hough 1984).

Despite the many positive attributes of encouraging natural environments within the city, in large parts of most cities nature has been increasingly subjugated to the needs of production and reproduction, as humankind has attempted to tame the fury of nature through the construction of isolated, highly controlled environments (Plant 1990). Over time, there has been a decrease in open space per capita in most cities (Hough 1984), whilst the use of open space has changed, usually becoming more intensive. Over time the design of open spaces has become increasingly artificial, as many urban parks, for instance, become carefully manicured and reliant on imported plant species (Smyth 1987). For these reasons, at the heart of the concern of most advocates of improving the natural environment in cities is not simply the question of how much urban space is provided, but also of where it is located and how it is designed and used.

Although most environmentalists advocate the use of natural spaces within urban areas, this does not simply imply turning formal parks into wildlife spaces; it is the mix of open space types which is important (Hough 1990). Not only do formal parklands play their own valuable role in providing safe play space for children and adults, they can also develop their own aesthetic appeal. However, some urban designers have expressed concern over the value of large parks in particular, as they tend to break up the connectivity between different urban functions and therefore increase car usage (Jacobs 1961, Elkin, McLaren and Hillman 1991) and also raise questions over safety for pedestrians at night (Murrain 1993). In part following from this analysis, Sherlock (1991) advocates that in addition to providing at least one park in every district of the city, greening the city should be achieved with measures to spread greenery throughout the cities, with trees and shrubs on pavements and the use of plots in front of, behind and between buildings. Tree planting can be important in filtering local air pollution, providing a noise barrier, providing visual screening and enhancing neighbourhood identity; where planted in large numbers in close proximity, trees may help reduce carbon dioxide pollution (Dole 1989e)

In a similar vein, Horsbrugh (1990) advocates the use of selected wall-creepers, urban roof gardens, and the greening of transport corridors, adding to their aesthetic appeal and the support of wildlife. Wall-climbing vines can reduce summer temperatures on a street by 5%, and reduce household heat loss by up to 30% in winter (Hough 1984). Roof gardens and other forms of roof greening are now required in some German cities on houses with slopes of 1–10%: they can be especially valuable in adding insulation, improving water retention, and helping reduce summer temperatures and air pollution (Osmundson 1990)

In ecological and wildlife terms, the interconnection of natural spaces is of particular value, not least in facilitating the migration of animals safely away from the motor car. This has led to an emphasis in many nature conservation plans for creating green corridors and wedges as axes for the development of wildlife, for instance, along rail and canal corridors. A precursor to this way of thinking, working on a grander scale, can be found in Patrick Geddes' (1915) *Cities in Evolution*, which advocated bringing the country back into the city along selected axes. One advantage of this form of wild space maintenance is that where it is accessible to the general public, it may bring both nature and recreational opportunities closer to the home than fewer, distant large parks would. This in turn may even reduce the weekend rush to the country of some urban residents. It also emphasises that commercially unused land within cities may secretly be harbouring a rich natural life.

On a larger scale of activity, there has been a move towards creating 'urban community forests' in recent years, both for recreational and more purely environmental purposes. These are usually located around the edges of cities, and at one level may simply represent a change in use of open land, from agriculture to recreational use: in the case of Britain a trend made possible, temporarily at least, by the increased productivity of agriculture and the resultant European Community-funded set-aside agricultural land which is no longer deemed necessary for production. Although perhaps preferable to peripheral housing encroachment, it has to be asked whether a better policy would be a less intensive use of remaining agricultural land, with less input of fertilisers and pesticides, and a more extensive style of agricultural production. Alternatively, in the Netherlands, considerable experiments have been undertaken with urban forestry, creating a zoning within them to allow some areas to be fairly intensively used by humans, whilst others are left relatively untouched to allow birds to breed. Most importantly, planners in The Hague have long sought to encourage development around existing trees, rather than destroy them and plant new ones, whilst in some areas trees are being planted prior to development, acknowledging that they will need time to mature (Deelstra 1990). In the USA, experiments have shown the value of urban forests as living filters for urban sewerage, where waste water is used to irrigate the forest (Sopper 1990).

Not all urban greening is so purposeful or as recent in origin as some of these urban forests. Incidental greening has long been a feature of cities, and remains important in many cities in developing countries (Furedy 1990), including the growing of food on garbage dumps in Calcutta, the composting of kitchen wastes around the world, and the use of nightsoil (human manure) for agriculture, which remains important on the fringes of some Chinese cities.

Agriculture is perhaps one of the most valuable and productive uses of open space in the city. Retaining agriculture in various forms within the city is particularly important in that most cities, unless strictly planned, tend to allow continuing encroachment on to agricultural land, regardless of its productive value, because of the disparities in land prices between most urban and agricultural uses. None the less, urban agriculture can be found in various guises, including large-scale agri-businesses on the edges of the city and market gardening closer to the centre. In the more built up areas, urban agriculture can take the form of backyard production, charitable, community city farms in the centre, and in the case of some developing-country cities, informal sector agriculture can be found, in such varied locations as road and rail verges, river and drainage banks, and other public lands (Dorney 1990, Lado 1990).

A recognition of the importance of urban agriculture in both economic and environmental terms has led to active supportive policies in countries such as Papua New Guinea, where a pilot project has been established in the city of Lae to develop an urban agro-ecosystem, with the establishment of allotment gardening and fuel wood production to take the pressure off surrounding forested areas, urban composting and sewerage treatment for fertilisers and fruit-tree production (Newcombe 1984). Whilst support can also be found in countries such as Japan, China and the Philippines, with government assistance for urban farmers provided in land use regulation and tax systems, in other nations and cities there is considerable discouragement of both formal and informal urban agriculture (Lado 1990), in part in order to reduce the noise and odour nuisance of livestock in densely populated urban areas.

Even for very large, densely populated cities, urban agriculture may still be feasible (Friedman 1984), but it is not without tensions such as those experienced in Hong Kong, where a total livestock ban was introduced in 1988 for urban and urban fringe areas. This has already resulted in improved water quality and reduced odour nuisance: some streams which had been blocked solid with waste are now running freely (Reed 1992). Alternatively, as Dorney (1990) has noted for cities in Canada, Japan, Spain and Costa Rica, agriculture is still often the dominant land use within legally defined metropolitan areas.

More experimental forms of combining urban living with agricultural production can be found across the world, most notably in the permaculture-influenced developments in Germany, Australia and Denmark. Here the emphasis is on increasing self-reliance in terms of food production, involving the conservation of fuel energy and use of renewable energy sources, recycling of wastes, organic food production and community cooperation (Mollison 1979). Perhaps the most important aspect of this type of argument is that it is important to recognise the different obstacles and possibilities in different parts of the city region, with Berg (1990b), for instance, advocating different forms of rehabilitation for the four areas which he says will typically constitute a bioregion: cities, suburbs, rural areas and wilderness. This plea to recognise diversity within the regions has an element of resonance with Breheny and Rookwood's (1993) proposals, noted earlier, to use a mix of greening strategies across the British social city region.

3.6 CHANGING THE CITY FROM WITHIN

This chapter has sought to emphasise the importance of the internal structure of the city as both a contributory factor to environmental degradation, and as a means of reducing urban environmental problems. Processes of change need to be encouraged which, where possible, emerge organically over time, making full use of those natural and human-made assets of the region which are conducive to sustainable development. High levels of diversity within the city are an inevitable outcome of the diversity of activities undertaken in the city and the wide range of desired lifestyles of those who live and work there. Policies to bring about sustainable urban development must seek to work with such internal variations, rather than suppress them in the name of some grand masterplan for the cities. The different policies suggested for different parts of the social city region suggested by Breheny and Rookwood (1993) provide one approach to this more locally sensitive approach to fostering sustainable urban development. Similarly, as Stretton (1989) has advocated, residential densities should be allowed to differ in different parts of the cities, whilst some recreational and retail activities should be concentrated in particular areas, and so on. This is not a call for an abnegation of land use policy in the city, letting market forces rip. Rather, it provides a flexible framework within which the very fundamentals of the urban fabric can be remoulded, preferably growing organically out of the existing diversity of the city region.

Key themes for this remoulding of the urban fabric include the value of 'concentrated decentralisation' policies in large city regions, either through developing stronger subcentres within the main city area, or through promotion of separate towns linked to the main city centres by strong public transport links (Owens 1992). The analysis also suggests that the neighbourhood is the most important building block for urban planning, accompanied by policy emphasis on diversity of building styles and ages, proximity, accessibility, community participation, and mixed uses. The provision and use of open space can and should vary in different parts of the city region, but urban residents should always have ready access to relatively secure open space in some form, whether parkland, allotments, naturally regenerated wasteland or a city farm, in order to retain their links with nature in some way.

In the past, some of the very poor policies were brought in to many cities from outside, as part of the bandwagon of modernisation in urban development. It will be important to be more sensitive in future: to learn good practice from networks of sustainable cities, but also to consider and consult more widely at the local level on what local needs and existing resources there are.

FURTHER READING

Many of the issues raised in this chapter are also dealt with in greater detail in Breheny (ed) (1992) *Sustainable Development and Urban Form*. On urban design, Jane Jacobs' (1961) *Death and Life of Great American Cities* still merits a read, whilst some of the chapters in Hayward and McGlynn (eds) (1993) *Making Better Places: Urban Design Now*, provide a good view of the current state of the debate.

KEY THEMES

- Urban consolidation and compact cities
- Concentrated decentralisation
- Unequal access to urban facilities and social disadvantage
- Designing *with* nature rather than *against* nature

DISCUSSION POINTS

- Boxes 3.1 and 3.2 illustrate some of the environmental arguments for and against low-density living. Provide your own boxes to illustrate some of the environmental arguments for and against high-density living, backing up your points with illustrations from a city with which you are familiar.

- Celebrating urban diversity is a key theme for the 1990s and indeed the next century. But diversity on whose terms? Critically analyse what it is that the festival city, the showpiece city, the post-modern collage city and so on are celebrating.

- Devise two lists, one of ten principles for good urban design, and one of ten principles for bad urban design. Where possible, provide illustrations of each point. Discuss the main interrelationships between your different principles.

PART B

INTRODUCTION TO POLLUTION

In order to appreciate more fully the nature and magnitude of urban-related environmental stresses, it is necessary to focus in on selected issues. We have chosen problems associated with air and water pollution to demonstrate current unsustainable practices in cities, and the strains these impose on the Earth's air and water resources on local, regional and global scales.

There are a number of reasons for this focus on air and water pollution. Air and water are clearly fundamental resources for life on Earth. The degradation of these resources via numerous forms of pollution is, arguably, the most significant threat to the integrity of the Earth's ecological balance and the sustainable use of its resources. It is slowly becoming accepted that human societies cannot rely on nature to provide a continuous supply of clean air and water to sustain human activities, whilst at the same time expecting these resources to absorb and neutralise the waste products of human activities cheaply and effectively. Moreover, cities, as centres of resource consumption and waste production, exert an influence over the contamination of air and water which is greatly disproportionate to their physical size. Cities are, therefore, responsible for very many air and water pollution problems, both within and beyond urban boundaries. Furthermore, pollution arises from many different activities (e.g. energy production, transport, industry, domestic waste disposal etc.) and as such provides a useful insight into the range of human endeavours which impact on the quality and functioning of the natural environment. Finally, the sources and effects of air and water pollution, although very far from being fully understood and appreciated, have been widely investigated around the world. These studies have contributed to a growing disquiet concerning pollution impacts on human health and the functioning of natural ecosystems. At present, much of the world's pollution is sourced in the developed countries; the North, with 25% of the world's population, consumes 70% of the world's energy, 75% of its metals, and 85% of its wood, whilst the citizens of developed countries also own 92% of the world's cars (Tolba and El-Kholy 1992).

THE NATURE OF POLLUTION

Pollutants are substances or forms of energy which cause environmental changes over and above those associated with natural background variation. A commonly-used description of pollution stresses its anthropogenic (human-made) nature: the introduction by humans into the environment of substances or energy which may result in hazards to human health, harm to living resources and ecological systems, damage to structures or amenity, or interference with the legitimate use of the environment (Holdgate 1979). Pollution may arise when the waste products of human activities are released into the environment at a point (e.g. a sewage outfall pipe), along a line (e.g. a road), or over a particular area (e.g. a landfill site used for domestic waste).

The range of pollutants commonly generated by urban activities is enormous, and encompasses forms of energy (such as excess heat, noise and radioactivity) as well as substances. A bewildering 'cocktail' of organic and inorganic materials is continuously emitted to air, water and soil through routine urban living. These materials may react with each other or with natural constituents in the environment to produce yet more, secondary, pollutants. A great deal of technical expertise is required to untangle the importance and effects of individual pollutants or pollutants acting in combination. However, specialist knowledge is not required to appreciate the sources and consequences of pollutants in the environment. The following two chapters aim to provide such a broad perspective.

Chapter Four considers air pollution, and Chapter Five is concerned with water pollution. This division according to environmental sector is commonly adopted, but is somewhat arbitrary and largely based on convenience. In reality, many pollutants are readily transferred between air, water and land, thanks to precipitation, dry deposition from the atmosphere to land and water, gas exchanges between the atmosphere and water bodies, and the storage and movement of pollutants through the actions of organisms. The problem of acid deposition (acid 'rain') provides a well-known example where pollutants released into the atmosphere can be converted into forms which may be harmful to aquatic ecosystems. (Acid deposition problems are, therefore, discussed in Chapter Five.) Gravitational settling and the 'capture' of atmospheric pollutants by falling precipitation ensure that pollutants of the air may become pollutants of soil and water; the converse can also occur. In Mexico City, for example, there are some 21 million residents. At least

5 million of these live in slum conditions without sewerage facilities. As a result, tonnes of human waste are deposited into gutters and open spaces every day. When this dries out and is picked up by the wind, a 'faecal snow' of dried excrement frequently falls on parts of the city (Miller 1991).

In addition, some pollutants such as heavy metals and potentially toxic organic compounds may be emitted to more than one environmental sector in significant quantities. Some potentially toxic metals and organic compounds which may be released into either air or water are given in Tables B.1 and B.2, respectively. Even the briefest examination of a relevant research journal, such as *Environmental Pollution*, would

Table B.1 Some toxic metals, their emission sources and their major health effects

Metal	Major emission sources	Health effects
Arsenic as arsenic trioxide	Smelting of non-ferrous ores; pesticides; catalyst and reagent for inorganic chemical production; additive to glass and non-ferrous alloys.	Carcinogenic, possibly teratogenic.
Beryllium	Combustion of coal and oil; mining; production of beryllium metal, cement plants, alloys, ceramics and rocket propellants.	Can cause contact dermatitis, ulcers, and inflammation of mucous membranes; known animal carcinogen.
Cadmium	By-product of zinc processing; used in electroplating, plastics, pigments and batteries; waste disposal by incineration; fertiliser processing and combustion of fossil fuels.	Carcinogen (animal); teratogen; can cause damage to liver, kidneys, lungs and blood (anaemia).
Lead	Manufacture of lead–acid batteries; lead-based paint; gasoline combustion and non-ferrous smelters.	Can impair haem synthesis in children; may cause subclinical neurological problems.
Mercury	Electrical apparatus; electrolytic preparation of caustic soda and chlorine; antifouling paint; pharmaceutical products and coal combustion.	Can cause low-level chronic poisoning, associated with confusion, headaches, fatigue and tremors.

Source: OECD 1985a

confirm that in recent years pollution by toxic metals and organic compounds has been of great concern to researchers studying the atmospheric, water and land environments. Tables B.1 and B.2 are, therefore, referred to in both Chapters Four and Five.

Table B.2 Some known or potentially toxic organic compounds and their emission sources

Organic Compound	Major Emission Sources
Acetaldehyde (ethanal)	Coffee roasting; manufacture of acrylic acid, acetic acid and vinyl acetate; car exhaust. (Atmospheric half-life: 1–2 days.)
Benzene	Petrol-fuelled internal combustion engines; as a raw material in the production of other chemicals; petroleum refineries; gasoline storage and handling; coke ovens.
Benzidine	Manufacture of dye, paper, textiles and leather. (Atmospheric half-life: 1–4 days.)
Benzo(a)-pyrene	By-product of incomplete combustion of coal, wood, charcoal and diesel fuel.
Carbon tetrachloride	Dichlorodifluoromethane and trichlorofluoromethane production; fire extinguishers; dry cleaning agents; cleaning agents for machinery and electrical parts. (Atmospheric half-life: 10 years; half-life in water: 70,000 years.)
Chlorofluoro-carbons	Aerosol propellant; refrigerant; foaming agents in carbons from plastics industry. Potential effect on stratospheric ozone layer with possible increase of ultra-violet radiation and possible climatic changes.
Chloroform	Miscellaneous, e.g. industrial solvent, fumigant, solvent, rubber industry and pharmaceuticals. (Atmospheric half-life: 1–2 years.)
Dioxins	Waste incinerators; herbicides. (Half-life in soil: 10–12 years.)
Ethylene oxide	Production of polyester fibre and film. (Atmospheric half-life: 3 hours – 1.6 days.)
Formaldehyde	Charcoal manufacturing; petroleum refining; internal combustion engine exhausts; resin production; formaldehyde production and storage.
Methyl chloroform	Metal cleaning and cleaning of plastic moulds.

Methylene chloride	Major component in paint strippers. (Atmospheric half-life 1–2 years.)
Nitrosamines	Limited commercial production but formed in air, water and food from precursors (amines, nitrogen oxides and nitrates).
Phenol	Manufacture of explosives, fertiliser, coke, illuminating gas, lampblack, paints, paint removers, rubber, asbestos goods, wood preservatives, synthetic resins, textiles, drugs, perfumes, bakelite and other plastics; disinfectant in petroleum, leather, paper, soap, tanning, dye and agricultural industries.
Phosgene	Manufacture of some dyestuffs; carbonic acid esters (polycarbonates); manufacture of some insecticides and pharmaceuticals.
Polychlorinated biphenyls	Production, storage and transport of PCBs; incineration of waste PCBs (electrical transformers and capacitors); solid waste disposal; evaporative losses of plasticisers; volatilisation of PCB-containing paints and coatings. (Atmospheric half-life: 26 days. A widespread pollutant of fish and wildlife.)
Trichloro-ethylene	Solvent in degreasing operations; PVC production; inks; surface coatings; adhesives; dry cleaning and pharmaceuticals.

Source: OECD 1985a

CHAPTER FOUR

The Urban Climate and Air Pollution

4.1 INTRODUCTION

This chapter examines the main causes and effects of the most important atmospheric pollutants which have a significant, day-to-day urban origin. Not included are pollutants released into the atmosphere as a result of accidents or those, such as certain radioactive isotopes, where human-made emission sources are normally outside urban boundaries. In omitting such pollutants, we do not seek to minimise their importance, but rather focus our analysis on those pollutants whose release can be attributed to specific characteristics of urban areas, such as dense traffic volumes.

Cities can bring about substantial changes to the local climate, and these may have important consequences for the nature and extent of air pollution both within and beyond urban boundaries. Conversely, urban air pollution can be an important contributing factor in the production of an urban climate which differs significantly from that of the surrounding countryside. The context for appreciating the impacts of urban air pollution is set here by a brief review of urban climate modification in section 4.2.

This is followed by sections on specific urban air pollutants. From the 1950s and 1960s, some pollutants, most notably sulphur oxides, carbon monoxide, nitrogen oxides and particulates, have been monitored, their effects researched and their emissions (to some extent) controlled in many developed countries. These so-called 'traditional' pollutants are discussed in section 4.3, followed by descriptions of the more 'exotic', less well understood pollutants. While many cities in developed countries regularly monitor many traditional air pollutants, any form of monitoring is still comparatively rare in cities in developing countries, and very little data exists on pollution trends over time. The chapter concludes with a review of the potential for global climate change through ozone depletion and the enhanced 'greenhouse effect', recognising that the links between air pollution and climate change may have major global ramifications.

4.2 THE URBAN CLIMATE

It has long been appreciated that the climate of towns and cities often differs substantially from that experienced in surrounding rural areas. As long ago as 1792, the physician William Currie complained of New York that it became insufferably hot in summer because of its narrow streets and high and crowded buildings (Meyer 1991). Urbanisation alters the nature of local atmospheric processes to produce discernable changes in the local climate. Almost all aspects of climate can become altered over cities, including the radiation–heat balance, wind speed, humidity and precipitation characteristics. Most work carried out on urban climate modification has been done for mid-latitude cities in temperate areas of developed countries. Selected findings are summarised in Box 4.1.

The average changes to elements of climate given in Box 4.1 are just that: these values hide much important detail, not least intra-urban differences in local climate associated with differences in urban land use and design. For example, although urbanisation frequently reduces average wind speed, the positioning of buildings can create long, narrow streets producing an unpleasant 'wind tunnel' effect on occasion, resulting in very strong gusts of winds. Similarly, the urban 'heat island' effect (see Box 4.1) will rarely, if ever, be uniform across a city, due to the uneven distribution of dense building materials (which can store heat for subsequent release) and heavily trafficked streets (vehicle engines release heat) (Bryson and Ross 1972). Therefore, shopping centres, the central business district and areas of high-density housing in cities often have more elevated air temperatures than parks or low-density housing areas. The use of brick as a housebuilding material in tropical countries can greatly add to the night-time discomfort of occupants, although the provision of tree shade and the east–west orientation of houses can alleviate this problem (Sani 1984). Ironically, human comfort frequently demands a greater expenditure of energy in air conditioning and the cooling of buildings in summer when urban air temperatures can become oppresive. More seriously, uncomfortably high air temperatures during summer months can contribute to higher-than-average death rates, especially among older people (Gunn 1978).

Vegetation cover and green open space can be important in ameliorating the build-up of heat in cities. Natural or semi-natural spaces tend to lose heat more rapidly at night, while during the day a dense vegetation cover helps to divert more of the heat available at or near the ground surface to the evapotranspiration process, creating a cooling effect on the lower atmosphere. Vegetated areas can also help to reduce noise and filter pollutants from the urban atmosphere (Dole 1989d). Imaginative and sympathetic urban design which works with nature can bring great benefits to city dwellers.

Box 4.1 Average Changes in Selected Climatic Elements Over Cities in Mid-Latitude Areas, as Compared with Surrounding Countryside

- **Solar radiation** received at the ground surface (0–20% lower) and the **duration of bright sunshine** (5–15% lower). This loss of energy and heat from the sun arises principally because of increased levels of atmospheric pollutants over urban areas, such as dust and smoke particles and gaseous admixtures, which absorb, scatter and reflect a proportion of the solar radiation which would otherwise reach the ground surface. However, generally this loss of solar energy is more than compensated for by factors giving rise to the urban 'heat island' effect (see below).

- **Air Temperature** (annual mean – 0.7 °C higher; winter maximum – 1.5 °C higher). This so-called urban 'heat island' effect arises through the burning of fossil fuels in power generation, space heating and transport; the high heat storage capacity of building materials; human metabolism; and lower average wind speed which reduces the potential for heat transport away from urban areas. The urban heat island effect is generally most pronounced at night and during winter months, and has been found to be proportional to the logarithm of urban population size.

- **Wind speed** (annual mean – 10–30% lower; extreme gusts – 10–20% lower; frequency of calms – 5–20% higher). These effects are due to the greater frictional drag exerted by relatively tall buildings and the uneven urban landscape which present a 'rougher' surface to airflow.

- **Relative humidity** (annual mean – 6% lower). Related to the lack of open water: transpiration is reduced as vegetation cover is removed, and the capping of water-holding soils with impermeable materials.

- **Cloudiness** (cloud frequency and amount – 5–10% higher) and **fogs** (winter frequency – 100% higher; summer frequency – 30% higher). This is because of the greater emission of dust and smoke particles into the urban atmosphere, which act as nuclei around which water vapour can condense to form the liquid droplets of cloud and fog.

- **Precipitation** (annual total – 5–15% higher; days with greater than 5mm of rainfall – 10% higher; frequency of rainstorms – 10–15% higher). Urban-induced increases in precipitation are frequently most prevalent downwind of large cities. Contributing factors include a greater number of condensation nuclei over urban areas, the enhanced upward thermal convection of air because of the heat island effect, and the increased upward mechanical convection of air caused by the presence of tall buildings.

(Adapted from Landsberg (1981) and Goudie (1989))

Design, climate and atmospheric pollution are, therefore, intimately interwoven facets of urban living. Consider again the urban heat island effect. Under certain circumstances, this fosters the build-up of air pollution over cities by producing a distinctive pattern of air circulation in and around the city. Since the relatively warm air over cities tends to rise, this may produce a weak thermal low-pressure centre which draws in air from the surrounding countryside. As this air rises, so more air is drawn in and a semi-closed circulation system becomes established which redistributes air pollution to form a 'dust dome' which 'hangs' over the city, often trapping pollutants close to the ground surface (see Figure 4.1). If a significant horizontal wind exists, this dust dome may be transformed into a plume, sometimes several hundred kilometres long, which carries pollutants downwind far into the countryside (Nicholas 1982). In this way, a combination of pollution-generating urban activities and urban climate modification may produce higher-than-average rainfalls, both in the city and in downwind rural areas (see Box 4.1). In a detailed study of the precipitation characteristics of La Porte in Indiana (some 50 km east of Chicago) from 1925, it was found that total precipitation and the number of days with rain increased by 30–40% (Changnon 1968). These changes were found to be closely related to the intensity of iron and steel production in Chicago, suggesting that air pollution from these complexes was partly responsible for the changes in precipitation observed downwind in La Porte.

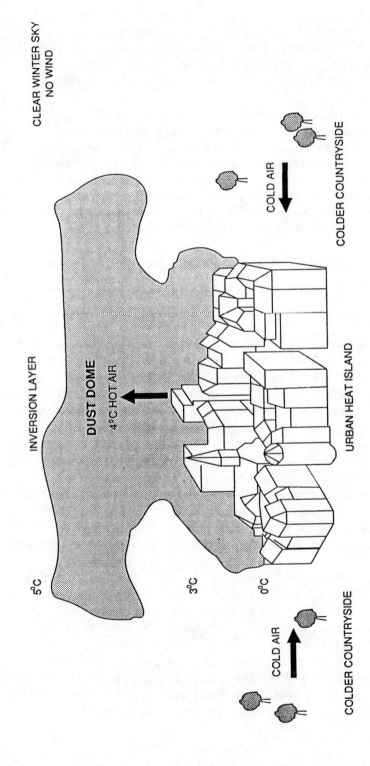

Source: Adapted from Commission of the European Communities 1990

Figure 4.1 The urban dust dome

The eventual breakdown of an urban dust dome may be inhibited by topographic characteristics. Both Los Angeles and Mexico City, for example, are located in topographic basins, in part surrounded by mountains, and are both subject to frequent temperature inversions which exacerbate air pollution containment over these cities (Cunningham and Saigo 1990, Miller 1991). Lower-than-average wind speeds in cities also contribute to the formation of urban heat islands and dust domes.

Clearly, urban air pollution and climate modification are interrelated concerns. The significance of appreciating this interrelationship lies in the opportunity this presents for the sympathetic design of our cities, in order to minimise adverse impacts on environmental resources, human health and quality of life.

4.3 GENERAL AIR POLLUTION

Urban areas are the major areal sources for many forms of air pollution, being centres of industrial activity, energy production and use, and vehicular traffic. As a prelude to the discussion of individual air pollutant groups, this section provides a few selected illustrations of the general scale of air pollution problems. It is only too easy to forget that individual pollutants do not exist in isolation, and can combine in a synergistic fashion to produce a much greater impact than the sum of their individual properties would indicate. Recent years have seen a growing recognition of the deleterious effects on human health and environmental quality of synergistic action and the production of secondary pollutants as a result of chemical chain reactions in the atmosphere (van Houdt 1990).

Without wishing to be over-dramatic, it is nevertheless true to say that the 'cocktail' of pollutants found over our cities kills and injures people, causes and aggravates chronic diseases, damages buildings and other structures, and damages or kills vegetation. The impacts of general air pollution are most frequently couched in national or international terms, with only very limited information available for individual urban areas. This said, it must be remembered that air pollution is largely a problem generated by urban activities, or activities (such as power generation) which serve the needs of cities, and so the urban association with air pollution, and its attendant impacts, is a profound one.

Miller (1991) provides a disturbing insight into the human health effects of general air pollution by suggesting that as many as one-quarter of all deaths in children under five years old, worldwide, may be a direct result of air pollution; the death-toll in this age group for Mexico City alone may may total 45,000 annually. Miller further suggests that 60%

of the population of the USA may be breathing unsafe air. Indeed, a large-scale study in the USA concluded that at least 11%, and more likely 21%, of lung cancers could be attributed to general air pollution (OECD 1985a). Urban areas are almost inevitably associated with the highest air pollution levels and this is reflected in the greater risk to urban dwellers of developing diseases of the respiratory system. Lung cancer mortality in Chinese cities, for example, is four to seven times higher than in the nation as a whole, while in Calcutta 60% of the population suffers from other air pollution-related diseases such as bronchitis and pneumonia (WCED 1987).

Table 4.1 Major classes of air pollution

Class of pollutant	Major members of the class
Carbon oxides	Carbon monoxide, carbon dioxide
Sulphur oxides	Sulphur dioxide, sulphur trioxide
Nitrogen oxides	Nitric oxide, nitrogen dioxide, nitrous oxide
Volatile organic compounds (VOCs):	
Hydrocarbons (gaseous and liquid compounds containing carbon and hydrogen)	Methane, butane, ethylene, benzene, benzopyrene
Other organic compounds	Formaldehyde, chloroform, methylene chloride, ethylene dichloride, trichloroethylene, vinyl chloride, carbon tetrachloride, ethylene oxide
Suspended particulate matter (SPM):	
Solid particles	Dust (soil), soot (carbon), asbestos, lead, cadmium, arsenic, beryllium, nitrate and sulphate salts
Liquid droplets	Sulphuric acid, nitric acid, oil, pesticides
Photochemical oxidants formed in the atmosphere by the reaction of oxygen, nitrogen oxides and VOCs under the influence of sunlight	Ozone, PANs (peroxyacetyl nitrates), formaldehyde, acetaldehyde, hydrogen peroxide, hydroxy radicals

Source: Miller 1988

Air pollution damage to human health has economic consequences, as does its degradation of other resources and assets such as crops, forests, buildings and other materials. Taking into account imputed costs for damage to human health, materials, agriculture, forestry and disamenity, air pollution in Germany was calculated at levels as high as 2.6–2.9% of GDP between 1983 and 1985 (Pearce 1993). Air pollution in the USA reportedly costs at least $110 billion a year in health care and lost productivity (Miller 1991). According to the OECD (1985a), total yearly damage costs calculated for health care, soiling/cleaning, vegetation and materials amounted to 1% of GDP in France and 2% in Netherlands in the early 1980s. More recently, Simmons (1991) has suggested that annual air pollution damage in developed countries amounts to some 1–2% of GDP.

The major classes of air pollution are shown in Table 4.1, with some of the most important human health and ecological effects of traditional air pollutants outlined in Table 4.2. It is important to note that the combustion of fossil fuels contributes pollutants to each one of the categories in Table 4.1. However, the type of fossil fuel is important. Sulphurous brown coal, for example, is still widely used in power generation in some east European countries adding greatly to urban and transfrontier (acid deposition) pollution: in Halle, in the former East Germany, high dust and sulphur dioxide levels from the combustion of this fuel have been linked to respiratory problems up to 15% higher than in neighbouring areas and a five-year reduction in life expectancy (ZumBrunnen 1990). Alternatively, the conversion from oil to natural gas and urban steam boilers in Russia has contributed to selective reductions in pollution levels in some cities (Peterson 1993).

4.4 TRADITIONAL AIR POLLUTANTS

4.4.1 Sulphur compounds

A number of sulphur compounds are emitted to, or formed in, the atmosphere in significant quantities. Sulphur may enter the atmosphere in gases (especially sulphur dioxide and hydrogen sulphide), or in liquid droplet particulate form (especially sulphuric and sulphurous acids), or in the form of sulphate salts perhaps attached to particulate matter. Also, sulphur dioxide in the atmosphere may react with oxygen to form sulphur trioxide, which may in turn react with water to form sulphuric acid.

Approximately half of all global sulphur emissions to the atmosphere are the result of natural processes (OECD 1991). However, the majority of emissions of sulphur oxides are of anthropogenic origin, of which sulphur dioxide is the most important. In many urban/industrial areas, such as eastern North America, more than 90% of all the sulphur dioxide emitted is the result of human activity (OECD 1985a). Anthropogenic sulphur dioxide emissions largely stem from the combustion of fossil fuels and the release of the sulphur contained within these fuels. In the majority of developed countries anthropogenic sulphur dioxide emissions come mainly from the energy sector, with industry being the next most important contributor. In the USA, 68% of all sulphur dioxide emissions come from coal- and oil-burning power stations (Miller 1988). Space heating systems, smelters, oil refineries, metal processing mills and sulphuric acid plants also emit significant quantities of sulphur dioxide. Hydrogen sulphide, with its very pungent smell of rotten eggs, may also be a localised problem around oil refineries and some pulp mills.

Table 4.2 Major potential health and ecological effects of 'traditional' air pollutants

Pollutants	Effects on human health	Effects on the natural environment
Carbon monoxide (CO)	Can affect the cardiovascular system, exacerbating cardiovascular disease symptoms, particularly angina; may also particularly affect foetuses, sickle cell anaemics and young children. Can affect the central nervous system, impairing physical coordination, vision and judgement, creating nausea and headaches, reducing worker productivity and increasing personal discomfort.	
Nitrogen oxides (NOx)	Nitrogen dioxide (NO_2) can affect the respiratory system. Nitrogen monoxide (NO) and nitrogen dioxide (NO_2), where they play a part in photochemical smog formation, may contribute indirectly to increased suscept-ibility to infections, pulmonary disease, impairment of lung function and eye, nose and throat irritations.	NO and NO_2 can contribute significantly to acid deposition, damaging aquatic ecosystems and possibly other ecosystems such as forests; NOx can also have a fertilizing effect on forests.

Sulphur oxides (SOx)	Sulphur dioxide (SO$_2$) can affect lung function.	SO$_2$ and other sulphur oxides can contribute significantly to acid deposition causing impairment of aquatic and possibly other ecosystems.
		Sulphates can affect the perception of the environment by reducing visibility even at low concentrations.
Particulate matter	Fine particulate matter may be toxic in itself or may carry toxic (including carcinogenic) trace substances, and can alter the immune system.	High dust and soot levels are associated with a general perception of dirtiness of the environment.
	Fine particulates can penetrate deep into the respiratory system irritating lung tissue and causing long-term disorders.	Fine particulates can significantly reduce visibility.

Sources: OECD 1985a, 1988; Tolba and El-Kholy 1992.

Sulphur dioxide emissions in almost all developed countries declined, or at least stabilised, during the 1970s and 1980s thanks to a number of factors, including the imposition of more stringent emission standards, economic incentives, fuel-switching away from high-sulphur coals and oil, a shift towards electricity and natural gas for domestic heating, increased energy efficiency, the installation of desulphurisation equipment in power stations and stagnant or decreasing rates of economic growth during the 1980s (OECD 1991, UNEP 1991, Tolba and El-Kholy 1992). In OECD countries, urban sulphur dioxide concentrations have fallen on average by between 30% and 75% since the early 1970s (OECD 1991), and generally declining atmospheric sulphur dioxide concentrations have been recorded in a number of cities around the world (see Table 4.3), where current levels compare favourably with the World Health Organisation (WHO) recommended concentration range of 40–60 µg/m^3 (micrograms per cubic metre). Except for a few cities in northern Europe and rather more in southern Europe, the annual averages of daily sulphur dioxide concentrations for most cities in OECD countries are generally less than 60 µg/m^3 (OECD 1985a).

Table 4.3 Recent trends in the relative average concentrations of three air pollutants in a number of selected cities

Pollutant	City	1980 Reference Value (µg/m3)	1970	'75	'77	'78	'79	'80	'81	'82	'83	'84	'85	'86	'87
								Concentration as a percentage of the 1980 reference value							
SO_2	Montreal	40.8	—	99	104	99	92	100	92	66	44	52	44	40	—
	New York	37.5	—	115	113	109	105	100	104	113	105	107	98	93	—
	Tokyo	48.0	227	125	125	98	100	100	90	88	63	56	52	48	48
	Paris	89.0	137	129	109	122	117	100	80	76	69	64	61	56	54
	Frankfurt	80.0	—	139	106	109	110	100	94	90	71	66	90	73	80
	Amsterdam	25.0	304	136	116	136	136	100	104	84	80	80	64	56	—
	Oslo	36.0	—	133	122	128	117	100	89	56	44	44	42	42	44
	London	69.0	—	172	125	130	116	100	104	83	72	70	55	58	—
NO_2	Montreal	54.7	—	55	107	—	97	100	83	86	83	90	—	—	—
	New York	66.2	—	104	99	94	100	100	92	100	101	98	96	93	—
	Tokyo	66.0	—	105	102	114	105	100	94	95	94	89	86	88	95
	Caen	34.0	—	—	—	—	109	100	88	97	100	97	103	109	97
	Frankfurt	83.0	—	86	98	95	—	100	114	112	98	78	86	107	69
	Amsterdam	40.0	68	105	90	93	103	100	110	113	108	103	113	128	—
	Oslo	70.0	—	—	—	—	—	100	—	100	—	127	117	121	129
	London	64.1	—	168	132	109	103	100	103	127	115	127	87	103	—

Table 4.3 Recent trends in the relative average concentrations of three air pollutants in a number of selected cities (continued)

Pollutant	City	1980 Reference Value (μg/m3)	Concentration as a percentage of the 1980 reference value												
			1970	'75	'77	'78	'79	'80	'81	'82	'83	'84	'85	'86	'87
SPM	Montreal	82.0	—	135	98	95	94	100	88	77	74	74	—	—	—
	New York	55.6	—	91	91	87	90	100	97	94	91	95	96	87	—
	Tokyo	48.0	—	169	154	125	98	100	108	106	98	108	110	121	123
	Paris	51.0	143	112	92	102	118	100	98	92	90	92	96	90	90
	Frankfurt	29.0	—	210	114	107	117	100	90	93	169	117	166	134	152
	Amsterdam	66.0	—	106	92	106	112	100	102	95	97	98	97	80	—
	Oslo	30.0	—	123	97	93	80	100	97	107	117	87	97	97	97
	London	22.0	—	200	127	141	132	100	114	91	109	95	91	86	—

Note: SPM = Suspended pariculate matter.

Differences between the cities in terms of the number of sampling sites, the measurement technique used in pollutant analysis, periods used in the calculation of mean pollutant concentration etc., make the comparison of data between cities inappropriate.

Source: OECD 1989

However, it is still true that urban concentrations are generally well above those experienced in rural locations, where concentrations are usually less than 2 $\mu g/m^3$, and levels can still reach well over 100 $\mu g/m^3$ in some cities (Goudie 1989, OECD 1991). In southern Europe, cities such as Athens and Naples have shown a significant increase in most air pollutants in recent years, due to rapid growth and an increase in industrial and vehicular emissions (Commission of the European Communities 1990).

The main world regions which have witnessed continuing increases in sulphur oxides are parts of Asia and Africa (Tolba and El-Kholy 1992). Some of the highest observed concentrations of sulphur dioxide occur in cities in southern China because of the burning of large amounts of high-sulphur coal in domestic stoves and the use of such coal in small-scale industries. Annual average concentrations in the cities of Chongqing and Guiyang, for example, are several times above the WHO's guideline level. A similar problem exists in Shanghai, where high-sulphur coal is used in seven power stations, eight steel works, 8000 industrial boilers, 1000 kilns, 15,000 restaurant stoves and 1 million domestic cooking stoves (Hardoy, Mitlin and Satterthwaite 1992).

Compared to most other forms of air pollution, the impacts of sulphur compounds have been relatively well studied. Apart from problems associated with acid deposition on to natural aquatic and terrestrial ecosystems (discussed in Chapter Five), sulphur compounds are known to exert pressures on human health, damage crops and human-made materials, and reduce visibility (see Table 4.2). The aerosol sulphuric acid form is highly corrosive of iron, steel, copper and nickel, and building materials, such as limestone and sandstone, containing carbonates (Simmons 1981). According to Milne (1988), the Dutch spend some £6.6 million per year repairing acid-damaged buildings, and in the USA acid damage to buildings costs some $8000 million annually. However, it is the primary pollutant, sulphur dioxide, which has received much of the research attention. As already mentioned, sulphur dioxide concentrations tend to be significantly higher over urban areas than in the rural environment and this has been demonstrated by the direct measurement of the gas along urban-to-rural transects and also indirectly by observations of the distribution of lichens which are particularly sensitive to sulphur dioxide in the atmosphere. Sulphur dioxide can act as a phototoxin (inhibitor of photosynthesis in plants). Measurements of sulphur dioxide made between central Nottingham in England and a rural area some 15 km to the south-west of the city, for example, showed that sulphur dioxide generally increased towards the city centre during the winter, when heating and power requirements were greatest (Berry and Colls 1990).

The effects of sulphur dioxide on plants have been studied for many years. Studies in the English cities of Leeds (on radish and lettuce), Manchester (on rye-grass) and London (on several garden flowers) showed decreases in the yield of these plants in areas of the cities subject to high concentrations of sulphur dioxide pollution (Edwards 1972). In the Manchester study, a decline in yield was noted at a sulphur dioxide concentration of only 60 μg/m^3. Sulphur dioxide pollution can reduce dry matter production, photosynthesis and yield without producing visible effects on plants, but concentrations of around 2700 μg/m^3 can cause visible damage and death (Last 1982). At this concentration, a physiological response in humans, such as inflammation of the upper respiratory tract, may become apparent (Simmons 1981).

4.4.2 Carbon oxides

Anthropogenic emissions of carbon dioxide through the burning of fossil fuels are causing great concern because of their contribution to the enhanced 'greenhouse effect'. This phenomenon has global climate implications: carbon dioxide production is discussed at the end of this chapter, together with the other main greenhouse gases. In this section attention is focused on carbon monoxide, a major contributor to general urban air pollution.

Approximately 65% of total global carbon monoxide emissions are of natural origin, being primarily the result of the oxidation of methane produced by decaying organic matter (OECD 1991). However, anthropogenic emissions from the incomplete combustion of fossil fuels are responsible for relatively high local concentrations in most industrialised countries. Up to 90% of anthropogenic emissions of carbon monoxide worldwide stem from the transport sector, mainly automobile emissions (OECD 1989). It has been suggested that motor vehicles contribute approximately 55% of the total anthropogenic emissions of carbon monoxide in the cities of the USA (Singh *et al.*, 1990).

The overwhelming importance of road vehicle emissions is clear, although it is important to note the much lower quantities emitted by diesel engines relative to petrol engines. In petrol engines, the highest concentrations of carbon monoxide in exhaust fumes occur during deceleration or when the engine is idling, both frequent occurrences in congested urban areas. Carbon monoxide emissions are usually most concentrated along major highways or near congested urban streets where vehicle density is high, engine efficiency is low and ventilation is restricted by buildings (Oke 1978). Other, non-vehicular anthropogenic sources of atmospheric carbon monoxide include metal processing industries, petroleum refineries, paper processing factories and cigarette smoke.

During the 1970s, total anthropogenic carbon monoxide emissions decreased significantly in North America and Japan, with a mixed picture in European countries. The 1980s have seen a decline or stabilisation of urban and total national emissions in nearly all OECD countries, which nonetheless accounted for 71% of the global total (OECD 1985a, 1989, 1991). This downwards trend can be attributed largely to the introduction of environmental controls on exhaust emissions in the 1970s, the effects of which were delayed with the progressive replacement of vehicle stocks. For instance, the mandatory introduction of catalytic converters on motor vehicles in the USA has been a major factor in the 40% fall in carbon monoxide production since 1970, despite a rise in car use (Tolba and El-Kholy 1992). However, there is little room for complacency. The problems associated with carbon monoxide pollution in many cities around the world are still causing great concern. Singh *et al.* (1990), for example, refer to carbon monoxide as the most common and widely distributed air pollutant in urban areas. They argue that frequent winter temperature inversions in Delhi, India, combined with increasing traffic volumes make carbon monoxide pollution a growing threat to public health in the city.

High levels of carbon monoxide in the atmosphere cause concern for a number of reasons. Carbon monoxide can be oxidised to form carbon dioxide, which is an important contributor gas to the 'greenhouse effect' (see section 4.9). Carbon monoxide also interferes with the uptake of oxygen by red blood cells in animals and humans. This can lead to a number of adverse effects in humans (see Table 4.2) including the exacerbation of cardio-vascular disease symptoms and headaches. The US National Ambient Air Quality Standard for carbon monoxide is set at 35 ppm (parts per million), whereby this value is not to be exceeded more than once a year, based upon hourly observations. Detectable clinical symptoms appear at a concentration of 100 ppm and death can occur at 1000 ppm. Urban areas generally experience the highest atmospheric concentrations of carbon monoxide, ranging between 1 and 100 ppm, with an average of around 10 ppm, the WHO recommended eight-hour maximum (Simmons 1981; OECD 1988, 1989, 1991). A concentration of 350 ppm has been recorded in London (Edwards 1972). The city of Los Angeles has established carbon monoxide alert levels at 100, 200 and 300 ppm.

4.4.3 Particulates

Suspended particulate matter (SPM) in the atmosphere can exist in a variety of solid and liquid forms (see Table 4.2), including soil, soot, smoke (black soot), metals, salts, acids and pesticides. Particulates vary in size from greater than 100 μm (micrometres) in diameter to less than 0.1 μm in diameter. Particles greater than 10 μm, or so, in diameter tend to settle out of the atmosphere relatively quickly, close to the emission source under the influence of gravity. This group includes dust, fly ash (the incombustible remnants of solid fuel combustion) and visible smoke. Those particulates with a diameter of less than 10 μm, often referred to as aerosols, may remain suspended in the atmosphere for many days. Particulate pollution has long been a feature of the urban atmospheric environment, arising from a number of anthropogenic sources, including combustion for heating and energy generation, vehicles, refuse incineration, industrial processing, surface disturbances caused by building activities, the action of heavy vehicles, and the action of strong wind on stockpiles of various materials.

In most developed countries, power generation accounts for the major proportion of anthropogenic emissions of particulates. Only in Canada, out of all the OECD countries, does industrial activity emit more particulates than the energy sector (OECD 1989). Concentrations of SPM have tended to decrease rapidly in recent years in the cities of many developed countries (Table 4.3). Anthropogenic emissions of particulates have declined since the early 1970s by almost 50% in OECD cities; this tends to have involved a number of factors, including: changing energy policies, particularly the use of alternative fuels, low-sulphur fuels and making energy savings; environmental control policies, particularly the installation of smoke and dust control equipment in power stations and industrial combustion units; and urban deindustrialisation and generally slower economic growth during the early 1980s (OECD 1985a, Clarke 1986).

It should be noted, however, that whilst the installation of particulate control equipment has reduced the total output of particulates from industrial combustion units and power stations, this has not greatly affected the background concentration of fine aerosol particles in the atmosphere, which still appears to be increasing (Simmons 1991). Fine aerosol particles resulting from human activity are principally formed in the atmosphere as secondary pollutants from gaseous emissions (Table 4.4), and are discussed in more detail below. Also, although long-term data from many developing countries are very limited, some appear to have witnessed increasing SPM concentrations; for instance in Calcutta and Delhi (Singh *et al.*, 1990).

Table 4.4 Estimates of atmospheric aerosol production rates

source	Production rate (tonnes per day)	Weight of total in %
Natural Sources		
a) Primary sources:		
wind blown dust	2×10^4 to 1×10^6	5.6
sea spray	3×10^6	33.4
volcanic	1×10^4	0.11
forest fires	4×10^6	4.5
b) Secondary sources:		
vegetation	5×10^5 to 3×10^6	22.2
sulphur cycle	1×10^5 to 1×10^6	5.6
nitrogen cycle	2×10^6	22.2
volcanic (gases)	1×10^3	0.011
Sub-total	6×10^6 to 10×10^6	93.6
Anthropogenic Sources		
a) Primary sources:		
combustion/industrial dust	1×10^5 to 3×10^5	2.2
cultivation	1×10^2 to 1×10^3	0.005
b) Secondary sources:		
hydrocarbon vapours	7×10^3	0.078
sulphates	3×10^5	3.3
nitrates	6×10^4	0.67
ammonia	3×10^3	0.033
Sub-total	5×10^5 to 7×10^5	6.4
Total	6.5×10^6 to 10.7×10^6	100

Source: van Houdt 1990

The European Community and USA standards for particulates (annual mean values of 80 and 75 $\mu g/m^3$, respectively) are still not satisfied in many regions of developed countries, particularly in heavily industrialised cities. Approximately 40 million people in the USA, for example, live in areas where the USA Environmental Protection Agency standard for particulates is exceeded (OECD 1991). This disappointing degree of exposure may be due to several factors of varying relevance in different countries, including high rates of production of secondary aerosol pollutants from increased gaseous emissions, a switch back to the use of coal in power stations in some countries and an increase in the use of diesel vehicles in many countries. A recent study conducted in Santiago in Chile, for example, concluded that 74% of the suspended particulates over the city could be attributed to emissions from diesel engines (Romo-Kroger 1990), and it has been estimated that over 50% of smoke readings in the central areas of UK cities may be contributed by diesel engine emissions, mainly from heavy goods vehicles (Clarke 1986). Diesel exhaust particulates comprise chain aggregates of carbon microspheres, covered with any of hundreds of organic compounds, some of which are known carcinogens (Tolba and El-Kholy 1992).

The importance of cities as areal generators of particulate pollution is emphasised by comparing the levels of particulates in the atmosphere typically found over cities with levels occurring in adjacent rural areas. Goudie (1989) reports the average concentration of SPM (in $\mu g/m^3$) found in the commercial areas of a number of cities as: 400 in Calcutta; 170 in Madrid and Prague; 147 in Zagreb; 43 in Tokyo; and 24 in London and Brussels. These values compare with rural concentrations of generally less than 10 $\mu g/m3$, prompting Goudie to conclude that, on average, the number of particles present in the air over urban areas is some ten times greater than over adjacent rural areas. It is interesting to note that the concentration reported by Goudie for Calcutta would, according to the USA Environmental Protection Agency, result in the aggravation of symptoms in people with heart and lung disease and cause irritation amongst the population as a whole. According to Simmons (1991), annual mean particulate concentrations during the 1980s in Kuwait, New Delhi and Beijing were 603, 405 and 399 $\mu g/m^3$, respectively. In some cities, a combination of geographical and meteorological factors may compound pollutant emissions. The air above Santiago in Chile, for example, is often heavily polluted with particulates, such that the annual mean concentration of particulates is greater than 200 $\mu g/m^3$ (Romo-Kroger, 1990). This is in part due to the location of the city in a valley surrounded by a chain of mountains, which encourages the formation of strong, low-level temperature inversions.

Recently, research on particulate pollution has focused on small aerosol particles (see Table 4.4). These are small enough to penetrate deep into the lungs, where they may cause long-term health disorders especially if the particles carry with them known toxins such as some metals and organic compounds (see Tables B.1 and B.2). Lung cancer, for example, has been linked to the inhalation of particles of asbestos, beryllium, arsenic, chromium and nickel (Miller 1988). A number of known mutagenic and/or carcinogenic organic compounds, principally emitted from vehicle exhausts in urban areas, have been detected on air-borne particulates, especially those less than approximately 3 μm in diameter (van Houdt 1990). Analyses of the chemical composition of particulates found over the Chinese cities of Beijing and Tianjin, showed relatively high levels of benzo-pyrene, which is a known carcinogen (Hardoy, Mitlin and Satterthwaite 1992).

Apart from direct effects on human health, particulates cause the soiling of buildings, statues, clothes, paintwork and vehicles. The acidic nature of some suspended particulate matter (principally sulphate and nitrate salts) is thought to be responsible for the soiling and corrosion of the Taj Mahal in Agra, India, for example, (Joshi *et al.* 1989). Aerosol particulates with a diameter comparable to the wavelength of visible light are effective in the scattering and absorbtion of visible light in the atmosphere, thereby reducing solar radiation input and creating a hazy atmosphere, which reduces visibility (Lee 1990). Suspended particles can also act as nuclei around which atmospheric water vapour can readily condense to form water droplets, which may in turn enhance the formation of fog (see section 4.2 on urban climate above). The soiling of leaf surfaces by particulates may also reduce photosynthetic activity in plants and, through the blockage of stomata, interfere with normal processes of gas and water exchange (Edwards 1972).

4.4.4 Nitrogen oxides

The majority of the total worldwide emissions of nitrogen oxides are thought to be of natural origin (about 60%), arising from the decomposition of organic matter, natural fires and fixation in the atmosphere by lightning. Anthropogenic releases stem principally from the burning of fossil fuels, with outputs from transport being roughly equal to those from power stations and industrial combustion combined in developed countries. Minor emissions also come from factories producing fertilisers and explosives (OECD 1989). Whereas natural biological processes of organic matter decomposition release all of the major oxides of nitrogen (nitric oxide, nitrogen dioxide and nitrous oxide), anthropogenic activities involving the combustion of fossil fuels emit only nitric oxide and nitrogen dioxide in significant quantities. However, nitrogen dioxide usually forms only a small proportion of the primary waste gases from combustion (less than 10%) and so the principal primary pollutant is nitric oxide derived from the nitrogen present in the fuel. Nitric oxide is thought to be a relatively harmless gas, but once in the atmosphere it readily oxidises to form nitrogen dioxide and so the relative proportions of these two oxides may then become comparable. Nitrogen dioxide is a yellow-brown-coloured gas which is a known irritant and may affect the respiratory system (see Table 4.2). It is this gas, therefore, which has been the main focus of research attention in urban areas.

Concentrations of nitrogen dioxide over many cities have not declined as rapidly or consistently as concentrations of sulphur dioxide or total particulates (see Table 4.3). In the major urban areas of India, for example, concentrations have increased in recent years (Singh *et al*. 1990). These disappointing findings may well reflect a general trend for increasing road traffic volumes in recent years (OECD 1990). Despite these problems, the USA National Ambient Air Quality Standard for nitrogen dioxide (an annual average of 100 $\mu g/m^3$ or 50 parts per billion) is achieved in most OECD cities (OECD 1989), although peak hourly values are normally double this standard.

Apart from direct effects on human health, nitrogen dioxide absorbs sunlight and so may reduce visibility, and can also directly impair plant growth (Edwards 1972). According to Simmons (1981), a concentration of 8000–10,000 parts per billion can decrease visibility to one mile. Nitrogen oxides also contribute to acid deposition problems (Table 4.2 and Chapter Five) and are instrumental in the formation of photochemical smog, which produces a wide range of adverse impacts.

4.5 SMOG

Smog is an all too apparent feature of many urban areas. The term 'smog' was actually first used by the author of a report into a coal-smoke air pollution disaster which occurred in London, killing some 1150 people in 1911. It succinctly describes the mixture of smoke and fog which often 'hung' over London at this time and, indeed, until much later. More recently, smog has been used to describe not just this London type of air pollution (often referred to as industrial or sulphurous smog), but also the production of secondary photochemical oxidants (photochemical or Los Angeles-type smog) in the atmosphere over many cities. Both types of smog are found to some degree over most urban areas, although one type commonly prevails during the summer (photochemical) and the other during the winter (sulphurous).

Sulphurous smogs have generally become less of a problem, even in highly industrialised cities, than was the case two or three decades ago. This trend reflects declining emissions of sulphur dioxide and suspended particulate matter (particularly smoke), which are the main constituents of sulphurous smog. Sulphurous smog is generated by fossil fuel combustion, when a proportion of the sulphur dioxide in the atmosphere forms secondary sulphur pollutants, especially sulphuric acid droplets and sulphate salts, which in association with soot particles coincide with a fog (or at least high humidity) to form a thick greyish haze. Cities which are especially prone to this type of smog can be generalised as being heavily industrialised and reliant on the combustion of large quantities of sulphur-bearing fuels, especially coal and oil during the winter. Most also suffer from cold, wet winters during which the atmosphere may become very stable, resulting in poor pollution dispersal. Such cities would include London, Chicago and Pittsburgh, for example. It was the irritative and congestive effects of this type of smog which resulted in approximately 4000 excess deaths, mostly among elderly people with respiratory and cardiac disorders, in London during the winter of 1952 and a further 2500 deaths during similar incidents in London in 1956, 1958 and 1962 (Holdgate 1979). In the USA, periods of sulphurous smog have also resulted in human deaths, for example in 1948 in Donora, Pennsylvania, when 6000 (from a total population of 14,000) people fell ill and 20 died, and in 1963 in New York City when approximately 300 excess deaths occurred during a sulphurous smog (Miller 1988).

The formation and make-up of photochemical smog are complex, involving a wide range of primary and secondary pollutants in gaseous and particulate forms. Essentially, the photochemical oxidants which make up photochemical smog are compounds with a strong oxidising potential formed by atmospheric chain reactions between nitrogen oxides, volatile organic compounds (VOCs), especially reactive hydrocarbons from vehicle exhausts, and oxygen in the presence of strong sunlight. (VOCs are discussed in the following section.) Ozone is the most prevalent oxidant formed in photochemical smog, and its concentration is often used as an indicator of the degree of photochemical smog pollution. Other particulate and gaseous oxidants are also typically formed in the atmosphere, including hydrogen peroxide, peroxyacetyl nitrates (PANs), various aldehydes and peroxybenzoyl nitrate (PBzN).

The prime meteorological conditions for the formation and accumulation of photochemical smog occur under conditions of strong sunshine and light winds. Unlike sulphurous smog, photochemical smog tends to predominate during the summer for countries outside the tropics. The long-range transport of photochemical oxidants, such as ozone, may also take place under suitable conditions. Typically, the concentration of photochemical oxidants reaches a peak in cities in the afternoon, when precursors to smog formation (e.g. nitric oxide and hydrocarbons) have built up in the atmosphere following morning rush-hour traffic and are then subject to strong early afternoon sunshine (Barry and Chorley 1982). The effects of photochemical air pollution first became apparent in the 1940s in the Los Angeles basin of the USA (OECD 1985a). Here, motor vehicle traffic is generally very dense and in the late summer and early autumn, periods of clear skies, light winds and temperature inversions combine to provide ideal conditions for the generation and accumulation of photochemical oxidants. The city of Los Angeles also lies in a topographic basin, which restricts air movement and pollutant dispersal. However, photochemical smog occurs to some degree in almost all modern cities, having been reported in Denver, Sydney, Mexico City, Buenos Aires, Tokyo, Athens and London, to name but a few (Miller 1991).

Considerable research has been devoted to the occurrence and effects of ozone in the lower atmosphere (troposhere), both for its own sake and as an indicator of the degree of photochemical smog pollution. The WHO recommended maximum hourly levels of 100–200 $\mu g/m^3$ and the USA National Ambient Air Quality Standard of 235 $\mu g/m^3$ (or 0.12 ppm) for ozone are both frequently exceeded in many cities around the world. According to the OECD (1989), maximum hourly concentrations in large cities in North America and Australia range between 340–860 $\mu g/m^3$, while concentrations of up to 340 $\mu g/m^3$ occur in the large cities of Europe and Japan. It is rare for background concentrations in remote rural areas to exceed 100 $\mu g/m^3$, although high levels of photochemical oxidants have been recorded in rural areas downwind of large cities. In 1988, New York was above the Federal health standard for ozone on 34 days during the summer, while this standard was exceeded on 172 days during the year in Los Angeles (Simmons 1991).

Photochemical oxidants can have wide-ranging impacts. In humans, high concentrations may result in an increased susceptibility to infections; impairment of pulmonary function; pulmonary disease; eye, nose and throat irritation; and headaches. It is likely that more than a billion urban dwellers are now breathing air which breaches international safety limits (Simmons 1991). It has been calculated that a small reduction of 0.01 ppm in ground-level ozone concentration in the USA would result in a million fewer cases of chronic respiratory disease in the workforce, bringing a financial saving of about a billion dollars a year (Odum 1989). Ozone concentrations of around 1.25 ppm can result in pronounced respiratory difficulties: in the summer in Athens, it is estimated that 300–350 people per day are admitted to hospital with respiratory difficulties related to the occurrence of photochemical smog. Relationships between ozone concentrations and human health and welfare parameters have also been identified. Whittemore and Korn (1980), for example, demonstrated a relationship between ozone levels and the incidence of asthma, while Portney and Mullahy (1986) found a relationship between ozone concentrations and the number of days when various human activities were restricted. In an intriguing recent paper by Brucato (1990), an attempt was made to assess the economic benefits (accrued through health and welfare savings) of a 10% reduction in the ambient ozone level in the heavily urbanised San Francisco Bay area of the USA. It was estimated that over a 30-year period, based on current costs, a 10% reduction in ozone levels might save between $115 and $813 million, with a best estimate value of $316 million.

Photochemical oxidants can also cause significant damage to vegetation, accelerate the deterioration of materials (especially rubber) and contribute to haze formation and visibility reduction. Losses to crops in California from direct photochemical smog-related injury and growth impairment may have cost approximately £50 million per year in the late 1960s and early 1970s (Edwards 1972). The plant damage area from photochemical smog in California grew from a few square kilometres near Los Angeles in 1942 to cover some 30,000 km^2 of California by 1966 (Smith 1975). More recent research has shown that photochemical oxidant pollution has affected both agricultural crops and native forest species elsewhere in the USA, and in Europe and Japan (see Furukawa 1984, Krupa and Manning 1988). It has been assumed in the majority of these studies that ozone was the primary toxic agent which directly influenced plant growth, and this was confirmed by Olszyk, Bytnerowicz and Takemoto (1989) for the Los Angeles basin, although they also reported the detrimental effects of acid fogs (thought to have a partial photochemical origin) and PANs on some plant species.

4.6 VOLATILE ORGANIC COMPOUNDS (VOCS)

Volatile organic compounds (VOCs) enter the atmosphere from both natural and anthropogenic sources. The term is usually used to describe a general group of chemicals, including gases, solvents and liquid fuels, which evaporate easily at normal temperatures. The potentially toxic organic compounds listed in Table B.2 are also VOCs, as are the hydrocarbons discussed above with reference to photochemical oxidant pollution. Plants are natural emitters of a variety of VOCs, so that forest, grassland, swamp and agricultural areas may emit significant quantities of VOCs, including a number of light hydrocarbons, several aldehydes and various essential plant oils (Molnar 1990). Major anthropogenic emission sources include the chemical industry (e.g. the production of synthetic materials such as ethylene, polypropylene and chlorofluorocarbons from natural gas, and the evaporation of industrial solvents); incinerator plants; and the incomplete combustion of fossil fuels (including motor vehicle traffic as a major source).

According to Molnar (1990), approximately 44% of total VOC emissions in Hungary are from natural plant emissions, especially from forests and agricultural crops, while emissions from the chemical industry and from traffic account for the great majority of anthropogenic VOC emissions, approximately 49% of the overall total. Emissions of VOCs in OECD countries have remained broadly stable or have increased over the past decade. In general the proportion of VOCs emitted by road traffic is increasing (OECD 1991).

The data available on the occurrence of VOCs in the atmosphere, although still limited, indicate that people in city-centre locations may be exposed to one thousand times the concentration of VOCs experienced by those in remote rural areas. A difference of several orders of magnitude in the concentration of benzene, for example, has been observed between urban and remote rural environments (OECD 1985a). Levels of formaldehyde, which can occur as a primary VOC pollutant or as a result of photochemical chain reactions, in air samples and rainwater over Mexico City were found to be amongst the highest ever recorded (Baez *et al.* 1989). A number of VOCs (e.g. aldehydes, polycyclic aromatic compounds, benzene and organic acids) may adversely affect human health, while others (e.g. ethene) may affect plant growth. Chronic exposure to some organochlorine solvents has caused central nervous system disorders and liver dysfunction in humans, while aldehydes are well known respiratory, eye and skin irritants (OECD 1985a).

Of particular recent concern has been the apparent potential of some VOCs to mutate cells and possibly cause cancer, perhaps especially when they occur together, compounding the risk to humans through synergistic effects (Table B.2). Both benzene and benzidine, for example, have been shown to be carcinogenic in humans, and VOCs such as carbon tetrachloride and PCBs are also potential teratogens: that is, they may produce abnormal changes in foetus development. Some 10,000 tonnes of benzene are released into the atmosphere over the USA each year. Benzene is known to cause leukaemia in humans (OECD 1991). According to the OECD (1985a), the concentration of gaseous organic mutagens and carcinogens in the atmosphere over major OECD cities ranges from at least 17 μg/m^3 to 59 μg/m^3. This range compares with a natural background concentration of about 1.9 μg/m^3 and concentrations of up to 4.1 μg/m^3 in rural areas. The OECD further suggests that the concentration of gaseous organic mutagens may be fifteen to twenty times higher in urban areas than the natural background level. In a study of the organic fraction of airborne particulates in Athens, Viras, Athanasiou and Panayotis (1990) found that all the organic extracts of airborne particulate matter showed direct mutagenic activity and that the degree of mutagenicity was well correlated with benzo(a)pyrene (a polycyclic aromatic hydrocarbon, or PAH) concentration and was greatest for particles with a diameter less than 3.3 μm. Generally, higher values of mutagenic activity were found during the winter, with maximum values occurring in the morning. These trends were explained by the greater burning of fossil fuels for space heating in the winter and the importance of morning rush-hour traffic in the generation of organic compounds. Morning and evening peaks in mutagenic activity associated with rush-hour traffic have, in fact, been reported in a number of urban-based studies (van Houdt 1990).

4.7 METALS

Few, if any, metals have not found some application in modern society, and the pollution of air, water and soil by toxic metals, especially arsenic, cadmium, lead, mercury and their compounds is of great current concern given their persistence in the environment (non-biodegradability) and predisposition to accumulate in organic tissues along food chains. It has recently been estimated that the toxicity of all the metals being released annually into the environment is far greater than the combined total toxicity of all radioactive and organic wastes. Nriagu (1988) argues that over one billion 'human guinea pigs' are now being exposed to elevated levels of toxic metals and metalloids in the environment. Furthermore, the number of people suffering from subclinical metal poisoning may be several million.

With reference to air pollution, anthropogenic emissions of lead, cadmium, mercury and arsenic to the atmosphere are some 20–300 times higher annually than natural emissions and are approximately 2,000,000, 5500, 11,000 and 78,000 tonnes per year, respectively (OECD 1989). As with so many other forms of air pollution, human activities within urban areas are responsible for the majority of this output (WCED 1987). Anthropogenic releases of metals into the atmosphere arise from the smelting of metallic ores, various industrial processes, the commercial use of metals and the burning of fossil fuels, including petrol. The burning of petrol in motor vehicle engines is a major source of atmospheric lead, since lead is used as an anti-knock agent in much of the petrol currently produced. Data on the deposition of metals released into the atmosphere suggest that metal deposition rates are several orders of magnitude greater in urban areas than rural areas, and up to one million times higher than observed deposition rates in Antarctica (OECD 1985a).

Research attention on metals in the atmosphere has focused on human health effects, particularly on urban populations and on effects in children. As Table B.1 indicates, toxic metals may have wide-ranging impacts on human health. Some toxic metals are carcinogenic, some are associated with reproductive impairments, some may be involved in immune suppression and others may produce or exacerbate cardiovascular diseases. In one study conducted in twenty-six states in the USA, the concentration of cadmium in the atmosphere was found to be highly correlated with the incidence of certain heart diseases (Carroll 1966). More recently, it has been found that approximately 20% of children in the Katowice region of Poland have elevated blood cadmium concentrations, probably due to the activity of many metal processing plants in the region (Hardoy, Mitlin and Satterthwaite 1992). Lead can impair the synthesis of haem which may adversely affect oxygen transport in the blood, neurotransmitter functions and cellular energetics (Nriagu 1988). These effects may become expressed as an impairment of intelligence, behaviour and performance in children (Holdgate 1979).

A nationwide survey carried out between 1976 and 1980 in the USA found that 3.5% of children under the age of five had blood lead levels of 300 µg/l (micrograms per litre) or more. This level is above the threshold for possible medical intervention, set at 250–300 µg/l in the USA. Many biochemical and neurological changes associated with lead toxicity have, in fact, been observed at concentrations as low as 60 µg/l (DHHS 1982). Smith (1986) reports that up to 70% of the total body burden of lead in the UK population as a whole may be derived from motor vehicle emissions. While this proportion may be expected to decline with the increasing use of unleaded petrol in many developed countries, Nriagu (1988) still argues that lead poisoning should be regarded as the most pressing public health problem in many parts of the world. Lead compounds are still widely used as petrol additives in the cities of most developing countries. Progress, however, has been made: since the early 1970s urban atmospheric lead concentrations have fallen by an estimated 85% in North America, and by around 50% in large European cities (OECD 1991).

With their generally less stringent environmental control measures, there is good evidence to suggest that the environmental levels of many toxic metals in developing countries will rise steadily in the future. The highest concentrations of lead in the atmosphere are, in fact, already being found in the urban areas of developing countries (Lansdown and Yule 1986). In Mexico City, for example, blood lead levels in residents have been found to be above those recommended by the WHO, and significantly higher than levels recorded in cities where the use of low-lead or lead-free petrol is more prevalent. Currently, over a quarter of the newborn babies in Mexico City may have blood lead levels high enough to impair neurological function and motor-physical development (Hardoy, Mitlin and Satterthwaite 1992).

4.8 NOISE

Although not listed as a major atmospheric pollutant in Table 4.1, noise can be regarded as an atmospheric pollutant since noise depends upon the ability of air to transmit sound waves. Moreover, noise pollution is an increasing feature of urban life and has received growing research attention in recent years. While the more acute biological effects of noise on humans may still be confined to some working environments and leisure pursuits (e.g. those involving loud music), it is increasingly being recognised as a serious threat to human welfare, especially in urban areas, through irritation and stress.

The major anthropogenic sources of noise pollution are road traffic, general neighbourhood noise, and aircrafts. Other significant noise sources include industrial activity, construction work, railway traffic, and leisure activities. In the 1970s it was estimated that some 100 million people living in the urban areas of OECD countries were exposed, in the course of 24 hours, to noise levels in excess of 65 dBA ('equivalent sound level' in decibels, A-weighted) (OECD 1980). An exterior noise of 55 dBA is generally considered an acceptable limit, with penetration to building interiors generally reducing this to 10–15 dBA (Nicholas 1982). Currently, it is estimated that some 130 million people in OECD countries are exposed daily to noise levels over 65 dBA, with traffic noise affecting approximately 110 million (OECD 1989, OECD 1990). The social cost of damage caused by transport noise in western Germany was recently estimated at nearly 2% of GDP (OECD 1991). Studies conducted in some cities in developing countries also point to significant noise pollution. In Bangkok, for example, noise levels exceed 70 dBA in many parts of the city because of noise from buses, trucks and motor-cycles. Moreover, in many countries major airports are located in the middle of densely populated areas, causing noise problems (e.g. Mexico City, Lima, Bogota and Buenos Aires) (Hardoy and Satterthwaite 1989).

Noise pollution can have a variety of effects on human health and welfare. Research is beginning to demonstrate that far from having transient effects, some forms of noise, particularly regular exposure to sudden, loud noises and noise which results in sleep disturbance, may cause long-term, and even permanent, physiological changes. These include constriction of blood vessels and high blood pressure, which may contribute to heart disease and circulatory disorders (OECD 1991). Long-term exposure to noise in the range 75–80 dBA may result in the permanent impairment of hearing ability. The stress engendered by excessive noise can also manifest itself in terms of psychological effects, such as increased general 'annoyance' and the fuelling of personal grievance.

4.9 GLOBAL AIR POLLUTION ISSUES

Whilst it has long been acknowledged that urban air pollution can have profound effects on the environment at local and regional scales, for the first time in human history air pollution may now be capable of destabilising the global environment. The depletion of the stratospheric ozone layer and global warming (the so-called enhanced 'greenhouse effect') are perceived by many to be the most important contemporary threats to the sustainability of natural processes at the global scale. A huge, international scientific and political effort is now underway in anticipation of profound impacts on human populations around the world from these distinguishable, but related phenomena. In contributing to global sustainability, cities will have a crucial role to play in the minimisation of activities contributing to ozone depletion and global warming. For these reasons, the causes and potential effects of global warming and ozone depletion are considered below.

4.9.1 Ozone depletion

Whilst high concentrations of ozone in the troposphere (lower atmosphere) may cause many adverse environmental effects, ozone in the stratosphere (upper atmosphere) plays a crucial role in regulating the amount of solar ultraviolet radiation received at the Earth's surface. Ozone occurs naturally throughout the stratosphere, although it is most concentrated in a layer at the base of the stratosphere some 20–25km above the Earth's surface. It is formed when oxygen gas reacts with ultraviolet light to give a molecule of three oxygen atoms. Ozone is also continually being broken down naturally in the stratosphere, so that its concentration remains roughly constant under natural conditions. However, in recent years this natural breakdown rate has been accelerated by certain pollutants which, when carried up into the stratosphere, have been implicated in the creation of ozone 'holes' in the stratosphere. The most widely noted ozone hole has been identified as occurring over the Antarctic, with severe depletion also occurring in winter in middle and high latitude areas in the northern hemisphere. At the moment, these holes are temporary and only occur at certain times of the year, principally during winter and spring. However, ozone layer depletion appears to have accelerated since the 1960s, and the frequency, duration and scale of ozone holes appears to be increasing (Tolba and El-Kholy 1992). Current predictions are that the stratospheric ozone layer will be eroded by 10% over the next 50–75 years.

The ozone layer provides a natural barrier to a large proportion of the ultraviolet radiation from the sun which is received by the Earth's atmosphere. Any significant increase in the amount of ultraviolet radiation received at the Earth's surface due to ozone depletion could have severe impacts on human health and the functioning of ecosystems, and may also contribute to climate change. The main ozone depleters are chlorine and bromine atoms, released by the breakdown in the strato-sphere of a variety of relatively long-lived compounds of anthropogenic origin. Research interest has focused on halocarbons, including various chlorofluorocarbons (CFCs) and halons, although, theoretically, any long-lived chlorine- or bromine-containing compound can break down ozone. Research interest has also turned towards the role of less well known compounds, such as the solvents carbon tetrachloride and methyl chloroform (see Table B.2), in ozone layer depletion. There is also an important natural element to ozone layer fluctuations, which is still little understood. Indeed, some scientists have prioritised natural factors such as volcanic activity and solar cycle changes over CFCs as major con-tributors to fluctuations in the ozone layer. It has been suggested that the eruption of Krakatoa in 1895 may have destroyed almost one-third of the ozone layer, but the Earth survived without major further catas-trophe (Allaby 1989).

Currently, the most important anthropogenic ozone depleters are the CFCs. CFCs were invented by the Du Pont chemical company in the 1930s and quickly became widely used for a number of purposes, including cooling fluids in refrigerators and air conditioning systems, propellants in aerosol cans, solvents for cleaning electronic materials and silicon chips, and as foam blowing agents used in hamburger packaging, insulation materials and general packaging. Halons are used in fire extinguishers and although their role in anthropogenic ozone depletion is minor, they are very long-lived in the atmosphere and are, therefore, significant.

The effects of ozone depletion are still little understood. It has been estimated however, that a 1% reduction in stratospheric ozone leads to a 1–2% increase in ultraviolet radiation, and that this in turn may yield a 3–4% increase in non-melanoma skin cancers in the global human population (Turner, Pearce and Bateman 1994). Depletion of the ozone layer may also increase eye damage and reduce immunity to infectious diseases (UNEP 1991). In addition, an increase in the penetration of ultraviolet light may trigger the creation of harmful levels of a number of substances in the troposphere, such as hydrogen peroxide, a range of acids and ozone. Work on a number of US cities suggests that for every 1% drop in stratospheric ozone, average tropospheric ozone concentra-tions may increase by between 0.7% and 0.9% (Adams and Rowe 1990). Natural or semi-natural ecosystems may also be affected; the yield of some commercial food crops may be reduced, as may fish stocks (Tolba and El-Kholy 1992; Turner, Pearce and Bateman 1994). In a preliminary

assessment of the annual economic costs of stratospheric ozone depletion on crop agriculture in the USA, Adams and Rowe (1990) calculated
that a 15% reduction in stratospheric ozone might result in losses of
between $1.3 and $2.5 billion a year. These costs were calculated based
upon both the direct effects of ultraviolet radiation on selected crop
species and using estimates of tropospheric ozone accumulation due to
stratospheric depletion.

Although poorly understood, the weight of scientific evidence impli-
cating the growing use of halocarbons until the mid-1980s in ozone
depletion has been sufficient to convince governments to cooperate
internationally to reduce their use dramatically. Moves are now in
motion to limit the manufacture of CFCs and halons and to recycle
them better. The Vienna Convention for the Protection of the Ozone
Layer was adopted in 1985, and in 1987 twenty-five countries adopted
the Montreal Protocol, which aimed to reduce the use of CFCs from
1986 levels by 50%, by 1998. The 1990 London Meeting of the Protocol
countries accelerated this process, with the 50% reduction target
brought forward to 1996, to be followed by a total phasing out of CFC,
halon and carbon tetrachloride consumption by the year 2000, and
methyl chloroform by 2005. Nonetheless, sufficient quantities of these
chemicals already exist in the stratosphere to affect the ozone layer for
the foreseeable future. The lesson is an important one: the environmental impacts of new technologies need to be scrutinised with much
greater vigour than ever before. The use of CFCs provides a particularly
good example from which we should learn. This is because they are not
only implicated in ozone depletion, but also in global warming, an issue
which is discussed below.

4.9.2 Global warming

The Earth is surrounded by a layer of natural 'greenhouse gases',
principally water vapour, carbon dioxide, methane and nitrous oxide.
Without them, the average surface temperature of the world might fall
from its current +15°C to -18°C (O'Riorden 1990). These gases trap
longwave radiation emitted by the Earth generating heat in the atmosphere, some of which is re-radiated back to the Earth's surface. Essentially, the greenhouse gases allow the transmission of solar radiation to
the Earth whilst retarding radiation back out. Any anthropogenic incre-
ment to these gases, or the emission of other chemicals such as halocarbons, carries the risk of enhanced global warming through an enhanced
'greenhouse effect'. The term 'greenhouse' is appropriate in the sense
of holding heat, though somewhat inappropriate in that much of the
heat of a garden greenhouse comes through shielding from cooling

winds (Milne 1988). This is rather ironic since one of the effects of global warming may be an increase in the ferocity and unpredictability of surface wind flows (Gribbin 1990).

Table 4.5 Greenhouse gas contributions to global warming

	Contribution to 'radiative forcing' in 1980s (%)	Contribution over 100 years (%)	Atmospheric lifetime (years)
Carbon dioxide	55	61	50–200
Methane	15	15	10
CFCs	24	9	65–130
Nitrous oxide	6	4	150
HCF 22	n.a.	0.4	n.a.
Other	n.a.	10.6	n.a.

Note: Contribution over 100 years takes into account the relative lifetimes of different gases and policies to reduce emissions.
n.a. = not available/known.
Sources: Adapted from: Houghton, Jenkins and Ephraums 1990, Pearce 1990, McMichael 1993.

It is important at this stage to stress that the scientific evidence on global warming and its true significance for the global environment is still equivocal, since we do not know whether current patterns of climate behaviour are within the existing parameters of natural variation. Nor can we be certain of the precise contributors to climatic change (Allaby 1989, O'Riorden 1990). Indeed, the 0.5°C average increase in global temperatures which has emerged over the past 90 years, though high, is in fact within the 'natural' climatic range of variation, also 0.5°C (Gribbin 1990). This said, the weight of scientific evidence is such that most scientists and politicians now accept that there is a high likelihood that human-induced global warming is taking place (O'Riorden 1989, 1990; Tolba and El-Kholy 1992).

If an enhanced greenhouse effect is occurring, then the primary causative agent is likely to be the carbon dioxide emitted during the combustion of fossil fuels (see Table 4.5). Atmospheric levels of carbon dioxide have increased by around 25% over the past 200 years, albeit at an accelerating rate; half of the increase is accounted for by the last forty years (Kelly and Karas 1990). Carbon dioxide emissions are hugely varied across the world, ranging in 1988 from 0.2 tonnes per capita in India to 2.7 tonnes in the UK, 3.8 tonnes in the USSR and 5.3 tonnes in the USA (Tolba and El-Kholy 1992). Measured in per capita terms, urban residents in the USA and Australia have carbon dioxide emission levels up to twenty-five times higher than in Dhaka, India (Hardoy, Mitlin and Satterthwaite 1992). This said, the fastest growth rates in production are now generally in developing countries, whose present growth rates could equal the carbon dioxide outputs of developed countries within 30 years (Warrick and Farmer 1990).

Methane is more difficult to account for in terms of its contribution to the enhanced greenhouse effect. It is produced as natural gas resulting from organic decomposition (e.g. in swamps and paddy fields) and as a result of bacterial action in the digestive tracts of termites and cattle. It can also enter the atmosphere from waste disposal sites. Methane concentration has been increasing at the rate of 1% per annum in the post-war years, and has more than doubled over the past 200 years (Kelly and Karas 1990). Nitrous oxide has been discussed previously, and is thought to have contributed only 6% to global warming during the 1980s, although it generally has a very long atmospheric residence time. Further contributions to global warming come from modern industrial chemicals released into the atmosphere which also absorb longwave radiation, most notably chlorofluorocarbons (CFCs). CFCs absorb longwave radiation approximately 1000 times more effectively than carbon dioxide, so that only relatively small amounts can have detrimental effects in terms of global warming (Kelly and Karas 1990). The relative contributions of the different gases to the enhanced greenhouse effect will change over time, according to different atmospheric lifetimes, different heat absorptive capacities and the anticipated impacts of global protocols to reduce emissions of CFCs in particular (see Table 4.5).

The effects of global warming are difficult to predict accurately because of the number of cumulative, interactive, and sometimes countervailing impacts involved, compounded by thermal lags built into the Earth–atmosphere system by the oceans (Warrick and Farmer 1990). During this century global average air temperature has increased by between an estimated 0.3 to 1.0°C (Milne 1988, O'Riorden 1990). The consequences of future changes of this magnitude could be immense, but also hugely variable between countries. For instance, an average global rise of 3°C might readily see winter temperature increases in the polar regions of 7–10°C (Simmons 1989). In the UK by 2030, mean winter temperatures might rise by 1.5–2.1°C, precipitation could increase by 5%, and the chances of hot summers would increase considerably, together with seasonal droughts (Warrick and Barrow 1991). In tropical countries, monsoon timing might change and intensities increase (Warrick and Farmer 1990). Increases in temperatures in these areas may also increase the spread of vector-borne diseases, raise health problems related to heat exhaustion, and where high humidity prevails, add to skin disorders (McMichael 1993).

Early estimates of dramatic sea level rises resulting from the melting of ice sheets and the thermal expansion of the oceans have recently been revised downwards. The Intergovernmental Panel on Climate Change (IPCC) now predicts an average 65 cm sea level rise by the end of the next century. A rise of one metre, the IPCC's top estimate, would none the less involve the flooding of considerable lowland areas. In Bangladesh, for example, this would displace 15–35% of the country's population (McMichael 1993), with problems exacerbated by the increased likelihood of temporary flooding and coastal erosion. Watertables would become more vulnerable to invasion by seawater, threatening drinking supplies (see Chapter Five).

Global warming has also been predicted to bring with it greater, more extreme climatic fluctuations, plus changes to existing wind and precipitation patterns and ocean currents. For some areas, there may be a rapid extension of desertification, with higher temperatures leading to greater evaporation, lower river flows and reduced lake levels. Bushfires might also increase in dry countries. These types of adverse impact are particularly anticipated in Mediterranean countries. In areas subject to tropical cyclones, warmer seas may increase their likelihood, affecting impoverished low-lying, coastal communities in particular (McMichael 1993).

4.10 CONCLUSIONS

The nature of urban air pollution varies enormously between cities, and for particular cities the key 'ingredients' of air pollution have changed over time, reflecting changing sources and urban activities. In many developed countries, air pollution from stationary sources, such as industrial chimneys, power stations and domestic solid fuel fires, has declined, as problems associated with traditional pollutants have (to some extent) been addressed through regulatory controls and technological advances. However, these gains need to be set against a background of increasing concentrations of other pollutants, perhaps especially those associated with vehicular traffic. In 1987, transport sources accounted for 70% of pollution in Moscow, 48% in Warsaw, 22% in Krakow, and 80% in Mexico City (ZumBrunnen 1990, Peterson 1993).

Although we are a very long way from a full understanding of the local, regional and global effects of air pollution, a number of things are clear. Air pollution kills and damages human beings, other organisms and even whole ecosystems. It also degrades the built environment. In short, urban air pollution imposes unsustainable costs on both urban and rural environments. Ultimately, it may also cause irreversible changes to the functioning of the global environment with, as yet, only partially glimpsed consequences for future generations. There is a growing conviction among scientists, environmentalists decision-makers and the general public that the potential risks associated with air pollution are not worth taking, and that concerted action must be taken now to lessen or prevent adverse impacts in the future.

FURTHER READING

A very comprehensive treatment of the nature and impacts of pollution is provided in *Pollution: Causes, Effects and Control* edited by Harrison (1990). With reference to air pollution, the chapters by Harrison, and Colbeck and Farman are particularly useful, covering the major air pollutants and the issue of stratospheric ozone depletion in detail. Allaby's (1989) *Green Facts: The Greenhouse Effect and Other Key Issues* provides a highly accessible review of the global warming debate. The *State of the Environment* report (OECD 1991) usefully summarises air pollution trends in a very succinct fashion.

KEY THEMES

- Interrelationships between urban form, climate modification and air pollution impacts
- Urban activities as major sources of air pollution
- Diversity of air pollutants and their impacts
- Secondary reactions in the atmosphere and synergistic action between pollutants
- Transboundary nature of air pollution (urban/rural; transnational; global)
- Changing sources and trends of air pollution

DISCUSSION POINTS

- Referring back to Chapter One, prepare a list of the ways in which urban-generated air pollution works against the requirements of sustainable urban development.
- For some air pollutants, such as ozone in the lower atmosphere, there are specific air quality standards. These are

frequently based on the levels at which some impairment to human health can be detected for that particular substance. Given your knowledge of urban air pollution and the requirements of sustainable urban development, discuss the limitations inherent in such an approach.

- For a city with which you are familiar, try to find out which air pollutants are monitored on a regular basis. How frequently are they monitored? Who carries out the monitoring work? How easy is it to access the information? Evaluate the scope and relevance of the monitoring programme.

- Adopt the role of someone who has been given the task of reducing general air pollution levels in the city with which you are most familiar. You are to set up a local action committee to tackle the problem. Who do you feel should be on the committee, and why?

- Outline the 'pros' and 'cons' of the modern attachment to the private car. Do you detect any moral dilemas which need to be addressed and, if so, how might these be resolved?

CHAPTER FIVE

Fresh Water Resources and Water Pollution

5.1 INTRODUCTION

Water pollution, the main theme of this chapter, is inextricably linked to issues of water demand and the working of natural ecosytems. Fresh water is required to supply the needs of agriculture, industry and domestic users. It is also required as a means of disposing of, and transporting, wastes from these users. If fresh waters become polluted, then their use for supply purposes becomes limited, unless treated. Moreover, urbanisation changes the way in which fresh water is stored and transported at or near the ground surface. Such changes have important implications for urban water supply, waste-water disposal and water pollution. Therefore, a full appreciation of urban water pollution requires some understanding of the related issues of water demand and urban hydrology.

5.2 FRESH WATER RESOURCES, URBAN DEMAND AND URBAN HYDROLOGY

The Earth contains some 1400 million km^3 of water, over 97% of which is contained in the oceans. Of the fresh water remainder, some 2% is locked up in the polar ice caps, icebergs and glaciers. Some 0.6% is stored beneath the ground surface as groundwater (below water tables) and soil moisture storage (above water tables). Only 0.02% of total planetary water is stored at the surface in the form of streams, rivers and lakes (McDonald and Kay 1988). Human needs for fresh water are almost exclusively met by the groundwater and surface stores. It has been estimated that the global capability for the stable supply of fresh water for human use is approximately 9000 km^3 annually (Simpson 1990). At a global scale this should be more than enough to meet human needs into the foreseeable future, given that current global consumption is less than 4000 km^3 annually (Golubev 1993). However, water supplies are unevenly distributed, poorly managed, wasted, inappropriately consumed and subject to increasing demands from population growth, agriculture and industry. Every human being needs an average of 1 litre of water a day to stay alive (assuming an adequate diet), and it takes some 300 tonnes of water to grow an adequate supply of food for one person in a year. Some examples of industrial water requirements include 100 litres for 1 kg of paper, 4500 litres for 1 tonne of cement, 4.3 tonnes for 1 tonne of steel, and 50 tonnes for 1 tonne of leather (Clarke 1991).

Not only is the increasing world population imposing greater stress on water supplies, but global average per capita water consumption is also increasing. Between 1940 and the present day, global average per capita water use has increased from below 400 m^3 per annum to at least 800 m^3 per annum. Per capita water use varies greatly in different countries. The USA, for example, is the world's largest water user with per capita consumption at nearly 2000 m^3 per annum. The equivalent figure in Switzerland is 150 m^3 per annum (OECD 1991). Globally, the urban population accounts for just 10% of total water withdrawals, but this is the most expensive form of demand, given the need for complex supply and maintenance systems (Golubev 1993). Increasing per capita consumption is related to a number of factors including growing urban and industrial activity and demand, and the increasing use of water-consuming domestic appliances, such as washing machines and dishwashers, as a result of higher living standards. In the UK recent decades have seen a considerable growth in domestic water consumption during a time of almost stable population, suggesting profligate use (McDonald and Kay 1988). Recent figures for England and Wales add weight to this view. A family of two adults and two children consumes approximately 500 litres a day, on average. This rate of consumption is understandable when one considers that (on average) each toilet flush requires 10 litres, a shower takes 30 litres, a bath takes 80 litres, a dishwasher cycle takes 50 litres and a washing machine cycle requires some 100 litres (Hamer 1992). In dry parts of the USA and Australia, the watering of lawns and gardens can account for up to 80% of daily household water use (Miller 1991). Frequently, it is high quality, potable water which is used for watering gardens and washing cars.

High consumption is frequently compounded by the wastage of water, with urban leakages absorbing up to 50% of water in urban distribution systems (Golubev 1993). In the UK, approximately 30% of water supplies are lost from the supply system through pipe leakages (Simpson 1990), while in the USA leakages waste 20–35% of the water withdrawn from public supplies (Miller 1991). In addition, the use of surface waters for waste disposal should not be forgotten. It has been estimated that worldwide every year some 450 km^3 of waste-water flows into streams and rivers from industry, coolant water from electricity generation and domestic sewage, and that a further 600 km^3 is required to dilute and transport this water before it can be used again. By the year 2000, the equivalent of the entire global river flow might be needed for waste transport and dilution (Clarke 1991). Clearly, then, the issue of water quality cannot be divorced from concerns over water supply availability. This has recently been recognised in Australia, where urban domestic and industrial consumers are using an increasing share of available water resources, and, at the same time, degrading these re-sources with their wastes. According to Cairnes (1993), unless the twin problems of water scarcity and pollution are tackled urgently, the cost of water will become an overriding constraint on national economic growth.

Such problems have led a number of commentators and environ-mental institutions to predict an impending global water crisis by the early part of the next century. This crisis may even affect the so-called water-rich countries because economic and industrial development cannot proceed without adequate water supplies. Such may be the case for the western and northern regions of Canada, for example (Kierans 1980). The potential for urban/industrial development may be strictly limited in parts of a number of countries, including Israel, Cyprus, Malta, Poland, Romania, the Ukraine, Bulgaria, Greece, Hungary, western USA, Australia, northern China, Luxembourg and Turkey. In addition, a number of regions in the Third World, including northern Africa and parts of India, are already facing water shortages and these are likely to intensify throughout the 1990s as population growth proceeds (Clarke 1991, Miller 1991). The growing proportion of city dwellers in developing countries will further add to the pressures on water resources because of the associated industrial development and the generally higher proportion of dwelling taps in urban areas (McDon-ald and Kay 1988). One recent estimate suggests that only 25% of the 1.5 billion urban residents in developing countries have adequate access to a clean drinking water supply (Cairnes 1993). If this problem is tackled, as it should be, then urban pressures on water resources will surely increase further. As Homewood (1991) points out with reference to Brazil, it is the massive migration of people from countryside to cities (some 30–40 million people in recent decades in Brazil) which is a much more significant contributor to water resource pressures than the coun-try's total population growth.

If we reduce the scale and consider water resources at the regional level, then the demands of urban areas become clearer. The task of supplying cities with wholesome fresh water requires major engineering works, often with profound environmental consequences. Many cities import water from a considerable distance and this often involves the construction of large reservoirs (with the attendant flooding of large areas of countryside), aqueducts, pipelines, smaller storage reservoirs, groundwater pumping stations, and the re-routing or alteration of existing water-courses to facilitate water supply. New York, for example, acquires only 5% of its water locally, with the remainder coming from the Croton, Catskill and Delaware reservoir systems as far as 200 km away. The cities of San Francisco, Oakland and Los Angeles depend on water transported by aqueducts from the Sierra Nevada and even the Colorado River hundreds of kilometres distant (Nicholas 1982). A substantial proportion of the water supply for Dakar in Senegal now has to be brought from the Lac de Guiers, some 200 km away, following the overuse and pollution of local groundwater supplies (Hardoy, Mitlin and Satterthwaite 1992).

In the south-east of England, the statutory water company (Thames Water) is currently planning to construct a new £300 million reservoir in the countryside to the south of the city of Oxford (Tickell 1991). This controversial proposal is a response to the water company's anticipation of rising per capita consumption combined with thousands of new urban domestic supply connections, especially in the Upper Thames region in the town of Swindon. Swindon is already facing severe water shortage and at the time of the development of the county structure plan, Thames Water objected to the plan because it sanctioned rapid growth in Swindon. Frequently, development plans pay very little (if any) attention to water resource issues. Another controversial dam and reservoir proposal is currently being considered to accommodate the projected water demand of the city of Melbourne in Victoria, Australia (Buckley, Buxton and McKenzie 1991). In Victoria, there are growing tensions between the water demands of Melbourne and the use of water for crop irrigation. The nature of urban development can also be an important consideration. Unwin and Searle (1991), for example, argue that the growth of low-density suburban housing around many of Australia's cities has increased water consumption through the watering of large gardens. This is backed up by other evidence which suggests that high-density urban residential communities may use only 65% of the water consumed by low-density housing areas (Spiller 1993b).

Potentially, one way to overcome the apparent need for an increased stable water supply to many cities which avoids the expense, land loss and ecological consequences of dam construction, might be to make much greater use of groundwater for urban and other forms of supply, where possible (World Resources Institute 1986). Extensive use is already made of groundwater. Often, nearby groundwater is easier to utilise than distant surface water supplies, and it is frequently cleaner than surface waters. Approximately 20% of total water withdrawal in OECD countries, for example, is from groundwater sources (OECD 1991). In the countries of the former Soviet Union, 60% of towns are supplied exclusively from groundwater, 25% have mixed surface and groundwater supplies and only 15% rely exclusively on surface waters (Clarke 1991). Tucson in Arizona is the largest city in the USA to rely on groundwater for virtually its entire supply, pumping some 370 million m^3 of water from underground every year (Charles 1991). While the potential for the much greater utilisation of groundwater does exist, this is not without its problems. Many groundwater aquifers have very long resumption times. The time taken for an aquifer to replenish itself may run into thousands or even millions of years. The utilisation of these sources would represent a form of mining rather than the sustainable tapping of a renewable resource (McDonald and Kay 1988).

Currently, about a quarter of the groundwater withdrawn in the USA is not being replenished (Miller 1991). In the aquifer which supplies the city of Tucson in Arizona, the natural regeneration rate is only half the rate at which water is being pumped out, and the water table has fallen by an average of 1m per annum for the past 50 years (Charles 1991). The city of Bangkok provides another example of the use of mined groundwater for supply (Clarke 1991). Furthermore, there are some well known problems associated with the lowering of water tables following the pumped abstraction of groundwater. These include land subsidence, increasing pumping costs as the resource diminishes, and the incursion of saline or polluted waters into the aquifer.

Groundwater subsidence was first noted in Mexico City in the 1850s. A considerable number of cities are now affected by subsidence predominantly resulting from groundwater extraction, including Houston, Beijing and Osaka (Table 5.1, World Resources Institute 1986, OECD 1991). In the Beijing area of China, so much groundwater has been pumped out in recent years that the water table fell by 4m in just one year (Clarke 1991). Land surface subsidence often leads to costly remedial engineering work and damages buildings, roads, railway lines and pipelines. The removal of water from an aquifer may also allow adjacent water, which may be saline or polluted, to intrude, thereby contaminating the supply. Salt water intrusion threatens to contaminate the drinking water of many towns and cities along the Atlantic and Gulf coasts of the USA, and in coastal areas of Israel, Syria and the Arabian Gulf states (Miller 1991). In Jakarta, Indonesia, many houses, shops and other businesses can no longer use groundwater supplies for drinking purposes because of saline intrusion. Also, because streams and rivers depend on groundwater input to sustain flow during dry spells, the lowering of water tables may cause these surface channels to suffer reduced flows, or even disappear altogether. Tickell (1991) reports the severely reduced flows of many rivers in the south-east of England as a result of several years of drought, exacerbated by the abstraction of groundwater to serve the (often still growing) towns and cities of the region and their associated industries. Some forty rivers in the region have been identified as being at risk as urban demand increases (Hamer 1992).

Table 5.1 Examples of land subsidence in cities due to groundwater extraction

Locality	Maximum subsidence (m)	Area affected (km^2)
Tokyo	4.60	2400
Venice	0.14	400
London	0.35	450
Mexico City	8.70	225

Source: Simmons 1989

Such pressures on water resources are leading to increasing tension between different users. This is not new. The Mesopotamian cities of Lagash and Umma were in conflict over access to fresh water supplies some 6500 years ago (Clarke 1991). However, the scale of the problem is much greater nowadays. The conflict over water supplies currently has an international dimension, with disputes occurring between the USA and Mexico, Jordan and Israel, and Iraq and Turkey, for example (UNEP 1991, Tolba and El-Kholy 1992). On a regional scale, it is the competing demands of urban areas and crop irrigation which frequently appear to be the most problematical. Usually, the outcome appears to be that urban demand takes precedence over other users. Miller (1991) suggests that this is the case in China, where water shortages are expected in 450 of the country's 644 cities by the turn of the century. In the west, south-west and mid-west of the USA, there are also many urban centres where water shortages are projected by the end of the century.

Recent events in the Avra Valley, Arizona, illustrate the growing concern of urban authorities to secure future water supplies (Charles 1991). The city of Tucson lies close to the Avra Valley and has a growing demand for groundwater. The population of Tucson is approximately 600,000 and each resident consumes an average of 625 litres of water

Box 5.1 A Summary of the Effects of Catchment Urbanisation on Local Hydrological Processes

Urban development is frequently associated with the replacement of natural or semi-natural soil and vegetation surfaces with human-made, impermeable surfaces (e.g. concrete, brick, tarmac and various roofing materials), and the rapid routing of urban rainwater along gutters, drains and sewers into a nearby water-course. Typically, these activities reduce evapotranspiration losses from the catchment area, increasing its water-yield potential. In many long established cities, surface rainwater is routed into the domestic sewer network, although in some countries (e.g. Australia) the sewer and storm water systems are separate. In consequence, the overland and sub-surface (in drains and/or sewers) movement of water is greatly accelerated, whilst the replenishment of groundwater is reduced. These changes result in a number of general and frequently observed alterations to river flow downstream of a partially urbanised catchment compared to an equivalent rural catchment:

- **A higher proportion of rainfall** becomes surface run-off so the average discharge (volume of flow per unit time) in the river is increased.

- There is **an accelerated catchment response** for a specific rainfall event, so that the lag time between rainfall and increased river discharge is reduced, as is the time to peak river discharge.

- There are **increased peak flood** discharges.

- **Discharges are decreased at times of low flow** reflecting the reduced contribution of groundwater.

- **Water quality is degraded** through effluent discharges and the pick-up of urban street pollutants via enhanced overland flow.

(Adapted from Shaw 1988)

per day. The statutory water company, Tucson Water, has purchased some 8900 ha of farmland (which now lies fallow) in the Avra Valley over the past 15 years. The water company has been prepared to offer farmers top land prices because land ownership gives rights to utilise groundwater supplies, and the water company is anxious to stop farmers pumping groundwater for crop irrigation. The cities of Phoenix and Los Angeles, where each citizen consumes an average of 984 litres per day and 1287 litres per day, respectively, have also resorted to the purchase of farmland to reduce competition for water supplies. Despite such measures, it is unclear if these cities have a secure future unless their residents cut water consumption considerably.

Urban pressures on fresh water supplies are already intense in many parts of the world. These appear set to increase where urban populations and industries continue to grow. The seemingly inexorable rise in per capita domestic consumption can only heighten the difficulties. The urban influence on water resources is not, however, restricted to considerations of water supply. Urbanisation also alters local hydrological processes of water storage and movement, summarised in Box 5.1.

Of these changes, the one which frequently causes greatest concern is the increased peak flood discharge of a river downstream of an urbanised catchment. This increases the risk of the river breaking its banks and flooding the surrounding area, which may be countryside or another urban area. A study in Texas, for example, found that urban development resulted in peak river discharges 100–300% higher than those in equivalent undeveloped areas (Ward and Robinson 1990). The study of a small catchment on the fringe of Exeter in England demonstrated that following the urbanisation of the area (to cover some 12% of the catchment), total river flow and peak discharge increased by between two and three times. Also, the lag time to peak flood in the river was reduced by half (Gregory 1974). A further increase in total river discharge may also occur if water is imported into an urban area from an adjacent catchment or from groundwater, and then released as effluent (e.g. from industry) into the nearest water-course (White, Mottershead and Harrison 1992).

Floodplain development is often favoured in many cities because of the locational advantages for transportation, water supply and waste disposal (Nicholas 1982). Many urban areas, therefore, may already be prone to flooding, and the risk will increase following the significant urbanisation of upstream catchment areas. The situation for many urban dwellers is bad enough without any increase in the risk of flooding. In many large cities in developing countries, the poorest people frequently settle in areas prone to flooding and landslides. In Mexico City, for example, some 1.5 million people live on the drained bed of Lake Texcoco which frequently floods or becomes a 'bog' following rainfall (Clarke 1991). The risk of flooding is heightened where upstream urban areas seek to dispose of surface water as quickly as possible, without considering downstream effects. It is not uncommon for various modifications to existing water-courses to be undertaken in order to facilitate rapid surface water drainage. These include water-course realignment (e.g. straightening) and the lining of channels with an impermeable material such as concrete (Shaw 1988). Floodplain areas within cities may be protected by the construction of dikes, levees and by the alteration of the existing river channel (e.g. the deepening of the channel by dredging). Urban areas may attempt to lessen their impact on downstream flow by building water storage basins, for example, which detain storm run-off before it moves downstream. Such basins, however, may take up valuable land and involve additional construction and maintenance costs (Ferguson 1987). Many of the changes outlined above involve deliberate alterations to the size, shape, texture and positioning of stream and river channels. These in turn change the nature of the flow in channels and the extent, range and quality of habitats available to aquatic organisms. For example, channel enlargement to provide increased flow capacity changes the physical dimensions of the channel ecosystem which may result in reduced water depth under low-flow conditions and a change in water velocity for a given discharge. Many modifications of channel shape, in profile, plan or cross-section, will reduce habitat and species diversity (see Haslam 1990).

Of the other hydrological changes which frequently follow urbanisation, the reduction in groundwater replenishment is ironic given the lengths that some urban authorities are going to in order to secure groundwater supplies (see previous section). Nevertheless, reduced groundwater replenishment is an important issue for urban areas. Groundwater recharge in Moscow, for example, was found to be 50% less than in another, rural, site in the Moscow River basin (Ward and Robinson 1990). This phenomenon provides another example of the way in which water quantity and water quality considerations are interlinked. Reduced river flows between storms, brought about by decreased groundwater recharge, effectively reduce the pollution dilution potential of the river, thus leading to poorer river water quality at certain times. Even during periods of high river flow when pollution dilution potential is greatest, water quality may still be poor. One reason for this may be the use of combined storm water and sewage systems in many urban areas. The provision of overflows in the sewage system to cater for surface water run-off during storms often permits mixed sewage and storm-water to bypass sewage treatment works and enter nearby streams and rivers untreated. This can create severe pollution problems.

5.3 GENERAL WATER POLLUTION

Water pollution can adversely affect the functioning of aquatic ecosystems, human health, agriculture, industry, transport, mineral exploitation and the aesthetic and amenity value of water resources. Pollution of fresh waters and the marine environment is a major local and regional problem around the world, especially near large urban/industrial centres. Where pollution is severe, the complete loss of an economically valuable biological resource may result. In the estuary of the River Tees in northern England, for example, rapid industrial development and dramatic increases in the human population over two or three decades eliminated the fishery there by 1937 (Abel 1989). Similarly, the Huangpu River which flows through the city of Shanghai in China is treated as an open sewer for domestic and industrial waste, and has been essentially devoid of aquatic life since 1980 (McMichael 1993). Lake Maryut in Egypt receives much of the domestic and industrial wastes from the nearby city of Alexandria. This pollution has resulted in an 80% decline in fish populations over the last decade (Hardoy, Mitlin and Satterthwaite 1992).

Water pollution comes in a huge variety of forms. Lack of space prevents all of these being discussed here in any great detail, and the following sections concentrate on a number of pollutants which have a significant urban origin and which are currently giving cause for concern. The major classes of water pollution and their sources and effects are given in Table 5.2. No attempt is made below to separate pollutants of the fresh water and marine environments. While some forms of water pollution are more prevalent in one or other of these aquatic environments, all of the pollutants listed in Table 5.2 can occur in both. Furthermore, some water environments, such as estuaries, do not fall neatly into either category, and gravity ensures that much of the pollution released into rivers will end up in the marine environment in any case.

As with air pollution, the impacts of water pollution arise both through the actions of individual pollutants, and through the effects of pollutants in combination. Multiple point sources of pollution along a river (e.g. a series of effluent discharge pipes) can create cumulative problems, often resulting in a rich mix of different pollutants, sometimes reacting to give secondary pollutants. General river water pollution is a major problem in most Chinese cities, for example; unsurprising in a country where 90% of urban waste-water is returned untreated (Smil 1984). If present at all, sewers in Chinese cities are inadequate and poorly maintained. Many rivers running through urban areas contain multiple industrial pollutants including oil products, phenolic compounds, cyanide, arsenic, heavy metals (lead, chromium, cadmium and mercury), chlorinated hydrocarbons, nitrates and sulphates. It is often extremely difficult to determine the full range of substances and their precise quantities, in an effluent discharge or stretch of polluted river. General urban run-off, for example, may contain a wide range of

Table 5.2 Major classes of water pollution

Class of pollutants	Major sources	Effects
Organic wastes	Human domestic sewage; animal and plant wastes; industrial wastes (e.g. pulp and paper waste, waste from food processing plants and oil refineries).	Main effects associated with depletion of dissolved oxygen in the water by excessive growth of oxygen-consuming bacterial populations. Death of fish and other higher aquatic organisms; destruction of plant life; poisoning of livestock; water may develop a foul smell.
Pathogenic micro-organisms	Human sewage and animal wastes.	Outbreaks of water-borne diseases such as hepatitis, poliomyelitis, typhoid, dysentery and cholera; infected livestock.
Radioactivity	Nuclear power generation; processsing of nuclear fuels; uranium mining; nuclear weapons testing.	Can cause cancer and genetic defects.
Heat	Cooling water from industrial and power generating installations.	Decreases solubility of oxygen in water; can kill some fish; increases susceptibility of some aquatic organisms to parasites, disease and chemical toxins; disrupts and changes composition of aquatic ecosystems.
Inorganic chemicals and minerals: a. Plant nutrients (nitrates & phosphates) and ammonia	Agricultural run-off; sewage and animal wastes; mining; food processing industries; fertiliser plants; phosphates in detergents.	May cause an excessive enrichment of water (accelerated eutrophication) leading to algal blooms (which can produce toxins) and a reduction in dissolved oxygen levels. Fish kills and disruption of aquatic ecosystems. High nitrate concentrations in drinking water can be dangerous to infants and have been linked to stomach cancer.

b. Metals	Vehicle exhausts; some pesticides; mining; smelting; large range of industrial activities.	Can be very persistent in the environment and accumulate in the tissues of organisms along food chains (bioaccumulative); toxic to many organisms, including humans.
c. Acids and alkalis	Wide range of industrial activities; mine drainage (acids); acid deposition.	Toxic to many organisms; disruption of aquatic ecosystems; acids may increase the solubility of some potentially harmful minerals.
d. Salts	Industrial wastes; mining; urban storm run-off.	Can kill freshwater organisms; can make water unfit for human consumption, irrigation and many industrial uses.
e. Sediments	Agricultural run-off; urban storm run-off; dredging activity; mining; forestry; construction activities.	Disrupts aquatic ecosystems; reduces shellfish and fish populations; reduces ability of water to assimilate oxygen demanding wastes; fills in water bodies.
Organic chemicals	This grouping includes a very wide range of chemical substances with very varying effects. Sub-groupings in this class could include: oil, detergents, petrochemicals (e.g. plastics and plastic intermediates and by-products); chlorine compounds and industrial bleaching agents; pesticides and herbicides (e.g. the toxic and persistent organochlorine compounds and their residues; the toxic, but less persistent, organophosphorus compounds and PCBs); solvents; phenols etc.	

Sources: Holdgate 1979; Fish 1986; Miller 1988

substances including rubber, bitumen and other tyre derivatives; metals; petrochemicals and other hydrocarbons from exhaust fumes; petrol and oil; glass; aggregate; tarmac derivatives and particles; derivatives from shoes; de-icing salt in winter; and spills from any type of transported load (Haslam 1990). To this list can be added animal wastes. It has been estimated that in New York City, for example, some 0.5 million dogs deposit up to 20,000 tonnes of faeces and up to 3.8 million litres of urine onto the streets each year, to be transported by urban run-off into the sewer system (Goudie 1990). As a brief aside, it is also worth noting that (as with urban climate) different patterns of urban development may have different environmental implications. The Council on Environmental Quality in the USA found that high-density urban residential communities generated 42% less water pollution (from surface run-off) than low density communities (CEQ 1975).

As we learn more about the sources and effects of pollution, so our appreciation of potentially dangerous urban/industrial activities grows. In the UK in recent years, for example, one disturbing aspect of the country's industrial legacy has received considerable attention. Approximately 65% of derelict land in the UK may be potentially contaminated because of past activities (Hawkins 1992). Perhaps the biggest fear surrounding such land contamination, is the subsequent pollution of groundwater supplies by a 'cocktail' of potentially toxic substances, including chemicals, oil, petroleum and metals, which might migrate underground (Crowcroft 1992). We have seen above how precious groundwater can be for many urban areas, and Odum (1989) argues that groundwater contamination is a potential disaster because, once contaminated, it is difficult and perhaps impossible to cleanse completely. Already, several cities in the industrial heartlands of the USA can no longer use local groundwater for domestic supply because of contamination by a range of substances (Pye and Patrick 1983), and Simmons (1991) reports that as many as 7300 landfill sites for municipal and other wastes in western Europe may need immediate action to prevent leakage and subsequent pollution of groundwater.

Many of the world's urban/industrial centres are situated on coastal areas. These centres exert great pressures on the quality of the oceanic margins (estuaries, coasts, harbours, inland seas and salt marshes), and it is at the oceanic margins that the effects of multiple pollutants are often the most severe and potentially damaging. Coastal margins witness the coming together of different pollutant transport pathways, including river flows and urban effluent discharge points. Yet, coastal areas generally have a high natural biological productivity and are vital as breeding, hatching and feeding grounds for coastal and deep water marine species. Although the oceans can dilute, disperse and break down large quantities of waste, the sheer magnitude of discharges around coasts can overload natural purifying processes. The scale of general water pollution impacts, then, is perhaps best appreciated by considering some of the problems encountered in marine areas adjacent to heavily urbanized regions of the world. Some of these issues are summarised in Box 5.2, for selected marine areas. Many of the individual pollutants mentioned as problematical in Box 5.2 are discussed in the following sections.

Box 5.2 A Summary of the Pollution Pressures and Issues Facing Selected Marine Areas

The shoreline of the Seto Sea, along the southern edge of Japan, contains a number of major cities, including Osaka and Hiroshima, and has been under very heavy pressure from industrial, tourist and urban development over the last 35 years. Industrial activity, for example, increased by 34% between 1975 and 1981. The result of all this development has been a dramatic decline in the quality of the natural environment of the area. Only 41% of the coastline now remains in its natural state, while excessive inflows of organic pollution and nutrients (particularly nitrates and phosphates) have contributed to the frequent and extensive occurrence of 'red tides' caused by the growth of certain algae. To protect fish stocks from these algal blooms, cultivated fish have had to be removed from sea areas most prone to the red tides.

The Baltic Sea is under heavy stress from its surrounding countries, being bordered by seven industrialised nations, containing around 70 million people. The Baltic is semi-enclosed and the inflow of clean, well-oxygenated water is, therefore, restricted. This makes it particularly prone to the impacts of pollution. The Baltic receives urban and other industrial pollution from the Gulf of Finland, central Sweden and along the coasts of Poland, Germany and Denmark. Among the major pollution-related concerns identified in the Baltic are: a decrease in the dissolved oxygen content of deep water layers this century to almost zero, resulting in severe stress for, or the complete absence of, higher organisms; a dramatic drop in the reproductive rate of female grey seals, linked to contamination by PCBs; the virtual extinction of the white-tailed eagle; a high degree of contamination of fish in some areas by metals and organic compounds; and signs of accelerated eutrophication in areas of the Baltic affected by urbanisation.

The Mediterranean is a shallow, enclosed sea having an average depth of 1.5 km and taking over 70 years to completely renew its waters. These characteristics make it very vulnerable to the effects of multiple pollutants. It is surrounded by a permanent population of over 100 million people, although as the world's primary tourist area it attracts a further 100 million people during the summer season. Polluted discharges via some 170 refineries and chemical plants, agriculture, seventy rivers and numerous ships total approximately 1.5 million tonnes annually. To this can be added a largely untreated sewage load of 30–50 million tonnes per annum from 120 coastal towns and cities. Industrial pollution comes mainly from heavily urbanised areas in the north, including areas in and around Barcelona, Marseilles, Genoa and Athens. The combined effects of this degree of activity and pollution are severe and include sewage pollution of beaches, extensive contamination of marine life including fish for human consumption, destruction of wetland habitats and interference with the breeding grounds of endangered species including the Monk seal, Loggerhead turtle and Dalmation pelican. Eutrophication problems result in 'red tides' of algae in heavily nutrient-enriched areas found from Gibraltar to Alexandria and along the north African coastline. Identifiable health hazards and/or ecological damage now affect 25% of the Mediterranean coastline.

The New York Bight is a shallow marine area some 19 km off the New York/New Jersey coast near the mouth of the Hudson River. It is the most intensively used ocean dumping site for dredge spoils, industrial wastes and sewage sludge in the world. Some 8.6 million tonnes of waste are dumped into the area off the mouth of the Hudson River each year. The site has been used as a dumping site for over 60 years and, as a result, an area of some 105 km^2 of the sea bed is covered by a black sludge containing high levels of bacteria, long-lived viruses, toxic metals and organic compounds. Storms have caused some of this sludge to move landwards on occasion, contaminating Long Island and New Jersey beaches and shellfish beds. Disease outbreaks have occurred amongst people consuming raw shellfish (mostly clams and oysters) from contaminated areas.

(OECD 1985, Miller 1988, Abel 1989, Goudie 1990, Simpson 1990, OECD 1991)

5.4 ORGANIC WASTES

Animal and plant waste organic material in the aquatic environment is naturally broken down into inorganic nutrients by the action of microorganisms and other detritus feeders. Bacterial populations are the most prevalent of these decomposers. Under natural conditions, the limited supply of organic matter ensures that the populations of microbial decomposers are restrained and that the dissolved oxygen in the water required by these organisms to decompose the organic matter remains relatively stable through time. However, excess anthropogenic inputs of organic matter to an aquatic ecosystem can lead to an 'explosion' in the numbers of microbial decomposers, resulting in a decrease in the dissolved oxygen concentration of the water and bottom sediments around the source of the organic pollution. Oxygen depletion may be at its worst during summer months in rivers, when water flow is at a minimum, and water temperature is at a maximum. There is an inverse relationship between the amount of dissolved oxygen which water can hold and water temperature. Problems associated with dissolved oxygen depletion arising from excess organic matter can, therefore, be exacerbated by thermal pollution resulting from cooling water discharges from power stations and industrial units (Holdgate 1979, Table 5.2). Under severe organic pollution loads, the water and bottom sediments may become almost completely devoid of oxygen (anoxic conditions) and the water can appear and smell foul. The production of hydrogen sulphide as a by-product of anaerobic microbial metabolism is often responsible for the foul smell.

There are many substances which may result in an increased demand on the dissolved oxygen content of water in this way (known as *biological oxygen demand*). The most prevalent of these oxygen-demanding pollutants is human domestic sewage, but wastes from some industries (e.g. pulp and paper waste, and waste from food processing plants) may also cause severe problems (see Table 5.2). Sewage is a mixture of wastes from laundry, bathing, cooking, as well as human faeces and urine. Wherever human populations are dense and sewage undergoes little or no treatment before being discharged or dumped into fresh waters or the marine environment, oxygen depletion will occur. Cities, inevitably, are a major contributor to this problem. Ever since the link was first made between outbreaks of certain water-borne diseases, such as typhoid and cholera, and the sewage contamination of domestic water supplies, much effort has been invested in the supply of clean and wholesome water to urban residences. Generally speaking, considerably less attention has been paid to how the sewage from urban areas is disposed of. The tendency has been, and often still is, to treat water bodies as cheap and convenient conduits and disposal sites for domestic and industrial effluents from urban areas. In OECD countries only 60% of the population was served by waste treatment plants in 1989 (OECD 1991). Between 1981 and 1991 the number of people in cities globally without access to sanitation facilities grew by 81 million, whilst in many cities in developing countries little or no domestic waste is treated (Tolba and El-Kholy 1992). In many cities no attempt is made to separate industrial and domestic waste, these being discharged together into the sewer system. Fish (1986) argues that the major cause of water pollution, particularly of streams, estuaries and the inshore waters off many coastal towns, are the discharges of waste waters from urban areas.

Table 5.3 gives recent trends in water quality indicators, including dissolved oxygen concentration and biological oxygen demand (BOD), for a number of major rivers/estuaries which drain large, partially urbanised catchments. Up to a temperature of 10°C most waters in a natural state contain approximately 11–14 mg/l (milligrams per litre) of dissolved oxygen (Jeffries and Mills 1990). While the dissolved oxygen status of many major rivers and estuaries in developed countries has improved in recent years, owing mainly to the provision of greater sewage treatment capacity and tighter controls of industrial discharges, Table 5.3 shows that many of these waters still fail to achieve dissolved oxygen concentrations within the range expected under natural conditions. In some cases (e.g. the Seine and Po) the disparity is still marked. Similarly, while it is rare for unpolluted waters to exhibit a BOD of greater than about 1 mg/l, the rivers and estuaries in Table 5.3 generally show values above the natural background. This is not surprising, as even treated sewage typically shows a BOD of 3–50 mg/l. Raw, untreated sewage typically has a BOD of 200–800 mg/l. Studies involving several cities in the USA have shown that urban run-off has a BOD of 10–250 mg/l (Goudie 1990). Where urban areas are still growing quickly, increased sewage treatment capacity may be required merely to ensure no further deterioration in oxygen levels, let alone an improvement.

Table 5.3 Recent trends in selected water quality indicators at the mouths or downstream frontiers of eight major rivers/estuaries draining large watersheds in their countries

| | Indicator and Date | | | | | | | | | |
| | Dissolved oxygen (mg/l) | | | | | Biological oxygen demand (mg/l) | | | | |
Location	1970	1975	1980	1985	Latest	1970	1975	1980	1985	Latest
St. Lawrence, Canada	8.1	10.0	–	9.7	10.4	–	–	–	–	–
Mississippi, USA	8.4	8.5	8.3	8.6	8.7	2.4	2.2	1.7	1.4	1.4
Brisbane estuary, Australia	–	5.6	6.4	6.0	–	–	1.6	1.0	1.2	–
Seine, France	–	3.3	4.9	5.2	5.4	–	10.2	6.6	3.2	3.4
Rhône, France	7.5	7.7	8.7	8.6	9.2	9.2	9.2	7.8	5.0	5.3
Rhine, Germany	5.6	6.8	9.0	9.3	9.6	6.1	7.9	4.0	3.8	3.4
Po, Italy	8.3	–	7.7	8.6	8.5	–	7.3	6.1	5.0	7.7
Thames, UK	–	10.8	9.9	10.0	10.2	–	3.4	2.7	2.4	2.8

	Nitrate (mg/l)					Phosphate (mg/l)				
	1970	1975	1980	1985	Latest	1970	1975	1980	1985	Latest
St. Lawrence	193	230	160	160	200	18	10	24	18	19
Mississippi	–	980	1200	1230	137	–	190	230	140	210
Brisbane est.	–	340	850	1050	–	–	200	380	480	–
Seine	–	4181	5356	6170	6004	–	1446	760	1005	836
Rhône	881	904	1243	1605	1823	147	150	179	134	201
Rhine	1820	3020	3590	4200	3933	520	750	360	480	363
Po	946	1350	1630	2400	2467	–	231	280	260	300
Thames	–	6500	6890	7510	7073	–	1073	1160	1320	1430

	Lead (µg/l)					Cadmium (µg/l)				
	1970	1975	1980	1985	Latest	1970	1975	1980	1985	Latest
St. Lawrence	–	–	1.00	1.00	0.77	–	–	1.00	1.00	0.40
Mississippi	–	2.00	2.00	5.00	4.17	–	2.00	2.00	2.00	2.00
Brisbane est.	–	5.70	5.30	5.00	–	–	2.30	2.00	2.00	–
Seine	–	26.00	8.00	40.00	26.70	–	2.00	2.00	–	–
Rhône	–	30.00	29.00	–	–	–	10.00	5.00	–	–
Rhine	–	24.00	7.00	11.00	11.00	–	2.40	1.40	0.30	0.30
Po	–	0.40	0.55	–	–	–	0.16	0.05	0.30	0.28
Thames	–	–	10.00	9.00	7.33	–	–	1.04	0.79	0.61

	Chromium (µg/l)					Copper (µg/l)				
	1970	1975	1980	1985	Latest	1970	1975	1980	1985	Latest
St. Lawrence	–	–	–	1.00	1.00	–	0.01	1.50	1.30	1.30
Mississippi	–	7.80	10.00	2.00	2.27	–	4.00	6.30	5.60	5.67
Brisbane est.	–	–	20.00	20.00	–	–	9.70	5.60	5.00	–
Seine	–	12.00	13.00	20.00	20.00	–	52.00	11.00	30.00	23.30
Rhône	–	–	9.00	–	–	–	14.00	28.00	–	–
Rhine	–	40.00	22.30	10.00	9.97	–	24.00	19.90	13.00	10.60
Po	–	0.50	0.60	–	–	–	0.60	0.85	–	–
Thames	–	–	11.00	10.00	9.33	–	–	10.00	11.00	10.70

Note: Latest = the mean of the annual values for the last 3 years
available prior to 1989.
Differences between the rivers in terms of the number of sampling sites,
the measurement technique used in pollutant analysis, periods used in
the calculation of mean pollutant concentration etc., make the comparison of data between cities inappropriate.
Source: OECD 1989

Haslam (1990), for example, provides many examples of the devastating effects which sewage effluents can have on aquatic ecosystems, often associated with periods of rapid urbanisation with the consequent overloading of existing sewage treatment works. Even when sewage is treated, the concentrated solid waste (sludge) from the treatment process still remains to be disposed of, through landfill or dumping at sea, for example. The New York metropolitan area alone produces approximately 6.8 million litres of sewage waste-water per day, of which about 16% currently goes untreated before disposal in rivers (Goudie 1990). It is also worth noting that large discharges of even highly treated sewage effluent can markedly increase the turbidity of river and estuarine waters. This may reduce the degree of light penetration to the river or estuary bed and adversely affect the growth of rooted plants for several kilometres downstream of the discharge point (Jeffries and Mills 1990). The effects of oxygen depletion are normally restricted to a distance of several kilometres from the source of the organic wastes. Within this sphere of influence, however, the ecological impacts may be very marked. Although the overall biological productivity of the water ecosystem may not in fact show a decline as a result of organic pollution (thanks to the very high numbers of a few anaerobic or low-oxygen-tolerant microbial and invertebrate species), the ecosystem usually exhibits a marked decline in species diversity. This is especially true for higher vertebrate (e.g. fish) and invertebrate species, which are often very intolerant of low oxygen conditions (McLusky 1981). Fish kills are often one of the first signs of an oxygen depletion problem and many fish, such as salmon and trout, cannot survive in water with an oxygen concentration of less than 6 mg/l (Fish 1986). As a general rule, the full species complement characteristic of a healthy aquatic ecosystem requires an average dissolved oxygen concentration of 10 mg/l, or more. The considerable deterioration of aquatic ecosystems around the sewage outlets of many major cities indicates that dissolved oxygen levels are inadequate. Examples include Athens, Barcelona, Venice, Marseilles, New York, San Francisco and Sydney (OECD 1985a). According to Abel (1989), the northern Adriatic, Baltic and eastern North seas are in imminent danger from the sewage effluents being discharged from the inadequate treatment and disposal facilities of coastal towns and cities. In these areas, anoxic conditions prevail periodically in bottom sediments and the water column, with heavy losses of marine life, including economically important species. In addition, 'blooms' of toxic algae whose growth is encouraged by nutrient enrichment from sewage effluents are an increasingly frequent occurrence.

Similarly, concern has been expressed over depressed dissolved oxygen concentrations found adjacent to the world's largest resort city,

Virginia Beach in the USA. In this case sewage from the Chesapeake Bay area may be causing significant ecological impacts, posing a threat to the productive fisheries in the bay off Virginia Beach and reducing the aesthetic and recreational value of the area (Butt and Alden 1986). In developing countries, sewage (and industrial effluent) treatment facilities are often rarer and the tendency to use rivers as 'open sewers' is common. During the 1970s in Cairo, for example, the streets were regularly flooded with untreated sewage (Simmons 1991). In Nigeria, there is growing concern and awareness of the effects of rapid urbanisation on the sewage inputs to streams and rivers (Adeniji 1988). In India, only eight of the country's 3119 towns and cities have full sewerage and sewage treatment facilities, while on the River Ganges 114 urban centres, each with a population of 50,000 or more, discharge untreated sewage to the river (WCED 1987).

5.5 PATHOGENIC MICRO-ORGANISMS

Pollution resulting from the discharge of sewage into waters can, as we have seen above, adversely affect aquatic ecosystems, including commercial and recreational fishing activities. Human and animal sewage may also contain micro-organisms which are pathogenic (disease causing) in humans. Many diseases are water-borne and may be caused by bacteria (e.g. gastroenteritis, typhoid and cholera), viruses (e.g. poliomyelitis and hepatitis) and amoebas (e.g. amoebic dysentery and bilhardziosis) when water becomes contaminated through contact with human or animal faeces (see Table 5.2). Contaminated water also plays a central role in the transmission of many intestinal worms. Simpson (1990) argues that microbiologically impure water is the world's major cause of disease, and that untreated sewage is the world's most dangerous pollutant.

The health problems associated with the contamination of water supplies by pathogenic micro-organisms have their fullest expression in cities in developing countries, where many of the diseases listed above are endemic, owing to inadequate water supply, sewerage and sewage disposal infrastructure (WCED 1987). Throughout the world, some 1.5 billion people do not have a microbiologically safe supply of drinking water, and some 5 million people die each year of water-borne diseases. The number of people with access to a supply of clean water globally increased during the United Nations Drinking Water and Sanitation Decade (1981–1991), but given the increase in world population the proportion without access remained much the same (Tolba and El-Kholy 1992). In cities globally, the number of people without access to clean water increased during this decade by 31 million (McMichael 1993).

Most cities in Africa and many in Asia have no sewerage system at all and untreated household waste is discharged into open streams, rivers, canals and ditches. Where a sewerage system does exist, it is typically confined to richer residential, government and commercial areas (Hardoy and Satterthwaite 1989). Only 2% of the population of Bangkok is connected to a sewer system and approximately one-third of the population is forced to buy water from vendors, having no access to public water supplies (Sivaramakrishnan and Green 1986). The city of Jakarta has no piped sewerage system; septic tanks are used by about 25% of the city's population, and the rest use rudimentary pit latrines, cesspools and ditches along roadsides. Much of the population is forced to use heavily sewage-contaminated drainage canals for bathing and laundering, as less than a quarter of the population are served by piped water. Less than 60% of the urban population of Brazil has an adequate water supply or sewerage system (Homewood 1991). Generally, hundreds of millions of urban dwellers in Third World cities have no alternative but to use sewage-contaminated water, or at least water whose quality is doubtful.

The coliform group of bacteria is often used as an indicator of the sanitary purity of waters used for drinking, recreation and bathing. As a guide, water for drinking should contain no more than 10 coliform organisms per 100 ml. A coliform concentration of more than 3 million/100 ml has been reported in the canals of central Jakarta, and the incidence of various water-borne diseases increases downstream of those areas where sewage contamination is greatest. Downstream of Colombia's capital a concentration of 7.3 million/100 ml has been recorded (Clarke 1991). Along a 48 km stretch of the Yamuna River in India, a coliform concentration of 7500/100 ml has been noted above the city of New Delhi. After flowing through the city, however, and receiving an estimated 200 million litres of untreated sewage every day (to add to the 20 million litres or so of industrial effluents) the river carries a concentration of some 24 million/100 ml (World Resources Institute 1986).

The contamination of waters by pathogenic micro-organisms is not, however, a problem of developing countries alone. The discharge of untreated or only partially treated sewage from urban areas situated on the coast is giving cause for concern where coastal waters and beaches are used for bathing, water sports and general recreation. In many locations, sewage is discharged at the shoreline or via short outfall pipes of only 100 m or 200 m in length (Abel 1989). In 1987 in the UK, for example, 109 out of 360 coastal holiday resorts tested in England and Wales showed bacterial water quality adjacent to popular beaches below the standard required by the European Community, and a number of studies in the UK and elsewhere have demonstrated a link between gastrointestinal infection rates and the degree of exposure to sewage-contaminated bathing water (Simpson 1990). Recreational beaches near Toronto in Canada had to be closed during the summer between 1984 and 1986 because of unacceptably high coliform counts in the water as a result of sewage contamination (Clarke 1991). Rapid urbanisation along many of the coastal areas of South Africa has led to growing fears over the safety of bathers due to sewage contamination (Schirnding *et al.* 1993). It is also known that shellfish living close to sewage outlet pipes can retain micro-organisms which they capture from the water whilst feeding, posing a health risk to humans eating them.

5.6 INORGANIC CHEMICALS AND MINERALS

This section examines just three of the substances listed under this category in Table 5.2: sediments, metals and plant nutrients.

5.6.1 Suspended sediment

Surface run-off from urban areas is often loaded with suspended inorganic material ('city dust'), especially during storms and from areas undergoing some form of building or construction work. Data from cities in the USA indicate that urban run-off typically contains 250–300 mg/l of suspended sediment, roughly the same as the suspended solid content of raw domestic sewage (Goudie 1990). Much of this particulate load will eventually find its way into streams and rivers that drain urban areas, thereby increasing the turbidity of these waters. In addition, coastal cities with port facilities need to keep shipping access open and this entails the frequent dredging of coastal waters and estuaries. This also increases water turbidity and necessitates the removal of significant quantities of sediment from one area, and its dumping in another. Coastal construction work (e.g. harbours and sea defences) may also increase turbidity and change current and siltation patterns.

Increased turbidity reduces sunlight penetration and, therefore, the photosynthetic activity of aquatic plants. Severe turbidity or the dumping of dredge spoil may halt photosynthesis altogether, smother and kill aquatic animals and block the gills of fish and other animals (McLusky 1981, Abel 1989). Dredge spoil and urban dust may also be contaminated with toxic substances such as metals and organic chemicals, thereby compounding the ecological impacts. A number of studies have demonstrated increased rates of erosion from construction projects associated with urban development, leading to higher sediment concentrations in local streams and rivers. In Devon, southern England, for example, the suspended sediment concentration in streams draining construction sites were found to be between two and ten times greater than those draining undisturbed sites. Studies in Virginia, USA, observed erosion rates from construction areas some ten times greater than those observed from adjacent agricultural land and some 2000 times greater than those measured from nearby forest areas (Goudie 1989). In Montgomery County, Maryland, a study of soil erosion found that some 4500 tonnes of soil was eroded from an 8 ha site during the construction of 89 houses over a five year period (Nicholas 1982). The coastal waters of developing countries with rapid urban growth are now often visibly laden with silt as a result of soil erosion inland, often caused by deforestation to supply urban areas with wood.

Reductions in the abundance of fish and large bottom-dwelling invertebrates during – and for a short time after – the construction of roads and road bridges over streams and rivers have been well documented (e.g. Ogbeibu and Victor 1989). Longer-term changes in the community structure at, and downstream of, road construction sites have also been noted. Taylor and Roff (1986), for example, observed changes in the relative abundance of different species downstream of a road construction site in southern Ontario for up to six years. In coastal waters, it has been found that filter feeders such as bivalve molluscs may be particularly prone to the dumping of dredge spoil and high water turbidity. These species are frequently commercially valuable.

5.6.2 Metals

The major sources of metals have already been discussed previously with reference to air pollution. This section provides a brief insight into the impacts of metals in the aquatic environment. The principal sources of metals for water pollution include domestic and industrial waste-waters and the dumping of sewage sludge. The River Mersey in northern England, for example, has a highly urbanised catchment area. It is severely polluted, affected by high concentrations of metals such as zinc from paper treatment, chromium from tanning and lead from battery manufacture, among many other substances (Moss 1988). Concentrations of metals in urban run-off can be extremely high: between 10 mg/l and 100 mg/l for several US cites, for example (Goudie 1990). Increasingly, fears are also being expressed over the contamination of groundwaters and streams by metals leached from waste disposal sites (Miller 1991).

Metals are generally very persistent in the environment and can become concentrated in living tissue along food chains (bioaccumulation), posing a threat to humans and other animals at the head of food chains. Low concentrations of metals in water and bottom sediments, therefore, do not necessarily signify a low degree of risk to aquatic ecosystems and to human health. As Table 5.3 illustrates, it is difficult to discern definite trends in the levels of many metals in water bodies, partly because monitoring programmes for these pollutants are relatively new (OECD 1985a, 1991). However, it is possible to compare these data with existing water quality criteria. The USA Environmental Protection Agency, for example, has guidelines for the protection of aquatic life. Some of these guidelines are based on toxicity tests which use the median lethal concentration (LC_{50}) for a given period of exposure (often 4 days: the 96-hour LC_{50} value). As well as ultimately causing the death of aquatic organisms, some metals have sub-lethal effects on aquatic organisms and predators such as birds and mammals, adversely affecting reproduction and behaviour (Aitchison, Henry and Sandheinrich 1987). Generally, molluscs and crustacea appear to be amongst the aquatic organisms most sensitive to metal pollution, while some insect species show relatively high tolerance (Whitton and Say 1975).

The US Environmental Protection Agency criterion for the protection of aquatic life with reference to cadmium is 4–12 µg/l (micrograms per litre). With the possible exception of the French Rhône in Table 5.3, none of the rivers/estuaries appear to exceed this guideline (on average) at the sampling stations used. More recent research, however, suggests that a safe environmental level with respect to aquatic life may well be below 1 µg/l (Hellawell 1988). Cadmium is known to accumulate in tissues and is thought to affect the way in which ions are regulated in aquatic organisms. Algae appear to be highly sensitive to cadmium and this metal is known to be capable of producing abnormal behaviour in fish (Woodworth and Pascoe 1982). For lead the 96-hour LC_{50} value is 0.01 µg/l and this is greatly exceeded in many rivers in Table 5.3. The LC_{50} value for copper is 0.1 µg/l. Chromium appears less of a problem, with a criterion value of 100 µg/l. Other metals, such as mercury and zinc, are also known to have adverse effects on aquatic life. The relatively recent discovery that inorganic mercury can be converted by microbial activity into the even more toxic methyl-mercury in water is causing concern. Mercury also appears to be rapidly accumulated in organic tissue. Concentrations in fish, for example, may be 10,000 times those observed in the surrounding water (Hellawell 1988). Mercury can also retard growth, inhibit reproduction and alter behaviour (Snarski and Olson 1982).

The bioaccumulative properties of mercury have resulted in episodes of epidemic methyl-mercury poisoning (Minamata disease) in human populations in Japan in the Minamata Bay area and in Niigata. These episodes, which occurred from the early 1960s to the mid-1970s, resulted from large industrial discharges of mercury compounds into the aquatic environment, with the subsequent concentration of methylmercury in fish and other organisms which were eventually consumed by humans (Smith 1986). It has been estimated that the number of people in Japan certified or suspected of having mercury poisoning is about 8000 (Asami 1984). The Japanese government has officially designated 2252 people as victims of Minamata disease, of whom 1228 have already died. Over forty victims of the disease have been awarded damages of about £16,000 each (*New Scientist* 1992a).

The contamination of drinking water supplies by metals is another potential risk to human health. With reference to lead, Levin (1987) has estimated the reduction in the numbers of people at risk in the USA from a variety of disorders which would accrue from a reduction in the concentration of lead in drinking water from 50 µg/l to 20 µg/l. Among the findings of this study, were the following estimates:

- 29,000 fewer children requiring medical treatment
- 230,000 fewer children suffering a loss of 1–2 IQ points
- 29,000 fewer children requiring compensatory education
- 82,000 fewer children at risk of stature decrement
- 680,000 fewer foetuses at risk
- 130,000 fewer cases of hypertension in adult males aged 40–59
- 240 fewer heart attacks in white adult males aged 40–59
- 80 fewer strokes in white adult males aged 40–59
- 240 fewer deaths among white males aged 40–59.

Action is being taken in the USA to reduce lead in drinking water, most of which normally originates from the corrosive action of acidic water on lead-bearing materials in the domestic plumbing system (e.g. lead pipes and the lead solder used to join copper pipes). The preferred method of reducing the problem in the USA is the addition of an alkali, such as bicarbonate, to public water supplies in order to reduce corrosion (OECD 1991).

Lead and cadmium are known to possess cardiotoxic properties, which may lead to damage to cardiac tissues and increased blood pressure (NAS 1979). Synergism between metals and between metals and organic compounds with respect to heart disease may be a possibility (Nriagu 1988). The contamination of drinking water, especially groundwater supplies, by arsenic is also a threat. A number of epidemiological studies in Europe, North and South America and Asia have demonstrated a close association between exposure to arsenic in drinking water and the occurrence of various skin disorders, including skin cancer (Pershagen 1983).

5.6.3 Plant nutrients: nitrates and phosphates

Normally, the growth of rooted aquatic plants and algae is limited by a restricted and balanced supply of the major plant nutrients, nitrates and phosphates. Through time, the productivity (particularly the biomass of plant organic material) of an aquatic ecosystem may gradually increase. This process is known as eutrophication. There is still considerable debate over whether or not eutrophication generally occurs as a natural process (see, for example, Moss 1988). However, it is known that the anthropogenically-enhanced input of plant nutrients, particularly nitrates and phosphates, to water bodies can greatly accelerate the eutrophication process. Lakes and reservoirs are particularly prone to accelerated eutrophication given their relative lack of water movement and renewal compared to rivers and marine environments. The principal anthropogenic sources of nitrates and phosphates in aquatic ecosystems include run-off from agricultural land, where inorganic fertilisers are used extensively; sewage and animal wastes; food processing industries; urban run-off; mining; fertiliser factories; and the use of domestic and industrial detergents (see Table 5.2).

The evidence available from developed countries suggests that nitrate concentrations have increased over recent years in many rivers and lakes, and that phosphate concentrations have remained consistently high in areas affected by one or more of the above sources (OECD 1985a, 1989). The data in Table 5.3 reflect these trends. To enable some comparison of the data in Table 5.3, the reader should note that it is rare for unpolluted fresh waters to contain more than 20 mg/l of nitrate and 1 mg/l of phosphate (Jeffries and Mills 1990). Studies of run-off quality in several cities in the USA, indicate typical concentrations of 0.5–5.0 mg/l for nitrate and phosphate concentrations. Raw sewage typically contains 25–85 mg/l of nitrate and 2–15 mg/l of phosphate (Goudie 1990).

The principal concern over accelerated eutrophication is the excessive growth of some plankton and algal species ('algal blooms'), which makes water more turbid, often turning it a green or brown colour. Some algae may even produce toxins dangerous to human and livestock health. In recent years episodes of livestock poisoning have occurred in Australia, for example, whilst the presence of 'toxic algae' in a number of UK water supply reservoirs has led to their closure to the general public in the summer months during 1989 and 1990. The general decline in water quality associated with accelerated eutrophication may also adversely affect the recreational potential of water bodies and their use as sources of drinking water. Excessive algal growth may also lead to periodic dissolved oxygen depletion in the water body and bottom sediments, resulting in the ecological effects outlined above with reference to pollution by organic wastes. Fish kills, for example, frequently accompany algal blooms. Although it is difficult to isolate the effects of accelerated eutrophication from the impacts of other water pollutants, it has recently been estimated that about one-third of the USA's 100,000 medium to large lakes suffer from some degree of accelerated eutrophication. The proportion rises to 85% for those lakes close to large urban areas (Miller 1988). The death of large areas of coral along the Florida coastline has prompted calls to limit further urban development of the Florida Keys. Most of the damage appears to be the result of the sewage-related nutrient enrichment of coastal waters which has encouraged coral disease following infestations of blue-green algae (Charles 1992).

5.7 ORGANIC CHEMICALS

This category covers a huge range of natural and human-made carbon-containing chemical compounds. Plant and animal tissues are composed of many organic compounds, as are fossil fuels. Fossil fuels provide the raw materials for the synthesis of a wide range of human-made organic chemicals, including solvents used in industry, pesticides, bleaching agents and detergents. The manufacture of many different products such as plastics, dyes, inks, adhesives and paper also requires fossil fuels.

From this bewildering range of compounds, research attention has focused particularly on those which are toxic to plants, animals and humans, and which are persistent in the environment and show a tendency for bioaccumulation in individual organisms and along food chains. Of these, organochlorine (chlorine containing organic chemicals, including the chlorinated hydrocarbons) compounds have received much attention. These compounds include CFCs (see Chapter Four); polychlorinated biphenyls (PCBs); the 'drin' pesticides, aldrin, dieldrin and endrin; the pesticide dichloro-diphenyl-trichloroethane (DDT); and, various dioxins (see Table B.2). A feature of these substances is their high resistance to breakdown in the environment. Moreover, some are more soluble in fat than in water and will, therefore, tend to accumulate in living fat tissue. Much has been written on the effects of pesticides, especially DDT. Although by no means a consequence of agricultural activities alone, the dominant source of these substances in water is not urban (Jeffries and Mills 1990). By contrast, urban/industrial areas are largely responsible for outputs of PCBs to the wider environment. The term 'polychlorinated biphenyls' is generic, covering a possible 200 chemical compounds depending on the quantity and configuration of chlorine atoms (Moss 1988). Their stability, cheapness and non-inflammability have resulted in a number of applications in industry, including insulating fluids in chemical transformers and capacitors; use in cutting oils; as a means of increasing the pliability of plastics; and as a constituent of paint, printing ink and carbonless paper.

The production of PCBs in OECD countries reached a peak towards the end of the 1960s. Since the discovery of widespread environmental contamination by PCBs from the mid-1960s, PCB production has decreased, although significant quantities are still in use primarily in older electrical equipment (Tanabe 1988). Research since the 1960s has demonstrated the environmental persistence of PCBs, which have been detected in the air, water and tissues of animals in both the Arctic and Antarctic (Atlas, Bidleman and Giam 1986). In short, PCBs have penetrated throughout the global environment. On a more local scale, heavy contamination has been found in urban and heavily industrialised areas such as the Great Lakes, the Baltic Sea and Tokyo Bay (Tatsukawa 1976, Olsson 1987). Estimates suggest that approximately 374,000 tonnes of PCBs exist in the global environment (Tanabe 1988). Interestingly, of the estimated total world production of PCBs, some 1.2 million tonnes – only 4%, has been degraded or incinerated. Of the remainder, some 31% exists in the free environment, while the majority (65%) is 'land-stocked', i.e. deposited in landfills or still in use in electrical equipment (Tanabe 1988). Given these figures, it is unlikely that PCB releases to the global environment will decline appreciably in the near future and may not in fact reach a peak until some time this decade. This is worrying because of the many and varied effects of PCBs on animals, especially marine life.

Because so many of the factories which produced or used PCBs were located adjacent to rivers, lakes, estuaries and on coasts, fears concerning the effects of PCBs have focused on aquatic organisms (Tatsukawa 1976). The consumption of contaminated fish, etc. would also appear to be the main routeway for the ingestion of PCBs by humans and domestic livestock (Sawhney and Hankin 1985). Even when concentrations of PCBs in water are very low, this may give a misleading impression of the risk to aquatic organisms. Accumulation along food chains may in effect magnify concentrations, so that in higher predators at the end of food chains PCB concentrations in body tissues may be up to 10 million times higher than in the surrounding water (Tanabe 1988). Magnifications of over 50,000 have been observed in fish species (Mauck, Mehrle and Mayer 1978). Marine mammals appear particularly at risk and there is growing evidence of reproductive impairment in these animals (Subramanian *et al.* 1987). The slow leakage of PCBs from landfill sites in the UK, perhaps 600 tonnes per per annum, has been implicated in the decline in otter populations in lowland rivers (Simmons 1991). What effects, if any, long-term PCB contamination may have on human health are unknown, although PCBs may sometimes be carcinogenic (Moss 1988). According to Park (1991), there is increasing evidence that PCB contamination of the Great Lakes in Canada is causing neurological damage to children, impairing their learning abilities, and it may also be a factor in the otherwise unexplained decline in human fertility rates.

Ironically, attempts to destroy PCBs through high temperature incineration may pose continued threats to the environment if the incineration temperature is not high enough (at least 1200°C) and oxygen is not plentiful during the incineration process. This is because the incomplete combustion of chlorinated chemicals may lead to the formation of dioxins (see Table B.2). Normal waste incinerators can release large quantities of dioxins, although dioxins are also found in effluents from paper and pulp mills which utilise chlorine-based bleaching agents. Dioxins can be highly toxic and are persistent in the environment. Traces of dioxins have now been found around the world, including appreciable quantities in both human and cows' milk (Price 1991).

Earlier in this chapter, we outlined the importance of groundwater as a source of supply for many urban areas. It is perhaps surprising then that the contamination of groundwater supplies by organic chemicals from urban/industrial activities is not uncommon. As previously stated, the city of Tucson in Arizona is entirely dependent on groundwater sources. In 1981, however, high concentrations of the toxic solvent trichloroethylene, or TCE, (see Table B.2) were found in an aquifer under the city (Charles 1991). In the USA, the Environmental Protection Agency has set a drinking water standard for TCE of 1.5 parts per billion (ppb). Concentrations of up to 15,000 ppb were found in the aquifer under Tuscon. The major source of the contamination was thought to be an industrial dumping site, which produced a 'plume' of contaminated water some 6.5 km long and 1 km wide under the western side of the city. In all, nine water supply wells threatened by the plume had to be closed, and since the pollution was first detected the city has been pumping out and treating the contaminated water at considerable expense. This treatment will probably have to continue for another 20 years, although the TCE can never be completely removed. Similar problems have been experienced in the San Gabriel Valley of California, where thirty-nine wells that supplied water to thirteen cities had to be closed in 1980 when they were found to be polluted by TCE (Clarke 1991).

5.8 ACID DEPOSITION

Acid deposition is among the best known and highly publicised pollution issues, and was remarked upon in Manchester as early as the 1850s (Ponting 1991). It results from air pollution and is considered in this chapter both because it represents pollution of rain water, and also because its most serious impacts are frequently associated with effects on the quality of fresh waters. Chapter Four has already provided information on the atmospheric releases of sulphur and nitrogen compounds, the precursors of acid deposition.

Acid deposition can occur as the wet deposition of sulphuric and nitric acids (the so-called 'acid rain') in rain, snow, sleet, hail, fog and dew, or in dry particulate form (sulphate and nitrate salts) through gravitational settling and capture by natural and human-made surfaces. Generally, dry acid deposition is prevalent relatively close to the pollution source, up to perhaps 300 km, while at greater distances wet deposition becomes more important. Under natural conditions, precipitation is normally slightly acidic, with a pH of between 5.0 and 5.6. This is because naturally occurring carbon dioxide, sulphur and nitrogen compounds may combine with water in the atmosphere to form weak acids; carbonic acid derived from carbon dioxide and water being the most prevalent. However, it is the anthropogenic excess of nitrogen oxides and sulphur dioxide released by the burning of fossil fuels which can result in severe direct and indirect effects on ecosystems.

Since the precursors of acid deposition and the acid substances themselves can be transported over long distances, up to several thousand kilometres, their effects are felt not only in the source vicinity, but also in relatively remote, non-urbanised areas. Such movement of pollutants can become an international issue as pollutants from one country affect another. In Europe, for example, it has been established beyond reasonable doubt that emissions of precursors from the UK have contributed to acidification problems in Scandinavian countries. Similarly, more than half of the acid deposition over Canada comes from USA emissions (Miller 1991). It is in Scandinavia, Germany, parts of the UK, north-east USA and eastern Canada where the effects of acid deposition appear to be giving the greatest concern. Other countries, such as China, however, are also affected (OECD 1991). These areas are heavily industrialised, or lie downwind of such regions, and have relied upon the burning of coal for energy generation over many years (Simpson 1990).

In the USA, for example, acid deposition problems are most acute in north-eastern states. This comes about because the prevailing south-westerly airflow transports the acid substances and their precursors from the industrial heartland of the USA located in a number of central and mid-western states (Miller 1988). At a smaller scale, the predominantly urban origin of acid substances or their precursors has been highlighted in a number of studies which compared the concentrations of nitrogen and sulphur compounds and hydrogen ions in precipitation over urban and (upwind) adjacent rural areas. Shaw (1982), for example, attributed 50% of the wet deposition of sulphate and hydrogen ions at a rural site in Nova Scotia, Canada, to emissions from Halifax, some 25 km distant. Downwind of Philadelphia, increases in the deposition rates of nitrate and sulphate of 200% and 90%, respectively, have been observed compared to upwind locations (Patrinos 1985).

At the present time, it is generally thought that sulphur compounds contribute more to acid deposition than do nitrogen compounds, but recent evidence suggests that the latter are becoming more important as emissions of sulphur dioxide decline in many of the affected countries, whilst those of nitrogen oxides (especially from motor vehicles) remain relatively constant or have increased. Data from both Scandinavia and the USA, for example, demonstrate increasing nitrate concentrations in precipitation, streams and lakes over the past two decades (Moss 1988). The pH of precipitation, rivers and lakes may be on average some 1.0–1.5 units lower than normal in affected areas of the USA and Scandinavia, while sulphate and nitrate deposition rates may be twice those normally observed. The average pH of rainfall in affected areas typically ranges between 3.5 and 5.5.

Acid deposition can have a number of direct and indirect effects on terrestrial and aquatic ecosystems, buildings (see Chapter Four) and human health. Where soils are thin and poor in base minerals, a characteristic of many remote upland areas, their ability to 'buffer' acid deposition, is limited. Thus a progressive acidification of these soils is possible, as is the acidification of water moving through the soils to streams, rivers and lakes which may also have an inherently poor buffering capacity. The liming of agriculturally important soils to combat acid deposition is now commonplace in continental Europe (Milne 1988). Freshwater aquatic organisms can be severely affected by acidic pollution, either through the gradual alteration of the chemistry of the water as base minerals become neutralised (the so-called 'titration effect'), or by occasional and temporary 'acid flushes' to the ecosystem following snow-melt or heavy rain. Even in fresh waters with a neutral or nearly neutral pH for most of the time, occasional acid flushes can result in ecological changes and fish kills. Fish kills occur because soil acidification leads to the mobilisation of metals, aluminium being particularly toxic to fish, which are then leached out of the soil in run-off into streams and lakes. It is the elevated concentration of aluminium and other metals often observed in acid deposition affected areas which is causing the greatest concern regarding acid deposition effects on human health. Recently, high levels of aluminium in drinking water have been implicated in the early onset of senile dementia (Alzheimer's disease) in humans, for example (Simpson 1990).

Fish losses in lakes and rivers have now been observed in many European countries, the USA and Canada. Approximately 4000 of Sweden's 85,000 lakes suffer from severe acidification problems (OECD 1985a). In Ontario, Canada, at least 1600 lakes now contain no fish because of excess acidity (Miller 1988). Fish populations have disappeared from some 1700 lakes in southern Norway (Simmons 1991). Ironically, lakes suffering from severe acidification can appear very appealing, having a crystal-clear quality due to the lack of algae in the water. Typically, acid-sensitive organisms such as crayfish, fresh water shrimps, molluscs and flatworms quickly disappear from acidified waters, while other species, such as resistant insects and water beetles, may remain. The general effect, however, is a decline in biological productivity and in species diversity. Terrestrial ecosystems may also become severely affected. The deteriorating condition of forests in many European countries, for example, is at least partly due to acid deposition, which can directly impair physiological function and indirectly affect plant performance through soil degradation (Heliotis, Karandinos and Whiton 1988). The decline in numbers of some invertebrate soil organisms has also been linked to soil acidification, while a close correlation between lichen decline and tree bark acidification has been noted in parts of the UK (Gilbert 1986).

5.9 CONCLUSIONS

When the impacts of urban areas on the quantity and quality of water resources are considered, there appear to be many inconsistencies and contradictions. On the one hand, towns and cities contribute to an unsustainable drain on regional fresh water supplies. Yet water is often wasted and inappropriately used in urban areas. While a city may go to great lengths to secure its water supply, often creating tensions with other users, much effort is frequently made to dispose of rain water and surface run-off from its streets as rapidly as possible. In doing so, a city may increase the downstream flood risk in another urban area despite, perhaps, being all too familiar with the devastation that urban flooding can bring. Urban areas rely on salt and fresh waters for drinking water, industrial activities, food supply, amenity and recreation. Yet, they pollute these resources to the detriment of aquatic ecosystems and organisms and, therefore, ultimately of themselves. It is almost beyond belief that urban activities are allowed to pollute groundwater, for example, when this source is so often of crucial importance in maintaining urban life. Furthermore, as we have tried to demonstrate, the water pollution costs of urban living extend far beyond urban boundaries.

Much of the evidence presented above suggests that cities do not operate on a sustainable basis with reference to water resources: this situation is clearly unacceptable. It is in the long-term self-interest of city authorities to instigate changes in the way urban activities operate, so that urban areas minimise their wider impacts and sustainable urban development becomes possible.

FURTHER READING

Many of the water resource issues raised in Chapter Five, including water quality, are discussed in much greater detail by McDonald and Kay (1988) in *Water Resources Issues and Strategies*. A less academic, but nonetheless highly informative, account is given by Clarke (1991) in *Water: The International Crisis*. Descriptions of urban modifications to hydrology are provided by Shaw (1988) in *Hydrology in Practice* and by Haslam (1990) in *River Pollution: An Ecological Perspective*. The chapter by Fish on fresh water in *Understanding Our Environment: An Introduction to Environmental Chemistry and Pollution* (edited by Harrison 1992) summarises many water pollution issues. Highly detailed accounts of individual aspects of water pollution appear in *Pollution: Causes, Effects and Control* (Harrison 1990).

KEY THEMES

- Sustainable yield of fresh waters
- Utilisation and modification of fresh waters for cities
- Interrelationships between urban form, local hydrological modifications, water utilisation and water pollution
- Urban areas as major generators of water pollution
- Diversity of water pollution: sources, types and impacts
- Transboundary nature of water pollution

DISCUSSION POINTS

- For a town or city with which you are familiar, identify the sources of domestic water supply. Describe the tensions which might exist in your area between urban and rural demands and impacts on these supplies. Consider both water quality and quantity.

- Using a point or stretch of your local river as an example, try to determine the general status or classification of the quality of the river from your local water utility and/or pollution control authority. What water quality parameters are used in classifying the status of the river? List the parameters which are regularly monitored in the river. Analyse the activities which might impinge on the quality of the river upstream of your selected point or stretch.

- Locate the sewage treatment works nearest to where you live or work. Determine the types of waste treated at the works. Where is the liquid effluent from the works discharged? What happens to any solid waste from the works? Can the works cope at all times with the wastes received?

- You are a local planning officer charged with the production of a land use plan which minimises the stresses on the status of fresh waters in your area. Describe and explain the activities which might cause you concern, and the factors you would wish to consider in finding appropriate locations for different types of new development in your area. Whom would you seek advice from and liaise with, and why?

- Formulate a list of as many management tools as you can devise which could be used to encourage both the more efficient use of water in urban areas and a reduction in water pollution. Try to think beyond the imposition of legal requirements to more subtle actions which might change behaviour. Explain how each of your management instruments would operate.

PART C

FROM PRINCIPLES TO POLICIES
ADDRESSING URBAN ENVIRONMENTAL PROBLEMS

In this final section, the analysis shifts towards bringing about sustainable urban development. In Chapter Six a series of twenty guiding principles are drawn out from the earlier analysis, and some of the policy implications discussed. Chapter Seven examines two sets of policy instruments for improving the urban environment: environmental impact assessment and economic tools. This chapter makes some important links between guiding principles for policy development and actual policy implementation, and in particular demonstrates the interrelatedness of different policy principles. In Chapter Eight the analysis is concluded with an overview of progress towards sustainable urban development, from the development of different land use planning models, to recommendations of various pressures groups and the 1992 Rio Earth Summit.

CHAPTER SIX

Guiding Principles for Sustainable Urban Development

6.1 INTRODUCTION TO THE GUIDING PRINCIPLES

In addition to the three foundation principles for sustainable development outlined in Chapter One, there are a considerable number of other important, second-tier principles, which we refer to here as guiding principles. It is valuable to recap briefly on the three fundamental basic principles for sustainability. *Inter-generational equity*, or futurity, asserts that each generation is entitled to expect an environmental stock of natural resources of at least equivalent worth to that of preceding generations. *Social justice*, or contemporary equity, demands that the basic needs of all people are met. Economic and social development should be self-reinforcing, where healthy and well-educated people are economically more productive as well as more fulfilled human beings (WCED 1987). More than this, for poor people, despoliation is most often a necessity forced on them by hunger, whilst starvation itself stems in considerable part from marginalisation within economic systems which exploit the land and people. *Transfrontier justice* is a recognition that political and administrative boundaries have in the past provided a means for shirking environmental responsibilities, and passing on the costs of environmental damage across boundaries without recompense. The need for global stewardship of the environment needs to be at the heart of the political process at all levels if sustainability is to be achieved.

This chapter goes beyond these three principles to elaborate upon the underlying conditions for sustainability. Where possible, we seek to examine how the resulting twenty guiding principles affect cities. It is for this reason that we refer to them here as principles for sustainable urban development, although in fact all of them can be adapted with very little effort to become general principles for rural, regional or global sustainable development.

To clarify the analysis, the guiding principles for sustainable development in cities are divided here into three categories: ecological, socioeconomic, and management. The categorisation of principles is made according to where each of the principles has its primary basis and the area of most immediate application for the principle. This divide represents none the less a tremendous oversimplification: not only could many of the principles fit into more than one category, they overlap and intermesh with each other, to varying degrees. This interrelatedness is one reason why we do not attempt to prioritise the principles in any way. It is the way in which these sub-elements mesh to contribute to the broader goal of sustainability which is the paramount concern.

In setting about the task of clarifying the underlying conditions necessary to achieve sustainability, the analysis draws on a considerable body of work which has sought to outline the principles for environmental management or sustainable development. Principles such as 'prevention is better than cure' or 'minimum waste' have been stated so often with reference to environmental protection that they have almost descended into the realm of environmental management jargon. Most analyses highlight just a small number of underpinning principles (e.g. Ahmad 1989, Bosworth 1993). The main exception to this is Miller (1992), who outlines 66 principles under four headings, 'resources, pollution and environmental degradation', 'scientific', 'economics and politics' and 'world view and ethics'.

A number of analyses with a specific urban dimension have also been provided, sometimes tending to be partial in the images they paint, albeit painting in thoroughly imaginative ways. Hough (1990), for instance, concentrating on urban open space issues, outlines five principles:

1. **Economy of means**, where the least effort is used to get the greatest returns. Examples might include shifting from 'manicured' parklands to more natural habitat construction, or farmers mowing road verges for hay, at the same time keeping the roads clear.

2. **Diversity**, both social and biological, as a means towards reducing stress and improving health. Cities should be interesting: they need quiet areas and noisy ones, such as markets; they need both cultivated green spaces and more natural habitats.

3. **Productivity** and **environmental relevance**, where waste-water is recycled, urban forests are planted to modify the urban climate, and gardens and parks converted in some part to food production.

4. **Capitalising on the nature of place**, in particular not attempting to adapt the outdoor environment as radically as we do the indoor environment, for instance creating grass lawns in near desert conditions, requiring excessive watering.

5. **Environmental education**, which should begin at home, so that knowledge of the immediate environment helps in taking steps to

improve it, as well as fostering awareness of broader environmental issues.

The analysis here implies a three-tier system of guidance: fundamental principles, guiding principles, and generally desirable policy directions. The first two categories should have a high level of universality, whilst the third level may be tailored more to particular regional or national circumstances. In this chapter, the analysis is concentrated on those guiding principles applicable globally. As such, it avoids widespread Western solutions to Western problems, such as greater urban containment. These are policy possibilities specific to particular circumstances, not generally applicable principles.

It is perhaps those principles advocated by others but which are missed out in this chapter, or which are adopted in variant themes, which are the most controversial and most interesting in terms of academic debate. For instance, we advocate working with the grain of the market where possible, but altering it through direct intervention where necessary. This sidesteps the polar extremes of calls to overthrow the existing global order and the market-led economy paradigm on the one hand, or to rely almost solely on the market on the other hand. Nor do the principles include a call for higher urban densities, not least because the case for this is not yet proven, and because high densities in themselves can be the source of many urban problems. For us the issues lie more in the combination of urban design, open space provision and use, the shape and function of the city, and so on, in addition to population density. Finally, although we agree with the policy of reducing military expenditure, we do not see this as a universal guiding principle for sustainable development, as has been advocated elsewhere.

Many of the guiding principles outlined in this chapter (summarised in Boxes 6.1, 6.3 and 6.4) have gained widespread acceptance already, and in recent years have increasingly found their way into legislation and official statements of policy. The main exception is the need to create new indicators for economic and environmental productivity. Despite the emerging consensus over certain principles, it is important to recognise that many environmental concerns have to be seen as trade-offs, even possibly at the level of guiding principles: when it comes down to translating principles into policy action there is rarely one and only one valid policy option, or one valid viewpoint. However, some of these trade-offs between economic and environmental development may have been working against the security and stability of the global environment (Ahmad 1989). These trade-offs commonly transcend national boundaries in their impacts, so that effective action requires international cooperation, in avoiding damage and in securing advantages for all. One of our ecological principles says that 'nothing stands alone'; in a similar vein, neither cities nor nations stand alone, economically, socially or politically. Principles for sustainable urban development only make sense if they are also principles for global sustainable development. Similarly, sustainability principles need to be constructed which are sufficiently flexible, yet also sufficiently meaningful and workable, to allow policies to be devised which move society towards an overall objective of increasing global environmental sustainability and economic well-being. The principles which are adopted in this chapter are not uncontentious therefore: for this reason they are put forward in the spirit of providing a starting point for debate, not an end point. As our understanding of the environment changes, and as our understanding increases of human impacts on the environment and of our capacity to change, so the principles of sustainable development will change.

Box 6.1 A Summary of the Guiding Ecological Principles for Sustainable Urban Development

Prevention is better than cure. This stresses the importance of a precautionary approach to urban development; environmental impact assessments must be conducted on all major development projects.

Nothing stands alone. Account should be taken of the local, regional and global implications of urban activities and urban environmental policies.

Minimise waste. In moving towards greater urban self-reliance, maximise reuse and recycling of materials; minimise unnecessary wastage of resources; and encourage built-in longevity in products.

Maximise the use of renewable and recyclable materials. The use of low- and non-waste technology should be especially encouraged; maximise the use of renewable resources within sustainable limits.

Maintain and enhance 'requisite variety'. This should be encouraged in the natural, cultural and even economic environments.

Identify and respect local, regional and global environmental tolerances. This ensures that urban development is sensitised to its capacity to interact with, and indeed alter, local and global capacities to cope with environmental disturbances.

Enhance environmental understanding through research. This ensures that complex environmental and economic interdependencies are better understood as a basis for informed decision-making.

6.2 ECOLOGICAL PRINCIPLES FOR SUSTAINABLE URBAN DEVELOPMENT

6.2.1 Prevention is better than cure

Implicit in this principle is a recognition of the role of a precautionary approach to development. This principle advocates that unless people are clear about the environmental impacts of their activities, they should refrain from activities which might potentially damage the environment. In particular, if policy makers are to take the idea of maintaining and enhancing the quality of the environment seriously, they must attempt to concentrate their efforts on preventing environmental degradation from occurring, rather than be forced to embark upon – often very expensive –'end-of-pipe' cures at a later date. Too often, both large-scale development projects and the unquestioned use of new technologies or products have resulted in unforeseen impacts on ecosystems through pollution, for example.

The principle of 'prevention is better than cure' has been at the heart of much of the environmental policy and legislation of recent years. This principle continues to be expounded by writers and organisations concerned with environmental protection. The UK based pressure group Friends of the Earth (FoE), for example, recently stated in their *Charter for Local Government* (1989) that

> Prevention is better than cure: it is always preferable to prevent a negative environmental impact occurring than cleaning up afterwards...great advances can be made if we assume that an activity is environmentally damaging unless proven otherwise. This puts the onus onto the potential polluters. (p.ii)

The intriguing and difficult issue central to the 'prevention is better than cure' principle is how to 'prove' that a given activity is not environmentally damaging. The short –and partial –answer to this is that some form of rigorous investigation needs to be made of the likely environmental implications of a particular activity prior to its commencement. This, however, is not adequate in itself, as it is the interrelationships of activities which need to be assessed, and for this it is important to adopt a more holistic approach to environmental impact assessment at policy-making level, possibly requiring area-wide environmental audits, against which the range of policies can be assessed (the theme of environmental impact assessment is returned to in Chapter Seven). When the environmental impacts of single or multiple activities are predicted to be potentially unacceptable in the light of the other ecological principles outlined here and, more profoundly, our societal sense of well-being (Sagoff 1988), one option available must be to prevent them from commencing in the form originally envisaged.

The ability to assess and censure projects in this way will inevitably require international agreement and appropriate national legislation, rigorously enforced. Even with better information for decision-making purposes, the question of whether a project should go ahead will remain subject to the need to consider what constitutes an acceptable environmental risk. If we accept that most human activities carry both personal and environmental risks, it quickly becomes apparent that the precautionary principle is a guide, not a rigid criterion. Risk-taking is a necessary part of human existence but it is an activity which requires continual questioning of the degree of acceptable risk, and analysis of the ethics of who bears the burden of any problems which emerge.

The related question arises of who should decide on the 'acceptability' of a particular development project. One of the principles which follows emphasises the need to engage the capacities and knowledge of local people in environmental policy decision-making and implementation. Taking this point, it becomes important to consult a wide range of professional and community expertise and viewpoints, whilst recognising the urban environment as a complex mixture of natural, built and cultural aspects. Whilst increased education on environmental matters for decision-makers is an important issue, and one which is returned to later, it is rarely beneficial to have development decisions being left solely to the wishes of any 'single' grouping.

6.2.2 Nothing stands alone

As we have sought to demonstrate in Chapters Four and Five, individual pollutants may combine in the environment to produce more severe effects than their individual characteristics might suggest. Similarly, individual pollutants may be altered in the environment by natural environmental constituents, resulting in more damaging compounds. Such is the case with acid precipitation, for example. This is a good example because it reminds us that pollutants of the atmosphere may also become land and water pollutants. In these senses, it is clearly important to recognise that 'nothing stands alone'. Unfortunately, many of the adverse environmental impacts of pollution have been unforeseen precisely because of a failure to appreciate such environmental interconnections. Ecology is concerned with and recognises environmental interrelationships, and so it is appropriate to consider this principle under an ecological banner.

Box 6.2 Examples of 'Nothing Stands Alone' from the Energy Sector

Coal-fired electricity generation

One means of reducing the sulphur dioxide content of flue gases from power stations which burn fossil fuels is to filter them out before emission from the chimney stack, using limestone (the process is commonly referred to as *flue gas desulphurisation*). However, the limestone required is almost invariably quarried in rural areas, which may sometimes be of exceptional value in terms of landscape and wildlife. (For instance, the Derbyshire Peak District and the Yorkshire Dales supply much of the limestone used by coal-fired power stations in central and northern England.) There is inevitably scope for major conflicts of interest in such cases, not least reducing urban pollution at the expense of exporting environmental problems to rural areas.

Renewable energy sources

The case for the greatly increased use of renewable energy is not always as straightforward as first appears. If wind, for example, is to become a large-scale, viable source of energy for urban areas, this may require the setting aside of large tracts of countryside to be used as 'wind farms'. Such activity could have severe impacts on wildlife, visual amenity and noise levels in these countryside areas. Similar forms of disamenity might also result from the operation of near-shore wave power generators or large solar power installations.

'Carbon' taxes

Increases in petrol prices or car taxes, designed to internalise into the market the full environmental costs of private vehicle use, may be important in relieving adverse environmental impacts in urban areas. These same policies, however, may exercise disproportionate negative impacts on rural vehicle users, many of whom need to travel further than their urban counterparts and do not contribute to the same extent to traffic congestion and noise pollution. Such potential differential impacts on urban and rural residents need to be recognised before policies designed to tackle predominately urban issues are devised and enforced.

The recognition that changes, whether unforeseen or deliberate, to one part of a system will almost inevitably impact elsewhere has broader implications. For example, it is important to consider some of the geographical interdependencies between cities and the wider environment, including the global economy, and the links between the prosperity of the world's economically richest countries and the economic impoverishment of developing countries (Box 6.2).

Inevitably there is a global dimension to these types of interdependencies. For example, the suggestion from some pressure groups (such as FoE 1989) that, in the interests of the global environment, the use of unsustainably produced materials (e.g. hardwood derived from the destruction of tropical rainforest) should be discontinued by UK local authorities appears laudable. However, many developing countries with rainforest resources depend upon the export of hardwood to earn foreign currency. The rapid decline of the market for this resource could cause hardship for the rural people of these countries and merely result in the unsustainable exploitation of other natural resources. Similarly, the Montreal Protocol limiting the use of CFCs may exercise disproportionate negative impacts upon the economies of developing countries, since they are less able than developed countries to afford the initially more expensive alternatives. For this kind of reason, transitional aid and development strategies for developing countries must be an integral part of sustainable development programmes.

As previous chapters have already emphasised, it is important to recognise the links between urban, regional and global activities in creating environmental problems at all scales and in moving towards their resolution. This is particularly relevant in the geographical sense of understanding that urban environmental problems may be manifestations of activities outside the city (such as water supply contamination from agriculture and rural industries), whilst problems which originate within the city can be transferred to surrounding areas (such as urban industrial air pollution). Instances where problems emerge solely in and impact solely on cities are, therefore, just one collection of urban environmental problems.

The key point here is that cities can exercise profound direct and indirect impacts on the environment of surrounding areas at regional, national and even global scales. It is important that policy makers attempt to understand such environmental interdependencies, in order to minimise the creation of undesirable impacts outside the city as well as inside it. The principle that 'nothing stands alone' requires a recognition of both the currently known and the as yet undiscovered links between environmental problems and environmental degradation at both urban and wider scales. As we have already noted, this principle is

not simply an ecological issue, it is also a socioeconomic and management concern.

6.2.3 Minimise waste; maximise the use of renewable and recyclable materials

The third and fourth ecological principles are combined in this section,
since they are in some respects more closely interrelated than any of the
other principles. Minimising waste means both reducing the wastage of
resources (e.g. the loss of high-quality water to urban domestic users
through pipe leakages), and reducing waste outputs to the environment
from households and industry. The minimisation of human resource
demands implies reduced resource use, the maximisation of reuse and
recycling initiatives and a greater reliance on repair rather than replacement.

The minimum waste principle once again has its roots in our growing
understanding of the functioning of natural ecosystems. Natural, fully-
developed (climax) ecosystems tend to be characterised by the efficient
use of resources, such as nutrients and water. They exist in a 'stable' state
(dynamic equilibrium) in which the loss of resources to the system is
minimised and growth is self-regulatory. It is now widely accepted that
cities should, as far as is possible, be made to behave in a more cyclic
manner, akin to the functioning of mature, natural ecosystems (see, for
example, OECD 1990).

In the past there was too little understanding of the stages where
adverse impacts occurred, from the materials required for manufacture,
through manufacture itself, to waste disposal. Only a small part of a
product's life cycle was considered as the responsibility of producers, an
attitude which can no longer be tolerated (OECD 1990). Simpson
(1990) similarly notes that

> Waste minimisation is a principle to be applied to the whole product
> life-cycle, not merely at the end of it. Targets are thus to be applied
> to raw material extraction, production, product use and disposal,
> which require technology, planning and a redefinition of what
> constitutes good house-keeping practices. (p. 84)

The principle of minimising waste requires a wide range of initiatives,
including increasing the life of products, cutting out unnecessary car
journeys, eliminating the over-packaging of goods in shops, and reducing and reusing the waste heat of large power stations. For example, it
implies a move away from the current heavy reliance on fossil fuels for
energy, towards energy derived from renewable resources and in particular sources which produce fewer waste products, such as hydro-elec-
tricity, wave power, tidal power, solar power, wind power and geothermal

energy. Increased energy efficiency in homes, offices and factories has the potential to lower significantly the consumption of fossil fuels, reducing the need to build new power stations, with all the attendant financial and environmental costs of construction and operation.

Attempts to reduce resource demand should precede attempts to meet it. It is important to note that many of the social problems which might accompany the introduction of full externality pricing in terms of increased charges could be countered by cost savings if resources were used more efficiently and effective incentives found to encourage greater waste minimisation and lower consumption. As various research programmes and project prototypes have shown, it is generally more efficient to reduce demand than to satisfy it. For instance, the OECD (1990) cite the example of Least Cost Utility Planning for electricity supply in the USA. Using this technique, investment in demand management and energy conservation must be placed on an equal basis with new plant installation. In Wisconsin this has led to a proposed $500 million investment in new generating capacity being replaced by a $70 million programme to reduce demand, with the further benefit in terms of the enhanced greenhouse effect of reducing generation by 250 megawatts.

Implicit also in this principle is the need to choose the most environmentally appropriate alternative. So for instance, in the case of energy production, although it may be preferable to turn to renewable sources, there are also important differences to consider between alternative non-renewable energy sources. It could be argued that, where resources permit, it is preferable to use natural gas rather than coal, as it produces less carbon dioxide per unit of energy. As an approximate guide, for a given unit of energy output, coal produces 100 units of carbon dioxide, oil 80 units, and natural gas 60 units (Toke 1990). Any such shift would only be one necessary element of a conservation policy, which should also involve improving the energy efficiency of homes, offices, factories, machinery, cars and so on. The mode of transmission of energy is important too, especially in the case of electricity, where losses of power are substantial over long distances, whilst large conventional power stations also generate considerable amounts of unused heat. According to Commoner (1976, p. 216) 'about 85 per cent of the work available in the energy presently consumed is not applied to the work-requiring tasks of the production system – it is wasted'. Finally, it will be important to change consumer behaviour through information on conservation measures and education on the environmental impacts of energy demands. Minimising waste is therefore intimately connected to principles concerning improved education and information, as discussed later.

Minimising the output of waste to the environment necessarily involves a greater reclamation, recycling and reuse of materials and products than is currently the case, especially in the more prosperous countries, where greater affluence has to varying degrees fostered a 'throw away' mentality in society. This imperative requires not just building longer-life products, but also ensuring simple repairs can be made, and that spare parts are readily available. In Germany, the 'whole product lifecycle' approach has now led to many products being designed so that they can be readily dismantled and different parts reused or recycled.

Cities have been identified as disproportionate contributors to waste generation and to the problems of disposal, with both total waste and waste generation per capita increasing not only with city affluence but also city size (Elkin, McLaren and Hillman 1991). The need to minimise urban waste generation is becoming more urgent given the growing shortage of landfill sites for the disposal of solid waste, particularly household refuse which accounts for around 80% of municipal waste in many Western cities, and problems of groundwater contamination associated with landfill disposal (see Chapter Five). A high proportion of substances such as paper, oils, plastics and glass, for example, which contribute to municipal and industrial wastes can be recycled, reprocessed and reused and would be more appropriately classified as residues (Simpson 1990).

Minimising waste will require the development and implementation of technologies which reduce waste, whether this is with reference to power generation or in industry. The adoption of low- and non-waste technology (LNWT), that is, technology which seeks to maximise efficiency and the potential for recycling, has generally been slow. This can be attributed to a number of factors, including a lack of economic incentives for industry and potential distortions of international trading conditions. Certainly, in the initial stages of developing LNWT, unless it is uniformly adopted, some companies could effectively penalise themselves relative to users of traditional methods, because they no longer 'externalise', or pass on, their environmental costs. For this reason, it is important that all environmental costs are absorbed by producers and consumers, and that a strong national and international regulatory framework exists to control the use and abuse of 'environmental commons' by industry and individuals (see Chapter Two). The potential distortions to international competitiveness illustrate the need for greater international cooperation to provide a framework for the development and use of LNWT. Ideally, however, waste minimisation should be achieved by preventative means (prevention is better than cure), rather than a heavy reliance on 'end-of-pipe' technologies.

The principle of minimum waste is usually discussed with reference to energy production and use, recycling of various wastes and LNWT. However, the principle also applies to the often wasteful use of resources used in other processes. In Chapter Five, we described the the wastage of valuable water resources through pipe leakages and the inappropriate use of high quality water for activities such as the watering of lawns and car washing. There is certainly much room for improvement in water conservation in urban areas, and this theme is returned to below. Similarly, whilst many urban areas are running out of land for development purposes, significant areas of land are left unused owing, among other things, to industrial dereliction and land contamination. The minimum waste principle, therefore, also requires making more efficient use of the land resource through, for example, appropriate land use strategies and reclamation of derelict and contaminated land.

In recent years there has been considerable attention paid to minimising waste and, relatedly, to reducing profligate or wasteful consumption. The inappropriate and wasteful use of fresh water supplies in the UK could be discouraged by the introduction of domestic water metering and subsequent payment according to use. A domestic water metering trial on the Isle of Wight resulted in an average drop in consumption of about 20% (Hamer 1992), while Charles (1991) suggests that an increase of 10% in the cost of domestic water reduces consumption by approximately 6%, on average. Domestic consumption can also be reduced in other ways. For example, the redesign of domestic appliances such as toilets and showers could produce a 50% saving in household water use, while the use of indigenous plants in gardens, rather than water-hungry alien species, might help to reduce household water consumption, especially in arid areas (Clarke 1991).

Treated sewage effluent, other waste-waters and urban storm water run-off can be reclaimed/recycled for subsequent use, thereby minimising water wastage and reducing demand. The city of Tucson, Arizona, for example, recycled some 6.4 million m^3 of waste-water in 1990 for use in industrial cooling, the watering of golf courses and as a means of recharging the local groundwater aquifer (after the waste-water had been treated) (Charles 1991). Clarke (1991) reports that in Israel, total waste-water reuse is now the declared national policy. Some 30% of all urban waste-water is currently being reused, mostly for crop irrigation. This has resulted in an effective increase in available water resources and has reduced the pollution of rivers and coastal areas. The use of waste-water in this way also supplies most of the nutrients required by the agricultural crops, and all sewage discharges to the Mediterranean coast of Israel are now being returned to the land. The use of reclaimed water in the home, however, may prove more problematical given the preference of many householders for high-quality, potable water even for purposes (such as washing cars, flushing toilets and watering gardens) for which it is not required. Cairnes (1993) argues that education is necessary to change peoples' attitudes since continued urban growth may force the use of reclaimed water in the home. In the north-west of Sydney, Australia, a large-scale trial is already underway of a new approach where urban blocks are being supplied with both potable and reclaimed water.

Industry also has an important role to play in conserving fresh water supplies. Again using the example of Israel, this country reduced its industrial consumption of water, between 1962 and 1975, from an average of 20 m^3 per \$100 worth of production to 7.8 m^3 per \$100 worth of production. Such savings do not necessarily require complex measures. A large textile factory in Sao Paulo, Brazil, for example, managed to cut its water use by 39% over two years, simply by turning off taps when water wasn't needed and by reusing wash water more frequently (Clarke 1991). Water savings can also follow the greater recycling of other materials. Miller (1991) suggests that manufacturing aluminium from recycled scrap rather than virgin ores can reduce water needs by 97%.

6.2.4 Maintain and enhance 'requisite variety'

This principle is most commonly associated with the need for continued biodiversity on both global and more local levels (see Box A.3). For many writers concerned with the use of open space in urban areas and particularly those interested in the 'greening' of cities, open spaces provide tremendous opportunities for the creation of diverse habitats and communities and for continued investigations into ecological processes in cities (see for instance Hough 1984, Gordon 1990). Areas such as parks, water and sewage treatment works, derelict land sites, railway sidings and road verges can be utilised much more than is currently the case to encourage variety in provision for wildlife. Some observers (e.g. Smyth 1987) argue that the creation of a variety of wildlife habitats within urban areas is a necessity rather than a nicety. This is central to the principle of requisite variety. Hough (1990, p.17), for instance, comments that

> If health can be described as the ability to withstand stress, then diversity may also imply health... Diversity makes social as well as biological sense in the urban setting. The quality of life implies, among other things, being able to choose between one place and another, between one life-style and another. In design terms, it implies interest, pleasure, stimulated senses and varied landscapes.

In a similar vein, Odum (1969) argues that the most pleasant and safest landscape to live in contains a rich mixture of crops, forests, lakes, streams, marshes and waste places. There are other compelling reasons for encouraging a variety of open, vegetated areas in cities. These may have a cooling influence on the urban climate (see Chapter Four), and facilitate the replenishment of soil water and groundwater (see Chapter Five).

It is important to note that the principle of requisite variety can also be applied to the cultural and built environments of cities. People who live in cities need continuous exposure to a variety of different stimuli, in respect of natural, social and economic environments. In Chapter Three the case for greater mixed-use zoning in land use planning was argued, providing a means of increasing the variety of activities in any given urban district and reducing transport problems. Although zoning of land uses is still necessary in cities, it must be undertaken within a broader remit to retain or regain the fine-grained diversity of activities at the neighbourhood level, involving a rich texture of different kinds and sizes of open space, and mixed residential and commercial usages. These changes will require cross-sectoral strategies which, for example, combine land use and transport planning to reduce the need to travel between home and work, and to increase the viability of public transport.

6.2.5 Identify and respect local, regional and global environmental tolerances

This principle relates to the 'nothing stands alone' principle. At its heart is an acceptance of the enormous importance of local variability in capacity to cope with differing environmental disturbances. For instance, the winter inversions of air in many non-tropical cities create an important localised constraint on the environment's ability to disperse air pollution. Similarly, local microclimates can affect the environmental capacities within cities, from the wind corridors created by high-rise buildings to the effects of local topographical variation on precipitation. Taking this further, local microclimates are not simply a natural factor which urban development needs to take into account: urban development can create its own microclimates, as well as ameliorating or accentuating existing local variations. The point to be emphasised here is that externally imposed developments, especially large-scale ones, still only rarely display a sensitivity to such local environmental tolerances and capacities.

Although increasingly evident in the context of the discovery of 'holes' in the ozone layer and the emergence of an apparent global greenhouse effect, it is important to emphasise continually that environmental tolerances at a global scale are not infinite either (MacNeill,

Winsemius and Yakushiji 1991). More than this, there are hidden limits which no one is aware of yet: only when these are breached, or close to be being breached, will society become aware. And by that time it may not be possible to repair any damage done. The need for caution, as stressed earlier, is paramount.

At the urban level, planners in some Australian cities are now considering the option of only sanctioning urban development in areas best able to cope with air and water pollution. In Sydney, for example, this might mean a return to development nearer the coast where the environmental capacity to absorb pollution is higher than in inland areas, and the provision of pollution control measures is easier (Unwin and Searle 1991, Cairnes 1993).

6.2.6 Enhance environmental understanding through research

Crosscutting all the principles in this chapter is a need to understand environmental processes better, including the economic and social causes and consequences of degradation. Further basic research is needed in areas as diverse as pollution sources and effects, and appropriate systems for managing the urban environment. Achieving and disseminating the results of this improved knowledge is an important element in improving the decision-making behaviour of individuals, companies and governments.

6.3 SOCIAL AND ECONOMIC PRINCIPLES FOR SUSTAINABLE URBAN DEVELOPMENT

This section covers those principles which relate to policies to control the abuse of the environment by individuals and businesses. Also in this section are those principles which relate to some of the interdependencies between the environment and the economy (Box 6.3).

6.3.1 Use of appropriate technologies, materials and design

Technological solutions to environmental problems too often tend to work against nature, to be more expensive than they need to be and to create work as the preserve of a scientific elite by creating products which ordinary people cannot understand or service themselves. Schumacher (1974) provided the most widely read commentary on this principle in *Small is Beautiful*, in which he argued that large businesses and state organisations combine with the functional specialisation of mass production to create massive economic inefficiency, inhumane working conditions and environmental pollution. Instead of high technology,

Schumacher advocated the use of intermediate or appropriate technologies, which would allow the poor to help themselves within the financial constraints of their circumstances. The idea here is that imported, sophisticated technologies may be inappropriate in developing countries, being labour-saving in societies where this is not a huge priority, whilst the machines themselves are expensive to buy and maintain.

Box 6.3 A Summary of the Guiding Social and Economic Principles for Sustainable Urban Development

Use of appropriate technology, materials and design. This is particularly useful where low cost indigenous solutions take precedence over expensive imported models.

Create new indicators for economic and environmental wealth. Move away from relying on Gross National Product as the primary indicator of national wealth, since it ignores environmental 'capital stocks'.

Create new indicators for economic and environmental productivity. This will encourage a shift away from wasteful production and from unsustainable use of non-renewable resources; productivity must be gauged as an outcome of the inputs of natural resources.

Establish acceptable minimum standards through regulatory control. Improved market incentives will always need to be accompanied by legislative back-up which sets minimum standards in environmental matters.

Continue action to internalise environmental costs into the market. This guideline subsumes such well-known environmental principles as 'polluter pays' and 'user pays'.

Ensure social acceptability of environmental policies. Policies designed to improve the urban environment should not result in a net decline in the quality of life of disadvantaged groups, both in cities and globally.

Widespread public participation. This should be encouraged in strategy formulation, policy implementation and project management.

Similar criticisms of the inappropriateness of imported development models, technologies and materials have been levelled at Western aid programmes to developing countries (Conroy and Litvinoff 1988, Hardoy, Mitlin and Satterthwaite 1992), which at least until recent years tended to favour bringing in outside expertise rather than tapping local knowledge and creating stronger indigenous development capacities. In addition, many aid and development programmes have proved to be ecologically destructive, such as building huge dams and cutting down forests.

According to Heaton, Repetto and Sobin (1991), the intergration of economic development and environmental protection objectives requires a transformation of technologies, such that two criteria are met. Firstly, technologies must be able to change industry and transportation from materials-intensive, high-throughput processes to those which use raw materials and fuels highly efficiently, rely on inputs with low environmental costs, generate little or no waste, recycle residues and release effluents which the natural environment can cope with. Secondly, technologies must be transformed or developed so that societies can 'live strictly off nature's income rather than consuming nature's capital' (p. 2). In terms of pollution prevention by industry, the potential range of options is enormous:

> Sometimes it is as simple as placing a lid on a vat of solvent. In other cases, significant changes in product or process – for instance, eliminating the use of heavy metals or replacing organic solvents with aqueous or mechanical processes – are required. (p.17)

Many companies have managed to make very significant reductions in pollutant outputs to the environment, whilst at the same time profiting from the reductions within only one or two years (Hirschhorn 1990). Some generalised examples of successful pollution prevention are given below.

- **Pharmaceutical production**. By replacing organic solvents with water-based solvents a 100% reduction in waste generation is possible.
- **Equipment manufacture**. The use of the ultrafiltration of wastes can reduce solvent and oil outputs by 100% and paint wastes by 98%.
- **Automotive manufacture**. The replacement of caustic cleaning with pneumatic cleaning processes can reduce sludge waste output by 100%.
- **Microelectronics**. The replacement of caustic cleaning with vibratory cleaning can reduce sludge waste by 100%.

- **Photographic film processing**. Electrolytic recovery by ion exchange can reduce developer waste by 85%, and a 95% reduction of fixer, silver and solvent releases can be achieved. (Huisingh, 1988)

In the urban context, the call for greater use of appropriate technologies, materials and design is common to many cities. This can be seen in the calls for 'sympathetic' development in English cities by critics such as Prince Charles, who favours a return to classical principles of architecture and more traditional building materials. In addition, nature needs to be designed into rather than out of the development process. This concept is as true of urban development as it is more generally. Many of the contemporary ills of cities stem from attempts to create artificial environments, both on the level of the whole neighbourhood and the individual home and office.

In a similar vein, policy-makers have begun to recognise the value of trams, which have recently returned to Manchester's city streets after an absence of 40 years. In Britain, some forty other urban areas are working on plans to do the same, aiming to reduce congestion and pollution in city centres (Hamer 1992).

The newly rediscovered technology of urban storm water harvesting promises to allow the positive use of rain which falls on impermeable urban surfaces (see Chapter Five), thereby reducing the need to import large quantities of water from often very distant sources. A harvesting system can also aid in attenuating storm water run-off from urban areas. As we have already noted, not all the water used in urban areas needs to be of high quality, potable standard. Urban water harvesting can provide a significant supply source for a wide range of industrial and domestic purposes. Storm water harvesting systems at their most basic involve the immediate spreading of captured rainwater (e.g. through land surface contouring) over land or water surfaces. Such systems are often referred to as 'water spreading' or 'run-off irrigation' techniques, and may route run-off to excavated and partially vegetated basins, for example, thereby providing a public amenity. With some additional expense and engineering, harvested water may be formally stored allowing a better balance between times of water supply and times of maximum demand. Storage may be open in ponds or reservoirs, or may be in covered tanks. Controlled gravity flow or pumping can then deliver water as required for irrigation purposes, or harvested water can be connected to indoor plumbing systems (e.g. for use in toilet cisterns). With further expense, captured water can be treated and used for drinking supply, especially if steps have been taken to isolate the relatively clean water draining roofs, from the normally heavily polluted water derived from urban streets (Ferguson 1987).

The city of Canberra in Australia, for example, now captures and stores urban rainfall to irrigate public open spaces. At the household level, the capture of water in rainwater tanks (e.g. sited on roofs) provides a 'free' supply of water for such activities as the watering of gardens and car washing. Some local urban councils in Australia are now encouraging the use of rainwater tanks, while a few have made their provision a requirement to help conserve town water supplies (Cairnes 1993).

There is nothing inherently bad about new technology, it is whether this technology is appropriate in terms of its mixture of environmental benefits and, if applicable, costs, and whether it is the most economically and socially appropriate form for a given country. For instance, Coghlan (1992a) reports the development of a new piece of water pollution detection technology. Water pollution inspectors could soon be using a device which identifies pathogenic water-borne micro-organisms in sewage-contaminated waters much more quickly than conventional techniques. The new instrument can detect the presence of pathogens in minutes rather than hours or days. This should aid in the rapid pinpointing of pollution sources.

It is in the cities of developing countries that some of the issues of appropriate technology, materials and design can be most starkly presented. In the shanty towns, for instance, abundant evidence can be found of people creating their own houses and communities, drawing on readily available building materials, often recycled. These can provide excellent examples of community self-help, using the best available means and technologies to provide a stepping stone on the ladder to decent housing (Turner and Roberts 1975). In some countries, this is now being recognised, and shanty town dwellers are being encouraged by the government to improve their housing still further, helped by the provision of infrastructure support in the shape of water and electricity supply connections (Hardoy and Satterthwaite 1989). There have also been some important advances using appropriate technologies in recent years. For instance, approximately 40% of China's small towns receive most of their power from mini-hydropower units. These only need the construction of small ponds to operate and are easily maintained by local communities (Clarke 1991).

6.3.2 Create new indicators for economic and environmental wealth

There is a need to broaden the way in which nations measure their well-being. At the minimum, rather than only using economic output measures, such as Gross National Product, a nation's wealth should also take into account the amount and status of its natural resources. If we adopted a wider perspective (OECD 1990), rapid rates of economic growth based on exploiting the natural resource base would be seen as what they are: signals of illusory gains in income and permanent loss of wealth. (p.37)

One of the fundamental weaknesses of reliance on the economic indicators used to compile Gross National Product figures, the currently most common way of measuring national wealth, is that they recognise only human-made and not natural assets. One result of this is that a country can gain a false sense of growth by rapid depletion of its environmental and natural resource stocks, in the process running down its long-term capacity for growth. Recognising this concern, the United Nations is currently reviewing its system of keeping national accounts, in order to take into account the depletion of national resources capital (see Chapter Seven).

At the local level, improved knowledge of environmental assets can be valuable, often measured physically rather than financially (e.g. areas of forest, kilometres of badly polluted river). The adoption of locality-wide 'environmental audits' by a number of local authorities in the UK provides a good example of the growing concern to take account of the quality of natural resources at the local level. The completion of a regular, independent environmental audit by a local authority is seen as a method of providing a baseline against which to gauge the changing status of an area's natural resource base, as a way of providing an agenda for action, and as a benchmark in assessing the efficacy of environmental policies (Association of Metropolitan Authorities 1989, Friends of the Earth 1989). The first such environmental audit to be carried out in the UK was the *Kirklees State of the Environment Report* for Kirklees Metropolitan District Council by Friends of the Earth (Kirklees MDC/FoE 1989). The Metropolitan District of Kirklees covers an area of approximately 415 square kilometres on the eastern edge of the Pennines in northern England and contains two large towns, Huddersfield and Dewsbury, and a population of 378,000. The report examines the status of air, water and land, and the effects of pollution on people, vegetation and wildlife. It discusses the practical uses and usefulness of the region's natural resources and the ways in which raw materials have been, and are being, developed for agriculture and industry (Kirklees MDC/FoE 1989).

The Kirklees environmental audit also included a number of recommendations for policies designed to improve the environment. Assuming that these are implemented, their effectiveness can be measured at some future date by reference to the baseline environmental conditions gathered for the first audit report. In itself, an environmental audit however is not sufficient, not least because of the difficulties in integrating it into everyday policy actions and the issues of conflicts of interest which can beset attempts at positive action.

6.3.3 Creating new indicators for economic and environmental productivity

Following on from the previous principle, and very much linked to the principle of 'minimum waste', there is a need in both production and accountancy procedures to bring environmental productivity considerations to the fore. At present, the emphasis is very much on unit outputs expressed in terms of financial or human inputs (e.g. £5000 per car, or 40 working days per car). Important though these are, there is an urgent need to look at productivity also in terms of environmental demands, tonnes of steel or water per car and so forth. The aim should be to minimise both resource inputs and waste outputs. As part of this concern it is important to conduct whole life-cycle audits for products, to see where wastage and waste generation occurs and assess the potential to reduce these. One of the most often cited examples of moving towards waste and wastage reduction is the United States-based company 3M. This company has instigated a wide-ranging programme to reduce wastage and waste generation through product redesign, process modifications, and recovery of by-products for reuse (Elkington and Burke 1987, Elkin, McLaren and Hillman 1991). These measures have reduced the company's waste flows and pollution activities, and saved it considerable amounts of money.

6.3.4 Estatabishing acceptable minimum standards through regulatory control

Traditionally, national and local governments (and supra-national institutions like the European Community) have adopted a 'command and control' approach to the implementation of environmental policies. This approach relies on the appropriate use of legislation, coupled with systems for the monitoring of compliance and punishing failure to comply with legislation (Sandbach 1980). Assuming that a given piece of legislation is appropriate in scope and scale and is properly enforced, the most obvious advantage of this direct regulatory approach is that it offers authorities a strong grip on environmentally degrading activities, with reasonably easily predicted effects (OECD 1990).

The exclusive use of direct regulation creates a number of difficulties. One such problem is that of 'diminishing returns'. It has been argued that many developed countries have now reached a point with the use of direct regulation where the efficacy of this approach has been declining, given the high costs and practical difficulties of regulation enforcement (OECD 1990). More than this, as Skinner (1990, p.85) has put it, 'a piece of legislation itself is merely paper; to successfully transform the city, there must be community will and support, an effective program and implementation'. It is also now widely accepted that a 'command

and control' approach in isolation does not provide incentives for internalising the costs of urban environmental impacts, leading to changed behaviour patterns for both individuals and businesses.

Appropriate legislation and regulation can none the less bring about direct improvements in the quality of the environment, or impact indirectly by stimulating investment in new 'environmentally friendly' technologies, for example. We have noted several times previously the importance of groundwater supplies for the state of Arizona in the USA. In order to lessen the profligate use and wastage of water, Arizona passed the Groundwater Management Act in 1980. This requires that cities in the state must achieve the sustainable withdrawal of groundwater by the year 2025, and abstraction of groundwater from all wells is now metered in order to indicate progress towards this goal (Charles 1991). One way in which city authorities can respond to the target of sustainable withdrawal might be through the use of building regulations. Tickell (1991) suggests that new housing developments, for example, could carry stipulations on the nature of domestic appliances, including the installation of water-efficient toilets and the fitting of showers rather than baths. Such actions have indeed been adopted in law by the city of Tucson in Arizona, where new housing developments are required to be installed with more efficient toilets, taps and showers (the city contributes to the extra cost of installing water-efficient toilets). Furthermore, since one square metre of grassy lawn requires some 11 litres of water each year, it has been stipulated that no more than 10% of the area around any new development can be planted with grass. With reference to the hydrological changes associated with urban development (see Chapter Five), most metropolitan areas of the USA now require urban developers to control storm water run-off in order to reduce the down-stream flood hazard, and (less consistently) to restore groundwater recharge and/or water quality (Ferguson 1987).

Water quality was a focus of the recent Federal Water Law in Germany, which forces companies to destroy organic compounds in effluent discharges or convert them into a biodegradable form. This requirement has stimulated research into newly available (and inexpensive) oxygen treatment processes which render organic wastes from chemical plants biodegradable (Coghlan 1992b). With reference to air pollution, the recent Dutch National Environment Plan has helped to reduce emissions of nitrogen oxide, VOCs and sulphur dioxide to the atmosphere. The reduction in sulphur dioxide emissions can be attributed to new agreements under the Plan which limit the permitted emissions from power stations and oil refineries. Decreases in nitrogen oxide and VOC emissions may be explained by the increased use of catalytic converters in cars, encouraged by generous tax incentives to motorists from the Dutch government (*New Scientist* 1992c).

6.3.5 Continuing action to internalise environmental costs into the market

The essence of this principle is the need to make the market work for the environment, by moving away progressively from the situation where polluters can abuse the 'free goods' of the natural environment (see Chapters Two and Seven). By 'free goods' or 'environmental commons' are meant the many services of the environment which are too often taken for granted, for instance industries discharging pollutants into the atmosphere or sea, hoping that these will be diluted, dispersed or reabsorbed into natural ecosystems (see Chapters Four and Five). Instead of this approach, users of environmental goods should pay the full costs of their activities. As a result, economic policies are needed which encourage polluters and users of natural resources to pay for the true environmental costs of their activities, accumulated at all stages of the product life-cycle. This guideline combines the OECD's user-pays and polluter-pays principles.

As we outlined in Chapter Five, the issue of contaminated land in the UK currently has a high profile. Some 100,000 sites are potentially contaminated in some way in the UK as a result of past industrial activities including mining, gas works, chemicals production and landfill sites. Among the issues raised by the problem of contaminated land are questions of clean-up costs and who should meet these costs. According to Milne (1992), the UK government is considering levying some form of tax on industry to pay for the clean-up. Such a tax may be of the type currently employed in the USA where there is a clean-up fund raised partly by taxing petrochemical and other polluting companies and partly by taxing industrial feedstocks, including fuel oil and lubricants. From 1993, new car buyers in the Netherlands will be charged a recycling levy of up to £80 to fund the collection and recycling of scrapped cars. However, motorists who hand in vehicles at specified scrapyards will be entitled to rebates on the levy (*New Scientist* 1992b).

Urban water use provides another area where there is much scope for the greater internalisation of the full costs of supply. As we have noted previously, fresh water is frequently wasted and inappropriately consumed by urban domestic and industrial users. Miller (1991) argues that in the USA there is currently very little incentive for domestic and industrial users to conserve water because water supply costs are effectively subsidised from general tax revenue, and the extent of subsidy does not appear on water bills. The removal of subsidies, combined with metering so that users pay as they consume, could do much to raise awareness of the full costs of water provision. Miller also suggests that industry should be made more aware of the effective subsidy it receives through federally-funded water supply projects, and that more realistic pricing would foster reuse and recycling. Tickell (1991) makes a similar point with reference to the UK practice of charging urban developers a 'flat-rate' infrastructure connection fee which does not reflect the actual costs of connection in different parts of a region.

6.3.6 Ensure social acceptability of environmental policies

It is important to recognise that the requirement for the full costs of resource utilisation to be reflected in the prices charged for the consumption of the environment may place an unacceptable extra financial burden on disadvantaged groups in society, and also on certain areas (see Chapter Two). With reference to the water industry, for example, although water metering has much to recommend it in terms of curbing excessive use of water and relating water payments to actual usage, there are important complications. Increases in a household's water bill as a result of these charges could cause great hardship for some, such as those on low incomes and those who require large amounts of water because of illness or disablement. The implication is not necessarily to abandon the notion of water metering, but where it is introduced to ensure that certain categories of vulnerable people are not penalised for their unavoidable high water demands.

A similar scenario can be envisaged if electricity supply charges were made to reflect environmental damage (or the costs of preventing it) as a result of pollution from power stations. Since sustainable urban development should aim to enhance the net quality of life of all residents, the imposition of high charges on disadvantaged groups in society as a result of externality pricing may not be appropriate. For groups such as the elderly, systems must be evolved which take account of the need for resources and ability to pay for their use, to ensure 'social acceptability'. Such systems might involve exemption of certain groups from charges altogether, rebates, a multi-tier charging system or enhanced benefits to cover additional costs for welfare recipients (see Chapter Seven).

6.3.7 Widespread public participation

Much is made in international, national and local environmental policy documents of the need to involve the local community in the decision-making process. Elkin, McLaren and Hillman (1991) refer to the need for a greater community role as the principle of 'participation'. The principle of participation argues that greater community involvement provides an additional source of knowledge of environmental conditions and improvement needs. Greater participation should also encourage people to engage directly in improvement schemes, not least through local voluntary and charity organisations. In addition, widespread community participation in strategy formulation, and in policy implementation and management, increases public awareness of environmental issues and fosters a sense of community responsibility for improving and maintaining environmental quality. Equally importantly, work in developing countries has been particularly influential in demonstrating how technological, externally imposed, professional 'solutions' to local problems have too often focused on 'things', not people, often mis-specifying the problems (never mind missing the best solutions), because local people were not fully involved in the process of development (see Conroy and Litvinoff 1988, Hardoy and Satterthwaite 1989). Maximum use of local initiatives and knowledge is always desirable in guiding the local urban development process. This is not only about improving the local environment, but enhancing the sense of stewardship for the global environment. The principle 'think globally; act locally' summarises the responsibility of local residents and businesses not only to improve their own environment, but also to think of the broader consequences of their activities.

To aid in the fostering of a sense of local community responsibility for urban environmental conditions, it may be helpful if a local environment forum can be clearly identified by local people as having the primary responsibility for environmental policies. This may be achieved if a key local politician (e.g. a mayor) or high-profile administrator is given the task of chairing the environment committee (OECD 1990). It has also been argued that the successful organisation and continued existence of a coordinated, cross-sectoral management system (see below) requires dynamic and persistent leadership, without which the integrated approach would disintegrate.

6.4 MANAGEMENT GUIDELINES FOR SUSTAINABLE URBAN DEVELOPMENT

Much of the success, or otherwise, of urban environmental improvement policies depends upon the manner in which policies are planned, implemented, coordinated and monitored. The management principles outlined in Box 6.4 provide guidelines for the effective administration of environmental improvements in urban areas, and indeed more generally.

Box 6.4 A Summary of the Guiding Management Principles for Sustainable Urban Development

Subsidiarity. Responsibility for the implementation and management of urban environment programmes must rest at the lowest feasible appropriate level of government.

Flexibility in devising and implementing environmental policy regimes. Tackling environmental problems will be most successful using a variety of instruments (e.g. legislative, market, fiscal), allowing flexibility to meet local needs.

Long-term strategies are necessary for environmental management. This requires a strategic vision centred upon improving the quality of urban life, encouraging residents to 'think globally; act locally'.

Improved coordination across environment-related policies. Better inter- and intra-governmental coordination can enhance complementarities between environmental and other policies, and public–private partnerships.

Non-discrimination and equal right of hearing. This would ensure that transboundary pollution issues could be resolved by all those affected on a basis of equal rights.

Need for better availability and understanding of environmental information. Communities and businesses should be informed of environmental consequences of development proposals as a matter of right, including across national state boundaries if appropriate. Better availability of information is also important, to improve decision-making.

6.4.1 Subsidiarity

Schumacher (1974) made this the first of his principles which related to large-scale organisations. In essence, subsidiarity means higher-tier organisations should never do what lower-tier organisations could do, defying the false assumption that greater wisdom resides at the top of any hierarchy. Instead, functions and decision-making should be devolved to the lowest tier possible, not least since Schumacher claims that loyalty can only grow from the small to the large organisation, and not the other way round. Subsidiarity then implies the decentralisation of both power and responsibility, something which may apply equally within the state and within private companies.

In many countries, urban environmental policy initiatives have been formulated and implemented by national governments (OECD 1990). However, there is a growing awareness of the need to involve local government and community groups in environmental policy formulation and implementation, giving local authorities greater autonomy to manage the diversity of urban environmental issues. It is at the local level that the coordination of environmental activities and policies can most efficiently be organised to cope with local priorities and needs. Greater local autonomy means that (OECD 1990):

> Issues and functions should generally be allocated to the scale closest to the people receiving the flow of goods or services from the management activity. Administrative responsibility for the urban environment should be pushed as far down the administrative chain as possible and rest as close to the ultimate user groups as possible. (p.43)

It should be pointed out here that although such sentiments sound fine in abstract terms, there are ambiguities about how far down is appropriate for any given environmental policy function. A key issue, therefore, is not simply which functions belong with which administrative tier, but how effectively the chains of governmental, business, and community responsibility work, both vertically and horizontally.

Although the appropriate level of responsibility for the formulation and realisation of urban environmental policies will usually lie primarily at the local level, in every case there is a need for involvement from national (and, in some countries, regional) governments. Indeed, as this book has stressed so frequently already, the international nature of many pollution problems requires international cooperation, via organisations such as the European Community and the United Nations, in the formulation of environmental quality standards, and pollution control and waste disposal agreements, for example. Rather than prescribing specific approaches or 'solutions' to urban environmental problems which may not be optimal in the local context, the ideal function of national government may be to encourage local action by providing human and financial resources, improving environmental education and training for the individual, giving leadership on environmental awareness, monitoring the effectiveness of local initiatives, providing a legislative framework which enables local action, and disseminating innovative approaches to the solution of urban environmental problems.

6.4.2 Flexibility in devising and implementing environmental policy regimes

In the search for appropriate policies to enhance the environment, there is a danger, perhaps for reasons of political dogma or reducing the short-term financial burden, that too much reliance will be placed on one particular means of moving towards sustainable urban development. Given the wide range of urban and more general environmental problems, and the dynamic nature of urban areas, a flexible approach to urban environmental management is required. Complex problems demand complex solutions, especially given the variations in environmental tolerances and in government systems. Therefore rather than trying to utilise individual policy instruments derived from a particular philosophical approach or principle, it is more likely to be fruitful to consider a 'portfolio' of instruments (e.g. a combination of externality pricing, differential taxation, grants, subsidies and regulation) when responding to a set of interacting and changing environmental problems. As the OECD (1990) notes in recommending a greater emphasis on economic policy tools:

> In practice, pragmatic approaches to new economic instruments seem to prevail: economic instruments are adjuncts to direct regulations in mixed systems. In such combinations economic instruments raise revenues for financing environmental measures, provide incentives to better implement the associated regulation and can stimulate technical innovation. (p.51)

There is also the combination of policy life-cycles and the changing nature of environmental problems which needs to be taken into account in devising policies (Button and Pearce 1989). Some policies are more appropriate in some places and at certain times than others. This said, although one policy instrument or policy approach may be in the ascendancy at any one moment, it is also inevitable that other policies will be in place simultaneously. Without this diversity, there is likely to be little experimentation or innovation emerging with the next generation of policies, and little sensitivity to the peculiarity of place.

It is appropriate at this point to mention the need for continuing research into finding the most efficient combination of instruments to combat different forms of urban environmental degradation. This will involve better information on environmental baseline conditions, and continuous 'open' monitoring; that is, information being made available. Although for the sake of flexibility of action it is important to foster the use of a 'portfolio' of instruments, this does complicate the task of assessing how well urban environmental policy instruments interact with each other, and also with other non-environmental policies. Research into the efficiency, interaction and 'side-effects' of economic instruments is especially urgent given the relative youth of a market-based approach to urban environmental management and the likely increase in the use of economic instruments by many governments in the near future.

6.4.3 Long-term strategies are necessary for effective environmental management

Intergenerational equity necessarily requires a long-term perspective in environmental management. The concept of sustainable urban development must have at its core the need to consider the development of the city and wider region over the long term, with short-term development objectives derived from, and consistent with, long-term sustainability objectives.

The city region is not the sole level at which long-term strategy needs to operate, but it is perhaps one of the most important. Most cities are still surprisingly reliant on their immediate bioregional hinterlands. Indeed some resources are naturally better managed at the regional level, most notably water supply and disposal, which should be related to natural watershed areas (Geddes 1915, MacKaye 1928). A strategic, long-term vision for individual cities, should have the central aim of enhancing the quality of life for both present and future residents, whilst contributing to global sustainability. Quality of urban life, however, is determined by a wide range of factors. These need to be considered together in the formulation of a strategic vision, which includes at its heart the prioritisation of environmental concerns and actions.

6.4.4 Improved coordination across environment-related policies

The need to bring together and consider many aspects of the quality of urban life, underpins the principle of improved coordination across environmental policies in urban areas. Also, a well-defined, clearly identifiable authority or administrative system should have the responsibility of overseeing the formulation and implementation of such a coordinated strategic vision. Thus, the identification of the appropriate level of responsibility, already referred to, becomes critical.

A primary focus of the coordination drive needs to involve bringing local-level activities more closely together, to exploit potential synergies and reduce any overlaps. In particular, the work of traditionally separate departments within local government needs to be brought together much more consistently (Freeman 1994). This might be achieved, for instance, via environment committees or task forces, to formulate environmental strategies which maximise the use of local knowledge and initiatives. Such environmental strategies would seek to maximise cooperation between departments, integrate the environmental policies of

different departments and maximise the existing and potential complementarities between environmental policies and other policies. For
example, land use planning decisions should be based upon a local
development plan agreed by all local government departments, the local
community and local business interests, integrating the needs and
aspirations of those involved in such apparently diverse sectors as
transport, housing, pollution control, waste disposal, local economic
development and recreation. Perhaps most importantly of all, many
environmental policies will need to be coordinated and implemented
across governmental boundaries, given the nature of urban impacts on
wider environments. In a sometimes contradictory way, in many countries some environmental municipal powers and responsibilities have
been increasingly fragmented, set up as separate cost centres, or privatised in recent years, ostensibly to achieve greater financial efficiency
and sometimes greater local sensitivity. One result of this fragmentation
process, however, has been that the need for coordination at the local
level has grown dramatically. In the case of the UK at least, this has been
accompanied by a diminution of the powers and resources of democratic
local governments, most notably with the abolition of the metropolitan
counties in 1986.

Private companies and institutions will in many urban areas have
much to offer local public authorities which could benefit urban improvement schemes. As well as the potential for financial investment in
appropriate development schemes, local private organisations can prove
valuable sources of additional advice on local environmental improvement needs (e.g. areas where upgraded infrastructure might stimulate
investment) and suitable management techniques for the implementation, monitoring and evaluation of environmental improvement policies
and projects. Already public–private partnerships have played a major
role in the success of a number of large-scale urban redevelopment
schemes, although the involvement of the private sector in these partnerships is not without its tensions (Haughton and Whitney 1989). It
may well be central to the success of urban environmental policies that
representatives of major local private interests be included on any
environment forum. This may in turn heighten the local business
community's awareness of environmental issues, and improve their
sense of ownership of the environmental problems towards which their
activities contribute.

Initiatives to improve policy coordination have abounded in recent
years, though very little evaluation of their effectiveness appears to have
been undertaken. Newman and Mouritz (1991) argue that the most
critical aspect of the future planning of development in the Australian
city of Perth is the integration of water and land use planning to minimise

the impact of urban development on hydrology. Already, the urban expansion plan for Perth has excluded development over major ground-water source areas to prevent any reduced replenishment of the ground-water store.

Miller (1991) suggests that the wastage of fresh water supplies in the USA is exacerbated by the frequent over-division of responsibility for water supply among many different state and local government agencies. The Chicago metropolitan area, for example, has 349 separate water supply systems, divided among some 2000 local units of government over a six-county area. By contrast, the UK operates a system of large regional utilities responsible for water supply and sewerage disposal. Arguments for large, integrated (i.e. multi-functional) utilities include:

- Small systems may generate insufficient revenues to allow expansion and service improvements.
- The reduction of competition amongst utilities encourages a socially equitable distribution of resources within the region as a whole.
- The amalgamation of utilities facilitates economies of scale and allows the provision of specialist facilities and staff.
- Larger management units encourage the basin-wide integration of functions and longer-term planning.
- Water resource fluctuations are generally moderated at the regional scale.

Disadvantages include:

- Power is concentrated in one organisation.
- There is a danger of bias if one organisation both operates and polices a resource utilisation system.
- The growth in administrative bureaucracy may slow decision-making and remove this process from local communities. (McDonald and Kay 1988)

Overall, the prevailing view appears to be that the advantages of regional resource management utilities, such as the UK water companies, out-weigh the disadvantages. However, one of the most important issues in resource management is the maintenance or creation of effective com-munication, both between and within those public and private organi-sations with an interest in the resource in question. Thus, the creation of regional utilities may have advantages for water supply, but the resulting regional boundaries may be of little relevance to other agencies. McDonald and Kay (1988) argue that ultimately such a mismatch of administrative boundaries should not be allowed to occur if it compromises effective communication. Such tensions need to be addressed, as do possible means of overcoming them.

Ultimately, the need for better coordination and communication may lead to the creation of crosscutting agencies involved with environmental protection. With reference to pollution control, for example, this appears highly desirable as many pollutants can occur in air, land and water, and become transferred between these media. In this context, an overarching agency which is capable of keeping track of potentially toxic emissions across media appears logical. Such concerns underlie the formation of Her Majesty's Inspectorate of Pollution (HMIP) in the UK. HMIP was formed in 1987 and is part of the Department of the Environment. As well as taking on a new role in the control of water pollution, it brought together three existing inspectorates; the Industrial Air Pollution Inspectorate, the Radiochemical Inspectorate and the Hazardous Waste Inspectorate. Leaving aside views on the success, or otherwise, of HMIP (and the broader environmental protection system within which it operates), it was formed to fulfil a number of aims:

- to exercise efficiently and effectively statutory powers for controlling radioactive substances, emissions to air from scheduled industrial processes and water authority discharges to water
- to monitor the efficiency and effectiveness with which water and waste disposal authorities exercise their powers of control, and to secure improvements where appropriate
- to ensure the development of economically sound technical practices for disposing of waste in the most environmentally acceptable way
- to help develop feasible methods of applying a cross-media approach to pollution control
- to develop plans for implementing the government's strategy for radioactive waste management. (UK contribution to OECD 1991, p. 44)

With the formation of HMIP and associated legislation, the UK government has sought to develop a system of Integrated Pollution Control (IPC) for the most dangerous industrial (scheduled) and non-industrial processes which release toxic substances into the environment.

6.4.5 Non-discrimination and equal right of hearing

The OECD and other international bodies have attempted to confront transfrontier pollution issues through a series of international agreements. The United Nations in particular has played a central role in bringing nations together to consider environmental issues of common concern, not least the greenhouse effect, high-level ozone depletion and acid precipitation (see Chapters Four and Five). Related to the pollution dimension in particular, the OECD have formulated the principle of non-discrimination and equal right of hearing. This states that trans-frontier polluters should face statutory provisions at least equivalent to those in the host nation, whilst the 'polluter pays' principle should also apply on a transfrontier basis. Similarly, those adversely affected by this pollution should be treated in at least an equivalent way to citizens in the host country.

The equal right of hearing takes this further, and would provide citizens of affected countries with the right to be heard on a basis equal to those in the country of origin. Both these principles could also have important implications if adopted at a micro-scale for urban development. Urban development proposals which will have adverse impacts on other areas, whether in the immediate hinterland or not, should be subject to consideration on an equal basis by all those affected, not just the local population and business community. Regional government provides one possible way around local parochialism which favours urban development with adverse external impacts, but it is not clear that in itself it will necessarily be effective in resolving intra-urban and urban–hinterland conflicts.

6.4.6 Need for better availability and understanding of environmental information

The awareness of environmental issues needs to be continually height-ened among the general public, state bodies and private industry to achieve the most from a market-based approach to urban environmental management and to foster a more responsible attitude to environmental quality. Such heightened awareness requires a right to freedom of information on environmental impacts of development, and more gen-erally, education and advice policies for producers and consumers alike.

Environmental education campaigns, perhaps involving competi-tions and awards, provide one means of raising environmental aware-ness. In the UK, for example, an Environment Week has been organised every spring since 1984 by the National Civic Trust Organisation, during which local authorities, businesses, schools, community organisations and the media are encouraged to initiate environmental improvements. Environmental education in schools and higher education institutions has developed strongly over the last two decades in many Western countries, whilst a large number of community awareness campaigns have achieved considerable localised success (for various examples see:

JURUE 1987, 1988; Partnership Limited 1988; Gordon 1990). The need is to take these campaigns forward into the home and, with detailed training programmes, into the workplace.

Additionally, in order to enable the marketplace to work effectively for the environment, consumers need freely available information on the environment-'friendliness' of goods and services. This is something which businesses themselves are taking increasingly seriously, not just in search of the green consumer and investor, but also in recognition of tightening governmental regulation and of firms' own moral obligations (Roberts 1992). In this case, to 'enhance awareness of environmental issues' implies freedom of information, as a right for the consumer. This may be achieved through the comprehensive labelling of products, the growth of ethical investment trusts or by the publication of the pollution discharge records of industrial companies, for example.

As a result of European Community action, companies may be required to divulge data on their emissions of toxic chemicals to the environment within the next few years. This would help to bring Europe into line with the USA, where companies are legally bound to provide information on environmental releases of some 300 toxic chemicals. This information is held in the Toxic Release Inventory and is open to public scrutiny (*New Scientist* 1991).

The continual monitoring, evaluation and synthesis of environmental quality data at local, national and international levels is an important environmental management tool. Environmental audits at the local level, for example, can aid the identification of environmental problems and the prioritisation of action programmes and policies. National governments should monitor the compliance of local authorities with national or international quality standards and could allocate resources effectively to areas with pressing environmental problems. Local authority data could also be amalgamated by central government to assist in the compilation of a national 'sustainability index' of the kind noted in the next chapter.

As with the application of ecological and social/economic principles, much monitoring and evaluative work is needed on appropriate administrative structures and successful local projects. The aim must be to ensure the maximum dissemination of good practice at as wide a scale as possible, without creating a dull conformity in policy actions which may not be sensitive to local needs. In this context, the 'sustainable city networks' suggested at the Rio Earth Summit may be particularly valuable.

6.5 CONCLUSION

This chapter has identified a wide range of guiding principles which when used together creatively may help urban residents, businesses and governments to contribute positively to global sustainability whilst providing attractive urban environments. It was stressed at the beginning of this chapter that the principles outlined for sustainable urban development are interrelated and that neither they, nor the policies derived from them, should be viewed in isolation. Some of these interconnections have already been elucidated, and the next chapter, on policy approaches to sustainable urban development, continues this task.

FURTHER READING

Ahmad (1989) provides a good review of the development over time of environmental management principles, whilst the World Commission on Environment and Development (1987) is a key source on the principles developed specifically in the context of the sustainability debate. Further elaboration of these themes, particularly intergenerational equity, can be found in Pearce, Markandya and Barbier (1989) and Pearce (1990). Taking an economic approach, the OECD (1990) provides a small number of principles specifically for cities, whilst also applying these to three sectors: energy, (land use-led) regeneration and transport. Taking a more ecological approach, Hough (1990) also provides some principles for urban sustainability.

KEY THEMES

In this chapter, each of the guiding principles provides a key concept, and it would be invidious to isolate any of them here. Perhaps the most important concept is the interrelatedness of these principles: in terms of principles, too, 'nothing stands alone'.

DISCUSSION POINTS

- Are there any additional principles which you feel should be added to this list? Are there any principles noted in this chapter which you feel should be excluded, or perhaps treated as 'fundamental' rather than 'guiding' principles? Where would you place 'decrease and reorient military spending', and why?
- Grassroots participation in sustainable development is often regarded as a central principle. Discuss the case for and against

a major decentralisation of powers and responsibility for environmental issues to the neighbourhood level. Consider in particular approaches to pollution control.

- Diversity in terms of urban society is regarded as an important element of the 'requisite variety' principle more normally associated with the natural world. This guidance can be interpreted in a variety of ways. In practical terms, how would you suggest that urban planners might seek to operationalise this idea, and what potential dangers do you see?

CHAPTER SEVEN

Policy Instruments for Improving the Urban Environment

7.1 INTRODUCTION

In moving from principles for sustainable urban development towards policies, this chapter concentrates on two broad approaches to policy making and policy implementation, environmental impact assessment (EIA) and economic policy instruments. The main rationale for choosing the two tools highlighted here is that they help illustrate many of the points made in the previous chapter, whilst also illustrating some of the interconnections between the different guiding principles. The analysis also seeks to demonstrate how these two policy approaches can be successfully combined with other approaches to environmental management: as one of the guiding principles in Chapter Six noted, it is important to emphasise flexibility in devising and applying combinations of policy instruments.

Putting the principles for sustainable development into operation requires a complex inter-weaving of different policy approaches, involving a multitude of different individual policy instruments. The main forms of policy instruments relevant to sustainable urban development, can be condensed into six categories: legislative, technological, economic, planning, local enablement, and education and information (Box 7.1). Used creatively, in the context of effective systems of local, national and international governance, a combination of these different policy approaches will usually bring about more rapid and more effective change than would happen if any were used in isolation. The management of sustainable urban development is a theme which we return to in the final chapter of this book.

It is helpful to consider the evolution of environmental policy concerns and tools in the context of different stages of urban development. Noting that the types of problem faced by cities differ at each phase of their growth, Button and Pearce (1988) argue that this means that different mixes of policy approach will be valid at each stage of a city's growth (Figure 7.1). This approach highlights that just as both actual

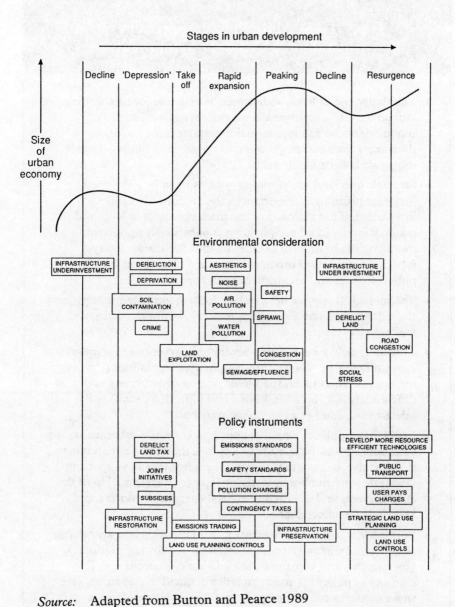

Source: Adapted from Button and Pearce 1989

Figure 7.1 A highly simplified representation of urban development and the use of policy tools

Box 7.1 The Main Policy Approaches to Sustainable Urban Development

- Legislative controls are widely seen as essential for establishing and policing minimum environmental standards, such as requirements on minimum quality standards for pollution discharges from industrial and other users, and limits on water usage, such as drought orders.

- Strategic and land use planning policies must be developed. Strategic planning is important in the coordination and integration of the activities of the main operators at local and regional levels. Land use planning is particularly important in moulding the built form of cities to enhance sustainability, especially policies on urban density, land use zoning, location of public services and provision of open space.

- Technological approaches can be adopted, for instance improving the efficiency of water-using appliances, stormwater reuse and waste-water treatment.

- Economic policy instruments centre on market-based solutions to environmental problems, through pricing externalities (e.g. water metering, carbon taxes, road tolls), introducing pricing differentials (e.g. between leaded and unleaded petrol) and selective subsidies (e.g. for public transport).

- Enablement policies work in support of collective schemes among communities and businesses to improve their local environments in particular, but not exclusively. The advantage of supporting non-state activities lies in fostering long-term stewardship of the environment, and in bringing in local energies, resources and knowledge to effect change.

- Policies which seek to provide better information and knowledge about environmental issues are essential in allowing producers, governments and consumers to make rational decisions. This category of policy approach includes demand management (e.g. water conservation campaigns), and the provision of better information on environmental impacts, from eco-labelling on products to full-scale environmental impact assessments.

and perceived problems change over time, so it may be that certain policy instruments are more appropriate or more feasible than others in particular places and at particular times. Add to this that our under-standing of problems and the sophistication of our policy instruments changes over time, and it becomes clear that there is no single solution or set of solutions which can readily be advocated as applicable to each and every city.

7.2 ENVIRONMENTAL IMPACT ASSESSMENT – A MECHANISM FOR ENVIRONMENTAL PROTECTION

The focus on *environmental impact assessment* (EIA) in this section, reflects the potential of this environmental management tool to translate principles of sustainable urban development into practice, whilst also demonstrating a range of links between principles. The aim of this section is not to provide a detailed overview of the workings of an EIA system. Rather, it seeks to give something of the flavour of the contri-bution that EIA could make to the realisation of sustainable urban development, particularly its potential as a vehicle for the parallel or synergistic application of several of the principles described in the previous chapter.

7.2.1 Background to EIA

Environmental impact assessment, sometimes referred to as environ-mental assessment (EA), provides a framework for the *prior* assessment of the potential impacts of urban, and other, developments such that adverse environmental effects can be eliminated or minimised before development commences. As a proactive development control tool, EIA, therefore, represents an attempt to apply and instigate the principle of 'prevention is better than cure'. The potential contribution of EIA to sustainable development was recognised by the World Commission on Environment and Development (1987), who suggested that nation-states should make, or require, prior environmental assessments of proposed activities which may significantly affect the environment or use of natural resources. Proposed activities which may affect urban environmental quality may take the form of development policies, plans or projects. To date, the use of EIA has been almost exclusively devoted to the appraisal of individual development projects, although the wider application of EIA is receiving greater attention and this theme is discussed later on. Most of what follows, however, focuses on the use of EIA at the project level.

From humble beginnings as a minor part of cost–benefit analysis (CBA) procedures used in the USA in the early 1960s, EIA has grown to become an accepted part of the development control procedures of many developed countries around the world. With the enactment of the National Environmental Policy Act of 1969 in the USA (United States Government 1969), EIA received its first formal recognition as an environmental management tool. Its primary function then, as now, was to enable those impacts on the (principally natural) environment which could not be measured in monetary terms to be included in the project appraisal process. Normally, a formal EIA system will require an *environmental impact statement* (EIS), or environmental statement (ES), to be produced for certain types of development project according to the potential for environmental disruption. Potential disruption is usually related to such factors as the size of the project, the nature of the processes associated with a particular development and its planned location.

EIA has been defined as (Wathern 1992):

> A process for identifying the likely consequences for the biogeo-physical environment and for man's health and welfare of implementing particular activities and for conveying this information, at a stage when it can materially affect their decision, to those responsible for sanctioning the proposal. (p. 6)

The formal adoption of EIA into environmental protection legislation has generally proceeded rapidly in developed countries in recent years. Indeed, it may not be too long before EIA is formally adopted in a number of countries in the former Eastern bloc (Starzewska 1992). The same may also be true of a number of developing countries (e.g. Htun 1992), although progress has, in the main, been slow. Many descriptions of the operation of a formal EIA system, such as the one given below, assume EIA to be part of a well developed and implemented legislative and planning base, both at national and local levels of government. However, while EIA can only be expected to operate optimally within such a context, many developing countries lack this development control base. As Kennedy (1992) points out, there remain serious obstacles to the operation of formal EIA systems in many developing countries, including: a general lack of political will or awareness of the need for EIA, insufficient public participation in decision-making, lacking or inadequate legislative frameworks, lack of an institutional base, insufficient skilled manpower, lack of environmental data, and insufficient financial resources. Moreover, Moreira (1992) suggests that since most Latin American countries lack national environmental policies or legislation, they would do better to formulate these before attempting to adopt a formal EIA system.

With reference to the siting of chemical plants in India, Bowonder, Prasad and Reddy (1987) recognise the need for EIA to become an integral part of project appraisal, rather than locational decisions being taken on economic and infrastructure availability grounds alone. They further suggest:

> The Bhopal accident clearly indicates the need for a proper industrial siting procedure co-ordinated with a comprehensive urban planning system under the broad framework of project evaluation, linking environmental impact assessment and project appraisal...Integration of the locational decisions, EIA, zoning of industries (polluting and non-polluting) and urban planning has to be achieved. (pp. 11, 19)

In the description of a typical EIA system given here it is important to bear in mind that while EIA has received recognition as a valuable environmental management tool around the world, many countries have yet to formally adopt EIA, and, arguably, lack the (immediate) basis to do so.

It is also important to appreciate that in no sense can EIA be described as solely or principally an urban management tool. Indeed, EIA has a critical role to play in the protection of the rich variety of natural biological and physical resources housed in rural or wilderness areas. Although urban areas do not generally provide a large reservoir of such natural resources, the importance of EIA in an urban context is not diminished. As has already been frequently emphasised, urban areas are unique, containing buildings, for example, which constitute a valuable cultural resource worthy of protection. Similarly, the construction of new urban buildings will require resources from urban hinterlands. Thus, a principally urban development may have implications for environmental quality far beyond urban boundaries. Also, the high population and industrial densities found in urban areas, combined with greater pressures for commercial development, create an enhanced potential risk of adverse impacts on the urban – and wider – environment and on human health from poorly conceived developments. Added to this is the great potential for damaging environmental interactions (e.g. the combination of many different pollutants) which may emerge in the urban realm.

Despite these factors, those areas rich in natural biological and physical resources most frequently appear to receive the attention of development agencies and environmentalists. Hyman (1990), for example, provides a summary and critique of World Bank projects and activities affecting urban environmental quality, stating that:

> Until recently, environmental considerations received little attention in the World Bank's work plans and policy statements concerning urban development... Much of the external pressure on the Bank from environmental organizations has surrounded rural development activities that cleared forests for roads and commercial agriculture, or inundated large land areas for dams (p. 204).

Indeed, up to 1989 the Bank appears to have assumed that its urban development projects could only have beneficial environmental impacts. This view appears to have been reached without the benefit of any project-based EIA and without any reference to the possible impacts of urban development on environmental quality (Hyman 1990).

A specific example which illustrates the relevance of EIA in an urban context is provided by the siting of a large petroleum refinery plant some 30 km north-west of the Taj Mahal monument (at Agra), near the city of Mathura in India (D'Monte 1985). The decision to site the plant at this location (taken by the government of India) was made on the basis of infrastructure availability, without any environmental consequences being considered, despite the already high air pollution levels at Agra from many small industries. Since the prevailing wind is from the north-west, it is now recognised that sulphur dioxide emissions from the plant threaten the Taj Mahal (not to mention the human population of Agra) through acid deposition. Had an EIA been conducted for the proposal, then such lack of foresight might have prevented the possible degradation of one of the world's most famous cultural assets. Thankfully, the refinery has installed sophisticated and complex pollution control equipment, although had other locations for the plant been considered through an EIA process, less costly pollution abatement technology might have been appropriate.

7.2.2 Basic features of an EIA system

Although EIA comes in a variety of systems, utilising a wide range of procedures, assessment methods and techniques, and thresholds of implementation, it is now widely accepted that most forms of EIA should attempt to conform to four fundamental tasks (Roberts and Hunter 1992):

1. They should identify the nature of the proposed and induced activities which are likely to be generated by a project or the introduction of a process.

2. They should identify the elements of the environment that will be significantly affected.

3. They should evaluate the initial and subsequent impacts.

4. They should be concerned with the management of the beneficial and adverse impacts which are generated.

Following from this, at least in theory, EIA is not merely a method of analysis, but a comprehensive framework which identifies, analyses, evaluates and manages the impacts associated with the introduction and operation of a development project. Seen in this broader context, EIA can be viewed as a means of integrating the concerns of economic development and environmental protection (see for example Htun 1992). The written output from the EIA, namely a detailed EIS, should provide the decision-maker(s) with a rational basis upon which to make a better decision. The EIS is not, in itself, a decision. The EIA may suggest to the decision-maker one of the following options:

- that the proposed development is acceptable at the suggested site
- that the proposed development is not acceptable at the site suggested, but may be acceptable at an alternative site
- that the proposed development is unacceptable at any site
- that a modified proposal may be acceptable either at the site suggested, or at an alternative site.

In reaching one of these decisions, it is important to recognise that the standards and criteria adopted by decision-makers will vary from country to country, according to national environmental legislation and policies, and even between different areas within one country, according to local conditions and priorities (Murphy 1981).

In more detail, Box 7.2 outlines the basic features of a typical EIA system. It is common to view the process of conducting an EIA as a linear progression through defined stages, such as those given in Box 7.2. While this simplifies a description of the EIA process, it does not necessarily represent the real-life situation. Commonly, there are cyclical as well as linear sequences of activities. These may arise through consultations between the developer and the competent authority (e.g. the local planning authority) responsible for sanctioning the project. Thus, feedback is possible at any stage in the EIA process resulting in modifications to the project's design or operation.

Box 7.2 Basic Features of a Typical EIA System

An EIS prepared for an individual project will normally be expected to cover the following *types* of items:

- description of the main characteristics of the project
- estimation of the residues and wastes that it is likely to create
- analysis of the aspects of the environment likely to be significantly affected by the project, including a description of the baseline condition of these aspects of the environment
- analysis of the likely significant effects of the proposed project on the environment including a description of the forecasting techniques and data used to assess these effects
- description of the measures envisaged to reduce harmful effects (this may be extended to include a consideration of alternatives to the proposed project and the reasons why they were rejected)
- assessment of the compatibility of the project with environmental regulations and land use plans
- non-technical summary of the total assessment.

The main *procedural elements* of the EIA process will normally include the following:

1. The developer (often with assistance from consultants, regulatory bodies and other organisations) prepares an EIS which is submitted, along with the application for project authorisation, to the competent authority (e.g. the local planning authority).

2. The study is published (possibly after checking its adequacy) and is used as a basis for consultation involving both statutory authorities, possessing relevant environmental responsibilities, and the general public.

3. The findings of the consultation process are presented to the competent authority.

4. The assessment study and consultation findings accompany the proposed project through the remainder of the competent authority's authorisation procedure.

Note: These basic features can be further elaborated by (for example) making arrangements for the preliminary screening and scoping of projects, for independent panels to vet the studies made for major projects, and for monitoring the environmental consequences arising from the implementation of the project.

(Adapted from Lee 1992)

In all EIA systems, some screening of projects is required to determine those to be subject to the full EIA process. In consequence, suitable selection criteria must be formulated which strike a balance between environmental protection and the unnecessary imposition of a full EIA where project characteristics do not warrant it. Many small-scale urban developments (such as house extensions or the repair of existing roads) which do not constitute a change in land use may require some form of regulation and planning permission from the local planning authority, but hardly merit a full EIA. However, it is difficult to formulate suitable screening criteria. Possibilities include the physical size of the project or its monetary cost. Clearly, these will not by themselves be adequate in all circumstances, as small and inexpensive proposals, in sensitive locations, may carry major impacts. Studies conducted to provide guidance in selecting projects to be subject to EIA highlight three criteria (Lee 1989). These are:

1. the size of the project, i.e. principally whether the physical scale of the project makes it of more than immediate local importance

2. the environmental characteristics of the area in which it will be located, e.g. a sensitive environment such as a nature reserve

3. the physical and process characteristics of the project, e.g. a project thought likely to give rise to particularly complex, dangerous or adverse effects.

Many countries have now developed lists of projects, based on criteria such as those given above, for which EIA is a development requirement. In Thailand, for example, the need for EIA is related to location, based upon the identification of environmentally sensitive areas (Wathern 1992). The use of rigid criteria has, however, been rejected in some countries because of perceived inflexibility of operation. Canada, for example, has adopted a phased screening process which can be applied to any type of project (FEARO 1978). In July 1988, member states of the European Community (EC) formally complied with the EC Directive on EIA (Commission of the European Communities 1985). This important piece of legislation contained two Annexes dividing projects into two broad categories. Those in Annex 1 of the Directive (generally large industrial or infrastructure developments) are normally subject to a mandatory EIA in all member states. For those in Annex 2, requirement for an EIA is at the discretion of each member state. The projects in each category are given in Boxes 7.3 and 7.4. The EC Directive has been much criticised for this division of projects (e.g. Haigh 1984). Those in Annex 1 are, by their very nature, not commonly encountered, while the day-to-day projects which perhaps generate the bulk of envi-

Box 7.3 List of Annex 1 Projects from the EC Directive Requiring an EIA

- Crude oil refineries (excluding undertakings manufacturing only lubricants from crude oil) and installations for the gasification and liquefaction of 500 tonnes or more of coal or bituminous shale per day
- Thermal power stations and other combustion installations with a heat output of 300 megawatts or more, and nuclear power stations and other nuclear reactors
- Installations solely designed for the permanent storage or final disposal of radioactive waste
- Integrated works for the initial melting of cast iron and steel
- Installations for the extraction of asbestos and for the processing and transformation of asbestos and products containing asbestos
- Integrated chemical installations
- Construction of motorways, express roads and lines for long distance railway traffic and of airports with a basic runway length of 2100 m or more
- Trading ports and also inland waterways and ports for inland waterway traffic which permit the passage of vessels over 1350 tonnes
- Waste disposal installations for the incineration, chemical treatment or landfill of toxic and dangerous wastes

(Adapted from Wathern 1992)

ronmental problems are not subject to mandatory EIA. Further refinement of these categories is clearly called for (Roberts and Hunter 1992).

The great majority of transport infrastructure projects, for example, are excluded from mandatory EIA under the EC Directive. Such projects can, however, have major impacts on urban environmental quality. With reference to road transport, Annex 1 of the EC Directive only covers new motorways (although not motorway improvements or the construction of motorway slip roads, which come under Annex 2) and express roads. The latter are described as roads accessible only from interchanges or controlled junctions, and on which parking and stopping are prohibited. Thus, most ordinary trunk roads are excluded from mandatory EIA. In recognition of the environmental degradation which trunk roads may cause, some countries have instigated mandatory EIA for trunk roads under certain circumstances, despite the inclusion of trunk roads in Annex 2 of the EC Directive. In the UK, for example, Annex 2 projects which require an EIA include roads through urban areas in which 1500 or more dwellings lie within 100m of the centre line of the proposed road. This should ensure that air quality and noise effects in heavily populated areas are properly investigated. Other trunk road proposals for which an EIA is required in the UK include:

- all new trunk roads over 10km in length
- all trunk roads over 1km in length which pass through, or within 100m of, a national park, a Site of Special Scientific Interest, a conservation area, or a nature reserve
- road improvements likely to have significant effects on the environment. (Simpson 1992)

Box 7.4 Categories of Projects Included in Annex 2 of the EC Directive

Agriculture	Food industry
Extractive industry	Textile, leather, wood and paper industries
Energy industry	Rubber industry
Processing of metals	Infrastructure projects
Manufacture of glass	Miscellaneous
Chemical industry	Modifications to Annex 1 developments
(Wathern 1992)	

Such schemes are assessed for their impact on a range of indicators, including traffic noise, visual impact, air pollution, community severance, agriculture, heritage and conservation areas, ecology, pedestrian amenity and driver stress (Department of Transport 1983). In the Netherlands, trunk road investment proposals are given a priority ranking on the basis of a complex project appraisal process. Although a wide range of environmental factors are taken into account in the project design process, only two aspects of environmental quality receive detailed attention in the prioritisation process: noise and local air pollution. It is interesting to note the relative weights given to different aspects of a trunk road proposal in this respect (Table 7.1).

Table 7.1 Relative weights given to aspects of a trunk road proposal in the Netherlands

Aspect	Weighting (per cent)
Economic (cost–benefit analysis)	35.0
Safety (deaths)	10.0
(injuries)	9.0
(damage)	0.5
Environment (noise)	15.5
(air pollution)	10.0
Land use planning	5.0
Transit role for freight	15.0

Source: Gwilliam and Gommers 1992

The inclusion of land use planning reflects the contribution that a particular road proposal will make to the realisation of a desired spatial structure, particularly in urban areas (e.g. effects on suburbanisation and access to development areas).

The consideration of environmental factors in the evaluation of transport infrastructure projects is perhaps most developed with respect to road proposals. Clearly, bus and light rail projects may also have significant impacts on the urban environment. However, an EIA does not normally form part of the appraisal process for such projects in the UK. With reference to potential congestion and air pollution reductions, for example, these schemes may not operate in an optimal manner (Tyson 1992).

In Box 7.2, the EIA process is shown to begin with the preparation of the EIS. In reality, it is highly desirable for EIA to be considered early on in the project planning and design stage, so that the project planning and EIA processes overlap. Ideally, the EIA process should be closely integrated with the ongoing planning and design work on the project, so that the developer can take account of environmental issues when considering alternative forms of the project. In the long run such integration can bring considerable benefits to the developer (Canter 1983), including:

- better compliance with environmental standards
- improvements in the siting of plant and machinery
- capital and operating cost savings
- the avoidance of costly adaptations to projects once in operation
- speedier approval of development applications.

British Gas, for example, has claimed significant cost savings through the early use of EIA, which has helped to reduce delays and identify and implement alternative, more cost-effective ways of achieving desired aims (HMSO 1981). Conversely, Bowonder, Prasad and Reddy (1987) report costly post-development pollution control measures which have had to be introduced at a steel works close to the city of Vizag in Andhra Pradesh, India, in order to prevent air pollution levels from breaching human health air quality standards. Problems associated with the siting of the plant so close to a major urban centre were exacerbated by the poor air pollution dispersion characteristics of the region, due to the Eastern Ghats mountain range. In retrospect, an alternative site would have been more appropriate.

According to Lee (1989), EIA should be contributing to matters like a review of alternative ways of meeting the developer's objectives (i.e. alternatives to the proposed project), a review of alternative locations for the project, and a review of alternative process designs, site layouts and ancillary facilities for the project. Such information can aid the developer in finding the most appropriate form of the project to submit to the remainder of the EIA process. Indeed, informal consultations with the competent authority may begin at the project formulation stage. Local community involvement is also a possibility at this stage.

Any formal EIA system hinges on the preparation of a detailed, written report of the environmental consequences of a development project, the EIS. This normally supports the developer's application for project authorisation, with both documents commonly being submitted to the competent authority for simultaneous consideration. Normally, it is the responsibility of the developer (or those acting for the developer) to prepare the EIS, covering the types of items given in Box 7.2, although ideally, the preparation of the EIS will involve consultations between the developer and representatives of the competent local authority, as well as other environmental control authorities. Giving responsibility to the developer in this way avoids public money being used to aid in the formulation of a (presumably profitable) private sector investment. In any case, experience suggests that the financial cost of conducting a satisfactory EIA normally accounts for a very small proportion of the total capital cost of a new project (UNEP 1988a). Putting the onus on the developer allows those with the greatest information on the proposal to conduct the EIA, and facilitates the integration of the project formulation and EIA processes. However, as Wathern (1992) points out:

> Without adequate safeguards, proponents may be tempted to regard EIA simply as a means of obtaining project authorization and present only those results which show proposals in a favourable light. (p.17)

For these reasons, a formal EIA system should require a developer to consider at least a minimum and proscribed range of development factors and environmental features during the EIA. Such is the case with the EC Directive, for example. The Directive requires that effects should be described and assessed for:

1. human beings, fauna and flora
2. soil, water, air, climate and the landscape
·3. the interaction between the two groups above
4. material assets and the built cultural heritage.

Under the Directive, the developer is required to supply at least the following information in the EIS (Commission of the European Communities 1985):

1. a description of the project with information on its site, design and size
2. measures intended to avoid, reduce or remedy significant adverse impacts
3. the data required to identify and assess the main environmental effects
4. a non-technical summary of the above three.

As indicated above, it is also important that the data used to make predictions of potential impacts is provided in the EIS, along with a clear explanation of the prediction techniques employed (see also Box 7.2). This can allow the proper scrutiny of the magnitude and significance of impact predictions. The EIS should only consider in detail those potential environmental impacts thought to be significant. This implies some kind of prior 'scoping' of potential impacts to identify priority issues. Scoping is an important part of the EIA process and is discussed later in this section. Although the majority of EIA legislation and guidance restricts the EIS to the consideration of significant impacts, frequently little help is given in the interpretation of the word 'significant'. Lee (1989) poses the following questions as a guide to deciding on significance:

- Is the impact in question likely to threaten the attainment of existing or proposed environmental quality standards?
- Is it likely to conflict with the objectives, policies or plans of the authority competent to authorise the project?
- Is it likely to be an issue of concern to an environmental control authority because it may conflict with its environmental objectives, policies or plans?
- Is it likely to be an issue of concern either to national environmental interest groups or to the local community in which the project would be located?

In predicting and assessing the significance of impacts a number of factors should be borne in mind. Changes to aspects of the environment brought about through a particular development project may be favourable or adverse. It is also important to note that the impacts to be assessed need not merely be restricted to those which are of a direct and immediate nature; knock-on, secondary effects should also be considered, if significant. These may arise through environmental interrelationships and interdependencies. Potentially, impacts can arise at any stage in the life of a project. The nature and magnitude of these impacts may vary considerably and it is common to find that project impacts are considered during both construction and operational phases, for example. New impacts may also occur if a project is subsequently modified in terms of its scale or operational characteristics. The implementation of one urban development project may also stimulate other developments, such as service facilities. The impacts associated with ancillary developments may be significant and, although frequently difficult to predict, should be kept in mind. On a related point, the cumulative impact of a series of projects may be greater than the sum of the impacts from individual developments. Impacts may become significant when a grouping of projects is considered together, but not on the basis of the effects of individual projects. Similarly, a point may be reached where one more urban development in an area poses a significant threat to environmental quality.

Additionally, although it is useful in gauging the likely impacts of a proposed development to refer to prior impact studies conducted for a similar project and in a similar location, caution must be employed if this is done. It is imperative that any impact study takes account of the specific environmental conditions which prevail at the location under consideration, and considers specific aspects of the development (stressor activities) within this context. Specific characteristics of the environment and of the development project should also be used to determine the geographical extent of the area around a proposed development to be considered in the EIA. Many urban/industrial projects may impact on the wider environment, and the area considered in the EIA might reflect factors such as:

- the dispersion patterns of various pollutants
- the relative importance of primary, secondary and tertiary impacts
- the specific locations of important ecological, archaeological and cultural sites in the vicinity. (Htun 1992)

On completion, the EIS usually accompanies the developer's application for project authorisation to the competent authority. At this stage in the EIA process it is common for the EIS to be made available to the local community. As a consequence of consultations between the developer and the competent local authority, the general public and other environmental control agencies, the detailed specification of the project may be altered, by including additional impact amelioration measures, for example. Following consultation, the competent authority will reach a decision on the proposal, with details of the decision often being made public. The competent authority may impose planning conditions on consenting to the development, such as the regular monitoring of actual environmental impacts.

7.2.3 Problems and opportunities in the use of EIA

With reference to the guidelines for sustainable urban development outlined in the previous chapter, the use of EIA in the appraisal of developments with an urban aspect appears commendable on a number of counts. Apart from the obvious relevance of EIA to the 'prevention is better than cure' principle of environmental protection, an EIA system may also, in theory, provide the framework which contributes (directly or indirectly) to:

- greater local community involvement in development decision-making
- enhanced awareness of environmental issues amongst developers, local communities and decision-makers
- better cooperation between the private and public sectors (e.g. through informal discussions in the preparation of an EIS)
- improved coordination between public development control authorities and other public agencies with environmental interests (e.g. discussions between a local planning authority, nature conservancy groups, pollution control agencies and water utilities during the evaluation of an EIS)

- greater use of technologies designed to minimise waste outputs
- better understanding of environmental processes and tolerances (e.g. through the post-development monitoring of actual environmental impacts)
- the better integration of environmental considerations with economic and social aspects of development proposals.

The efficient use of EIA provides tremendous opportunities to translate many of the guiding principles of sustainable urban development into action 'on the ground'. However, many EIA systems have been criticised for failing to realise their full potential in this regard. Some of these operational problems and limitations are discussed below, along with proposed actions to improve the use of EIA.

LOCAL COMMUNITY INVOLVEMENT AND SOCIAL SCOPING

The opportunity afforded by EIA – at least in theory – for early public involvement in the appraisal of development proposals has long been recognised. In reality, however, the lack of opportunity for full public involvement in the EIA process still remains a valid criticism of many formal EIA systems, although significant advances have been made in recent years. Increasingly, it is being recognised that the use of public meetings or enquiries held after an EIS has been produced is an inadequate mechanism for the full participation of the local population in project decision-making, and there is a need to involve local people early on in the EIA process (Wood and Jones 1991). This need arises for several reasons. The exclusion of the public at an early stage may foster anger and resentment and increase the likelihood of litigation and delay. Bailey and Saunders (1988), for example, in describing environmental assessments for a titanium dioxide plant near Bunbury in south-western Australia, state that, 'conflict resolution can be aided by early evaluation of what the community regards as valuable' (p. 38). Public exclusion also omits a potentially very valuable source of expert opinion and pressure regarding the quality of the local environment and the assessment of potential impacts. The last point recognises that the purpose of local community involvement in EIA should not be restricted to forestalling an adverse reaction to a particular development project, but rather that such participation can result in a positive and useful input to the EIA process. Specifically, the views of the local community can be critical both in the 'scoping' of potential impacts, and in assessing their relative importance. The concept of scoping is described below.

As we have already noted, an EIS should only consider in detail those potential environmental impacts thought to be significant. For the sake of the best use of time and resources in the operation of an EIA, and therefore the production of a high quality EIS, these significant potential impacts should be identified at a very early stage in the EIA process. This focusing of attention on selected impacts is known as *scoping*, and when it involves canvassing the views of the local community it is frequently referred to as 'social scoping'. Beanlands (1992) argues that the importance of scoping in EIA cannot be over-emphasised, because it directs the (frequently very expensive) collection of scientific data and subsequent impact prediction to those aspects of the development of most concern. Failure to do so may result in resources (monetary and human) being spread too thinly causing the inadequate coverage, or even exclusion, of some important impacts and the unnecessary wastage of time, money and effort on minor concerns. Scoping need not be an exercise confined to the environmental experts or professionals involved in EIA. A so-called objective assessment of significant potential impacts is often, in reality, based upon the subjective value judgements of only one or two professionals (Wathern 1992). The early involvement of the local community in the EIA process through social scoping lends more credibility to the output of an EIA.

Questions arise over how community involvement might best be achieved, the degree of importance to be accorded to community input and how such input might need to be balanced against professional judgement (Beanlands 1992). Although still very limited in use, social scoping has been formalised into some EIA systems. In Canada, for example, carefully mediated public meetings form the basis of project scoping. A similar system operates in the USA. However, it is perhaps worth ending this sub-section with a reminder that the people of many countries still lack any opportunity for involvement in development decision making. As Bowonder, Prasad and Reddy (1987) point out:

> In most developing countries, the system of public hearing is not institutionalized because government works mostly in a regulatory framework, and official information on project siting is mostly kept secret to reduce possible pressures by various interest groups. (p.19)

WIDENING THE INTERPRETATION OF ENVIRONMENT

It is apparent from both the general definition of EIA given earlier and the aspects of the environment considered to be relevant to EIA under the EC Directive (see above), that EIA has generally remained loyal to its roots, retaining a bias towards consideration of impacts on the biological and physical components of the natural environment. The EC Directive does make direct reference to potential impacts on human health and welfare, and to cultural heritage (meaning aspects of built heritage). Both of these may be especially pertinent for developments affecting the urban environment. In general, however, the EC initiative on EIA and other EIA systems appear preoccupied with the biophysical environment, and have been interpreted as such in EIS reports. Given the increasingly held view that the urban environment should be seen in a holistic light (see Chapter One), and the wide range of factors of relevance to sustainable development, the current focus of much EIA practice on the natural environment appears too narrow (see, for example Bronfman 1991). As Glasson (1993) points out, it is often the trade-off between biophysical and socioeconomic impacts that is the key focus of decision-making. Therefore, the view is growing that social and economic impact assessments should be subsumed within EIA systems (see for example Davies and Muller 1983). In other words, the interpretation of 'environment' in EIA should be widened.

In any case, the demarcation between social impacts (for example) and impacts on the natural environment may be very difficult to draw. Consider a semi-natural area of woodland within a city which provides a haven for a wide variety of wildlife. A development which threatened the integrity of this woodland would impact on the ecology of the area. However, it would also, almost certainly, detract from the area as an amenity and recreational resource for the local population, perhaps significantly reducing the quality of life of nearby residents. In this example, the loss of biological diversity may also have social implications. If EIA systems formally subsumed such social impacts, EIA practitioners might have a clearer idea of where to 'draw the line' in impact assessment.

Glasson (1993) suggests that the following socioeconomic aspects might be included in an EIA-based project appraisal system:

- direct impacts on the economic base – e.g. direct employment, labour market characteristics, local and wider trends
- indirect impacts on the economic base – e.g. non-basic services/employment, labour supply and demand
- demography – population structure and trends
- housing – supply and demand
- local services – supply and demand of health, education, police services, etc.
- socio-cultural effects – e.g. lifestyles/quality of life, social problems, community stress and conflict.

Some signs of integration do already appear in many EISs. Developers are often keen to stress aspects such as job creation and economic multiplier effects. Even the more comprehensive cost–benefit analyses (CBAs) often include some information on environmental impacts

(Wathern 1992). This may indeed become more popular as attempts to value natural environmental resources in monetary terms (see following section) become more prevalent and better understood. However, the formal and routine application of a fully integrated and comprehensive appraisal system to the assessment of development proposals still appears a distant prospect, although frameworks for such an integrated system have been proposed (see, for example, Nijkamp 1980).

An example of an EIS which included substantial socioeconomic impact information (largely in an urban context) is provided by Kennedy (1989), and relates to the construction of a stretch of motorway in the USA to extend the Interstate-69 route which runs from Indianapolis, Indiana, to the US–Canadian border in Michigan. The rationale for the project was to improve access and road links to the city of Lansing, the Michigan state capital. As well as potential impacts on the urban environment in and around Lansing, the proposal had potential impacts on the rural environment, including agricultural land and wetland and woodland wilderness areas. With reference to urban impacts, the following were considered appropriate for inclusion and consideration in the EIS:

- employment – e.g. through the stimulation of major retail or industrial developments
- accessibility – e.g. the effect of the project on residents' travel times and on commuter journeys
- safety – e.g. reduced congestion and traffic volumes on existing roads
- other central-city impacts – e.g. effects on air and water quality; noise pollution; the integrity of neighbourhoods
- urban sprawl – e.g. the conversion of agricultural land around the development to residential, commercial and light industrial uses
- displacement – e.g. the number of homes and businesses which would have to be relocated as a result of the project
- community facilities and services – e.g. changes to school bus routes; access for health, police and fire services; displacement of churches; effects on gas, electricity and telephone utilities
- tax base – e.g. loss of tax revenue to local authorities through the compulsory purchase of private land.

IMPACT PREDICTION AND EVALUATION

Clearly, the ability of methods and techniques to accurately predict and evaluate project-induced environmental change is critical to any EIA system. However, much of the available evidence suggests that the evaluation, prediction and assessment of potential environmental impacts is inadequate in a substantial proportion of EIA studies. The quality of EISs has come in for recent criticism in the UK, for example (Wood and Jones 1991), while in Australia, impact predictions are only 50% accurate on average, and occasionally incorrect by over two orders of magnitude (Buckley 1991). Problems with the use of methods and techniques may be compounded by inadequate environmental baseline information, the lack of formal scoping procedures and the natural variability of different sites in terms of environmental processes, making it difficult to translate the information gained from one area to another (Newson 1991). The availability and quality of baseline information on the status of the environment, for example, is critical to the efficacy of EIA, since without such information it is difficult (if not impossible) to make accurate predictions of environmental change. This relates to the continuing need for reliable environmental quality data to be gathered (e.g. through regular area-based environmental audits, as outlined in the previous chapter), so that this database of information can then be made available to EIA practitioners and decision-makers. The lack of baseline data is often particularly acute in developing countries. In India, for example, the government provides incentives for industries to locate in particularly underdeveloped areas. Yet, it is frequently in these areas where baseline environmental data are absent, encouraging development agencies to neglect long-term impacts on the environment (Bowonder, Prasad and Reddy 1987). Advances are, however, being made. In Peru, for example, government-sponsored research on natural resources may be used to provide baseline information for future EIAs (Moreira 1992).

Some of these problems relating to impact prediction and evaluation are summarised by Bisset and Tomlinson (1992), who suggest that EIA often involves the

> use of environmental information which is often characterized by scarcity and uncertainty, predictive techniques with unknown error margins and evaluation methods which assess and present information to decision makers in a variety of ways. (p.126)

Certainly, much more work is needed to refine the use of the various methods and techniques which can be applied in EIA. In this respect, post-development environmental monitoring combined with the auditing of EIA studies is crucial. Only through monitoring and auditing can

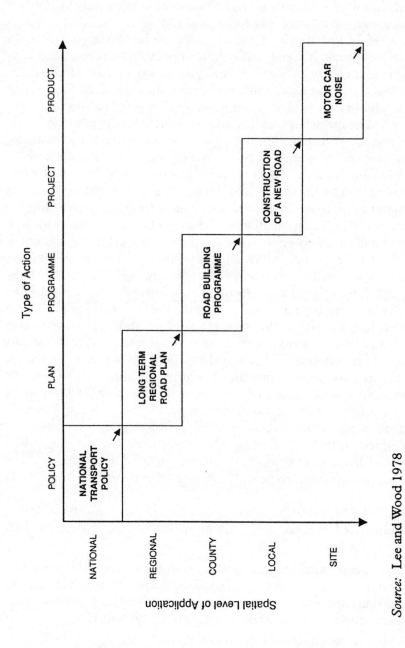

Source: Lee and Wood 1978

Figure 7.2 *A hierarchy of EIA application*

those involved in EIA learn through experience, and the use of methods and techniques be improved. Also, without post-development monitoring there can be no way of ensuring that any recommended mitigating measures have been implemented, or are working effectively, and there can be no early opportunity of modifying the development because of adverse impacts. A recent survey of EISs in Australia found that only 3% were suitable for the testing of predictive ability, because only this proportion had adequate post-development monitoring schemes (Buckley 1991). If EIA is really to become a comprehensive environmental management tool, then impact assessment must be extended beyond the decision which sanctions the project, and cover operational (and even decommissioning) impacts.

The importance of post-development project monitoring and appraisal was recently highlighted by Thompson, Whigg and Perker (1991), with reference to a number of urban flood protection schemes in England and Wales. In the case of the sea defence scheme at Harwich, it was found that changing 'best estimates' for sea level rise necessitated periodic reappraisal of the flood prevention scheme. At the time of construction, a sea level rise of 3mm per annum was assumed. The current best estimate is 6mm per annum. More generally, the post-development appraisals identified a need for flood protection schemes to take more account of urban development pressures (e.g. the location, extent and type of proposed developments), implying better coordination between developers, local planning authorities and those involved in initiating such projects.

BEYOND THE PROJECT LEVEL

Arguably, one of the most fundamental problems with the current status of much EIA practice relates to its project-specific emphasis. This means that while 'end-of-pipe' technical solutions to issues like waste minimisation may (rightly) attract much attention in EIA, less attention is paid to the potential application of EIA in the appraisal of development policies, plans and programmes (PPPs) (see Figure 7.2). Yet, it may be with reference to the appraisal of these 'higher-level' development proposals that EIA can best embrace the principles of sustainable development. Theoretically, there is no impediment to the extension of EIA to proposed PPPs (Wood 1992): EIA could be applied to a programme of projects (e.g. the building of a network of new roads in and around a city), a plan (e.g. the land use plan for a city), or a policy (e.g. a national transport policy). The term used to describe the application of EIA to PPPs before the authorisation of individual projects is *strategic environmental assessment* (SEA). Lee and Walsh (1992) explain the recent growth of interest in SEA with reference to the growing awareness of the limitations of traditional project-based EIA, and the need better to integrate environmental considerations into development planning in order to promote sustainable development. They argue that the limitations of project-level EIA include the following issues:

- **Coverage of ancillary developments**. A major project may give rise to significant impacts from induced and indirect activities which may not be properly assessed in the EIA for the initial project. Even if induced projects are subsequently subjected to EIA in sequence, this hampers investigation of cumulative impacts and, of necessity, provides for the consideration of fewer development options than is the case for simultaneous assessments through SEA.

- **Foreclosure of alternatives**. By the time it becomes possible to apply EIA to an individual project, it is likely that a number of development options (with different environmental consequences) will have been eliminated from consideration at a previous point in the planning process. These options will not have been subject to EIA. Therefore, it seems appropriate to introduce some form of environmental assessment at an earlier stage in the planning process.

- **Cumulative impacts**. These are unlikely to be handled in a satisfactory manner in the absence of previous sectoral and/or area-based environmental assessments where multiple developments or the expansion of activities associated with a particular sector are proposed.

- **Project exclusions from EIA**. Some projects may be excluded from EIA because they are individually too small, but may yet have significant impacts through cumulative effects.

The proper application of SEA could overcome many of these difficulties (Therivel *et al.* 1992). However, for Lee and Walsh (1992), among others, SEA is actually seen as a requirement of sustainable development, insofar as it allows the 'integration of economic, social and environmental considerations when planning or guiding future development' (p. 130). Thus, it is possible to envisage the combined use of SEA and EIA to allow such integration at all development proposal levels. Recently, the Commission of the European Communities (1992, para 7.3), for example, stated that:

> Given the goal of achieving sustainable development it seems only logical, if not essential, to apply an assessment of the environmental implications of all relevant policies, plans and programmes. The integration of environmental assessment within the macro-plan-

ning process would...enhance the protection of the environment and encourage optimisation of resource management.

Although formal provision for, and practical experience of, SEA is as yet very limited around the world, some countries (including Holland, France, Germany, the USA, New Zealand and Australia) have utilised SEA. Interestingly, the European Commission recently signalled its desire to formulate a new Directive on SEA for certain policies, plans and programmes (Commission of the European Communities 1992), although this has not generally been met with great enthusiasm by many governments of the member states (Glasson 1993).

7.2.4 Conclusions

Potentially, the use of project-level EIA is useful for the prior assessment of urban-based projects which may impact on the quality of the urban and wider environment, and for projects sited outside urban boundaries which may also have consequences for the urban environment. By minimising the demand for – and on – environmental resources, EIA can contribute to sustainable urban development. EIA can also provide the vehicle for the enactment of other desirable features of sustainable development policies, such as enhanced community involvement and better co-operation and integration in decision making.

However, there can be little doubt that the formal EIA systems and procedures currently in use do not allow EIA to fulfil its maximum theoretical potential for the translation of principles and policies of sustainable urban development into practice. Many of the methodological problems with EIA which have emerged at the project assessment level have been outlined above. Many of these problems may be solved in time, as the use of EIA becomes still more common and we learn from experience and good practice. This said, there may be some issues which cannot be overcome unless a more strategic view of the application of EIA is adopted. Moreover, there is a growing realisation that sustainable development requires the environmental assessment of all types of development proposal, whether these take the form of projects, programmes, plans or policies. Unless the appropriate use of SEA becomes commonplace, it will be difficult to claim that EIA is playing its full part in the realisation of sustainable development.

7.3 ECONOMIC POLICY INSTRUMENTS

7.3.1 Context

The potential of economic instruments to foster environmental improvements has been increasingly recognised in recent years by governments and environmental pressure groups alike (Sagoff 1988, Pearce, Markandya and Barbier 1989, OECD 1990, Pearce 1991). Agenda 21, from the 1992 Rio Earth Summit, summarises many of the benefits of economic policy approaches (Quarrie 1992):

> Within a supportive international and national economic context and given the necessary legal and regulatory framework, economic and market-oriented approaches can in many cases enhance capacity to deal with the issues of environment and development. This would be achieved by providing cost-effective solutions, applying integrated pollution prevention control, promoting technological innovation and influencing environmental behaviour, as well as providing financial resources to meet sustainable development objectives. (p.93)

Economic policies generally aim to make the market work better by improving the working of existing mechanisms, including altering the pricing mechanism to reflect 'hidden' costs, in particular environmental externalities (see Chapter Three), and adjusting fiscal mechanisms, such as counter-productive subsidies or tax concessions. More recent economic policy approaches have additionally emphasised the value of creating new markets, for instance by treating pollution as a tradeable commodity. Many of the goals of economic policy can be traced to market failure rationales (Box 7.5).

Improving the working of the market, and working with the grain of the market, provide the essential themes of economic approaches to environmental management. For instance, the UK government's environment White Paper, *This Common Inheritance* (Department of the Environment/Welsh Office 1990), argues that the economic approach gives

> consumers and industries clear signals about the costs of using environmental resources...it allows producers and consumers rather than regulators to decide how best to alter their demands in order to meet environmental needs. This has a number of beneficial consequences: freedom of choice is not constrained; those who find it cheapest to reduce emissions will make the biggest reductions; there will be an incentive to develop more efficient technology; there is a continuing incentive not to misuse the environment. (p.21)

Box 7.5 Market Failure Rationales for State Economic Intervention from Orthodox Economics

- Improving the economic competitiveness of the economy, by ensuring firms and individuals take proper account of the true (environmental) costs and benefits of their activities.
- Amending anarchic property rights, working against long-term stewardship of resources: market exchange cannot work without clear ownership rights.
- Enabling state decision-makers to take account of both positive and negative environmental externalities; for instance, creating parks may raise nearby property values, whilst building major roads can lower them.
- Providing widely available public benefits, e.g. public parks or public transport.
- Reducing risk and uncertainty, especially in new or uncertain product areas, e.g. recycling initiatives.
- Supporting projects with high capital costs and involving new technologies. Similarly, economies of scale may require public intervention, for instance in water provision where large dams are needed.
- Educating and providing information, to individuals and companies, so that their decisions can take into account the individual and collective (environmental) costs and benefits of activities.

There is a particular value to looking at economic instruments in an urban context, since many of the environmental problems of cities relate to what economists would refer to as a concentration of negative externalities, that is, non-costed environmental impacts. The use of economic instruments to improve the urban environment is, as yet, in its infancy, albeit rapidly evolving (see for instance Button and Pearce 1989; OECD 1990). The most widespread application of economic policy approaches to date has probably been in urban transport, a sector which is used later to illustrate some of the urban applications of economic policy.

7.3.2 Introduction to economic tools for environmental change

Economists generally argue that the case for economic approaches to environmental problems rests on their relative economic efficiency, and the rigour they add to deciding policy priorities, not least between economic growth and environmental change. Whilst many businesses favour the traditional regulatory controls because of the certainty they bring, it is now argued that these are often more expensive than alternative market-based approaches (Pearce 1990). The problems of the regulatory, or 'command-and-control' approach are usually held to be high administrative costs, often passed on straight to the consumer or taxpayer, the existence of widespread cheating, the lack of flexibility for the polluter in tackling the problem, and what some say is a reduced incentive for technological innovation and voluntary conservation (Pearce 1990, OECD 1990).

Box 7.6 Evaluating Different Policy Instruments

- The instrument must be capable of attaining its environmental objectives in a reliable and consistent fashion, whilst being adaptable to changing circumstances over time and sensitive to differences in local conditions.
- The instrument should be judged against costs, that is, its economic efficiency.
- The impacts of the policy instrument should not be socially regressive, and should involve a concern for equity of impacts.
- Compliance costs need to be weighed, as high administrative costs are undesirable, and heavy information burdens may make a scheme unworkable in practice.
- The instrument must be politically acceptable, easy to operatate and relatively transparent, so that those affected understand the need for, and objectives of, a particular approach.
- The instrument should be compatible with other policy approaches operating in parallel.

(Adapted in part from Young 1992, and Turner, Pearce and Bateman 1994)

Tietenberg (1990), reviewing a number of studies of the relative costs of command-and-control approaches and economic tools for pollution control, found the costs of regulation averaging four to six times higher than those of economic instruments, and sometimes considerably higher. However, the effectiveness of different policy approaches and of individual policy tools needs to be gauged against several additional non-cost criteria, not least equity (Box 7.6).

The challenge of global sustainability has encouraged the development of new thinking and new economic approaches to environmental management. Pearce (1993) summarises the four main components of this as: a greater emphasis on long-term well-being and on equity considerations; concern over the nature and assessment of trade-offs between the environment and economic development; measurement and valuation of environmental externalities, to assist in decision-making about environment–economic development trade-offs; and the emergence of mechanisms to decouple economic growth and adverse environmental impacts. An illustration of the latter point would be the reduced energy consumption per unit GDP, as GDP rises. The implication here is that economic growth can be viewed as environmentally acceptable in some respects, and not necessarily environmentally degrading, provided the rate of energy saving is greater than the rate of GDP growth. However, the links between higher GDP, efficient energy generation and higher energy demands makes this relationship a little less clear. To put it another way, the fuel consumption per kilometre travelled may improve in the more efficient cars found in a European city relative to a city in a developing country, for instance, but the beneficial effects may be more than cancelled out by higher vehicle ownership levels, longer distances travelled and greater proportions of engines idling in congested cities.

Although frequently presented as alternatives, the regulatory and economic approaches usually work best when they are linked in some way, as they usually are, with, for example, regulations to establish minimum technical or ambient environmental standards, and a system of fines and charges set for those breaching these standards. The main area of debate is the extent to which it is possible to introduce market incentives to achieve agreed standards.

As a prelude to more detailed discussion later, some of the main economic approaches to environmental management are outlined in the remainder of this section, adapting elements of the framework used by MacNeill, Winsemius and Yakushiji (1991).

Box 7.7 Examples of Environmental Charges and Taxes

Transgression and enforcement charges, including government fines, non-compliance fees and performance bonds to encourage producers to adhere to environmental standards and regulations (OECD 1991).

Effluent charges, where the polluter absorbs the full costs of compensation towards any damage caused by emissions, with consequent price rises encouraging shifts in producer and consumer behaviour towards more environment-friendly inputs, processes, and products.

User charges, encompassing the user-pays principle, anticipating the costs of pollution treatment and incorporating these into the price of goods and services, in the urban context most evident in garbage collection, effluent and water charges, and road tolls. According to the OECD (1990), polluter-pays and user-pays charges need to be combined and more widely applied within the urban environment.

Natural resource user-pays charges, so that inputs into the production system are fully costed in terms of their environmental impacts and replacement costs. Full costing of resource inputs should encourage greater efficiency in use and recycling of materials, and a shift from non-renewable to renewable resources, managed within a sustainable yield regime.

Market creation, in particular for pollution licences and tradeable permits, where polluters pay for the right to pollute within a given set of ambient standards, with a market created in pollution licences (Pearce 1990; Turner, Pearce and Bateman 1994; see Rees 1991, and Victor 1991, for some of the limitations of this approach).

Liability or risk insurance obligations, to help ensure compensation can occur for environmental damage.

Policing and administrative charges, so that the costs of implementing environmental policies are borne by those they are aimed at.

Deposit-refund measures to encourage recycling and environment-friendly waste disposal, for instance bottle banks, bottle return schemes, and schemes to collect refrigeration coolants, car oil, and car batteries. Performance and assurance bonds have been used with mining and logging companies to cover clean-up or restoration costs (Turner, Pearce and Bateman 1994). The OECD (1990) have also suggested that at the development stage of major urban projects deposit or bond schemes might be used to ensure subsequent site reclamation.

Ownership charges, such as car or road taxes.

INTRODUCING ENVIRONMENTAL CHARGES AND TAXES

In attempting to make the market work for the environment, a central concern is to ensure that the market takes account of all environmental costs, risks, and benefits. Market externalities need to be incorporated into the market through being allocated an imputed price or charge. The price mechanism can then be used to change producer and consumer behaviour in a variety of ways (Box 7.7). One of the most important underpinnings of environmental charges is the user-pays principle (see Chapter Six). Effluent charges, user charges and resource charges all exemplify some element of the polluter-pays principle.

Ownership charges, such as car taxes, are usually straightforward state revenue-raising systems, which do however have distorting effects, penalising for instance those who need a car but do not necessarily use it very often. In the case of an annual road licence tax, the regular commuter is in effect subsidised by the person in a remote rural area who needs a car for occasional shopping expeditions, visits to the doctor and so on. This has led the OECD (1990) to recommend that the balance of taxation change away from ownership charges and towards usage or resource input charges.

CORRECTING PERVERSE INTERVENTIONS IN THE MARKET

The distorting impacts of non-costed activities can be magnified through a range of perverse market charges, most notably involving direct and indirect government interventions in the market through the tax system, subsidies and grants, price setting, and production/waste/trade quota allocations. Examples of perverse market interventions include the public subsidy of suburban infrastructure costs, which in some countries has encouraged low-density housing sprawl and agricultural land encroachment. As we shall see later, there has also been considerable direct and indirect state subsidy of road transport (MacNeill, Winsemius and Yakushiji 1991). In the rural sector, subsidies of pesticides have led to their overuse, in turn leading to food, water and land contamination, plus the elimination of some beneficial natural predators.

CREATING POSITIVE PUBLIC INTERVENTIONS, INCENTIVES AND REGULATORY CONTROLS

Whilst some government interventions distort market mechanisms in a dysfunctional way, it is also possible for government involvement to intervene to correct market failings and sometimes to create the conditions for market activity which are beneficial to the environment. For instance, secure property rights are often important in encouraging long-term stewardship of natural resources. This has led to policies to intervene in markets which are failing, most notably perhaps in providing land ownership rights to squatter settlements in some cities, and land titles for rural farmers in Thailand (Panayotou 1992). Other important mechanisms include differential taxing of leaded and unleaded petrol, reduced taxes on energy-saving products, for instance home insulation, and the subsidy of research and development into environmentally benign products and processes, to reduce the commercial risk to those involved. In cities, local property taxes can be altered to reflect the benefits of access to public parks, including the beneficial impacts on property prices, whilst proximity to major polluting activities could lead to lower taxes. Where property taxes are based on property value, some element of the financial impacts of 'access to goods' and 'proximity to bads', is automatically captured. Another increasingly common policy tool is *least cost utility planning* (see Chapter Six, OECD 1990, Cairncross 1991), which requires that alternatives to building new facilities are considered as part of a project development strategy. For instance, an improved public transport system may reduce the need for a new highway.

REFORMING ECONOMIC ACCOUNTING SYSTEMS

Official indicators of national prosperity such as gross national product (GNP) have become a dominant element in national and international economic policy, as targets for growth are set and economic transformation measured according to these indicators. Economic growth as an objective in its own right, without reference to satisfying fundamental human needs and maintaining environmental well-being, has become one of the greatest distorting features of twentieth century economic development (van Dieren and Hummerlinck 1979). The use of GNP as a measure of progress is extremely problematic, as Chapter Six noted, since it is a very partial indicator of well-being, which incorporates productive capital investment and income, but not natural resource assets, human capital assets, or essential public services (Jacobs 1991, Repetto *et al.* 1992). One consequence of accounting systems which assume natural resource assets to be free gifts, or as infinitely reproducible, is that they can send distorting signals to policy makers (Repetto *et al.* 1992). Perhaps the most extreme illustration of this potential problem is the Australian study which showed that two-thirds of the money which changes hands after a road accident goes to lawyers and is counted towards GNP, so a country with safer roads would appear to reduce its income (Stretton 1976). More telling is the case of those countries which encourage felling of tropical rainforests and replacement with extensive agriculture on poor soils, gaining a temporary boost in income from logging but a long-term reduction in productive potential.

Michael Jacobs (1991, p.244) provides a definition that the 'standard of living equals real disposable income plus the quality of life', which captures some flavour of the elements which need to be incorporated into any new indicator of national well-being. However, as he readily acknowledges, this still leaves unanswered questions of what constitutes quality of life, and whether monetary values can capture this. None the less, considerable progress has been made in constructing better indicators of well-being, including natural resource accounting systems in Norway, Finland, Germany, Spain, Portugal and France (Lone 1992). More broadly constructed indicators have been suggested, for instance Ekins and Max-Neef (1992, pp. 298–99) who propose a four-component model which brings together: environmental and resource accounts, measured in physical units; an adjusted national product measure which takes account of natural capital depreciation and nets out military spending; a household production account, for instance, imputing a value for domestic work such as childcare; and a social indicator. The social indicator would incorporate aspects of quality of life and capital growth, in particular ecological capital, human capital, organisational capital (government, businesses, community organisations, family) and physical capital (infrastructure, buildings, etc.).

Promisingly, at the Earth Summit in Rio, 1992, a strong case was made for establishing systems which incorporate environmental and economic accounting, possibly as satellite accounts to the main economic indicators. Agenda 21 encourages all nations to set up such integrated accounts, particularly for natural resource assets and those engaged in productive but unpaid tasks. The existing UN Handbook on integrated accounting systems was proposed as the starting point for this work, but further work on developing the methodologies and applications proposed is needed.

At a more local level, the need to reform economic systems suggests that urban and regional well-being needs to be measured by more than just economic measures, or by indicators of social deprivation: instead a wider view of quality of life needs to be adopted. Although there are many studies which suggest what a sustainable city might be characterised by in terms of factors such as urban form, economic and ecological self-reliance and human health characteristics, there is as yet no widely agreed upon, comprehensive set of indicators for sustainable urban development. Given the disagreements about what urban sustainability entails, this is not surprising. None the less, as local environmental audits have shown in the UK, there is considerable advantage to be had in obtaining a comprehensive picture of an area's environmental condition, so that changes in well-being can later be evaluated against this baseline. Sustainable development, however, implies examining more than just environmental conditions, covering related aspects of human health, resource assets, and the social environment. This is something which the UK's Association of Metropolitan Authorities (1989) addresses in its document *Action for the Future,* which provides a wide-ranging checklist of issues to be gauged, and possible policy approaches at local and national levels. The main weak link of this approach, is that whilst it is very good on the micro-scale detail of the built environment, covering issues such as housing, community safety and access for the disabled, it is less informative on larger-scale issues of urban form and function. This possibly reflects the limited powers in land use planning which the UK government allowed local authorities in the late 1980s.

One of the most comprehensive academic attempts at bringing together something of this range of potential indicators at the urban level is that of Cappon (1990), who from a human health perspective provides indicators for the physical environment, the human environment, urban form, physical and mental health, and social well-being. The value of this approach is its breadth of coverage; its main problem the lack of depth in justifying each indicator, some of which appear to be highly subjective, difficult to quantify and, as in the case of the proposed optimum city size, open to dispute. In addition, the focus is essentially on humans, with scant regard for other life forms in the city.

MAKING ECONOMIC AND POLITICAL INSTITUTIONS ENVIRONMENTALLY RESPONSIBLE AND ACCOUNTABLE

Where most government environmental interventions have tended to be focused on actions post-development, there is now an increasing need for more anticipatory approaches to environmental management (Mac-Neill, Winsemius and Yakushiji 1991). This needs to be built into governmental and business thinking at all levels. The 1993 GATT agreement, for instance, has attracted considerable opposition from some environmentalists, who argue that it will lead to deteriorating environmental conditions as countries are exposed to more intense international competition, leading to a greater overexploitation of environmental assets as a source of competitive advantage. International trade agreements then need to be accompanied by strong, enforceable environmental protocols, including common target setting for pollution, standards of work safety, and mandatory publishing of environmental impacts associated with a product (e.g. eco-labelling), allowing consumers a choice based on environmental criteria.

At the urban level, making economic institutions more environmentally responsible, would entail measures such as encouraging transport authorities to take greater account of the hidden environmental and social impacts of their subsidies and infrastructure investments, adding these to economic efficiency and economic payback considerations. At the moment, such consideration is all too often merely a form of lip service.

7.3.3 The limits of economic policy

Although the shift towards correcting market mechanisms is generally undisputed as a policy goal, there none the less remains considerable debate about the extent to which the market can be expected to eliminate environmental problems without strong parallel legislation to impose controls. Where some economists and politicians appear to believe that it is largely sufficient to 'fine tune' the market through calculating and incorporating into the price mechanism full or near-full environmental costs, others remain convinced that taming the market in this way is not an adequate response to the scale and scope of change required (Jacobs 1989, 1991). Whilst the detractors generally agree that the market needs adjusting to take account of environmental externalities, they would argue that this needs to be just one element in a broader regulatory framework, whose parameters are set by ecological tolerances and constraints.

Those who are sceptical about the shift in policy emphasis towards economic tools point to the difficulties inherent in attempts to create a market for natural resources, not least the problems of costing certain environmental goods. There are specific problems with price setting in the face of scientific uncertainty or even lack of knowledge, as the case of stratospheric ozone illustrates. Twenty years ago, few 'consumers' would have placed a high value on the ozone layer, even if they knew it existed. Today, the problem would be how to place a value on something so fundamental to human existence. The same arguments apply to loss of biodiversity through the extinction of plant and animal species.

Even with less controversial areas, such as access to an urban park, the many techniques for evaluating what people might be prepared to pay for this aspect of the environment are open to dispute (for reviews of these techniques and surrounding debates see Pearce, Markandya and Barbier 1989, Jacobs 1991, Pearce 1991, Turner, Pearce and Bateman 1994.) For example, asking people how much they would be prepared to pay for the creation of a park, or to compensate for the loss of a park, might reveal that in an area of poor residents, parks appear less valuable in monetary terms than parks in a richer area, even though the need may be greater in the poorer area. Naturally this example is a crude caricature, but it does highlight that subjective opinions of the value of an environmental asset will vary widely between people, may vary over time and will almost certainly vary between areas.

A related problem is that the information base for consumers and producers in making decisions is never likely to be sufficiently reliable or widely available, because of incomplete scientific knowledge, commercial confidentiality and also the costs involved in data collection and dissemination. At its furthest extreme, the anti-market argument would hold that the market is incapable of ever catering for environmental limits and for adopting a sufficiently long-term horizon. Similarly, the reduction of the environment to the cash nexus is held to debase it (Sagoff 1988, Seabrook 1990). In particular, the notion that the market works effectively through the atomistic decisions of individuals taking decisions for their own benefit, and possibly by default for society's, is regarded as inevitably leading to short-term self-interestedness holding sway over the long-term needs of the economy, society and the environment. Viewed from this perspective, market-based policy is seen as potentially socially divisive, in the sense that it might simply allow the rich to pollute more than the poor, whilst failing to place a cap on antisocial behaviour. Its extreme social equivalent might be to allow thieves to pay for a licence to steal: the more people paid for their licence, the more they could steal. The unregulated market approach, being relatively amoral, can allow individuals to be immoral.

The ethical dimension is important since the market does not provide a sufficient basis for the resolution of the profound moral issues which face us every day; it can play a part in avoiding distorted decision making by individuals and organizations, but alone it cannot reconcile all of the environmental problems facing society. Indeed it is possible that the commodification of nature and environmental risk may 'crowd out' the environmental ethic, where businesses and consumers assume that the price mechanism will make decisions for them; alternatively regulatory controls retain legal and societal signals over what is and is not acceptable behaviour (Frey 1992). Sagoff (1988, p.22) takes this further, and argues that resource and welfare economics are largely obsolete, that the important decisions which we need to make in relation to the environment are not economic trade-offs gauged through the price nexus: instead to establish priorities, 'we need to distinguish the pure from the polluted, the natural from the artificial, good from bad, right from wrong. These are scientific, cultural, aesthetic, historical, and ethical – not primarily economic – distinctions'. This kind of argument is not especially convincing in that the proposed polarities are not absolutes, nor are they comparable. The natural environment is not necessarily wholly benign to the human condition, with a rich mix of hazards capable of challenging human survival every day. Nor is the artificial necessarily wholly bad: is the car more or less artificial than a train? Emotionally appealing though it is to appeal to moral absolutes, these are sometimes as ill-founded as some of the absolutes of orthodox economics, such as the individual as the rational decision-maker.

It is important to emphasise here that there is a problem with some critiques of economic tools, since they are rarely advocated as the sole tools for environmental management. More or less all advocates of economic tools start from a point of establishing minimum acceptable standards and targets, with economic tools seen as the most efficient and effective means of meeting these standards. Pearce (1991) answers critics of his earlier book, *Blueprint for Survival* (Pearce, Markandya and Barbier 1989), by arguing that, although it is an inexact science, to approximate and move towards improving, or indeed creating, markets for environmental goods, society is at least attempting to move forward rather than ignoring the problem.

Marxist analysis, whilst not necessarily denying the validity of the insights of orthodox economists into environmental externalities, places greater emphasis on understanding the underlying logic of the capitalist accumulation process. That is, Marxist analyses seek to examine how economic wealth is generated and shared, particularly through continuing societal and geographical concentration of the means of production. This form of analysis is much more firmly rooted in particular historical contexts, rather than the relatively atemporal assumptions of most neo-classical models. Central to the analysis is the perceived need of the capitalist system to reduce labour and the natural environment to commodities, valued and exchanged through the cash nexus. Whilst the commodification and concomitant exploitation of labour power has taken pride of place in most Marxist analyses, environmental exploitation has nonetheless been a recurrent if subordinate theme, where the production of nature is seen as an integral part of the social relations of economic production (Short 1985, Smith 1990, Benton 1991, Harvey 1993).

An intriguing contrast is emerging between some Marxian approaches and the assumptions of conventional economists. Where orthodox economics holds that the further commodification of nature, through externality pricing, is the best means of controlling environmental problems, others argue that nature cannot be readily reduced to an abstract, consumable, commodified input into the market mechanism. Assumptions that technology allows humans to control and commodify nature are seen as ill-founded, in part because of the volatility and unpredictability of nature, and indeed of humans.

Finally, it must be borne in mind that the capitalist system is not yet as all-pervasive as many commentators would lead us to believe, even in the wake of the move away from state socialist-planned economies in the countries of eastern Europe. The so-called command, or planned, economies clearly failed to pay adequate attention to environmental issues, which obtained only a low priority, particularly where environmental problems stood in the way of industrialisation (ZumBrunnen 1990). It is perhaps worth noting in a more general vein that the growth of government employment and state enterprises in many Western nations, too, effectively created a large non-market area which, until recent reforms in governmental practice, could not only absent itself from the disciplines of the market, but also often from general public accountability. Added to this there is the substantial role of the informal economy, which is strongly present in developing-country cities in particular, and in poorer areas generally. Subsistence economies in developing countries which do not revolve around the cash nexus have frequently proven to be highly robust in environmental terms, displaying considerable husbandry of nature's resources, together with a sometimes religious mixing of respect for and stewardship of the natural environment. Market-based policies then have only a limited sphere of applicability, and sometimes policies to further commodify the environment as a basis for applying economic tools may involve an unwarranted disruption of alternative societal structures and techniques for environmental management, which may have been highly effective for many centuries.

7.3.4 Sharing the burdens and benefits of economic policy

One of the key criteria for evaluating policy tools is equity, and this has certainly been one of the most hotly contested issues in terms of adopting economic policies for the environment: who benefits most, and who benefits least? For instance, a carbon tax may well be socially regressive, since poor people spend a higher proportion of their income on fuel. In response to this criticism it can be argued that this option is less regressive than some other solutions, whilst it does not preclude compensation through redirecting some proportion of tax revenues to support those hardest hit (Barrett 1991).

Pearce (1990) notes that it is possible to make environmental taxes fiscally neutral, simply displacing other sources of taxation. This option has the advantage of not creating tax disincentives in the broader fiscal control of the economy. In many countries none the less, a direct link has been established between environmental levies and spending on environmental projects (Tietenberg 1990). In the UK, however, hypothecation (directly linking a tax revenue source to specific expenditure programmes) is strongly resisted still by the Treasury.

Applying environmental taxes in a fiscally neutral manner would create incentives for changing consumer and producer behaviour. However, unless existing tax revenues are used to compensate all existing problems created by environmental externalities, there is still likely to be a shortfall in compensatory transfers. There might also be a socially regressive impact, such as using environmental tax revenues simply to reduce income taxes, if we accept the argument that the poorest people are both most subject to the adverse impacts of pollution (Hall 1972, Friedmann 1989) and least able to manipulate the tax system to their own advantage. The inability to work compensation through changing the tax system alone is exacerbated in that many vulnerable groups, such as the young, unemployed and elderly, are outside the income tax system, so that the benefits of income tax reductions would be in considerable part lost to them. Problems of social equity are not insurmountable under economic policy regimes, however, with a variety of ways existing for rebates or differential charging rates to assist those least able to pay (OECD 1987).

There is a related concern that those geographical areas where adverse impacts are most heavily concentrated will gain little direct compensation in a fiscally neutral system, unless government expenditure patterns are radically altered to favour environmental restoration in the most polluted areas. This relates to the concern raised in Chapter Two that the costs and benefits of urban development are unevenly shared between neighbourhoods within the city, and between the city and its hinterland area. It should be stressed that the flows are rarely one way, the city passing on its air pollution to rural areas, for instance, is matched by the passing on of rural water pollution to urban areas, such as contamination by pesticides and artificial fertilisers. On a related point, in implementing economic policies, it is also important to consider the differential impacts possible between areas, where a petrol tax, for instance, will impact more heavily on rural residents than urban residents, given the greater dependence on car transport in rural areas with poor public transport.

A concern with the geographical differences in access to a good-quality environment within the city has once again begun to vex planners and geographers, where for instance high-income areas in US cities 'zone' to keep industry out, impose pollution fees, shift new infrastructure investments (such as waste incineration plants) and lobby for low growth because of the possible 'dysfunctional' effects of growth in terms of environmental quality (Friedmann 1989). The costs of environmental degradation are in effect being foisted onto those people, and those areas, with lowest incomes, whilst the benefits in terms of jobs and local environmental quality continue to accrue to those with high incomes.

Many people in effect gain access to a higher quality of environment by moving out to enjoy the 'free goods' of a relatively undisturbed environment at the edge of the city, avoiding paying 'urban' taxes for schemes to improve the urban environment. In a similar vein the areas suffering from the highest motor vehicle emissions within Manchester, UK, are those inner areas with the lowest car ownership rates (Wood *et al.* 1974), relating in part to proximity to main roads used by edge-of-city commuters.

In some eastern European countries, including some countries in the former USSR, an approach which links local pollution fees to local restoration funds appears to be emerging, but with ambiguous results so far. In 1989, the State Committee of Environmental Protection, *Goskompriroda*, introduced stiff penalties for environmental infringements in 50 cities and regions, adding a further 64 areas the following year, with 85% of the resulting revenues going to municipal budgets (Feshbach and Friendly 1992). By 1991 the fee-fine system was operating nationally, with all revenues going to municipal budgets and none to national environmental protection work. This may have led some local authorities to be over-zealous in applying their charges, in an attempt to raise revenue. In Poland the experience of ecological charges on pollution emissions has been similarly equivocal, seemingly creating new distortions, with high levels of charges (up to four times the cost of treatment) forcing some companies out of business and making it difficult for them to finance investment in new, more environment-friendly equipment. Alternatively, some firms enjoying near monopoly situations have simply raised their prices and continued to pollute. Likewise environmental fines appear to have the extreme characteristics of not influencing firms' behaviour or forcing them out of business (Poskrobko and Cygler 1992).

In developed countries, too, it is possible to identify local sensitivity in the application of economic tools. For instance, tradeable permits for pollution rights, most associated with environmental policy in the USA, includes the practice of *offsetting*, introduced in 1976. In areas where Clean Air Act standards are not achieved, expansion of existing factories or the movement in of new plants is allowed only under stringent conditions, related to improving ambient standards (Tietenberg 1990). Offsetting allows firms to set up new plants in these areas, provided reductions at least equivalent to the new emissions are achieved, either by other local plants owned by the same firm, or by other local firms. In these cases pollution reductions in one plant are traded for the right to add pollution emissions elsewhere, although there have been some attempted abuses, such as a steel company in Detroit, which sought to offset its pollution against paving rural dirt roads (Cunningham and

Saigo 1990). In practice most offsetting activities have been between plants owned by the same owner, largely because of the difficulties of acquiring information from other firms (Turner, Pearce and Bateman 1994).

Charges for urban physical infrastructure, discussed in Chapter Three, provide another instance of economic policy instruments used to back up urban planning policies. It is now a common trend in OECD countries to charge for technical infrastructure: in Germany local governments receive about a quarter of their income from charges and fees, recovering 91% of the cost of garbage disposal and 85% of the cost of sewerage disposal (OECD 1989). Development impact fees, or planning gain, and linkage policies are also to varying degrees ways of introducing financial charges on the private developers of major projects. These schemes can have a variety of rationales, including a private-sector contribution to necessary public infrastructure expenditures, mitigation of adverse impacts, and a return of profit to the community as a form of betterment (Healey, Purdue and Ennis 1993). Planning gain in England and Wales has been only weakly addressed in terms of statutory powers, but in recent years it has become accepted that it can be negotiated for contributions to physical and social infrastructure, and to the conservation of the natural environment, but should not involve commitments to on-going maintenance costs (Lichfield 1992). The main areas of agreements to date appear to cover highways, sewerage and drainage, and landscaping, with community facilities, affordable housing, building restoration, and public transport all benefiting too, but only relatively rarely (Healey, Purdue and Ennis 1993). In the case of the USA, planning gain, or platting, has a more statutory basis, and conditions can be contained in development plans for charges to be imposed to recover some of the costs of state infrastructure provision (Purdue, Healey and Ennis 1992).

Linkage policies in the USA have been more commonly associated with the provision of social infrastructure, such as low-cost housing, public art and day care centres. In cities such as Boston, linkage fees are levied to compensate for the loss of low-cost housing and added road congestion resulting from city-centre commercial developments. Charges are levied per unit of floorspace constructed and then used to help finance, typically, the construction of low-cost housing in other parts of the city (Keating 1986, Smith 1988). An interesting variant exists in Dortmund, Germany, where a planning linkage policy requires developers encroaching onto green space on a particular site to provide funds for the purchase and restoration of green space. This replacement green space can be sited some distance away: the state helps by buying and improving a number of large, strategically located plots of land, which different developers can contribute towards rather than set up their own replacement scheme. What these policies demonstrate is something of the flexibility of incorporating economic mechanisms into the environmental management process, and in particular the scope for combining these with other policy instruments, not least land use planning.

It is possible, then, to devise economic tools which are sufficiently sophisticated to compensate equitably for the geographically uneven distribution of the costs and benefits of polluting activities. It is more often the case that political systems are insufficiently flexible to allow such local sensitivity and innovation in policy application. It should also be said that the administrative burdens for detailed calculations of the separate location of the causes and effects of adverse environmental impacts would be potentially substantial. But it is possible to use economic tools in urban environmental management, and in the case of urban transport, they arguably can provide one of the most effective means through which beneficial changes can be brought about, as the next section begins to illustrate.

7.3.5 Economic approaches to urban transport problems

Given the range and magnitude of problems associated with urban transport (see Chapter Three), it would be unreasonable to expect economic policies in isolation to make the decisive impact in bringing about beneficial change (Box 7.8).

It is in cities that the greatest prospects lie for changing transport habits and reducing car-dependence, in particular by encouraging public transport use and altering the urban form. Economic policies for urban traffic aim to change transport preferences, in particular seeking to encourage: a shift of both passenger and freight transport away from urban roads and towards public transport; greater reliance on vehicles which use fewer carbon fuels and which produce less air and noise pollution; reductions in the demand for journeys, including a removal of subsidies which encourage low-density suburban sprawl. In all these cases, one of the main policy objectives is to remove subsidy distortions which either directly or indirectly have favoured private motor vehicles and high petrol consumption. In the USA, for instance, huge subsidies during the 1980s continued to be given to highway construction (US$16 billion per annum or 31% of costs), oil exploration and research and development, and low-density suburban development (estimates of up to US$117 billion per annum) (Pucher 1990).

Box 7.8 Supportive Non-Economic Approaches to Urban Transport

- Regulatory standards, e.g. for emissions and noise, for road traffic speeds and for traffic management (i.e. traffic calming, heavy lorry bans, bus and bicycle priority lanes, car-free areas, car pooling schemes, and improvements in public transport coverage, coordination and quality)

- Encouraging technological improvements, e.g. 'zero'-emission vehicles, lean-burn petrol engines, catalytic converters for emission reduction, noise barriers, noise reduction through tyre design

- Strategic and land use planning, e.g. improved coordination of investment for public and private transport modes, facilities for inter-modal journey changes between bus, rail and car, and land use controls over urban densities and location of urban functions

- Encouraging self-help schemes, e.g. car pooling, provision of secure bicycle parking spaces outside shops

- Information and education, e.g. road safety and anti-drink-drive campaigns, publicising the fuel economy gains of lower-speed road travel

The Worldwatch Institute has estimated the hidden social and environmental costs of car-driving at over \$300 billion a year, or \$2400 per passenger car (Renner 1988). In contrast, public transport in US cities was largely neglected from 1945 to the mid 1970s, further encouraging the shift towards road transport, with subsequent investments largely failing to reverse this trend in transport preferences (Pucher 1990). The motor vehicle lobby has become so influential that it has become difficult politically to reverse these trends, although not impossible (Newman and Kenworthy 1989). The scope for changing the balance of public and private transport is enormous, not least since so much expenditure is involved, much of it public: counted together, private and public transport infrastructure provision and maintenance, plus vehicle building and maintenance, account for 4–8% of gross domestic product in industrialised countries, up to 4% of jobs, and in Europe around 10% of household consumption spending (OECD 1991).

Pucher (1990) has usefully highlighted differences in levels and forms of public-sector support, contrasting cities in the east European socialist countries in the late 1980s with Western cities. The Eastern bloc countries were much more firmly ideologically committed to the belief that the individual had the right of access to good public transport, whilst in the USA in particular, public transport was frequently regarded as the option of last resort. Not surprisingly, there are major variations by country in public transport reliance, with further marked variation also between cities within each country. In Hungary, the USSR, Czechoslovakia and Poland, cars accounted for between 11% and 15% of urban trips, in European countries between 31% (Italy) and 48% (West Germany), jumping to a massive 74% in Canada and 82% in the USA (Pucher 1990). Australian data measuring car dependence based on passenger kilometres appear to show a level of reliance on the private car similar to US levels (Newman and Kenworthy 1989).

There are many factors which underlie these differences, including urban density and form, but particularly important are the different approaches to pricing and subsidising public and private transport in each country. Pucher argues that the main reason for differences in public transport dependence is not the income of residents, but rather differences in the price of public and private transport. In the Soviet Union and Eastern Europe in 1988 a litre of petrol cost 7–12 times more than a single ride on public transport; in Western Europe on average twice as much, whilst in the USA the litre of petrol amounted to just 36% of the average public transport fare. These differences very much relate to the price and subsidy mechanisms. The base price of petrol varies little between countries, with differences largely related to taxation policy. Other taxes exacerbate this divide, with sales taxes on new cars on average four times higher in European countries than in the USA. Just as importantly, there are major differences in the support of public transport, with the former West Germany enjoying a per capita subsidy four times higher than that of the USA. Differences in coverage and quality of public transport also varies widely between cities, not necessarily reflecting differences in subsidy level alone.

It could be argued that price and subsidy policies have also had a more insidious effect, in the communist era allowing car production in the former Eastern bloc to continue to churn out cars with low fuel-efficiency, low safety standards and high pollution emissions. Alternatively, the low cost of petrol in particular in some Western countries distorted competition, so that it tended to increase demand for large, fuel-hungry models, not for more economical cars. At either side of the spectrum, pricing policy has encouraged car production unsuited to the needs of the city, not least allowing the continued output of cars with low fuel economy and high pollution. In the USA, competition centred on styling rather than fuel economy, leading to a major decrease in fuel economy between 1958 and 1973: styling rivalry alone is estimated to have artificially increased fuel consumption in the USA by 18 billion gallons of petrol during the 1950s (Adams and Brock 1986).

The scope for using economic tools to address the problems of urban transport is clearly enormous, but it is not necessarily easy to predict or even measure the outcomes of particular instruments. Moreover, it is not clear that many economic policies have been based on a rigorous attempt to cost environmental externalities, and even fewer have established direct compensatory mechanisms. At a national level the main direct areas of transport pricing alteration include: differential fuel prices, between leaded and unleaded petrol for instance; road taxes; car sales taxes, including differentials based on fuel efficiency; tax relief for research and development towards more environment-friendly forms of public and private transport; reduction of car ownership subsidies, including company car tax relief; increased public investment in inter-city and intra-city public transport; and greater use of road pricing mechanisms, including tolls.

Urban transport problems have their own particular complexion and require additional, more locally based policy approaches. Particularly important is peak period congestion in cities, with associated pollution, noise and time delay problems. In addition, there are problems such as the unnecessary intrusion of motor vehicles into residential areas, which are usually best treated with local traffic management schemes rather than economic tools. This said, in the case of limiting external traffic intrusion, resident-only parking schemes do often involve a small charge on residents. Policies to address peak period traffic congestion include higher fares on public transport at certain times of the day, increased car park fees for all day usage (that is aiming at commuters rather than shoppers), reduced all-day parking availability, higher fuel taxes in cities, higher urban car ownership taxes, and differential road charges (OECD 1985b, 1988, 1990). It is sometimes possible to link interventions across private and public transport directly. For instance, fuel tax revenues have been used to improve public transport in Stockholm, although an ownership tax may be more effective in targeting urban residents and employees (OECD 1985b).

Regulatory control, exhortation and education, and selective subsidy have all been experimented with, separately and in combination, by cities anxious to address their road transport problems in ways other than simply building new roads. In Los Angeles, ambitious plans have been put forward to limit reliance on petrol-powered cars, moving progressively towards cleaner fuels (OECD 1988, 1990). A combination of ambitious targets and restrictions on sales appears to have been successful in moving manufacturers to seek out new technologies. In addition, the Los Angeles plan aimed to promote work at home and telecommuting, and a regional approach among local governments to residential and employment centre location decisions. In Athens an emergency system was introduced in 1981 of restricting cars from entry on alternate days during the week in business hours, with access based on licence plates ending with an odd or even number (OECD 1988). Although this did appear to reduce traffic by 20% it also led many simply to buy a second car! Some local authorities have sought to reduce the costs of public transport, notably the Greater London Council which cut fares by 25% in 1983 and provided a pass valid for trains, buses and the underground, leading to a 16% increase in use of public transport and a fall of 10–15% in cars entering the city at peak times. The full benefits were estimated at £171 million, the costs at £75 million. A short-sighted national government abolished the Greater London Council in 1986 and proceeded to push up the fares for public transport and to reduce investment. Elsewhere, transport authorities have encouraged inter-modal transfer, between car, bus, rail and tram. 'Park-and-ride' facilities have also been introduced, for instance in the historic town of York in England: acute city centre congestion has led the local authority to provide parking and free bus transfers from edge-of-town locations.

Economic tools have also begun to emerge as important in their own right. Urban road pricing mechanisms have begun to attract considerable interest in many countries, and have been used in Singapore since 1975, and in Hong Kong, Stockholm and Cambridge (UK) on a trial basis. Methods include tolls at city entrance points, and electronic tagging systems allowing computerised monitoring and charging for car usage within the city. Road pricing policies cannot be implemented in isolation of other supportive measures: in the case of Singapore there is a mixture of road user charges, parking management and vehicle taxes (OECD 1988). The Singapore system involves commuters buying supplementary licences to enter the city in peak periods, with car pools, consisting of four or more riders in a car, allowed free access. Off-street car park fees were increased, as were hourly on-street parking charges, whilst a surcharge was introduced on privately owned car parks. A four-tiered vehicle tax system was used to encourage the scrapping of older, inefficient cars, and a shift towards smaller new cars, using a trade-in arrangement for old cars to mitigate against new car taxes. Evaluations of the scheme indicate a major success in reducing peak period road transport into the city, particularly in the morning, with a shift away from car-use, which accounted for 56% of city centre-bound work trips in 1975, but only 23% in 1983.

Other forms of innovative economic policies point to further possibilities for the creative use of economic approaches to urban transport management. In Los Angeles, the building of a new subway line has been accompanied by the creation of 'benefit assessment districts', where land owners whose property values increase because of the improved access to subway stations become liable to special taxes (OECD 1988). In California, tax concessions exist to promote car pooling, both for individuals and for companies. In the larger French cities a payroll levy exists on employers of ten or more (2% in Paris, 1.2% elsewhere) and is used to help fund public transport. In many countries the introduction of simplified fare structures and fare reductions has had notable successes in attracting passengers from road to rail, most notably in London during the early 1980s (see Chapter Three).

What such initiatives indicate is the valuable contribution economic policies can make towards beginning to incorporate social and environmental externalities into the pricing mechanism, thereby helping to shift urban transport preferences in favour of public transport. However, the most important ingredient in policies to relieve urban transport problems remains the need to maximise the synergies between the different policy instruments, economic and non-economic, and this in turn requires effective coordination of transport policies, possibly creating a single local agency responsible for private and public transport in each major city (OECD 1990). This leads us to two of the issues dealt with in the next chapter, the management of cities and the coordination of policies for sustainable urban development.

7.4 SUMMARY

Using the examples of EIA and economic policy instruments, this chapter indicates something of the flexibility and creativity with which policies for the urban environment can be applied in different cities. Themes which emerge from this analysis include the need for compatibility across different policy approaches, and most importantly, integration in the application of different policy instruments. To achieve this requires urban and environmental management systems which show a sensitivity to local problems and potentials at both inter- and intra-urban scales, and which seek to integrate policies for change across a range of time horizons, responding to both immediate and long-term needs. Within this framework, it is necessary to address policies with a view to the combined objectives of environmental effectiveness, social equity, and economic efficiency. Unfortunately, political expediency has frequently hindered this process: it is for this reason that the final chapter provides a closer examination of the management and political challenges of bringing about a move towards more sustainable forms of urban development.

FURTHER READING

Wathern (1992) provides an excellent reader on environmental impact assessment. Economic tools in an urban context are discussed in both Button and Pearce (1989) and OECD (1990).

KEY THEMES

- Precautionary approach to urban development
- Strategic environmental assessment
- Internalising 'externalities' into the pricing mechanism
- Regressive taxation systems

DISCUSSION POINTS

Six sets of policy instruments were suggested in the introductory section of this chapter as being fundamental to the move to creating sustainable cities.

- Can you suggest at least one additional category?
- Consider how any three of the policy categories can be usefully applied in an integrated fashion.
- Identify some of the main limitations of using any one of these policies in isolation in attempting to, for instance, curb large city growth.

CHAPTER EIGHT

Towards the Sustainable City

8.1 INTRODUCTION

Sustainable urban development is a process which is ceaselessly dynamic, responding to changing economic, environmental and social pressures. Although there are relatively few universal principles for sustainability, the ways of moving from these to policy implementation are many. Sustainable urban development, therefore, is a process which will necessarily vary between cities, and which will evolve in different ways in each city. Indeed, the very notion of what constitutes a sustainable city will inevitably change over time, as our understanding of global and local environments becomes more sophisticated. One of the most profound challenges at present is to create viable, indeed sustainable, political and institutional systems within which strategies, programmes and policies for sustainable urban development can be framed.

Given the importance accorded in previous chapters to various aspects of urban form and design, this chapter begins by examining some of the main grand visionary strategies proposed in the twentieth century to improve cities as places to live, work and play, through policies to alter urban size, shape, density and form. Almost inevitably, these strategies also contained either explicit or implicit social and political goals, in addition to more straightforward goals of raised quality of life, improved aesthetic appearance, and economic efficiency. This overview is helpful in reminding us of some of the dangers facing those seeking to bring about radical change to the urban fabric. Both top-down and bottom-up strategies for altering existing cities are examined following this, whilst the penultimate section examines some of the political and managerial challenges of making strategies work on the ground. In the concluding section the future challenges facing urban residents, urban businesses and urban managers are outlined.

Crosscutting all these sections are a number of important common challenges to the way in which strategies for sustainable urban development are constructed: creating political structures which promote collective benefits and avoid political alienation and fragmentation; the availability and allocation of resources for shaping urban change; developing social and environmental stewardship, and responsibility within urban communities; and the changing role of the different participants in the urban development process, not least the challenges facing the main professions, the architects, planners and so on.

8.2 CHANGING THE SHAPE AND FORM OF THE IDEAL CITY

A considerable body of innovative and experimental plans for creating variants on the theme of sustainable urban development has emerged in the twentieth century, sometimes bearing related titles such as organic, green or eco-cities. As we have already hinted, the sustainable city is not an end point, more a direction, something which the notion of organic planning seeks to capture. Drawing from work on human psychology and ecological systems, evolution in the organic sense is seen to entail a shift from simplicity to complexity, uniformity to diversity, and instability to stability. Human nature develops from the basics of searching for food and shelter towards more complex needs of creativity, drawing synergy from involvement in different activities. In a similar way, it is implied, the city should be encouraged to develop organically to support these human needs and the drive towards self-fulfilment at a continuously higher level, where the built environment supports and amplifies positive personal and environmental development (Hill 1992).

Urban development which in some way adheres to the notion of organic development has been widely advocated as the philosophical rationale for ideas of a startling variety. These have ranged from proposals to spread population thinly across the American continent, to proposals to create two-mile-high mega-structures; indeed, these two extremes were both proposed by Frank Lloyd Wright at different stages of his life (Hill 1992).

The main rationales and contradictions of some of the most influential proposals for radically altering the size, shape and form of cities are examined in this section, which identifies four main categories of approach: balanced regional integration with the natural environment; deconcentration and dispersal, returning the city to nature; dense urban concentration – technology taming nature; and concentrated decentralisation, with mixed-density development and ready access to green space.

8.2.1 Balanced integration with the regional natural environment

The need to plan urban development within the context of local features of the natural environment was a lesson which needed to be relearnt after the nineteenth century onslaught of urbanisation, which frequently sought to annihilate rather than accommodate nature. Most importantly, the growth of cities with large populations extending over ever larger physical areas required new thinking about how cities and their inhabitants could remain in contact with nature.

The development of city region structures which helped bring nature into the city, and created accessible green belt areas for urban residents found its most famous expression in the work of Ebenezer Howard and his followers. As Chapter Two indicated, Howard's (1898) Garden City proposal was a landmark in urban planning. It differed from other plans of its era in its formal expression of the need to decentralise the population away from the unpleasantness of the capital, the need to start again building cities from small settlement units on new sites, and aspiring to create an urban environment more closely connected to the natural environment. For Howard, the large city could never be a suitable place for living: ill-ventilated, ill-planned, unwieldy and unhealthy cities were doomed. The countryside, too, was an uncomfortable option for future living. Instead he proposed a third magnet, the Garden City.

Social motives were very much to the fore in the plans for the Garden City. Land would be bought collectively and the benefits of raised land rentals put to community benefit, and indeed to pay for the building of the Garden City. Taxes would be unnecessary; rents would suffice to run hospitals and so on. The key to good living was seen as the provision of good housing and the rational organisation of space, with an end to cluttered and jumbled towns. The new, orderly Garden City must of necessity have industries, but these had to be on the outskirts of town. Work, then, did not unify the town, this was left to leisure and civic enterprise. Although initially planned as heading social change which would provide an alternative to the growth of state power, the Garden City movement very quickly became simply a land use planning movement.

Patrick Geddes (1915) believed that urban planning needed to build from a knowledge of natural regions and their resources. In particular, he regarded the river basin as the natural unit for examining the different activities associated with cities. Within this context, it would be possible for residents to link with nature and with their own past. Geddes also foresaw the important influences on city size that would be exerted by new technologies such as electricity and motor vehicles. As the sprawling city would dissipate resources and energy, and alienate people from

a) 'Balanced' regional hierarchy

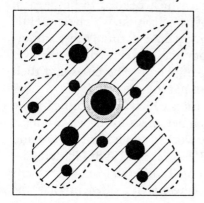

b) Concentrated centre

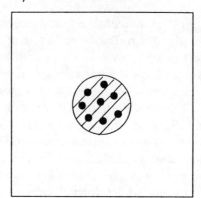

c) Concentrated decentralisation

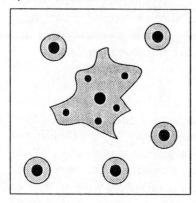

d) Deconcentrated development

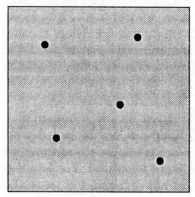

- - - - - - - - - Edge of metropolitan area (with axial development
along transport routes)

Urban open space

Low/Medium density

High density

Figure 8.1 Urban form and sustainability

nature, it would be important to bring nature back into the city. This, Geddes proposed, would be best achieved by encouraging urban settlements to develop in a star-like form, with axes of natural space intruding into the city (see, for example, Figure 8.1a). This proposal has a resonance with more recent advocates of 'fingers' of agricultural land stretching into cities, up to a mile wide, whilst built-up areas should generally be no more than a mile wide (Alexander, Ishikawa and Silverstein 1977). For Alexander and his colleagues, large cities are acceptable provided that multiple centres are supported within the city, and that growth is based on neighbourhood-level organic development from within, building upon historical development where appropriate (Alexander 1967, 1969).

Lewis Mumford (1961) took elements of the 'social cohesion' and city size thinking of Howard, as well as the river basin approach espoused by Patrick Geddes, to create a more direct link between ecological areas and city region development. His proposals involved new Garden City-type, decentralised urban development, located in river basin regions (Hill 1992). This approach is taken further in one direction in the work of Ian McHarg (1969), pursuing the theme of 'design with nature'. Like Geddes, McHarg advocated examining the environmental condition of an area in detail prior to initiating urban development, but advancing the level of analysis to incorporate variables such as aquifer recharge area and local climate. Aquifer recharge zones, for instance, are seen as best suited to agriculture, forestry, open space, low-density housing and industry not associated with toxic effluents. Taking various dimensions of the impacts of urbanisation on the natural environment, these are then examined together to help identify those areas where urbanisation would least damage natural ecosystems. McHarg, unlike Howard, Mumford and Alexander, had little concern with human interaction, neighbourhood development, regional hierarchies and even general principles for urban shape: the natural environment is too varied to allow such ready blueprints.

One of the most important implications of these various approaches is that attempts to fill in non-developed areas should usually be avoided. Policies for green belts, green wedges, green corridors may all need to be applied to ensure that the city region retains a mixture of built-up areas and readily accessible green spaces. In addition, the work of Geddes, Mumford and McHarg in particular, emphasises the need to plan for urban expansion and new towns from a sound knowledge of local ecological conditions, aiming to minimise the adverse impacts of urban development, and to ensure that urban development in itself makes the most of local natural assets, from simple issues like solar aspects of housing to maintaining existing sites of ecological value.

8.2.2 Decentralisation, dispersion and assimilation within the natural environment

One of the earliest advocates of low density living was Peter Kropotkin (1899) in the late nineteenth century, who saw the rise of electric power in particular as liberating the need for industry to locate in cities. He argued that large cities would quickly become unnecessary and could be replaced by a series of small settlements without a strong urban centre.

The promotion of dispersed or decentralised settlement development has since permeated much green thinking, with small villages and communes seen as the natural alternative to large cities (*Ecologist* 1972, Roszak 1973, Bookchin 1974, Schumacher 1974, Callenbach 1975). Key themes include: the centrality of small-scale economic and political organisational forms; grassroots political empowerment; the emphasis on collective action; local economic self-reliance, including farming and industry; use of appropriate technologies, recycling and reuse of materials; and the value of 'natural' ecological or resource areas as potential political boundaries.

One of the most articulate visions in this genre was provided in 1975 by the novelist Ernest Callenbach, in his novel *Ecotopia*. The inhabitants of Ecotopia secede from the USA in 1980, determined to lead an ecologically ethical life in the former west coast states of Washington and Oregon. Residents seal their borders to the rest of polluted America, recycle all metal, glass, paper and plastic, and introduce quiet magnetic-propulsion trains to join the new country together. The women-dominated Survival Party leads the new government, with Party meetings not having an agenda: people simply start out by sharing concerns, and no motions or votes occur. Instead, issues are argued out, and consensus reached, with members taking pains to assuage the feelings of those who give most ground. The old state and county boundaries are abandoned early on, being replaced by five metropolitan and four rural regions, based on regional ecological systems. Naturally, considerable levels of power are further devolved within local communities. Cars too are abandoned, and the former roads along waterfront areas in cities have been converted to recreational use, with riverside cafes, piers and parks. Attempts to use fines and special taxes on polluting industrial firms have failed because businesses simply passed the charges on to customers, who then complained they had to put up not only with the pollution but also higher prices. As a result many polluting activities have been simply prohibited, and despite a transition period with government assistance, many go out of business. In this slice of Ecotopia we can see some intriguing parallels with earlier Utopias, some radical extensions, and some portents of green city proposals which were to follow.

Taking the decentralisation theme to the extreme of a near-uniform dispersion of the population across the land are some of the ideas contained in the more nationalistic writings of the American Frank Lloyd Wright. Where Kropotkin and others promoted the values of small-scale cooperation, based around relatively small communities, Wright fought long and hard for individualism and private ownership, and against the 'tyranny of the majority'. Where writers such as Ebenezer Howard wanted to maintain something of the distinctiveness of town and country, Wright was happy to see the two merged by low-density development of individual households, at an average one family per acre (Wright 1974). In his low-density, high-technology 'exurbia' people would be closer to nature, encouraging the 'nomad hermit' instinct rather than the urge to be part of the city 'herd'. The neighbourhood concept is avoided, as is the notion of planning around any form of ecological region (Hill 1992). Wright had little time for the state or for collective action: suburbs of individuals living within ten to twenty miles of their work, recreational pursuits and services were all that was necessary for the realisation of his version of democracy and urbanism. This form of extreme dispersion would have been extremely energy-demanding and profligate of resources; people were envisaged as travelling with their own personal helicopters and cars, whilst long-distance provision of electricity and water would be likely to be extremely inefficient in terms of both infrastructure provision and leakage during transmission. This extreme form of non-city in fact serves to bring home how environmentally efficient cities can be, in some respects at least.

8.2.3 Urban concentration and the control of nature

High-density urban living experiments in the twentieth century are especially associated with high-rise residential buildings, made possible by advances in the availability of electric energy supply, and by new building materials and techniques. Earlier high-rise buildings in particular were largely built with the intention of creating highly controlled artificial environments, excluding nature almost completely. However, this high-density land use did frequently allow the provision of considerable open space in surrounding areas. It is very rare indeed, however, to find such space providing safe, aesthetically pleasing or ecologically valuable conditions. In addition, there have been various proposals to tame nature by incorporating cities within large structures, such as Buckminster Fuller's Geodesic Domes (Meller 1970). These were bubble-like frames which would enclose buildings, creating new, protected, artificial environments. This concept has been used in Pionersky in Siberia, developing Buckminster Fuller's attempts to create 'ideal climates' (Rosenau 1983). Paulo Soleri too (1990), as noted in Chapter Three, is attempting to create new compact, high-density communities, developing various ideas for high-rise and partly underground cities, argued for in part with reference to the need to save land, and to understand the contrast between the natural and built environments. As we have already noted, although Soleri's plans appear to excite some for their environmental concerns (such as Canfield 1990), there is a tension between some of the environmental benefits to be gained and the disadvantages of crowded living in artificial environments.

Control of the individual and control of nature both lay at the heart of the thinking of Le Corbusier (1929) perhaps still the most influential exponent of higher-density living. Whilst he is commonly blamed as the inspiration for the 1960s proliferation of residential tower blocks, his plans were actually for medium-height residential developments, with offices located in the skyscrapers (Hall 1988). In his Plan Voisin, intended for Paris, the medium-rise residential units would be clearly segregated along class lines in apartments, which were to be uniform in design and to have the same furniture. All areas, however, would have considerable provision of open space and generous tree planting. Higher-density living was to be the means to improving internal communications and to increasing the amount of open space within the city. Many of Le Corbusier's basic principles have a continuing resonance with environmental concerns put forward today. However, some of the original thinking, and most importantly, some of the later misinterpretation of his work have meant that in practice the ideas were largely unsuccessful. One example is his view that the existing city would have to be demolished to make way for the new city.

As with so many other grand visionaries, Le Corbusier drew on the possibilities of emergent technologies in developing his views of urban design as a means to elevate the human condition, through liberating people of some of the drudgery of everyday existence, whilst creating a new aesthetic for the urban environment. He is now, perhaps unjustly, regarded as the technocratic grandmaster, unable to resolve the conflicts his plans created between authority and participation. He saw the architect-planner as an inviolate artist, who had to be protected from parliaments and elections, relying instead on his or her own understanding of society, its structure, its values, its ambitions, its needs and its resources (Fishman 1977). Le Corbusier was full of contradictions which were never satisfactorily resolved, between wanting 'authority and freedom, organisation and individuality, mechanisation and craftsmanship, planning and spontaneity' (Fishman 1977, p 260). Lewis Mumford (1961) delivered an early indictment of his work which remains well known, lauding the Cartesian clarity and elegance, but deriding the

Baroque insensitiveness to time, change, organic adaptation, functional fitness, and ecological complexity.

It is easy to be cynical about visionary architects and master planners in retrospect, but as Hall (1984) points out, many of them showed extraordinary perspicacity for their time. Ebenezer Howard anticipated the decentralisation of population away from the cities; Frank Lloyd Wright anticipated the huge impacts the motor car would have on urban form; and Le Corbusier anticipated the importance of new building materials and techniques. None the less, the main contribution of Le Corbusier to the sustainable city debate is to reveal something close to the opposite of what a green city should be, not least in his disdain for the views of the ordinary people.

8.2.4 Concentrated decentralisation

Various forms of concentrated decentralisation have found favour in recent writings on sustainable urban development (see Chapter Three). Kevin Lynch (1961, 1981) has noted the possible value of creating a regional city, built up from a series, or 'galaxy', of separate medium-sized communities, surrounded by large amounts of open space and connected by major roads. Lynch (1961) also commented on the possibility of a ring city, with strong edge-of-city centres being developed, similar to the pattern which has since become well-established in some North American cities. Interestingly, in the context of the 'galaxy of cities' approach, Lynch warned against the danger of functional monotony occurring amongst smaller towns, unless each could be allowed to develop its own specialist functional niche. This sense of 'sameness' is perhaps one of the most persistent criticisms levelled at today's suburban centres.

Lynch's (1981) *Good City Form* has been one of the most influential books in shaping the ideas of how the design of the city might be improved, drawing together ideas of regional ecological planning and concentrated decentralisation. He argued that the city should be located as part of a distinct regional area, with clear boundaries based on ecological and social capacities. Within the city, places and people would be highly interdependent, with different order functions recognisable but not necessarily separated; the intimate neighbourhood would be the key building block, socially and economically heterogeneous, and urban communities would be cooperative rather than competitive.

Gruen (1964, 1973) also pursued the 'galaxy of settlements' approach, putting forward the notion of the cellular metropolis. He felt that this approach might help in retaining the 'feel' of urbanity, the diversity and vibrancy of cultural, economic and social life possible in the city centre. Rather than suburban sprawl or regional hierarchies of cities, Gruen proposed that high-density metropolitan living can be accommodated within a series of towns, each surrounded by natural areas, and each town made up of a series of smaller cells, or neighbourhoods. A central downtown area of around 50,000 people would be surrounded by thirty towns of 65,000 people, in may ways a scaled up version of Howard's similar Social City Region.

As Chapter Three highlighted, concentrated decentralisation has been increasingly advocated on environmental grounds, because of its potential to reduce energy usage, in particular by encouraging greater use of public transport and allowing the viable development of combined heat and power systems. Concentrated decentralisation can involve both development in separate towns outside the main city, connected by good public transport to the main urban centre, and strong suburban centres. In both cases, higher-density development around these development nodes is advocated, to encourage diversity of use and the support of viable public transit systems.

An intriguing variant on this theme has been the attempt to provide a new model for sustainable urban development in the Japanese–Australian multifunction-polis (MFP) initiative. The MFP follows the concentrated decentralisation model in its attempt to create a new subcentre within an existing city. MFP-Australia is currently slowly taking shape in Adelaide, South Australia (Haughton 1994). It represents an ambitious attempt to bring together elements of a high-technology production base, cosmopolitan living, and sustainability. Alternative plans for a multi-site plan within Sydney were rejected as likely to increase journeys across the city, whilst greenfield plans for development in coastal Queensland were also ultimately rejected, although more on political and financial grounds than environmental. The site chosen for Adelaide consists in considerable part of degraded land, located to the north of the city. In environmental terms, the advantage is seen to be the conversion of this 'waste' land (not all of it is waste) and promotion of development within an existing city rather than fuelling further urban land take.

The MFP concept has evolved over five years in a highly politicised atmosphere, where compromises have had to be made. Early claims of a city with high levels of internal containment, plus high levels of overseas investment and skilled labour, created fears that a new enclave was being created within Adelaide. Increasingly, the Australian input to the proposal has come to the fore, along with an emphasis on the integration of the MFP with the rest of the city and with linked MFP sites in other Australian cities. As one element of gaining popular support, the role of the city as a sustainable city exemplar has also risen in prominence, with schemes underway to improve stormwater capture and reuse. The new settlement is envisaged as consisting of small villages, and the prospect has been raised of these being internally linked by innovatory transport forms, such as small electric cars. There is a good deal of local scepticism about the likelihood of such tantalising developments taking place, adding to the existing doubts over the very desirability of choosing as the site for the MFP a polluted swamp with a municipal tip and considerable ground contamination, and surrounded by heavy industry, including a power station. There is also a perceived threat to the remaining mangrove reserves of the area, which are regarded as of regional ecological significance. As a private sector-led initiative, backed by federal and state governments, it is hardly surprising that many of the features of green cities elsewhere are missing: local political control is not proposed – instead a development corporation is to oversee the project; and collective community action is advocated, but appears to be an objective which is highly subordinate to the needs of private investors. In its early stages the MFP shows the limited commercial potential which 'sustainability' still has in such developments, despite its popular appeal. Whatever its long-term achievements, the MFP proposal has been valuable in opening up the debate on urban sustainability. The challenge will be to attract commercial investment and to remain true to the ideals of promoting urban sustainable development.

8.2.5 Drawing some conclusions for the green city

Urban form can be a major element in bringing about habits which are more conducive to global sustainability, in particular reducing reliance on private cars. Whilst most urban development of the twentieth century has tended to be incremental, rolling outwards and infilling, there have been some notable attempts to create new cities, to control urban expansion and to reorder urban form in an attempt to create a more 'rational' city. This sense of the 'rational' has often implicitly had an environmental dimension, in the attempts to ensure efficient movement of people and goods between and within cities. However, development forms which respect local natural environmental conditions have remained the exception rather than the rule. Instead, mass-produced housing has obliterated large sites, using relatively uniform housing styles and site layouts. Incorporating elements of the natural environment has been subordinate to the use and needs of new technologies, not least the car, and commercial viability.

Some of the most well-intentioned masterplans have gone badly awry. The main reason for this is perhaps that provided by Peter Hall (1984), who argues that those experiments which showed a strong grasp of the socioeconomic framework generally worked, and those that did not failed. Relating to this, it is frighteningly true to say that until the last twenty years very few of the grand urban masterplans involved meaningful participation by those whose lives would be affected. In consequence, we have seen a reaction to the early twentieth century deification of the urban expert, leading to the popular vilification of the main professions, the architects and the planners. Alexander (1969) captures something of this popular feeling, arguing

> While architects dream of utterly unimaginable futures, the planners talk about piece-meal incremental planning. The visionary architecture is imaginative, daring, but completely mad. The planners' plans are utterly and boringly sane; though based on facts, they offer no comprehensive vision of a better future. (p.78)

The time is certainly ripe for new approaches and for new partnerships of development professionals, communities, and politicians. Together the various interested parties need to think again about how to approach the task of creating cities that are not simply habitable today, but sustainable into the future.

8.3 RESTRUCTURING EXISTING CITIES FOR SUSTAINABILITY

Important though strategies which start from a base of idealised physical form for urban settlements are, they have been increasingly superseded by more holistic strategies, which incorporate land use issues, but which also place much greater emphasis on restructuring the political, social, economic and managerial dimensions of existing cities as the basis for bringing about sustainable urban development. In recent years proposals for reorganising and managing urban settlements have emerged in increasing numbers, from international bodies, national governments, local governments and environmental and community pressure groups. Most proposals acknowledge that successful policies for the urban environment require a combination of top-down and bottom-up approaches. This section provides an overview of some of the major dimensions of these approaches.

8.3.1 International and national governments and sustainable urban development

Sustainable urban development needs to be set within the context of global initiatives for environmental management, including agreements on meeting the transboundary challenges of ozone depletion, acid deposition and global warming, for example. It is also important that international agreement is reached on environmental goals for cities, aiming to ensure that they contribute more to global sustainability. There have been long-standing initiatives in this direction, including the UNESCO Man and the Biosphere programme, launched in 1971, plus more recent initiatives such as the World Health Organisation's Healthy Cities programme, and the Sustainable Cities Programme of HABITAT. Valuable though these initiatives have been, there has remained a tendency among international agencies promoting development to favour rural over urban initiatives. For instance, only 1% of UN grant-related expenditures went to human settlements in 1988, whilst just 5.5% of World Bank and International Development Agency loans were allocated for urban development, water provision and sanitation (Quarrie 1992). As the scale of urban problems in the developing world has become more apparent, some international funding bodies have in recent years begun to develop programmes with an explicit urban focus.

At the 1992 Earth Summit in Rio a detailed agenda specifically for human settlements was set out, encompassing both urban and rural settlements. In addition, many of the other policy agendas incorporated specific urban dimensions, most notably in the sections on the protection and promotion of human health, and on fresh water resources (Box 8.1). Although most of the individual measures are in themselves fairly unexceptional, what makes the Rio agenda different is that the policy elements are brought together in a single package which has the backing of virtually the whole international community.

At the supranational level, the European Union has been particularly active in uniting member states on environmental issues. The Fifth Environmental Programme, for instance, sets out to address the following issues: sustainable management of natural resources; integrated pollution control and prevention of waste; reduction in the consumption of non-renewable energy; improved mobility management, in favour of more environmentally rational location decisions and transport modes; coherent packages to improve urban environmental quality; and improvement of public health and safety (Commission of the European Communities 1992). The Commission has been particularly active in promoting debate on the changing nature of cities and on urban environmental issues, issuing a Green Paper on the Urban Environment in 1990. This pro-cities document advocated policies for the development of compact cities, high-density cities which would see a renaissance of urban living and urban quality of life. This approach has generated considerable debate, in particular challenging whether compact cities are as desirable and as environmentally efficient as the Commission claims (Breheny 1992). There are fears too that the generalised review of urban problems and broad blueprint ignores the particularities of cities in different nations, facing different sets of problems. For instance, for southern European cities it is argued that the Commission's call for attention to fine-detail planning for urban design, working to promote mixed-use neighbourhoods, should not lead to an abandonment of larger-scale urban planning (Hastaoglou-Martinidis, Kalogirou and Papamichos 1993).

Box 8.1 Summary of the Main Urban Dimensions of Agenda 21

A. Provision of adequate shelter for all

Adopt/strengthen national shelter strategies, including legal protection against unfair eviction from homes or land; provide shelter for the homeless and the urban poor; seek to reduce rural–urban drift by improving rural shelter; introduce resettlement programmes for displaced persons; develop multinational cooperation to support the efforts of developing countries.

B. Improve human settlement management

Improve urban management; strengthen urban data systems; encourage intermediate city development.

C. Promote sustainable land use planning and management

Develop national land inventory and classification systems; create efficient and accessible land markets, with land registers etc.; encourage public–private partnerships in managing the land resource; establish appropriate forms of land tenure; develop fiscal and land use planning solutions for a more rational and environmentally sound use of the land resource; promote access to land for the urban poor; adopt comprehensive land use strategies; encourage awareness of the problems of unplanned settlements in vulnerable areas.

D. Ensure integrated provision of environmental infrastructure: water, sanitation, drainage and solid waste management

Introduce policies to minimise environmental damage; undertake EIAs; promote policies to recover infrastructure costs, whilst extending services to all households; seek joint solutions where issues cross localities.

E. Develop sustainable energy and transport systems in human settlements

Develop and transfer technologies which are more energy-efficient and involve renewable resources; improve urban transport systems.

F. Encourage human settlement planning and management in disaster-prone areas

Promote a culture of safety; develop pre-disaster planning; initiate post-disaster reconstruction and rehabilitation planning.

G. Promote sustainable construction industry activities

Encourage greater use of local natural materials and greater energy efficiency in design and materials; strengthen land use controls in sensitive areas; encourage self-help schemes.

H. Meet the urban health challenge

Develop municipal health plans; promote awareness of primary health care; strengthen environmental health services; establish city collaboration networks; improve training; adopt health impact and EIA procedures.

(Quarrie 1992)

The Urban Affairs group of the OECD has also been active in promoting discussion of environmental issues for cities, most notably in *Environmental Policies for Cities in the 1990s* (OECD 1990). This document provides a series of policy principles (see Chapter Six), as well as policy guidelines for urban energy, urban transport and urban area rehabilitation. The main thrust of this document is that long-term, cross-sectoral, integrated and coordinated policies are necessary to improve the urban environment. In achieving this, market-based and regulatory approaches are held to be complementary forces in bringing about change. In addition, forms of urban environmental development are advocated that involve partnerships between the public and private sectors, and a building of local capacities, including community participation.

At the national level, whilst most governments have now developed policies for sustainable development, very few appear to have provided an explicitly urban focus to their policies. The Australian 'Better Cities' programme may turn out to be an example of a national framework for environmental policies for cities, given its attention to urban consolidation policy, but even two years after initiation its aims remain ambiguous and ill-articulated within the public realm (Spiller 1993a). Alternatively, national advisory bodies and pressures groups, such as the Association of Metropolitan Authorities and Friends of the Earth in Britain, have provided a series of valuable policy statements and guidelines for sustainable urban development (see for instance: Association of Metropolitan Authorities 1989, Elkin, McLaren and Hillman 1991). These guidelines can be extremely influential in promoting local level policies in support of sustainable development: policies which, as the next two sections reveal, can be extremely productive.

8.3.2 Local government and sustainable urban development

As environmental concern heightened in the late 1980s, local governments in many countries emerged as key protagonists in the attempts to ensure that the environment became and remained a political priority, and also an everyday concern of every department in the authority and of every resident in an area. Even in the UK, whilst local government powers have been eroded in other areas of activity, their acknowledged long-standing expertise in environmental issues and sensitivity to local conditions and needs have been acknowledged by central government. For the same reasons, local government in most countries is widely argued as the most appropriate focal point for coordinating and implementing environmental policies. Not only have they got a long track record, but they also typically bring their expertise and powers to a variety of important areas, including land use planning, transport, environmental health, parks, building control, waste disposal and education (Hollis, Ham and Ambler 1992, Stoker and Young 1993). Increasingly, the role of local government has switched from that of prime player, implementing its own policies, to that of the coordinator, facilitator and enabler of environmental strategies and policies. Central to this role has been a shift towards strategies which bring together actors and agencies at local, national and international levels, across public, private and voluntary sectors.

Within local governments there has been a shift away from relatively uncoordinated policies by different departments towards a more corporate approach. There are various ways in which this can be effected, including setting up a separate environmental unit to coordinate environmental policies (Freeman 1994). Encouraging though such trends may be, it is worth remembering that in 1973 a survey of 3000 North American local governments found 40% had an environmental coordinator and 24% had citizens' environmental boards, yet little was achieved, in large part because of underfunding, uncertainty, delay, poor communications with senior administrators and poor technical assistance. Similarly, it is possible to see that attempts to improve the management of urban environmental problems may be something of a red herring, aiming to reduce problems to bite-size administrative issues whilst denying large-scale, comprehensive polices to tackle major environmental problems (see Rees and Roseland 1991). A separate local environmental unit is fine, but not in itself enough to bring about far-reaching changes in the ways in which policies for the environment are conceived, coordinated and implemented.

When given adequate resources and powers, the record of local government, working in partnership with others, in instigating innovative environmental policies is often exemplary (see Box 8.2). However, during the last twenty years the political, social and economic cohesion of many cities in the West – and increasingly in developing countries too (Hardoy, Mitlin and Satterthwaite 1992) – has come under growing threat as powers have been centralised and local government resources denuded and powers diminished. Collective public services and spaces have been variously cut back, privatised, deregulated and fragmented: sometimes services have improved, but quite often they have deteriorated. Local democratic control has sometimes been severely eroded by the emergence of non-locally accountable bodies with responsibility for increasing amounts of public expenditure, such as the Urban Development Corporations in the UK.

The trend towards reducing local government financial resources and fragmenting and reducing local powers has largely worked against effective large-scale urban environmental strategies. The shift away from public service provision and public benefaction may also have reduced social cohesion within cities (Mulgan 1989). The public pronouncements of national governments and international governmental bodies on the need for subsidiarity and greater local responsibility have largely been empty rhetoric. Nowhere is this more apparent than in England, where the abolition of the whole tier of metropolitan-wide government in 1986 was brought about by the national government; in part this was in a fit of pique at the successes of innovative and popular local environmental policies, such as the low public transport fares and selective night-time lorry bans of the Greater London Council.

Box 8.2 Some Successful Local Programmes for the Urban Environment

Reducing pollution

- The *Hoy no circula* programme (day without a car), launched in Mexico City in 1989 saw air pollutant emissions fall 21% in its first year.
- In Cubatao, Brazil, since 1984 state and local governments, and some local businesses, have combined to reduce air pollution and have enforced tougher regulations.

Integrated land use and transport planning

- In Curitiba, Brazil, a sophisticated, integrated bus system with exclusive bus lanes has been developed along five main axes out of the city. High-density development was encouraged along the routes by land purchasing and land use orders. These policies have reduced car usage, achieving fuel savings of up to 25%.
- In Los Angeles a programme was introduced in 1989 to reduce air pollution. Policies with ambitious targets have been established to increase car occupancy rates, to encourage more telecommuting, and to increase low- and zero-emission vehicles. Regional growth management measures are proposed to help bring about a distribution of future jobs and employment compatible with reducing vehicle emissions.

Resource conservation

- Minneapolis, St Paul and Santa Monica provide free or low-cost installation of energy/water conservation devices.

Recycling

- A wide-ranging resource recovery operation in Shanghai province was established in 1957. It now employs nearly 30,000 people retrieving and reselling reclaimed and recycled products, including 3600 advisors working with factories on sorting and retrieving waste.
- Berkeley, California, changed its zoning rules to encourage repair facilities and used goods stores.
- Seattle operates a municipal compost operation and provides bins for backyard composting.

- In Curitiba, Brazil, 70% of households separate recyclable rubbish, and in squatter settlements food and bus fares are exchanged for garbage.

Phasing out harmful materials

- Local CFC emissions in Irvine, California, fell by 46% in just one year following comprehensive bans on the use, sale and manufacture of ozone-depleting compounds.

- Food packaging which is neither biodegradable nor recyclable is banned in Minneapolis and St Paul; polystyrene packaging has been banned in Berkeley.

(Skinner 1990, OECD 1991, Rees and Roseland 1991, Hardoy, Mitlin and Satterthwaite 1992)

Given this context, it is hardly surprising that in Britain many local authorities appear to be seizing the opportunity afforded by the Earth Summit call to produce local Agenda 21 statements, in the hope that they might provide the means for embarking upon far-reaching strategies to change the ways in which policies are constructed and implemented. As local Agenda 21s are being prepared around the world, it will be interesting in future years to see whether local innovation and beneficial impacts will correlate to national government attitudes to local government.

8.3.3 Local communities and sustainable urban development

Grassroots involvement in local environmental initiatives at every stage, from conception to implementation and management, is widely regarded as a central precondition for bringing about permanent beneficial change. This currently seems so blindingly obvious as to constitute a truism, since community empowerment has become a catch phrase within urban development. But it is only gradually that, over the past thirty years, community consultation in local planning, neighbourhood design and housing management has come to the fore. For all the lip service increasingly paid to the ideal of community empowerment in recent years, progress remains patchy. This is in part because effective means of community involvement are still only gradually emerging. In addition there are limits to what community-based projects can achieve in isolation from wider initiatives, whilst central and local government have displayed an inability to let go of some of their powers. This lack of willingness to devolve responsibility stems largely from inertia, including a protective fear of job losses among urban professionals, and also from a recognition that devolved community responsibilities and powers may occasionally result in perverse outcomes. So whilst neighbourhood-level organisation for resisting undesirable developments has grown in recent years, so has the tendency to improve or maintain an existing local environment by seeking to avoid responsibility for activities deemed necessary but undesirable, such as building hostels for the mentally ill and finding a location for waste tips. All too often it has been affluent neighbourhoods that have been able to mobilise to resist such 'intrusions', perhaps motivated more by a desire to maintain property values than to improve the environment.

Box 8.3 The New York Green City Program

The city must protect and expand its parks, gardens and open spaces

Encourage a regional food system, thereby encouraging regional farmers; raise the park budget to 1% of the city budget; protect and expand community gardens; widen sidewalks where possible and plant more trees; create a continuously accessible waterfront.

New Yorkers must have clean, healthy air to breathe

Encourage public transport, walking and cycling over car use; reduce bus and subway fares; close down inefficient city and apartment incinerators; plant trees to reduce carbon dioxide levels.

The city must ensure abundant clean, healthy water

Practice water conservation, upgrade infrastructure, enforce building codes; protect watersheds by purchasing development rights.

The city must conserve energy

Amend zoning and building codes to encourage use of natural ventilation; prohibit sealed buildings and include energy conservation; retrofit buildings for energy conservation; promote pricing for conservation; plant trees to cool the city; reduce car usage, improve public transport and eliminate commuter toll discounts and parking subsidies.

The city must be responsible for its garbage, sewage and toxic wastes

Recycle everything possible (60–85%); set up exchange facilities for reusable trash; eliminate non-recyclable packaging and other products; build holding tanks to contain sewer overflow during storms; enforce 'right to know' laws for local workplaces and industries; introduce low-interest loans for residents to remove asbestos.

The city must ensure environmentally sound development

Base development on carrying capacity of natural systems, the city's infrastructure and the need to create a liveable city; reinstate a comprehensive planning process which mandates the least environmentally damaging options and then site these equitably where they do least harm; provide full environmental analysis, including loss of open space, resource impacts, increased pollution, displacement of residents and businesses, shadows and wind created by new buildings.

The city must provide environmental education for all ages

Help schools acquire natural sites for field work; encourage intensive media campaigns; provide innovative, informal education for adults.

(Adapted from Andruss *et al.* 1990, Gardner 1990)

Known as the NIMBY ('Not In My Back Yard') syndrome in Britain, perverse local turf wars, however, are still far less frequent than benign local interventions, at both neighbourhood and city-wide levels (Stretton 1989). Examples abound of well-run, locally sensitive schemes tapping into local knowledge and resources to improve local environmental conditions and to educate local people about the natural environment. Partnership working is often central to such initiatives. In Australia in the 1970s, trade unions and local community groups united to impose 'green bans' on inner-city redevelopment schemes which were felt to damage open space or local neighbourhoods (Roddewig 1978). In Britain, a national network of local Groundwork Trusts has undertaken a wide range of local conservation and restoration projects, in every case seeking to build local partnerships between residents, businesses and local authorities. Housing associations across Europe have worked with local residents to improve both housing and the local environment. Local businesses have become more involved in local initiatives, from supporting neighbourhood and local environmental groups to coming together to discuss how they as businesses can improve their contribution to the environment, thereby learning from each other (Clark, Burrall and Roberts 1993). Schools, too, have often been important foci for local environmental initiatives. In many ways, however, the most notable initiatives involve the growing numbers of less formalised groups of local people, whose achievements are less widely trumpeted but often locally significant, such as improving eyesore land spots, removing graffiti and picking up litter.

From preventing problems arising to remedying those which have already arisen, working from the bottom up is necessarily an important dimension of any urban environmental strategy. Indeed, it is entirely feasible and highly valuable for bottom-up strategies to emerge which in a sense subsume the policies of 'higher' tiers of authority, such as local government. An example of this can be found in the wide-ranging strategy for change put forward for New York. The New York Green City Program (Box 8.3) was put together as a focus for debate in 1989 by a coalition of eighteen environmental and community groups in the city, and has since been endorsed by over 200 local groups (Andruss et al. 1990, Gardner 1990). Where the 'radical greens' tended to see a return to nature and to rural communities as a central goal in the past, in recent years the decentralisation emphasis has been largely superseded by attempts to change existing cities from within. Increasingly, radical policies are being proposed to change the city from within, to ensure that its development is more compatible with sustainable development, whilst also providing vibrant communities (see Andruss et al. 1990, Gordon 1990, Canfield 1990). Permaculture, for example, is now advocated as a way of bringing nature back into the town (see Chapter Three).

8.4 MANAGING THE SUSTAINABLE CITY

Changing the way in which people and industries behave is a fundamental requirement of sustainable development, at global and local levels. The European Commission (1992) argues that central practical requirements for sustainable development involve transforming patterns of growth through:

- addressing the issue of finite resources through implementing policies for reducing wasteful consumption and increasing reuse and recycling and reducing waste

- rationalising the production and consumption of non-renewable energy
- changing the consumption and behaviour patterns of society itself, by encouraging individuals and businesses to appreciate the full costs of their activities, particularly in the context of finite natural resources.

Box 8.4 Suggested Initiatives for Sustainable Urban Management from Agenda 21

1. Institutionalise a participatory approach to sustainable urban development, based on a continuous dialogue between all actors, especially women and indigenous peoples.

2. Promote social organisation and environmental awareness through community participation in identifying and meeting collective needs, such as infrastructure provision, enhanced public amenities and restoring the fabric of the built environment. 'Green works' programmes should provide formal and informal employment for low-income urban residents.

3. Strengthen the capacity of local governing bodies to deal with environmental challenges, especially through comprehensive planning which recognises the individual needs of cities; promote ecologically sound urban design practices.

4. Participate in international 'sustainable city networks'.

5. Promote environmentally sound and culturally sensitive tourism.

6. Establish mechanisms to mobilise resources for local initiatives to improve environmental quality.

7. Empower community groups, non-governmental organisations and individuals to manage and enhance their immediate environment through participatory approaches

(Adapted from Quarrie 1990)

At the urban scale, it has become more widely accepted in recent years that it is not necessary to retreat from the city to smaller settlements in order to address environmental problems. Similarly, although changing the nature of urban development to account for the natural environment by 'designing with nature' and changing urban form to encourage reduced energy consumption *can* be important elements in changing people's behaviour, they are not sufficient in themselves. Changes are also required to the way in which cities are governed and to the ways in which people acknowledge and respond to their individual responsibilities for environmental stewardship, both for their immediate locality and for the global environment.

Box 8.5 Strengthening The Management of Urban Development: WHO Recommendations

- Improve coordination of policies and programmes across sectors and actors.
- Rationalise the pricing and regulatory framework, including property rights.
- Decentralise decision-making to metropolitan and more local areas of government.
- Encourage involvement of communities, NGOs and the private sector, and better coordination across sectors.
- Make better use of resources, including a greater reliance on small-scale projects, and establish more local powers to raise revenues through taxes and user charges.
- Place maximum reliance on indigenous skills, drawing on networks of groups within the city and across cities.
- Reorientate and develop technologies, to be more 'humane' and 'user-friendly'.
- Promote community action partnerships.
- Develop community-based action and human resources, including providing community facilitators, public awareness campaigns on health and other issues, and training professionals to work better with the community.
- Provide better access to finance, including payment 'in kind' and cash, improving credit availability for low-cost housing initiatives, and reallocating unused public resources, e.g. land.

(Adapted from World Health Organization 1991)

There may now be an emerging consensus over the main ingredients necessary for managing the sustainable city (see Boxes 8.4 and 8.5). There is, however, considerably less agreement about what each approach actually entails, so that the different ingredients can be interpreted very differently by governments. For instance, expressed in broad terms, policies to delegate greater powers to the local level are easy commitments for national governments to make. However, this still leaves unanswered the questions of how much finance is committed, how much leeway is allowed for innovative fiscal policy, and what legislative and regulatory powers will be ceded to local-level control. In some countries responsibility has been devolved to the local level, for instance on pollution monitoring, but without being accompanied by major additional resources or powers to bring about changes in behaviour. Nor is it solely national governmental belligerence which results in inaction. At the local level, very real tensions remain on the ways of balancing environmental considerations and the needs for restructuring local economies in the face of external change and, indeed, the perceived imperatives of economic growth. The seeming consensus on the basics of managing sustainable urban development usually belies the practice.

Should this all sound too negative about the prospects for positive local action, it is worth mentioning a few of the valuable initiatives for sustainable urban development currently being developed, concentrating in particular on north European countries. (Box 8.2 has already noted examples from developing countries and from North America.) One of the most important elements of urban environmental policy in many cities has been the promotion of improved public transport infrastructure, with a view to encouraging people away from car travel, with new tram systems recently installed in Nantes (1985), Grenoble (1987) and Manchester (1991). All appear to have been highly successful in improving the character of the city and encouraging a shift towards public transport (Mega 1993).

In a European context, Denmark, the Netherlands and Germany have pioneered many of the recent innovations in policies for bringing about sustainable development generally, particularly through regulations, standards and targets on insulation, recycling and energy conservation. In Denmark, environmental consciousness has become a part of everyday habits, with a recycling rate of 9%, as opposed to 2.2% in the UK (Blowers 1993). On an urban level too there have been significant innovations. In Odense, Denmark, far-reaching policies have been instituted to integrate land use and transport planning. In addition, 95% of homes are served by district heating, mainly from the city's combined heat and power (D. Hutchinson 1992). The main advantages of CHP lie in distributing, rather than losing, the heat used in power production and in reducing energy loss in transmission. Danish law allows municipal authorities to require that all potential users in an area connect to the system, helping ensure the viability of the schemes (Owens 1992). CHP can provide energy savings of up to 80% relative to some forms of electricity generation (Webb and Gossop 1993).

In the Netherlands, urban environmental initiatives may have been laggardly (van der Valk and Faludi 1992), though the neighbourhood-level *woonerven* are internationally admired. These have been developed with a mixture of features designed to curb the intrusion of the motor car into residential districts, slowing down cars, and providing more open space and tree planting (Vale and Vale 1991). In recent years, far more ambitious plans for cities have been proposed and backed by the government, including greater use of indigenous and natural materials, such as houses with grass roofs. More radical still are proposals for self-contained neighbourhoods with green fields for water purification, and small-scale waste disposal and recycling facilities.

It is in Germany, however, that adventurous, innovative approaches for the urban environment are perhaps most widespread. Initiatives include the massive tree planting efforts which have accompanied attempts to restructure the Ruhr region, using approaches such as roadside planting to reduce noise and visual intrusion, and to filter pollutants. More ambitious still is the international demonstration project, the IBA Emscher Park, which aims to use ecological enhancement as the key to economic restructuring. A wide-ranging set of initiatives are in train to create a green corridor along the improved waters of the formerly highly polluted Emscher river, along with improvements to housing, the creation of an environmental technology park and the preservation and reuse of old buildings, including old coal mines. Experimental 'ecological housing' is being built in cities such as Kassel, where the emphasis is on the use of natural materials and reusing materials such as used vehicle tyres as part of earth-banked wall insulation.

8.5 FINALE

The imperatives of sustainable development add a further tier of complexity, tension and debate to the process of urban development. In political terms, the need for sustainable development should be seen alongside the need to address economic and social issues, such as unemployment and social exclusion. As we have stressed throughout this book, environmental issues are very much a part of such broadly constituted urban economic and social structures and dynamics. Policies for sustainable urban development need to place economic and social analysis at their heart. Equally, policies for urban economic and social restructuring need to have environmental considerations at their heart, if they are to bring about an improvement in the quality of life of residents and to effect a long-lasting improvement in local economies and communities.

Just as local economic policies have to come to terms with the vagaries of ill-understood international competitive forces, so too do local environmental policies have to be framed in relation to our still evolving understanding of the contribution which urban activities, both directly and indirectly, make to global environmental problems. Most importantly of all, policies for the urban environment need to consider the impacts of their activities outside the city, regionally and globally, for current generations and for future generations.

Sustainable City Manifesto

- The sustainable city is developed to respect and make the most of natural environmental assets, to conserve resource use and to minimise impacts on the local and wider natural environment.

- The sustainable city is a regional and global city: no matter how small or how large, its responsibilities stretch beyond the city boundaries.

- The sustainable city involves a broadly based, participatory programme of radical change, where individuals are encouraged to take on more responsibility for the ways in which their cities are run.

- The sustainable city requires that environmental assets and impacts are distributed more equitably than at present.

- The sustainable city is a learning city, a sharing city, an internationally networked city.

- The sustainable city is not rooted in an idealised version of past settlements, nor is it one given to a radical casting-off from its own particular cultural, economic and physical identity in the name of the latest passing fad for wholesale urban change.

- The sustainable city will seek to conserve, enhance and promote its assets in terms of natural, built and cultural environments.

- The sustainable city presents tremendous opportunities for enhancing environmental quality at local, regional and global scales.

This is the first of the eight points of our manifesto for the Sustainable City. We hope the manifesto provokes you to debate such issues, to alter some points, maybe even to delete some altogether, and certainly to add others. For each city requires its own manifesto, its own vision of the city it wants to become, and how it will get there.

FURTHER READING

Both Lynch (1981) and Hill (1992) discuss the different approaches to laying out the city as a means of improving its environmental impacts. In terms of changing the city from within, changing the behaviour of businesses, residents and visitors to be more in tune with the demands of sustainable development, it is valuable to look at Agenda 21 itself (Quarrie 1992) and the work of the World Health Organisation (1991). From the British perspective, Ekins, McLaren and Hillman (1991) provide an enormous range of suggestions. A variety of local approaches are also discussed in Williams and Haughton (1994) *Perspectives Towards Sustainable Development.* Also valuable in this respect is Blowers (1993) and Canfield (1990).

KEY THEMES

- Strategic planning
- Policy integration and coordination
- Community participation

DISCUSSION POINTS

- Does your local area have a Green Plan or Strategy, similar to the one shown earlier for New York? Using some of the themes introduced in this book, how effective do you feel it is likely to be? How does it measure against the various principles for sustainable development outlined in Chapters One and Six?
- Improved community education is frequently seen as a linchpin in achieving sustainable urban development. Suggest a strategy for achieving this in your own area.
- Devise your own manifesto for the sustainable city, based on your own experience of living in or visiting a large city.

References

Abel, P.D. (1989) *Water Pollution Biology*. Chichester: Ellis Horwood.

Adams, R.M. and Rowe, R.D. (1990) 'The economic effects of stratospheric ozone depletion on U.S. agriculture: a preliminary assessment'. *Journal of Environmental Management 30*, 321–335.

Adams, W. and Brock, J.W. (1986) *The Bigness Complex: Industry, Labor, and Government in the American economy*. New York: Pantheon Books.

Adeniji, K. (1988) 'Water resources and environmental pollution in Nigeria: some preliminary findings'. *Journal of Environmental Management 27*, 229–235.

Ahmad, Y. (1989) *Elements of Environmental Management*. London: Edward Arnold.

Aitchison, G.J., Henry, M.G. and Sandheinrich, M.B. (1987) 'Effects of metals on fish behaviour: a review'. *Environmental Biology of Fisheries 18*, 11–25.

Alcamo, J. and Lubkert, B. (1990) 'The city and the air: Europe'. In C. Canfield.

Alexander, C. (1967) 'The city as a mechanism for sustaining human contact'. In W.R. Ewald (ed) *Environment for Man*. Bloomington, IN: Indiana University Press.

Alexander, C. (1969) 'Major changes in environmental form required by social and psychological demands' *Ekistics 48*, 78–85. Reprinted in A. Blowers, C. Hamnett and P. Sarre (eds) (1974) *The Future of Cities*, London: Hutchinson.

Alexander, C., Ishikawa, S. and Silverstein, M. (1977) *A Pattern Language: Towns, Buildings, Construction*. Oxford: Oxford University Press.

Allaby, M (1989) *Green Facts: The Greenhouse Effect and Other Key Issues*. Third edition. London: Hamlyn.

Andruss, V., Plant, C., Plant, J. and Wright, E. (1990) (eds) *Home! A Bioregional Reader*. Philadelphia: New Society Publishers.

Angotti, T. (1993) *Metropolis 2000: Planning, Poverty and Politics*. London: Routledge.

Appleyard, D. (1981) *Livable Streets*. Berkeley, CA: University of California Press.

Asami, T. (1984) 'Changing biogeochemical cycles'. In J.O. Nriagu (ed) *Changing Metal Cycles and Human Health*. Berlin: Springer-Verlag.

Association of Metropolitan Authorities (AMA) (1989) *Action for the Future*. London: AMA.

Atlas, E., Bidleman, T. and Giam, C.S. (1986) 'Atmospheric transport of PCBs to the oceans'. In J.S. Waid (ed.) *PCBs and the Environment (vol. 1)*. Boca Raton, FL: CRC Press.

Babbage, D. (1993) 'The impact of medium density housing on adjacent property values'. *Urban Futures 3*, 2, 30–32.

Baez, A.P., Belmont, R.D., Gonzalez, O.G. and Rosas, I.P. (1989) 'Formaldehyde levels in air and wet precipitation at Mexico City, Mexico'. *Environmental Pollution* 62, 153–169.

Bailey, J.M. and Saunders, A.N. (1988) 'Ongoing environmental impact assessment as a force for change'. *Project Appraisal 3*, 1, 37–42.

Bairoch, P. (1988) *Cities and Economic Development: From the Dawn of History to the Present.* London: Mansell.

Banister, D. (1992) 'Energy use, transport and settlement patterns'. In M. Breheny (ed) *Sustainable Development and Urban Form.* London: Pion.

Barrett, S. (1991) 'Global warming: economics of a carbon tax'. In D. Pearce.

Barry, R.G. and Chorley, R.J. (1982) *Atmosphere, Weather and Climate.* Fourth edition. London: Methuen.

Barton, H. (1992) 'City transport: strategies for sustainability'. In M. Breheny (ed) *Sustainable Development and Urban Form.* London: Pion.

Beanlands, G. (1992) 'Scoping methods and baseline studies in EIA'. In P. Wathern (ed) *Environmental Impact Assessment: Theory and Practice.* London: Routledge.

Beaumont, J.R. and Keys, P. (1982) *Future Cities: Spatial Analysis of Energy Issues.* Chichester: Research Studies Press.

Begg, I. and Moore, B. (1990) 'The future economic role of urban systems'. In D. Cadman and G. Payne (eds) *The Living City: Towards a Sustainable Future.* London: Routledge.

Benton, T. (1991) 'The ecological challenge to Marxism'. *New Left Review 187*, 103–20.

Berg, P. (1990a) 'Growing a life-place politics'. In V. Andruss *et al.*

Berg, P. (1990b) 'More than just saving what's left'. In V. Andruss *et al.*

Berg, P. (1990c) 'A Green City program for San Francisco Bay area cities and towns'. In V. Andruss *et al.*

Berry, M. (1984) 'The political economy of Australian urbanisation'. *Progress in Planning 22*, 1–83.

Berry, R.D. and Colls, J.J. (1990) 'Atmospheric carbon dioxide and sulphur dioxide on an urban/rural transect – 2. Measurements along the transect'. *Atmospheric Environment 24A*, 10, 2689–2694.

Birrell, R. (1991) 'Infrastructure costs on the urban fringe: Sydney and Melbourne compared'. In Economic Planning Advisory Council (ed) *Background Papers on Urban and Regional Issues: Background Paper 10, February.* Canberra: Australian Government Publishing Service, 201–34.

Bisset, R. and Tomlinson, P. (1992) 'Monitoring and auditing of impacts'. In P. Wathern (ed) *Environmental Impact Assessment: Theory and Practice.* London: Routledge.

Blowers, A. (1993) 'Pollution and waste – a sustainable burden?' In A. Blowers (ed) *Planning for a Sustainable Environment.* London: Earthscan.

Bookchin, M. (1974) *The Limits of the City.* New York: Harper Colophon.

Bosworth, T. (1993) 'Local authorities and sustainable development'. *European Environment 3*, 1, 13–17.

Bowlby, S. (1988) 'From corner shop to hypermarket: women and food retailing'. In J. Little, L. Peake and P. Richardson (eds) *Women in Cities: Gender and the Urban Environment*. Basingstoke: Macmillan.

Bowonder, B., Prasad, S.S.R., and Reddy, R. (1987) 'Project siting and environmental impact assessment in developing countries'. *Project Appraisal 2*, 1, 11–20.

Boyden, S. (1984) 'Ecological approaches to urban planning'. In F. di Castri, F. Baker and M. Hadley (eds) *Ecology in Practice. Part II: The Social Response*. Dublin: Tycooly and Paris: UNESCO.

Boyden, S., Millar, S., Newcombe, K. and O'Neill, B. (1981) *The Ecology of a City and its People: The Case of Hong Kong*. Canberra: Australian National University Press.

Breheny, M. (1990) 'Strategic planning and urban sustainability'. *Proceedings of the 1990 Town and Country Planning Association Annual Conference*. London: TCPA.

Breheny, M. (1992) 'The contradictions of the compact city form: a review'. In M. Breheny (ed) *Sustainable Development and Urban Form*. London: Pion.

Breheny, M. and Rookwood, R. (1993) 'Planning the sustainable city region'. In A. Blowers (ed) *Planning for a Sustainable Environment*. London: Earthscan

Bronfman, L.M. (1991) 'Setting the social impact agenda: an organisational perspective'. *Environmental Impact Assessment Review 11*, 69–79.

Brookfield, H. (1975) *Interdependent Development*. London: Methuen.

Brotchie, J. (1992) 'The changing structure of cities'. *Urban Futures*, Special Issue 5, February, 13–23.

Brown, L.R. (1981) *Building a Sustainable Society*. New York: Worldwatch Institute.

Brucato, P.F. (1990) 'Urban air quality improvements: a comparison of aggregate health and welfare benefits to hedonic price differentials'. *Journal of Environmental Management 30*, 265–279.

Bryson, R.A. and Ross, J.E. (1972) 'The climate of the city'. In T.R. Detwyler and M.G. Marcus (eds) *Urbanization and the Environment*. Belmont, CA: Duxbury Press.

Buckley, K., Buxton, M. and McKenzie, F. (1991) 'Towards ecologically sustainable urban development'. *Urban Futures 4*, 47–54.

Buckley, R.C. (1991) 'How accurate are environmental impact predictions?' *Ambio 20*, 3/4, 161–162.

Burnett, J. (1978) *A Social History of Housing, 1815–1970*. London: Methuen.

Butina Watson, G. (1993) 'The art of building cities: urban structuring and restructuring'. In R. Hayward and S. McGlynn.

Butt, A.J. and Alden, R.W. (1986) 'Depressed oxygen levels offshore of Virginia Beach, Virginia, USA'. *Journal of Environmental Management 22*, 105–111.

Buttel, F., Hawkins, A. and Power, A. (1990) 'From limits to growth to global change: constraints and contradictions in the evolution of environmental science and ideology'. *Global Environmental Change 1*, 1, 57–66.

Button, K.J. and Pearce, D.W. (1989) 'Improving the urban environment: how to adjust national and local government policy for sustainable urban growth'. *Progress in Planning 32*, 3, 135–84.

Cadman, D. and Payne, G (eds) (1990) *The Living City: Towards a Sustainable Future*. London: Routledge.

Cairncross, F. (1991) *Costing the Earth: The Challenge for Governments, the Opportunities for Business*. Boston, MA: Harvard Business School Press.

Cairnes, L. (1993) 'Water resources: planning for sustainable water use'. *Urban Futures 3*, 1, 25–29.

Calder, N. (1993) 'Why CO2 is good for you'. *The Guardian*, 3 June, 12.

Callenbach, E. (1975) *Ecotopia*. New York: Bantam.

Canfield, C. (1990) (ed) *Ecocity Conference 1990*. Berkeley, CA: Urban Ecology.

Canter, L. (1983) 'Methods for environmental impact assessment: theory and application'. In PADC Environmental Impact Assessment and Planning Unit (ed) *Environmental Impact Assessment*. The Hague: Martinus Nijhoff.

Cappon, D. (1990) 'Indicators for a healthy city'. *Environmental Management and Health 1*, 1, 9–18.

Carroll, R.E. (1966) 'The relationship of cadmium in the air to cardiovascular disease rates'. *Journal American Medical Association 198*, 267–269.

Changnon, S.A. (1968) 'The La Porte weather anomaly – fact or fiction'. *Bulletin of the American Meteorological Society 49*, 4–11.

Charles, D. (1991) 'Squeezing the deserts dry'. *New Scientist*, 14 September, 30–34.

Charles, D. (1992) 'Mystery of Florida's dying coral'. *New Scientist*, 11 January, 12.

Cheshire, P. (1988) 'Urban revival in sight: the end is where we start from?' *Local Economy 3*, 2, 96–108.

Clark, M., Burrall, P. and Roberts, P. (1993) 'A sustainable economy'. In A. Blowers (ed) *Planning for a Sustainable Environment*. London: Earthscan.

Clarke, A.G. (1986) 'The air'. In R.E. Hester (ed) *Understanding Our Environment*. London: The Royal Society of Chemistry.

Clarke, R. (1991) *Water: The International Crisis*. London: Earthscan.

Clement, K. (1991) 'Environmental auditing for business: European perspective'. *European Environment 1*, 3, 1–4.

Coase, R. (1960) 'The problem of social cost'. *Journal of Law and Economics 3*, 1–44.

Coghlan, A. (1992a) 'Speedy detector will pinpoint polluters'. *New Scientist*, 8 February, 26.

Coghlan, A. (1992b) 'Oxygen treatment makes organic waste digestible'. *New Scientist*, 7 March, 24.

Coleman, A. (1985) *Utopia on Trial: Vision and Reality in Planned Housing*. London: Hilary Shipman.

Collective Design/Projects (eds) (1985) *Very Nice Work if You Can Get It: The Socially Useful Production Debate*. Nottingham: Spokesman.

Commission of the European Communities (1985) 'On the assessment of the effects of certain public and private projects on the environment'. *Official Journal L175*, 40–48.

Commission of the European Communities (1990) *Green Paper on the Urban Environment*. Luxembourg: Commission of the European Communities.

Commission of the European Communities (1992) *Towards Sustainability: A European Community Programme of Policy and Action in Relation to the Environment and Sustainable Development*. Brussels: Commission of the European Communities.

Commoner, B. (1973) *Ecology and Social Action*. Berkeley, CA: University of California Press.

Commoner, B. (1976) *The Poverty of Power: Energy and the Economic Crisis*. London: Jonathan Cape.

Confederation of British Industry (1991) *Corporate Environmental Policy Statements*. London: CBI.

Conroy, C. and Litvinoff, M. (eds) (1988) *The Greening of Aid: Sustainable Livelihoods in Practice*. London: Earthscan Publications.

Cooper Marcus, C. and Sarkissian, W. (1986) *Housing as if People Mattered*. London: University of California Press.

Corbridge, S. (1986) *Capitalist World Development: A Critique of Radical Development Geography*. Basingstoke: Macmillan

Correa, C. (1989) *The New Landscape: Urbanisation in the Third World*. Sevenoaks: Butterworth.

Council on Environmental Quality (CEQ) (1975) 'The cost of sprawl in the USA'. *Ekistics 40*, (239).

Crowcroft, P. (1992) 'Contaminative use of land – the implications for the future'. *Environmental Policy and Practice 2*, 1, 25–36.

Cunningham, W. P. and Saigo, B.W. (1990) *Environmental Science: A Global Concern*. Dubuque, IA: Wm. C. Brown Publishers.

D'Monte, D. (1985). *Temples or Tombs?* New Delhi: Centre for Science and the Environment.

Dankelman, I. and Davidson, J. (1988) *Women and Environment in the Third World: Alliance for the Future*. London: Earthscan.

Dauncey, G. (1986) 'A new local economic order'. In P. Ekins.

Davey, B. (1992) 'Eco-cities: strategies for urban survival'. *Permaculture 1*, 1, 13–14.

Davies, G.S. and Muller, F.G. (1983) *A Handbook on Environmental Impact Assessment for Use in Developing Countries*. Nairobi: United Nations Environment Programme.

Deelstra, T. (1990) 'The productive city: urban forestry in the Netherlands'. In D. Gordon.

Department of Health and Human Services (DHHS) (1982) *Blood lead levels for persons 6 months – 74 years of age: United States, 1976–80*. Hyattsville, MD: Public Health Service, National Center for Health Statistics, US Department of Health and Human Services.

Department of the Environment/Welsh Office (1990) *This Common Inheritance*. London: HMSO.

Department of Transport (1983) *Manual of Environmental Appraisal*. London: DoT.

Dicken, P. (1992) *Global Shift*. Second edition. London: Paul Chapman.

Dicken, P. and Lloyd, P.E. (1981) *Modern Western Society*. London: Harper and Row.

Dinham, B. (1985) 'Mass death at Bhopal – whose responsibility?'. *International Labour Reports 8*, 8–11.

Dole, J. (1989a) 'Greenscape 1: the place of buildings'. *Architects' Journal*, 12 April, 67–71.

Dole, J. (1989b) 'Greenscape 2: climate and form'. *Architects' Journal*, 19 April, 81–85.

Dole, J. (1989c) 'Greenscape 3: solar architecture'. *Architects' Journal*, 26 April, 55–59.

Dole, J. (1989d) 'Greenscape 4: tempering cold winds'. *Architects' Journal*, 26 April, 55–59.

Dole, J. (1989e) 'Greenscape 5: green cities'. *Architects' Journal*, 10 May, 61–69.

Dorney, R. (1990) 'Urban agriculture and urban land use'. In D. Gordon.

Douglas, I. (1989a) 'The rain on the roof: a geography of the urban environment'. In D. Gregory and R. Walford (eds) *Horizons in Human Geography*. London: Macmillan.

Douglas, I. (1989b) 'The environmental problems of cities'. In D.T Herbert anu D.M. Smith (eds) *Social Problems and the City*. Oxford: Oxford University Press.

Duval Smith, A. (1991) 'Triumphs and Trabants'. *The Guardian*, 17 May, 33.

Ecologist (1972) 'Blueprint for survival'. *Ecologist 2*, 1.

Edwards, R.W. (1972) *Pollution*. London: Oxford University Press.

Ekins, P. (ed) (1986) *The Living Economy: A New Economics in the Making*. London: Routledge and Kegan Paul.

Ekins, P. and Max-Neef, M. (eds) (1992) *Real-Life Economics: Understanding Wealth Creation*. London: Routledge.

Ekins, P., Hillman, M. and Hutchinson, R. (1992) *Wealth Beyond Measure: An Atlas of New Economics*. London: Gaia Books.

Elkin, T., McLaren, D. and Hillman, M, (1991) *Reviving the City: Towards Sustainable Urban Development*. London: Friends of the Earth.

Elkington, B. and Burke, T. (1987) *The Green Capitalists: Industry's Search for Environmental Excellence*. London: Victor Gollancz.

Endean, C. (1993) 'The buildings that are killing Rome's breeze'. *The European*. 19–22 August, 5.

England, K.V.L. (1991) 'Gender relations and the spatial structure of the city'. *Geoforum 22*, 2, 135–147.

Engwicht, D. (1992) *Towards an Eco-City: Calming the Traffic*. Sydney: Envirobook.

Federal Environmental Assessment Review Office (FEARO) (1978) *Guide for Environmental Screening*. Ottowa: FEARO.

Ferguson, B.K. (1987) 'Urban stormwater harvesting: applications and hydraulic design'. *Journal of Environmental Management 25*, 71–79.

Feshbach, M. and Friendly, A. (1992) *Ecocide in the USSR: Health and Nature Under Siege*. New York: Basic Books.

Fielding, A.J. and Halford, S. (1990) *Patterns and Process of Urban Change in the UK*. London: HMSO.

Fincher, R. (1991) *Immigration, Urban Infrastructure and the Environment*. Canberra: Bureau of Immigration Research, Australian Government Publishing Service.

Findlay, S.E. (1993) 'The third world city: development policy and issues'. In J.D. Kasarda and A.M. Parnell (eds) *Third World Cities: Problems, Policies and Prospects*. Newbury Park, CA: Sage.

Fish, H. (1986) 'Water'. In R.E. Hester (ed.) *Understanding Our Environment*. London: The Royal Society of Chemistry.

Fishman, R. (1977) *Urban Utopias in the Twentieth Century: Ebenezer Howard, Frank Lloyd Wright and Le Corbusier*. New York: Basic Books.

Forester, T. (1992) 'The electronic cottage revisited: towards the flexible workstyle'. *Urban Futures*. Special issue 5, 27–33.

Fothergill, S. and Gudgin, G. (1982) *Unequal Growth: Urban and Regional Employmant Change in the United Kingdom*. London: Heinemann Educational.

Fox, K. (1985) *Metropolitan America: Urban Life and Urban Policy in the United States, 1940–1980*. Basingstoke: Macmillan.

Freedland, J. (1993) 'America's free-trade cowboys are here'. *The Guardian*. 13 November, 40.

Freeman, C. (1994) 'Urban environmental planning in local authorities: developing a corporate approach'. In C.C. Williams and G. Haughton.

Frey, B.S. (1992) 'Pricing and regulation affect environmental ethics'. *Environmental and Resource Economics 2*, 399–414,

Friedman, Y. (1984) 'Towards a policy of urban survival'. In F. di Castri, F. Baker and M. Hadley (eds) *Ecology in Practice. Part II: The Social Response*. Dublin: Tycooly and Paris: UNESCO.

Friedmann, J. (1989) 'Planning, politics and the environment'. *Journal of the American Planning Association*. Summer, 334–41.

Friedmann, J. and Weaver, C. (1979) *Territory and Function: The Evolution of Regional Planning*. London: Edward Arnold.

Friends of the Earth (1989) *Charter for Local Government*. London: FoE.

Furedy, C. (1990) 'Incidental greening – saving resources in Asian cities'. In D. Gordon.

Furukawa, A. (1984) 'Defining pollution problems in the Far East: a case study of Japanese air pollution problems'. In M.J. Koziol and F.R. Whatley (eds) *Gaseous Air Pollutants and Plant Metabolism*. London: Butterworth.

Galtung, J. (1986) 'Towards a new economics: on the theory and practice of self-reliance'. In P. Ekins.

Gardner, J. (1990) 'Influencing big city environmental policy'. In C. Canfield.

Geddes, P. (1915) *Cities in Evolution*. London: Williams and Norgate.

George, S. (1984) *Ill Fares the Land*. Washington, DC: Institute for Policy Studies.

Gibbs, D.C. (1991) 'Greening the local economy'. *Local Economy 6*, 3, 224–239.

Gibbs, D.C. (1993) *The Green Local Economy*. Manchester: Centre for Local Economic Strategies.

Gilbert, A. and Gugler, J. (1992) *Cities, Poverty and Development: Urbanization in the Third World*. Second edition. Oxford: Oxford University Press.

Gilbert, O.L. (1986). Field evidence for an acid rain effect on lichens. *Environmental Pollution (Series A) 40*, 227–231.

Gillespie, A. (1992) 'Communications technologies and the future of the city'. In M. Breheny (ed) *Sustainable Development and Urban Form*. London: Pion.

Girardet, H. (1990) 'The metabolism of cities'. In D. Cadman and G. Payne.

Girardet, H. (1992) *Cities: New Directions for Sustainable Urban Living*. London: Gaia Books.

Glasson, J. (1993). 'Environmental impact assessment: only the tip of the iceberg yet?' *Professorial lecture to mark the inauguration of Oxford Brookes University, 24 November*. Oxford: School of Planning, Oxford Brookes University.

Goldstein, A. (1993) 'The impact of temporary migration on urban places: Thailand and China as case studies'. In J.D. Kasarda and A.M. Parnell (eds) *Third World Cities: Problems, Policies and Prospects*. Newbury Park, CA: Sage.

Golubev, G.N. (1993) 'Sustainable water development: implications for the future'. *International Journal of Water Resources Development 9*, 2, 127–54.

Goode, D. (1990) 'Introduction: a green renaissance'. In D. Gordon.

Goodey, B. (1974) 'Images of place: essays on environmental perception, communications and education'. *CURS Occasional Paper 30*. Birmingham: University of Birmingham.

Goodey, B. (1993) 'Urban design in central areas and beyond'. In R. Hayward and S. McGlynn.

Gordon, D.(ed) (1990) *Green Cities: Ecologically Sound Approaches to Urban Space*. Montreal: Black Rose Books.

Gordon, P. and Richardson, H.W. (1990) 'Gasoline consumption and cities – a reply'. *Journal of the American Planning Association 57*, 341–44.

Gordon, P., Kumar, A. and Richardson H.W. (1989a) 'The influence of metropolitan spatial structure on commuting time'. *Journal of Urban Economics 26*, 138–51.

Gordon, P., Kumar, A. and Richardson, H.W. (1989b) 'Congestion changing metropolitan structure and city size in the United States'. *International Regional Science Review 12*, 1, 45–53.

Gore, C. (1984) *Regions in Question: Space, Development Theory and Regional Policy*. London: Methuen.

Gossop, C. and Webb, A. (1993) 'Getting around: public and private transport'. In A. Blowers (ed) *Planning for a Sustainable Environment*. London: Earthscan.

Gottmann, J. (1967) 'Urban sprawl and its ramifications'. In J. Gottmann and R.A. Harper.

Gottmann, J. and Harper, R.A. (1967) *Metropolis on the Move: Geographers Look at Urban Sprawl*. New York: John Wiley.

Goudie, A. (1989) *The Nature of the Environment*. Second edition. Oxford: Basil Blackwell.

Goudie, A. (1990) *The Human Impact on the Natural Environment*. Third edition. Oxford: Basil Blackwell.

Gregory, K.J. (1974) 'Streamflow and building activity'. In K.J. Gregory and D.E. Walling (eds) *Fluvial Processes in Instrumented Watersheds*. Special Publication 6. London: Institute of British Geographers.

Gribbin, J. (1990) 'Did the greenhouse effect cause the storm?'. *New Scientist, 3 February*, p. 25.

Gruen, V. (1964) *The Heart of our Cities*. New York: Simon and Schuster.

Gruen, V. (1973) *Centers for the Urban Environment*. New York: Van Nostrand Reinhold.

Gugler, J. (1988) 'Overurbanization reconsidered'. In J. Gugler (ed) *The Urbanization of the Third World*. Oxford: Oxford University Press.

Gunn, M. (1978) *Habitat: Human Settlement in an Urban Age*. Oxford: Pergamon.

Gwilliam, K.M. and Gommers, M.J.P.F. (1992) 'Transport project appraisal in the Netherlands'. *Project Appraisal 7*, 4, 237–248.

HABITAT (1987) *Global Report on Human Settlements*. Oxford: United Nations Centre for Urban Settlements and Oxford University Press.

Hahn, E. and Simonis, U. (1990) 'Ecological urban restructuring: method and action'. *Environmental Management and Health 2*, (2), 12–19.

Haigh, N. (1984) *EEC Environmental Policy and Britain*. London: Environmental Data Services.

Hall, E.T. (1966) *The Hidden Dimension*. New York: Doubleday.

Hall, G. (1972) *Ecology, Can We Survive Under Capitalism?*. New York: International Publishers.

Hall, P. (1984) 'Utopian thought: a framework for social, economic and physical planning'. In P. Alexander and R. Gill (eds) *Utopias*. London: Duckworth.

Hall, P. (1988) *Cities of Tomorrow*. Oxford: Basil Blackwell.

Hall, P. and Hay, D. (1980) *Growth Centres in the European Urban System*. London: Heinemann.

Hall, P., Thomas, R. Gracey, H. and Drewett, R. (1973) *The Containment of Urban England*. Cambridge: Cambridge University Press.

Hamer, M. (1992) 'Down came the drought.' *New Scientist*. 2 May, 22–23.

Hardin, G. (1969) 'The tragedy of the commons' *Science 162*, 1243–8.

Hardoy, J. E., Mitlin, D. and Satterthwaite, D. (1992) *Environmental Problems in Third World Cities*. London: Earthscan.

Hardoy, J.E. and Satterthwaite, D. (1989) *Squatter City: Life in the Urban Third World*. London: Earthscan.

Hardoy, J.E. and Satterthwaite, D. (1990) 'Urban change in the Third World: are recent trends a useful pointer to the urban future?' In D. Cadman and G. Payne.

Hardoy, J.E. and Satterthwaite, D. (1991) 'Environmental problems of Third World cities: a global issue ignored?' *Public Administration and Development 11*, 341–61.

Hardoy, J.E. and Satterthwaite, D. (eds) (1986) *Small and Intermediate Urban Centres: Their Role in Regional and National Development in the Third World*. London: Hodder and Stoughton.

Harrison, R.M. (ed.) (1990) *Pollution: Causes, Effects and Control*. Second edition. London: Royal Society of Chemistry.

Harrison, R.M. (ed.) (1992) *Understanding Our Environment: An Introduction to Environmental Chemistry and Pollution*. Second edition. London: Royal Society of Chemistry.

Harvey, D. (1973) *Social Justice and the City*. London: Edward Arnold.

Harvey, D. (1989a) *The Urban Experience*. Oxford: Blackwell.

Harvey, D. (1989b) *The Condition of Post-Modernity*. Oxford: Blackwell.

Harvey, D. (1993) 'The nature of environment: the dialectics of social and environmental change'. *Socialist Register*.

Haslam, S.M. (1990) *River Pollution: An Ecological Perspective*. London: Belhaven Press.

Hass-Klau, C. (1990) 'Public transport and integrated transport policies in large metropolitan areas of Britain'. *The Planner*, 25 May, 13–20.

Hasson, F. (1985) 'Exporting death'. *International Labour Reports 8*, 7–8.

Hastaoglou-Martinidis, V., Kalogirou, N. and Papamichos, N. (1993) 'The revaluing of urban space: the Green Paper for European cities and the case of Greece'. *Antipode, 25*, 3, 240–52.

Haughton, G. (1994) 'Birthpangs in utopia: the emergence of a high tech, sustainable city in Australia'. *Geography*, January.

Haughton, G. and Whitney, D. (1989) 'Equal urban partners'. *The Planner*. 15 December, 9–11.

Hawkins, S. (1992) 'Clean-up of contaminated land: an assessment of the mechanisms available'. *Journal of Planning and Environmental Law*. December, 1119.

Hay, D. (1990) 'On the development of cities' in D. Cadman and G. Payne.

Hayward, R. and McGlynn, S. (eds) (1993) Making Better Places: Urban Design Now. London: Butterworth Architecture.

Henderson, J. and Castells, M. (eds) (1987) *Global Restructuring and Territorial Development*. London: Sage.

Healey, P., Purdue, M. and Ennis, F. (1993) 'Development impacts and obligations'. *The Planner 77*, 7, 11–14.

Heaton, G., Repetto, R. and Sobin, R. (1991) *Transforming Technology: An Agenda for Environmentally Sustainable Growth in the 21st Century*. Washington, D.C.: World Resources Institute.

Heliotis, F.D., Karandinos, M.G. and Whiton, J.C. (1988) 'Air pollution and the decline of the Fir forest in Parnis National Park, near Athens, Greece'. *Environmental Pollution 54*, 29–40.

Hellawell, J.M. (1988) 'Toxic substances in rivers and streams'. *Environmental Pollution 50*, 61–85.

Hill, D.R. (1992) 'America's disorganized organicists'. *Journal of Planning Literature 7*, 3–21.

Hirschhorn, J. (1990) 'The technological potential: pollution prevention'. *Paper prepared for the World Resources Institute Symposium, Toward 2000: Environment, Technology and the New Century. Annapolis, Maryland, 13–15 June.*

HMSO (1981) *Environmental Assessment of Projects*. House of Lords Parliament Debates Official Report. London: HMSO.

Hoch, I. (1969) 'The three dimensional city: contained urban space'. In H. Perloff (ed) *The Quality of the Urban Environment: Essays on New Resources in an Urban Age*. Washington: Resources for the Future.

Holdgate, M.W. (1979) *A Perspective of Environmental Pollution*. Cambridge: Cambridge University Press.

Hollis, G., Ham, G. and Ambler, M. (1992) *The Future Role and Structure of Local Government*. Harlow: Longman.

Holyoak, J. (1993) 'The suburbanisation and re-urbanisation of the residential inner city'. In R. Hayward and S. McGlynn.

Homewood, B. (1991) 'Dirty cities head Brazil's environmental ills'. *New Scientist.* 7 September, 21.

Horsbrugh, P. (1990) 'Plants in urban well-being'. In C. Canfield.

Hough, M. (1984) *City Form and Natural Processes.* London: Croom Helm.

Hough, M. (1990) 'Formed by natural process – a definition of the green city'. In D. Gordon.

Houghton, J.T., Jenkins, G.J. and Ephraums, J.J. (eds) (1990) *Climate Change: The IPCC Scientific Assessment.* Cambridge: Cambridge University Press.

House of Lords Select Committee on the European Communities (1993) *Industry and the Enviroment.* London: HMSO.

Howard, C.I. (1976) 'The psychology of urban life'. In G. Harrison and J. Gibson (eds) *Man in Urban Environments.* Oxford: Oxford University Press.

Howard, E. (1898) *Tomorrow: A Peaceful Path to Real Reform.* London: Swan Sonnenschein. Subsequently republished in slightly modified form as *Garden Cities of Tomorrow* (1946). London: Faber and Faber.

Htun, N. (1992) 'The EIA process in Asia and the Pacific region'. In P. Wathern (ed) *Environmental Impact Assessment: Theory and Practice.* London: Routledge.

Huisingh, D. (1988) *Good Environmental Practices – Good Business Practices.* Berlin: Science Center.

Hutchinson, C. (1992) 'Environmental issues: challenges for the chief executive'. *Long Range Planning 25, 3,* 50–59.

Hutchinson, D. (1992) 'Towards sustainability: the combined production of heat and power'. In M. Breheny (ed) *Sustainable Development and Urban Form.* London: Pion.

Huxley, M. (1991) 'Planning as a framework of power'. *Paper to the 8th Urban Change and Conflict conference, 10–13 September. University of Lancaster.*

Hyman, E.L. (1990) 'An assessment of World Bank and AID activities and procedures affecting urban environmental quality'. *Project Appraisal 5,* 4, 198–212.

Issel, W. (1985) *Social Change in the United States 1945–83.* Basingstoke: Macmillan.

Jacobs, J. (1961) *The Death and Life of Great American Cities.* Harmondsworth: Penguin.

Jacobs, J. (1984) *Cities and the Wealth of Nations: Principles of Economic Life.* Harmondsworth: Penguin.

Jacobs, M (1989) 'Green dilemma'. *New Socialist 62,* 11–13.

Jacobs, M. (1991) *The Green Economy: Environment, Sustainable Development and the Politics of the Future.* London: Pluto Press.

Jeffries, M. and Mills, D. (1990) *Freshwater Ecology: Principles and Applications.* London: Belhaven Press.

Johnston, R.J. (1989) *Environmental Problems: Nature, Economy and Society.* London: Belhaven Press.

Jones, G. (1993) 'Planning and the reduction of transport emissions'. *The Planner 77,* (7), 15–18.

Jones, H. (1990) *Population Geography.* Second edition. London: Paul Chapman.

Joshi, S.D., Pandya, G.H., Phadke, K.M., Tajne, D.S., Jain, A.K., Gajrani, C.P. and Yennawar, P.K. (1989) 'An investigation into the acid content of aerosols in the ambient air at the Taj Mahal, Agra'. *Environmental Pollution 58*, 87–96.

JURUE (1987) *Greening City Sites: Good Practice in Urban Regeneration*. London: HMSO.

JURUE (1988) *Improving Urban Areas: Good practice in Urban Regeneration*. London: HMSO.

Keating, M. (1986) 'Linking downtown development to broader community goals'. *Journal of the American Planning Association 51*, 133–141.

Kelly, P.M. and Karas, J.H.W. (1990) 'The Greenhouse Effect'. *Capital and Class 38*, 17–27.

Kemp, D. (1990) *Global Environmental Issues: A Climatological Approach*. London: Routledge.

Kennedy, W.V. (1989) 'Environmental impact assessment of two adjacent segments of a highway'. In C. Wood (ed) *Environmental Impact Assessment: Five Training Case Studies*. Occasional Paper 19. Second edition. Manchester: EIA Centre, University of Manchester.

Kennedy, W.V. (1992) 'Environmental impact assessment and bilateral development aid: an overview'. In P. Wathern (ed.) *Environmental Impact Assessment: Theory and Practice*. London: Routledge.

Keyder, C. and Oncu, A. (1993) *Istanbul and the Concept of World Cities*. Istanbul: Friedrich Ebert Foundation.

Keyfitz, N. (1991) 'Population growth can prevent the development that would slow population growth'. In J.T. Matthews (ed) *Preserving the Global Environment: The Challenge of Shared Leadership*. London: W.W. Norton.

Kierans, T.W. (1980) 'Thinking big in North America: the Grand Canal concept'. *The Futurist 14*, 6, 29–32.

King, A.D. (1990a) *Urbanism, Colonialism and the World-Economy: Cultural and Spatial Foundations of the World Urban System*. London: Routledge.

King, A.D. (1990b) *Global Cities: Post Imperialism and the Internationalisation of London*. London: Routledge.

Kirklees Metropolitan District Council/Friends of the Earth (1989) *Kirklees State of the Environment Report*. Huddersfield: Kirklees MDC.

Kitamura, R. (1991) 'Home work clears air'. *New Scientist*. 5 October.

Knox, P. and Agnew, J. (1989) *The Geography of the World Economy*. London: Edward Arnold.

Kropotkin, P. (1920) *The State: Its Historic Role*. Fifth edition. London: Freedom Press.

Kropotkin, P. (1899) *Fields, Factories and Workshops*. London: Hutchinson.

Krupa, S.V. and Manning, W.J. (1988) 'Atmospheric ozone: formation and effects on vegetation'. *Environmental Pollution 50*, 101–137.

Lado, C. (1990) 'Informal urban agriculture in Nairobi, Kenya: problem or resource in development and land use planning?'. *Land Use Policy 7*, 3, 257–263.

Landsberg, H.E. (1981) *The Urban Climate*. New York: Academic Press.

Lansdown, R. and Yule, W. (1986) *Lead Toxicity*. Baltimore, MD: John Hopkins University Press.

Last, F.T. (1982) 'Effects of atmospheric sulphur compounds on natural and man-made terrestrial and aquatic ecosystems'. *Agricultural Environment 7*, 299–387.

Le Corbusier (Charles Édouard Jeanneret) (1929) *The City of Tomorrow and its Planning*. London: John Rodher.

Lee, D. (1973) 'Requiem for large-scale planning models'. *Journal of the American Institute of Planners 39*, 117–42.

Lee, D.O. (1990) 'The influence of wind direction, circulation type and air pollution emissions on summer visibility trends in southern England'. *Atmospheric Environment 24A*, 1, 195–201.

Lee, N. (1989) *Environmental Impact Assessment: A Training Guide*. Occasional Paper 18. Second edition. Manchester: EIA Centre, University of Manchester.

Lee, N. (1992) 'Training requirements for environmental impact assessment'. In P. Wathern (ed.) *Environmental Impact Assessment: Theory and Practice*. London: Routledge.

Lee, N. and Walsh, F. (1992) 'Strategic environmental assessment: an overview'. *Project Appraisal 7*, 3, 126–136.

Lee, N. and Wood, C.(1978) 'EIA: a European perspective'. *Built Environment 4*, 2, 101–110.

Leff, E. (1990) 'The global context of the greening of cities'. In D. Gordon.

Lemnitz, L. (1988) 'The social and economic organization of a Mexican shanty town'. In J. Gugler (ed) *The Urbanization of the Third World*. Oxford: Oxford University Press.

Levin, R. (1987) 'Reducing lead in drinking water: a benefit analysis'. *Report Number EPA 23–09–86–019*. Washington, DC: Office of Policy and Environmental Protection Agency.

Lewis, W.A. (1978) *The Evolution of the International Economic Order*. Princeton, NJ: Princeton University Press.

Lichfield, N. (1992) 'From planning obligations to community benefit'. *Journal of Planning and Environment Law*, December, 1103–1118.

Linton, M. and Greco, T. (1990) 'LETS: the local exchange trading system'. In V. Andruss *et al.*

Lipietz, A. (1992) *Towards a New Economic Order: Postfordism, Ecology and Democracy*. Cambridge, UK: Polity Press.

Lipton, M. (1977) *Why Poor People Stay Poor: Urban Bias in World Development*. London: Maurice Temple Smith.

Lloyd, P.E. and Dicken, P. (1977) *Location in Space*. Second edition. London: Harper and Row.

Lone, O. (1992) 'Environmental and resource accounting'. In P. Ekins and M. Max-Neef.

Lynch, K. (1961) 'The pattern of metropolis'. *Daedalus*, Winter, 79–98.

Lynch, K. (1981) *Good City Form*. Cambridge, MA: MIT Press.

MacKaye, B. (1928) *The New Exploration: A Philosophy of Regional Planning*. New York: Harcourt Brace.

Mackenzie, S. (1988) 'Balancing our space and time: the impact of women's organization on the British city, 1920–1980'. In J. Little, L. Peake and P. Richardson (eds) *Women in Cities: Gender and the Urban Environment*. Basingstoke: Macmillan.

Mackenzie, S. (1989) 'Women in the city'. In R. Peet and N. Thrift (eds) *New Models in Geography, volume two*. London: Unwin Hyman.

Maclennan, D. and Mega, V. (1992) 'Land use management and environmental improvement in cities: an introduction to the issues'. In D. Maclennan and V. Mega (eds) *Land Use Management and Environmental Improvement in Cities: Proceedings of a European Workshop, Lisbon*. Dublin: European Foundation for the Improvement of Living and Working Conditions.

MacNeill, J., Winsemius, P. and Yakushiji, T. (1991) *Beyond Interdependence: The Meshing of the World's Economy and the Earth's Ecology*. Oxford: Oxford University Press.

Massey, D. And Meegan, R. (eds) (1985) *Politics and Method: Contrasting Studies in Industrial Geography*. London: Methuen.

Matthews, P. (1993) 'The road to nowhere'. *Independent on Sunday Review*, 7 November, 9.

Mauck, W.L., Mehrle, P.M. and Mayer, F.L. (1978) 'Effects of the polychlorinated biphenyl Aroclor 1254 on growth, survival and bone development in brook trout'. *Journal of Fish Research Bulletin. Canada 35*, 1084–1088.

Mayur, R. (1990) 'Vision and joy of green cities'. In D. Gordon.

McDonald, A.T. and Kay, D. (1988) *Water Resources Issues and Strategies*. Harlow, Essex: Longman Scientific & Technical.

McGlynn, G., Newman, P. and Kenworthy, J. (1991) 'Land use and transport: the missing link in urban consolidation'. *Urban Futures*, special issue 1, July, 8–18.

McHarg, I.L. (1969) *Design With Nature*. Philadelphia: Natural History Press.

McLusky, D.S. (1981) *The Estuarine Ecosystem*. Glasgow: Blackie.

McMichael, M. (1993) *Planetary Overload: Global Environmental Change and the Health of the Human Species*. Cambridge: Cambridge University Press.

Meadows, D.H., Meadows, D.L., Randers, J. and Behrenv III, W.W. (1972) *The Limits to Growth*. New York: University Books.

Mega, V. (1993) 'Innovations for the improvement of the urban environment'. *European Planning Studies 1*, 4, 527–41.

Meller, J. (ed) (1970) *The Buckminster Fuller Reader*. London: Jonathan Cape.

Meyer, W.B. (1991) 'Urban heat island and urban health: early American perspectives'. *Professional Geographer 43*, 1, 38–48.

Michelson, W. (1970) *Man and his Urban Environment: A Sociological Approach*. Reading, MA: Addison-Wesley.

Miller, G.T. (1988) *Environmental Science: An Introduction*. Second edition. Belmont, CA: Wadsworth.

Miller, G.T. (1991) *Environmental Science: Sustaining the Earth*. Third edition. Belmont, CA: Wadsworth.

Miller, G.T. (1992) *Living in the Environment: An Introduction to Environmental Science.* Seventh edition. Belmont, CA: Wadsworth.

Milne, A. (1988) *Our Drowning World: Population, Pollution and Future Weather.* Bridport, Dorset: Prism Press.

Milne, R. (1992) 'Industry should pay to clean its mess'. *New Scientist.* 22 February, 13.

Mishan E. J. (1967) *The Costs of Economic Growth.* Staples Press. Republished (1969) Harmondsworth: Pelican Books.

Mollison, B. (1979) *Permaculture Two: Practical Design for Town and Country in Permanent Agriculture.* Tasmania: Tagari Books.

Mollison, B. (1990) 'Strategies for an alternative nation'. In V. Andruss *et al.*

Molnar, A. (1990) 'Estimation of Volatile Organic Compounds (VOC) emissions for Hungary'. *Atmospheric Environment 24A*, 11, 2855–2860.

Moran, N. (1993) 'Energy saving office has air of a cathedral'. *Independent on Sunday.* 28 November.

Moreira, I.V. (1992) 'EIA in Latin America'. In P. Wathern (ed.) *Environmental Impact Assessment: Theory and Practice.* London: Routledge.

Moss, B. (1988) *Ecology of Fresh Waters: Man and Medium.* Second edition. Oxford: Blackwell.

Mulgan, G. (1989) 'A tale of New Cities'. *Marxism Today.* March, 18–25.

Mumford, L. (1961) *The City in History.* Harmondsworth: Penguin.

Murphy, T. (1981) 'EIA and developing countries'. *Planning Outlook 24.*

Murrain, P. (1993) 'Urban expansion: look back and learn'. In R. Hayward and S. McGlynn.

National Academy of Sciences (NAS) (1979) 'Geochemistry of water in relation to cardiovascular disease'. Washington DC: US National Academy of Sciences.

New Scientist (1991) 'Data on toxins'. 30 November, 17.

New Scientist (1992a) 'Minamata damages'. 22 February, 14.

New Scientist (1992b) 'Car recycling'. 29 February, 17.

New Scientist (1992c) 'Dutch cut pollution'. 2 May, 11.

Newcombe, K. (1984) 'Energy conservation and diversification of energy sources in and around the city of Lae, Papua New Guinea'. In F. di Castri, F. Baker and M. Hadley (eds) *Ecology in Practice. Part II: The Social Response.* Dublin: Tycooly and Paris: UNESCO.

Newman, P. and Kenworthy, J. (1989) *Cities and Automobile Dependence.* Aldershot: Gower.

Newman, P. and Mouritz, M. (1991) 'Ecologically sustainable urban development and the future of Perth'. *Urban Futures.* Special issue 4, November, 13–27.

Newson, M. (1991) 'Environmental assessment and the academic environmentalist'. *Planning Outlook 34*, 2, 72–74.

Nicholas, F.W. (1982) 'Managing the urban physical environment'. In C.M. Christian and R.A. Harper (eds) *Modern Metropolitan Systems.* Columbus, OH: C.E. Merrill.

Nijkamp, P. (1980) *Environmental Policy Analysis: Operational Methods and Models.* Chichester: John Wiley.

Nilles, J., Carlson, F., Gray, P. and Hannemann, G. (1976) *The Telecommunications–Transport Tradeoff.* New York: Wiley.

Nriagu, J.O. (1988) 'A silent epidemic of environmental metal poisoning?'. *Environmental Pollution 50*, 139–161.

Nyere, J. (1988) 'Let us pay heed to the peasant' in Gugler, J. (ed) *The Urbanization of the Third World.* Oxford: Oxford University Press.

O'Riorden, T. (1989) 'The challenge for environmentalism'. In R. Peet and N. Thrift (eds) *New Models in Geography: Volume One.* London: ⊘REFERENCES = Oberai, A.S. (1993) 'Urbanisation, development and economic efficiency'. In J.dKasarda, J.D. and Parnell, A.M. (eds) *Third World Cities: Problems, Policies and Prospects.* Newbury Park, CA: Sage.

Odum, E.P. (1969) 'The strategy of ecosystem development'. *Science 164*, 262–270.

Odum, E.P. (1989) *Ecology and Our Endangered Life-Support Systems.* Sunderland, MA: Sinauer Associates.

OECD (1980) *Noise Abatement in OECD Countries.* Paris: OECD.

OECD (1985a) *The State of the Environment.* Paris: OECD.

OECD (1985b) *Coordinated Urban Transport Pricing.* Paris: OECD.

OECD (1987) *Managing and Financing Urban Services.* Paris: OECD.

OECD (1988) *Transport and the Environment.* Paris: OECD.

OECD (1989) *Environmental Data Compendium.* Paris: OECD.

OECD (1990) *Environmental Policies for Cities in the 1990s.* Paris: OECD.

OECD (1991) *The State of the Environment.* Paris: OECD.

Ogbeibu, A.E. and Victor, R. (1989) 'The effects of road and bridge construction on the bank-root macrobenthic invertebrates of a southern Nigerian stream'. *Environmental Pollution 56*, 85–100.

Oke, T.R. (1978) *Boundary Layer Climates.* London: Methuen.

Oliver, P., Davis, I. and Bentley I. (1981) *Dunroamin: The Suburban Semi and its Enemies.* London: Barrie and Jenkins.

Olsson, M. (1987) 'PCBs in the Baltic environment'. In J.S. Waid (ed) *PCBs and the Environment (vol. 3).* Boca Raton, FL: CRC Press.

Olszyk, D.M., Bytnerowicz, A. and Takemoto, B.K. (1989) 'Photochemical oxidant pollution and vegetation: effects of mixtures of gases, fog and particles'. *Environmental Pollution 61*, 11–29.

Orishimo, I. (1982) *Urbanization and Enviromental Quality.* Boston, MA: Kluwer.

O'Riorden, T. (1990) 'Global warning'. *Marxism Today,* July, 12–15.

Orrskog, L. and Snickars, F. (1992) 'On the sustainability of urban and regional structures'. In M. Breheny (ed) *Sustainable Development and Urban Form.* London: Pion.

Osmundson, T. (1990) 'Rooftop gardens of the world'. In C. Canfield.

Ossenbrugge, J. (1988) 'Regional restructuring and the ecological welfare state – spatial impacts of environmental protection in West Germany'. *Geographische Zeitschrift 76*, 2, 78–93.

Ossenbrugge, J. (1991) 'Impacts of environmental production on regional restructuring of Northern Germany'. In P. Jones and T. Wild (eds)

De-industrialisation and New Industrialisation in Britain and West Germany. London: Anglo-German Foundation.

Owen, W. (1969) 'Transport: key to the future of cities'. In H. Perloff.

Owens, S. (1986) *Energy, Planning and Urban Form.* London: Pion.

Owens, S. (1991) *Energy Conscious Planning.* London: Council for the Protection of Rural England.

Owens, S. (1992) 'Energy, environmental sustainability and land use planning'. In M. Breheny (ed) *Sustainable Development and Urban Form.* London: Pion.

Owens, S. and Cope, D. (1992) *Land Use Planning and Climate Change.* London: HMSO.

Owens, S. and Owens, P.L. (1991) *Environment, Resources and Conservation.* Cambridge: Cambridge University Press.

Panayotou, T. (1992) 'The economics of environmental degradation problems, causes and responses'. In A. Markandya and J. Richardson (eds) *The Earthscan Reader in Environmental Economics.* London: Earthscan.

Parham, S. (1993) 'How has women's involvement in urban planning changed our cities?' *Urban Futures 3*, 3, 46–50.

Park, C. (1991) 'Transfrontier air pollution: some geographical issues'. *Geography 76*, 1, 21–35.

Park, P. (1991) 'Great Lakes pollution linked to infertility'. *New Scientist*, 28 September, 18.

Partnership Limited (1988) *Creating Development Trusts: Good Practice in Urban Regeneration.* London: HMSO.

Patrinos, A.A.N. (1985) 'The impact of urban and industrial emissions on mesoscale precipitation quality'. *Journal of Air Pollution Control Assessment 35*, 719–727.

Pearce, D. (1990) 'Economics and the global environmental challenge'. *Millennium 19*, 3, 365–87.

Pearce, D. (1992) 'Economics, equity and sustainable development'. In P. Ekins and M. Max-Neef.

Pearce, D. (1993) 'Sustainable development and developing country economies'. In R.K. Turner (ed) *Sustainable Environmental Economics and Management.* London: Belhaven.

Pearce, D. (ed) (1991) *Blueprint 2: Greening the World Economy.* London: Earthscan.

Pearce, D., Markandya, A. and Barbier, E.B. (1989) *Blueprint for a Green Economy.* London: Earthscan.

Pepper, D. (1984) *The Roots of Modern Environmentalism.* London: Croom Helm.

Perloff, H. (ed) (1969) *The Quality of the Urban Environment: Essays on New Resources in an Urban Age.* Washington, DC: Resources for the Future.

Pershagen, G. (1983) 'The epidemiology of human arsenic exposure'. In B.A. Fowler (ed) *Biological and Environmental Effects of Arsenic.* Amsterdam: Elsevier.

Peterson, D.J. (1993) *Troubled Lands: The Legacy of Soviet Environmental Destruction.* Boulder, Colorado: Westview Press.

Pickup, L. (1988) 'Hard to get around: a study of women's travel mobility'. In J. Little, L. Peake and P. Richardson (eds) *Women in Cities: Gender and the Urban Environment.* Basingstoke: Macmillan.

Piore, M. and Sabel, C. (1984) *The Second Industrial Divide.* New York: Basic Books.

Plant, J. (1990) 'Searching for common ground: ecofeminism and bioregionalism'. In V. Andruss *et al.*

Ponting, C. (1991) *A Green History of the World.* Harmondsworth: Penguin.

Porter, M. (1990) *The Competetive Advantage of Nations.* London: Macmillan.

Portney, P.R. and Mullahy, J. (1986) 'Urban air quality and acute respiratory illness'. *Journal Urban Economics 20*, 21–38.

Poskrobo, B. and Cygler, M. (1992) 'Effectiveness of environmental protection control at the period of general economy transformation in Poland'. *Paper given at the conference on Institutions and Environmental Protection, Krakow, Poland, June.*

Pratt, G. (1989) 'Reproduction, class, and the spatial structure of the city'. In R. Peet and N. Thrift (eds) *New Models in Geography: Volume Two.* London: Unwin Hyman.

Price, B. (1991) *P for Pollution.* London: Green Print.

Pucher, J. (1990) 'Capitalism, socialism, and urban transportation: policies and travel behaviour in the East and West'. *Journal of American Planning Association 56*, 3, 278–296.

Punter, J. (1990) 'The ten commandments of architecture and urban design. *The Planner.* 5 October, 10–14.

Purdue, M., Healey, P. and Ennis, F. (1992) 'Planning gain and the grant of planning permission: is the United States' test of the "rational" nexus the appropriate solution?' *Journal of Planning and Environment Law.* November, 1012–24.

Pye, V.I. and Patrick, R. (1983) 'Ground water contamination in the United States'. *Science 221*, 713–718.

Quarrie, J. (ed) (1992) *Earth Summit '92: The United Nations Conference on Environment and Development.* London: Regency Press.

Rainnie, A. (1989) *Industrial Relations in Small Firms: Small isn't Beautiful.* London: Routledge.

Ravetz, A. (1980) *Remaking Cities: Contradictions of the Recent Urban Environment.* London: Croom Helm.

Redclift, M (1987) *Sustainable Development: Exploring the Contradictions.* London: Routledge.

Redclift, M. (1992) 'The multiple dimensions of sustainable development'. *Geography 77*, 1, 36–42.

Reed, S. (1992) 'Managing Hong Kong's high pressure environment'. *Environmental Policy and Practice 2*, 1, 51–69.

Rees, J. (1990) *Natural Resources: Allocation, Economics and Policy.* Second edition. London: Routledge.

Rees, J. (1991) 'Equity and environmental policy'. *Geography 76*, 4, 292–303.

Rees, W. E. and Roseland, M. (1991) 'Sustainable communities: planning for the 21st century'. *Plan Canada 31*, 3, 15–26.

Reid, M. (1993) 'Paydirt down Mexico way'. *The Guardian.* 19 November, 14–15.

Renner, M. (1988) *Rethinking the Role of the Automobile.* Washington, DC: Worldwatch Institute.

Repetto, R., Magrath, W., Wells, M., Beer, C. and Rossini, F. (1992) 'Wasting assets: natural resources in the national income accounts'. In A. Markandya and J.

Richardson (eds) *The Earthscan Reader in Environmental Economics*. London: Earthscan.

Richardson, H. W. (1993) 'Efficiency and welfare in LDC Mega-Cities'. In J.D. Kasarda and A.M. Parnell (eds) *Third World Cities: Problems, Policies and Prospects*. Newbury Park, CA: Sage.

Richardson, H.W. (1978) *Regional and Urban Economics*. Harmondsworth: Penguin.

Roberts, J. (1981) *Pedestrian Precincts in Britain*. London: Transport and Environmental Studies.

Roberts, P. (1992) 'Business and the environment: an initial review of the recent literature'. *Business Strategy and the Environment 1*, 2, 41–50.

Roberts, P. and Hunter, C. (1992) 'Environmental assessment: taking stock'. *CUDEM Working Paper 11*. Leeds: Centre for Urban Development and Environmental Management, Leeds Metropolitan University.

Robertson, J. (1978) *The Sane Alternative: Signposts to a Self-Fulfilling Future*. London: James Robertson.

Robertson, J. (1989) *Future Wealth: A New Economics for the 21st Century*. London: Cassell.

Roddewig, R. J. (1978) *Green Bans: The Birth of Australian Environmental Politics*. Montclair, NJ: Allanheld, Osmun and Co.

Romo-Kroger, C.M. (1990) 'Elemental analysis of airborne particulates in Chile'. *Environmental Pollution 68*, 161–170.

Rosenau, H. (1983) *The Ideal City*. Third edition. London: Methuen.

Roseth, J. (1991) 'Urban consolidation – how decisions are made'. *Urban Futures*. Special issue 1, July, 1–7.

Ross, D. (1986) 'Making the informal sector visible'. In P. Ekins.

Rostow, W.W. (1960) *The Stages of Economic Growth: A Non-Communist Manifesto*. Cambridge: Cambridge University Press.

Roszak, T. (1973) *Where the Wasteland Ends*. New York: Anchor.

Rydin, Y. (1992a) 'Environmental dimensions of residential development and the implications for local planning practice'. *Journal of Environmental Planning and Management 35*, 1, 43–61.

Rydin, Y. (1992b) 'Environmental impacts and the property market'. In M. Breheny (ed) *Sustainable Development and Urban Form*. London: Pion.

Sagoff, M. (1988) *The Economy of the Earth: Philosophy, Law and the Environment*. Cambridge: Cambridge University Press.

Sani, S. (1984) 'Inadvertent atmospheric modifications through urbanization in the Kuala Lumpur area'. In Y.Y. Hoong and L.K. Sim (eds) *Urbanization and Ecodevelopment, with special reference to Kuala Lumpur*. Kuala Lumpur: University of Malaysia Press.

Sassen-Koob, S. (1984) 'The new labour demand in global cities'. In M.P. Smith (ed) *Cities in Transformation: Class, Capital and the State*. London: Sage.

Sawhney, B.L. and Hankin, L. (1985) 'Polychlorinated biphenyls in food: a review'. *Journal Food Production 48*, 442–448.

Schirnding, Y.E.R., Strauss, N., Robertson, P., Kfir, R., Fattal, B., Mathee, A., Franck, M., and Cabelli, V.J. (1993) 'Bather morbidity from recreational exposure to sea water'. *Water Science Technology 27*,3/4, 183–186.

Schumacher, E.F. (1974) *Small is Beautiful: A Study of Economics as if People Mattered.* London: Abacus.

Seabrook, J (1990) *The Myth of the Market: Promises and Illusions.* Bideford, Devon: Green Books.

Searle, G. (1991) 'Successes and failures of urban consolidation in Sydney'. *Urban Futures.* Special issue 1, July, 23–30.

Self, P. (1982) *Planning the Urban Region: A Comparative Study of Policies and Organisations.* London: Allen and Unwin.

Sennett, R. (1990) *The Conscience of the Eye: The Design and Social Life of Cities.* London: Faber and Faber.

Shaw, E.M. (1988) *Hydrology in Practice.* Second edition. London: Chapman and Hall.

Shaw, R.N. (1982) 'Deposition of atmospheric acid from local and distant sources at a rural site in Nova Scotia'. *Atmospheric Environment 16*, 337–348.

Sherlock, H. (1991) *Cities are Good For Us.* London: Paladin.

Short, J.R. (1985) 'Human geography and Marxism'. In Z.G. Baranski and J. Short (eds) *Developing Contemporary Marxism.* London: Macmillan.

Simmonds, R. (1993) 'The built form of the new regional city: a "radical" view'. In R. Hayward and S. McGlynn.

Simmons, I.G. (1981) *The Ecology of Natural Resources.* Second edition. London: Edward Arnold.

Simmons, I.G. (1989) *Changing the Face of the Earth: Culture, Environment, History.* Oxford: Basil Blackwell.

Simmons, I.G. (1991) *Earth, Air and Water: Resources and Environment in the Late 20th Century.* London: Edward Arnold.

Simon, J. (1981) *The Ultimate Resource.* Oxford: Martin Robertson.

Simon, J. and Kahn, H. (eds) (1984) *The Resourceful Earth.* Oxford: Basil Blackwell.

Simpson, M. (1992) 'Transport evaluation of highway schemes'. *Project Appraisal 7*, 4, 197–203.

Simpson, S. (1990) *The Times Guide to the Environment.* London: Times Books.

Sinclair, J (1990) 'Ozone layer will hit health and food'. *New Scientist 1702*, 27.

Singh, M.P., Goyal, P., Panwar, T.S., Agarwal, P., Nigam, S. and Bagchi, N. (1990) 'Predicted and measured concentrations of sulphur dioxide, SPM and nitrogen oxides over Delhi'. *Atmospheric Environment 24A*, 4, 783–788.

Singh, N (1989) *Economics and the Crisis of Ecology.* Third edition. London: Oxford University Press/Bellew Publishing.

Sivaramakrishnan, K.C. and Green, L. (1986) *Metropolitan Management: The Asian Experience.* Oxford: Oxford University Press.

Skinner, N. (1990) 'Ecocity legislation'. In C. Canfield.

Smil, V. (1984) *The Bad Earth: Environmental Degradation in China.* London: Zed Press.

Smith, K. (1975) *Principles of Applied Climatology*. London: McGraw-Hill.

Smith, M.P. (1987) 'Global capital restructuring and local political crises in US cities'. In J. Henderson and M. Castells (eds) *Global Restructuring and Territorial Development*. London: Sage.

Smith, M.P. (1988) 'The uses of linked development policies in US cities'. In M. Parkinson, B. Foley and D. Judd (eds) *Regenerating the Cities: The UK Crisis and the US Experience*. Manchester: Manchester University Press.

Smith, N. (1990) *Uneven Development: Nature, Capital and the Production of Space*. Second edition. Oxford: Basil Blackwell.

Smith, S. (1986) 'Assessing the ecological and health effects of pollution'. In R.E. Hester (ed), *Understanding Our Environment*. London: Royal Society of Chemistry.

Smyth, B. (1987) *City Wildspace*. London: Hilary Shipman.

Snarski, V.M. and Olson, G.F. (1982) 'Chronic toxicity and bioaccumulation of mercuric chloride in the fathead minnow (*Pimephales promelas*)'. *Aquatic Toxicology* 2, 143–156.

Soleri, P. (1990) 'Ecocity theory (based on a presentation by Paolo Soleri)'. In C. Canfield.

Solesbury, W. (1990) 'Cities as assets'. *Town and Country Planning*. December, 334–335.

Sopper, W. (1990) 'Forests as living filters for urban sewage'. In D. Gordon.

Spiller, M. (1993a) 'Federal initiatives on better cities'. *Urban Futures 3*, 1, 15–24.

Spiller, M. (1993b) 'Strategies for funding urban infrastructure: a response to the Industry Commission agenda'. *Urban Futures 3*, 2, 1–9.

Starzewska, A. (1992) 'The legislative framework for EIA in centrally planned economies'. In P. Wathern (ed) *Environmental Impact Assessment: Theory and Practice*. London: Routledge.

Stoker, G. and Young, S. (1993) *Cities in the 1990s*. Harlow: Longman.

Stretton, H (1989) *Ideas for Australian Cities*. Third edition (first published 1970). Sydney: Transit Australia.

Stretton, H. (1976) *Capitalism, Socialism and the Environment*. Cambridge: Cambridge University Press.

Stretton, H. (1978) *Urban Planning in Rich and Poor Countries*. Oxford: Oxford University Press.

Subramanian, A. Tanabe, S., Tatsukawa, R., Saito, S. and Miyazaki, N. (1987) 'Reduction in the testosterone levels by the PCBs and DDE in Dall's porpoises of northwestern North Pacific'. *Marine Pollution Bulletin 18*, 643–646.

Taafe, E., Morrill, R. and Gould, P. (1963) 'Transport expansion in underdeveloped countries: a comparative analysis'. *Geographical Review 53*, 503–29.

Tanabe, S. (1988) 'PCB problems in the future: foresight from current knowledge'. *Environmental Pollution 50*, 5–28.

Tatsukawa, R. (1976) 'PCB pollution of the Japanese environment'. In K. Higuchi (ed) *PCB Poisoning and Pollution*. Tokyo: Kodansha.

Taylor, B.R. and Roff, J.C. (1986) 'Long-term effects of highway construction on the ecology of a southern Ontario stream'. *Environmental Pollution (Series A) 40*, 317–344.

Taylor, P. J. (1989) 'The error of developmentalism in human geography'. In D. Gregory and R. Walford (eds) *Horizons in Human Geography*. Basingstoke: Macmillan.

Therivel, R., Wilson, E., Thompson, S., Heaney, D., and Pritchard, D. (1992) *Strategic Environmental Assessment*. London: Earthscan.

Thompson, P.M., Wigg, A.H., and Perker, D.J. (1991) 'Urban flood protection post-project appraisal in England and Wales'. *Project Appraisal 6*, 2, 84–92.

Thomson, J. M. (1977) *Great Cities and their Transport*. London: Victor Gollancz.

Tickell, O. (1991) 'Conflict looms over troubled waters'. *New Scientist*. 11 January, 59–60.

Tietenberg, T. (1990) 'Economic instruments for environmental regulation'. *Oxford Review of Economic Policy 6*, 1, 17–33.

Toke, D. (1990) *Green Energy: A Non-Nuclear Response to the Greenhouse Effect*. London: Green Print.

Tolba, M. K. and El-Kholy, O.A. (eds) (1992) *The World Environment 1972–1992: Two Decades of Challenge*. London: Chapman and Hall.

Troy, P. (1992) 'The new feudalism'. *Urban Futures 2*, 2, 36–44.

Turner J.F.C. and Roberts, B. (1975) 'The self-help society'. In P. Wilsher and R. Righer *et al. The Exploding Cities*. London: Andre Deutsch.

Turner, R.K. (1991) 'Environmentally sensitive aid'. In D. Pearce.

Turner, R.K., Pearce, D. and Bateman, I. (1994) *Environmental Economics: An Elementary Introduction*. Hemel Hempstead: Harvester Wheatsheaf.

Tyson, W. (1992) 'Appraisal of bus and light rail projects'. *Project Appraisal 7*, 4, 205–210.

United Nations Environment Programme (UNEP) (1988a) *Environmental Impact Assessment: Basic Procedures for Developing Countries*. Bangkok: UNEP.

United Nations Environment Programme (UNEP) (1988b) *The Montreal Protocol for the Reduction of Chlorofluorocarbons*. Montreal: UNEP.

United Nations Environmental Programme (UNEP) (1991) *Environmental Data Report, 1991/92*. Oxford: Blackwell.

United States Government (1969) *National Environmental Policy Act*. Washington, DC: United States Government Printing Office.

Unwin, N. and Searle, G. (1991) 'Ecologically sustainable development and urban development'. *Urban Futures*. Special issue 4, November, 1–12.

Vale, B. and Vale, R. (1991) *Green Architecture: Design for a Sustainable Future*. London: Thames and Hudson.

van der Valk, A. and Faludi, A. (1992) 'Growth regions and the future of Dutch planning doctrine'. In M. Breheny (ed) *Sustainable Development and Urban Form*. London: Pion.

van Dieren, W. and Hummerlinck, M.G.W. (1979) *Nature's Price: The Economics of Mother Earth*. London: Marion Boyars.

van Houdt, J.J. (1990) 'Mutagenic activity of airborne particulate matter in indoor and outdoor environments'. *Atmospheric Environment 24B*, 2, 207–220.

Victor, D.G. (1991) 'Limits of market-based strategies for slowing global warming the case of tradeable permits'. *Policy Studies 24*, 199–222.

Vidal, J. and Chaterjee, P. (1992) 'All the difference in the world'. *The Guardian*, 10 April, 31.

Viras, L.G., Athanasiou, K. and Panayotis, A.S. (1990) 'Determination of mutagenic activity of airborne particulates and of the benzo(a)pyrene concentrations in Athens atmosphere'. *Atmospheric Environment 24B*, 2, 267–274.

Vittorio, R. (1992) 'Development impact costs and infrastructure funding'. *Urban Futures 2*, 1, 18–23.

Walker, R. (1981) 'A theory of suburbanization: capitalism and the construction of urban space in the United States'. In M. Dear and A.J. Scott (eds) *Urbanization and Urban Planning in Capitalist Society*. London: Methuen.

Wallerstein, I. (1979) *The Capitalist World-Economy*. Cambridge: Cambridge University Press.

Ward, B. (1975) *Human Settlements: Crisis and Opportunity Ministry of State for Urban Affairs*. Ottawa, Canada.

Ward, C. (1985) *When We Build Again: Let's Have Housing that Works!* London: Pluto Press.

Ward, C. (1989) *Welcome Thinner City: Urban Survival in the 1990s*. London: Bedford Square Press.

Ward, R.C. and Robinson, M. (1990) *Principles of Hydrology*. Third edition. Maidenhead: McGraw-Hill.

Warrick, R.A. and Barrow, E.M. (1991) 'Climate change scenarios for the UK'. *Transactions, IBG, NS16*, 4, 387–99.

Warrick, R.A. and Farmer, G. (1990) 'The greenhouse effect, climatic change and rising sea level: implications for development'. *Transactions, IBG, NS15*, 1, 5–20.

Wathern, P. (1992) 'An introductory guide to EIA'. In P. Wathern (ed) *Environmental Impact Assessment: Theory and Practice*. London: Routledge.

Webb, A. and Gossop, C. (1993) 'Towards a sustainable energy policy'. In A. Blowers (ed) *Planning for a Sustainable Environment*. London: Earthscan.

Webber, M.M. (1964) 'The urban place and the non-place urban realm' in Webber, M.M. *et al.* (eds) *Explorations into Urban Structure*. Pennsylvania: University of Pennsylvania.

White, I.D., Mottershead, D.N. and Harrison, S.J. (1992) *Environmental Systems: An Introductory Text*. Second edition. London: Chapman and Hall.

Whitelegg, J. (1993) *Transport for a Sustainable Future: The Case for Europe*. London: Belhaven.

Whittemore, A.S. and Korn, E.L. (1980) 'Asthma and air pollution in the Los Angeles area'. *American Journal of Public Health 70*, 687–696.

Whitton, B.A. and Say, P.J. (1975) 'Heavy Metals'. In B.A. Whitton (ed) *River Ecology*. Oxford: Blackwell.

Williams, C.C. and Haughton, G. (1994) (eds) *Perspectives Towards Sustainable Development*. Aldershot: Avebury.

Winikoff, T. (1993) 'Changing places–cultural action and environmental design: women's needs, visions and creative work'. *Urban Futures 3*, 3, 23–26.

Wood, C. (1992) 'EIA in plan making'. In P. Wathern (ed) *Environmental Impact Assessment: Theory and Practice*. London: Routledge.

Wood, C. and Jones, C. (1991) *Monitoring Environmental Assessment and Planning*. London: HMSO.

Wood, C., Lee, N., Luker, J.A. and Saunders, P.J.W. (1974) *The Geography of Pollution: A Study of Greater Manchester*. Manchester: Manchester University Press.

Woodworth, J. and Pascoe, D. (1982) 'Cadmium toxicity to rainbow trout, *Salmo gairdneri*: a study of eggs and alevins'. *Journal of Fish Biology 21*, 47–57.

World Commission on Environment and Development (WCED) (1987) *Our Common Future*. Oxford: Oxford University Press.

World Health Organization (1992) *Report of the Panel on Urbanization*. (WHO Commission on Health and Environment.) Geneva: WHO.

World Health Organization (WHO) (1991) *Environmental Health in Urban Development*. WHO Technical Report Series 807. Report of a WHO Expert Committee. Geneva: WHO.

World Resources Institute (WRI) (1986) *World Resources 1986*. New York: Basic Books.

Wright, F.L. (1974) 'City of the future'. In A. Blowers, C. Hamnett and P. Sarre (eds) *The Future of Cities*. London: Hutchinson. Originally published in F.L. Wright (1932) *Disappearing City*.

Zelinsky, W. (1971) 'The hypothesis of the mobility transition'. *Geographical Review 61*, 219–49.

ZumBrunnen, C. (1990) 'The environmental challenges in eastern Europe'. *Millennium 19*, 3, 389–412.

INDEX

Town and Country
  Planning Association
  78
'town cramming' *see*
  urban consolidation
town planning *see*
  planning
toxins
  and acid rain 195
  algae 183, 190–1
  chemicals 6, 191, 192,
    193, 233
  and contaminated land
    177
  data on emissions 233
  and UK inspectorates
    231
  wastes 5
  see also metals; organic
    compounds
trade
  and barter 65–6
  GATT agreement
    (1993) 270
  global 30–1, 37, 38,
    55–6
  import substitution 65
  and Third World 6
  urban 67, 71
trade unions 42, 58, 305
traffic *see* cars; transport
transfer payments 75
transfrontier
  environmental
    problems 3
  justice 200
  pollution 5, 137, 194,
    225, 231–2, 297
  responsibility 16, 17, 23
transport
  access to 102
  air pollution 143, 148,
    149, 152, 153, 154,
    162
  congestion 36, 49,
    59–60, 96, 98
  and economic
    approaches 278,
    279–83
  energy-efficient 299

environmental costs 49,
  270–1
and greening the city 25
heavy goods vehicles
  111, 147
improvements 30, 41,
  47
infrastructure 42, 46,
  49, 82, 85, 91, 246,
  271, 279
and innovation 295
local planning 300, 302
national policy 259
pricing 280–1, 282
shift to road 62
traffic calming 111–12
traffic and development
  94–5, 256
traffic noise 156
traffic problems 7, 8
and urban environment
  248
and urban form 95–100
see also cars; public
  transport
trees/woodland 118–19,
  255, 256, 310
Tucson (Arizona) 169,
  170–1, 193, 211, 221
Turkey 43, 167, 170

Ukraine: water supplies
  167
ultraviolet radiation
  157–8, 159
Umma (Mesopotamia)
  170
unemployment 40, 54
Union Carbide plants 57,
  241
United Kingdom
  as acid rain source 194
  car industry 56
  carbon oxides 160
  coastal resorts 185–6
  contaminated land 193,
    222
  economics and
    pollution 262

energy use 67, 108
Environment Week 232
environmental audits
  219, 269
and environmental
  impact statement
  (EIS) 257
flood protection
  schemes 259
housing 93, 108
land use planning 270
local environmental
  projects 305
and local government
  207, 219, 229, 300,
  301, 303
New Towns 72–3, 87,
  110
pollution inspectorates
  231
racial tensions 71
and sustainable
  development 309
tax system 50–1, 65
telecommuting 60
transport pollution 97,
  155
trunk road projects 247
urban development
  223, 301
urban forestry 119
water companies 168,
  230
water wastage 166
see also individual
  locations
United Nations
  Conference on the
    Human
    Environment
    (Stockholm) 4
  Drinking Water and
    Sanitation Decade
    184
  Handbook 269
  and national accounts
    219
  and pollution issues
    226, 231–2

Regional Policy and Development Series

Retreat from the Regions
Corporate Change and the Closure
of Factories
Stephen Fothergill and Nigel Guy
ISBN 1 85302 101 6 hb
ISBN 1 85302 100 8 pb
Regional Policy and Development 1

Spatial Policy in a Divided Nation
Edited by Richard T Harrison
and Mark Hart
ISBN 1 85302 076 1
Regional Policy and Development 2

Regional Development in the 1990s
The British Isles in Transition
Edited by Peter Townroe and Ron Martin
ISBN 1 85302 139 3
Regional Policy and Development 4

An Enlarged Europe
Regions in Competition?
Edited by Sally Hardy, Mark Hart,
Louis Albrechts and Anastasios Katos
ISBN 1 85302 188 1
Regional Policy and Development 6

Union Retreat and the Regions
The Shrinking Landscape
of Organised Labour
Ron Martin, Peter Sunley and Jane Wills
ISBN 1 85302 255 1
Regional Policy and Development 8

The Regional Imperative
Regional Planning and Governance
in Britain, Europe and the United
States
Urlan A Wannop
ISBN 1 85302 292 6
Regional Policy and Development 9

The Regional Dimension of
Transformation in Central Europe
Grzegorz Gorzelak
ISBN 1 85302 301 9
Regional Policy and Development 10

Regional Policy in Europe
S S Artobolevskiy
ISBN 1 85302 308 6
Regional Policy and Development 11

The Determinants
of Small Firm Growth
An Inter-Regional Study
in the United Kingdom 1986–90
Richard Barkham, Graham Gudgin,
Mark Hart and Eric Hanvey
ISBN 1 85302 331 0
Regional Policy and Development 12

Unemployment and Social Exclusion
Landscapes of Labour Market
Inequality
Edited by Paul Lawless, Ron Martin
and Sally Hardy
ISBN 1 85302 341 8
Regional Policy and Development 13

Multinationals and European
Integration
Trade, Investment and Regional
Development
Edited by Nicholas A. Phelps
ISBN 1 85302 353 1
Regional Policy and Development 14

Regional Development Strategies
A European Perspective
Edited by Jeremy Alden and Philip Boland
ISBN 1 85302 356 6
Regional Policy and Development 15

British Regionalism and Devolution
The Challenges of State Reform
and European Integration
Edited by Jonathan Bradbury
and John Mawson
ISBN 1 85302 370 1
Regional Policy and Development 16

The Coherence of EU Policy
Contrasting Perspectives on the
Structural Funds
Edited by John Bachtler and Ivan Turok
ISBN 1 85302 396 5
Regional Policy and Development 17

Innovation, Networks and Learning
Regions?
Edited by James Simmie
ISBN 1 85302 402 3
Regional Policy and Development 18